SCREEN PRINTING TECHNIQUES

ALBERT KOSLOFF M.A.

Honorary Member, Member of Academy of Screen Printing Technology, and Consultant to Screen Printing Association International

THIRD EDITION

Published by
THE SIGNS OF THE TIMES PUBLISHING CO.,
Cincinnati, Ohio, U.S.A.

ISBN: 0-911380-52-3

To my mother and father

PREFACE

The aim of the previous edition of the book *Screen Printing Techniques* was to present in a clear and simple manner the processes and techniques used in screen printing or mitography. The purpose of this third edition is the same—to present the different phases of the process to varied individuals in screen printing and related industries, to the craftsman, student, teacher, artist, newcomer, hobbyist, T-shirt printer, and to anyone interested in this fascinating phase of graphic communications.

The constant changes and the impact of information in screen printing make it mandatory that original and newer standardized developments of processes and products be interpreted objectively. Since the industry's self-evaluation and self-repair have produced basic industrial values, it becomes more important to stress developmental information.

The writer considers it a privilege and a challenge to interpret screen printing objectively in order to supplement the efforts of the international industry to inform the graphic communications, the related industries, and the public about the contributions and potential of screen printing.

In writing this book, the author has drawn on his own experience (both vocational and avocational) and on the constructive aid of individuals and organizations of varied parts of the world in trying to articulate the industrial past with present developments. It is a pleasure to acknowledge the following sources which are as diverse as the subject itself:

Advance Process Supply Co., Chicago; American Screen Printing Equipment Co., Chicago; Anderson-Prichard Oil Co., Oklahoma City; Argon Services Ltd., Milan, Italy; Atlas Silk Screen Supply Co., Chicago; The Autoroll Machine Corp., Salem, Mass.; Autotype, London, England; Samuel Bingham Co., Chicago; BTU Engineering Corp., Waltham, Mass.; Burke Communications Industries, Inc., Chicago; Buser Limited, Wiler, Switzerland; Canrad-Hanovia, Inc., Newark, N.J.; Caprock Developments, New York; Carlson Handprints, Cowell, Calif.; Cellusuede

Products, Inc., Rockford, Ill.; Chemcut Corp., State College, Penn.; Chicago Decal Co., Chicago; Chicago Screen Print, Inc., Morton Grove, Ill.; Chicago Silk Screen Supply Co., Chicago; Chroma Glo, Inc., Duluth, Minn.; Ciba Co., Inc., New York; Cincinnati Printing and Drying Systems, Inc., Cincinnati, Ohio; Colonial Printing Ink Co., Rutherford, N.J.; Commercial Solvent Corp., New York; Comet Industries, Inc., Bensenville, Ill.; Cudner and O'Connor Co., Chicago:

J. H. Day Co., Cincinnati, Ohio; Drakenfeld, Division of Imperial and Chemical Dept., Washington, Penn.; E. I. Du Pont de Nemours and Co., Inc., Wilmington, Del.; Eastman Kodak Company, Rochester, N.Y.; Factory Enterprises, Inc., Pittsburgh, Penn.; Fasson Products, Painesville, Ohio; David A. Frindell Signs, Milwaukee, Wis.; Fostoria Industries, Inc., Fostoria, Ohio; General Research, Inc., Sparta, Mich.; Graphic Equipment Co., Inc., Boston, Mass.; Melvin and Sheldon Green, Chicago:

Homer Laughlin China Co., Newell, W.Va.; The O. Hommel Co., Pittsburgh, Penn.; Indev, Inc., Pawtucket, R.I.; Kalmus and Associates, Inc., Broadview, Ill.; John Key, Keyline, Solana Beach, Calif.; William Korn, Inc., New York; Kenro Corp., Cedar Knolls, N.J.; Lawson Printing Machine Co., St. Louis; Lawter Chemicals, Inc., Northbrook, Ill.; L and L Manufacturing Co., Twin Oaks, Penn.; Liebig Industries, Beaver Dam, Wis.; Lindberg Heavy-Duty, Watertown, Wis.; Linde Photocure System, Union Carbide Corp., Indianapolis; Litho Paint Poster Co., Chicago:

Minnesota Mining and Mfg. Co., St. Paul, Minn., Majestic Bolting Cloth Corp., Somers, N.Y.; McGraw Colorgraph Co., Burbank, Calif.; Frank Mayer and Associates, Inc., Grafton, Wis.; M and M Research Engineering Co., Oshkosh, Wis.; Moore Signs, Detroit; Naz-Dar Co., Chicago; Newark Wire Cloth Co., Newark, N.J.; nuArc Co., Inc., Chicago; Nu-Film Products Co., Inc., New York; Joseph E. Podgor Co., Inc., Philadelphia; Plastic-Vac., Inc., Charlotte, N.C.; Precision Screen Machines, Inc., Hawthorne, N.J.:

R-K Electric Co., Cincinnati, Ohio; Robertson Photo-Mechanix, Inc., Des Plaines, Ill.; Screen Printing Assn. Int., Fairfax, Va.; Sericol Group, Ltd., London, England; Signs of the Times Publishing Co., Cincinnati, Ohio; Stork Inter-America, Charlotte, N.C.; Stretch Devices, Inc., Philadelphia; Superior Silk Screen Industries, Inc., Chicago; Swiss Bolting Mfg. Co., Ltd., St. Gall, Switzerland; Switzer Brothers, Inc., Cleveland, Ohio; Tetco, Inc., Elmsford, N.Y.:

Ulano Products Co., Inc., New York; Union Ink Co., Ridgefield, N.J.; Varigraph, Inc., Madison, N.Y.; Vastex Machine Co., Roselle, N.J.; Viola Studio, Chicago; J. R. Wallace Co., Pasadena, Calif.; Western Technology Associates, Santa Ana, Calif.; Wire Cloth Enterprises, Pittsburgh; Wornow Products Dept., The Dexter Corp., Los Angeles; Maurice Yochim, Chicago; and Zurich Bolting Cloth Co., Zurich, Switzerland.

The author also expresses his gratitude to his wife for her encouragement and constant aid; to *Screen Printing* magazine and *Signs of the Times* magazine for permission to use material and illustrations which the writer had contributed to past issues of the journals; to the late D. R. Swormstedt, Sr.; and to Robert O. Fossett and David M. Souder, editors of the above publications for their courtesies.

Albert Kosloff

CONTENTS

Chapter 1

SCREEN PRINTING

Graphic arts or graphic communication deals with those industries or processes by which man records information in visible form and expresses his thoughts and feelings through the use of such processes as drawing, painting, application of symbols, photography, xerography, and printing. The most important phase of graphic communication is printing. Today's printing may be divided into four basic methods: (a) *relief* or *letter-press* printing, (b) *intaglio* printing (pronounced in-tal'-yo), (c) *planography,* and (d) screen printing. Because all industry in this technological age, like all of life, is interdependent, the screen printer should know how his process relates to or differs from the other methods of printing.

Relief printing, the oldest method, is done with a raised surface which stands out in bold relief. When ink is applied to the surface of the type face or engraving and the inked surface is pressed onto a paper, an impression is made. Hand-set printing, linotyping, stereotyping, electrotyping, and photoengraving belong to this phase.

Intaglio printing involves printing from a plate in which the lines are cut or scratched in with a sharp instrument by hand or etched chemically. The lines or grooves are filled in with ink and a prepared paper is pressed in to take up the ink. Etching, dry point, and rotogravure are methods which use intaglio printing.

Planography, sometimes called chemical printing, means printing from a plane or smooth surface. It is based on the principle that oil and water or grease and water do not mix. In this process, the design to be printed is applied upon the smooth surface of a stone or metal plate photomechanically or by hand. The surface is then treated chemically so that the ink will adhere to the design that was treated but not to the rest of the surface. When paper comes in contact with the surface, only the inked design will transfer onto the paper. Photo-offset, photo-lithography, and offset use this principle in printing.

Modern screen printing does not only differ from the other three basic methods in technique but in the fact that it is the most versatile of all of them. It is used for printing on paper, cardboard, wood, plastics, textiles, ceramic products, metal, leather, and combinations of the latter materials. It is a process that is done not only on flat surfaces but is successfully accomplished on round, convex, concave, and irregular shapes. It is the child born of necessity and reared behind closed doors, since most details of processing were kept as trade secrets. It is growing and has by no means reached its limits.

There is no specific period at which graphic communications can be said to have developed. While screen printing today occupies the position where it is both an international industry and a creative art, the principle of screen printing had its origin in the simple stencil. However, it differs from the old stencil as modern relief printing differs from the printing done during the time of Johann Gutenberg of Mainz. The stencil goes back to the ancient civilizations and may have been one of the oldest methods of reproduction.

Although the Japanese may be credited with the "tieless" stencil where the centers and loose parts of cut letters were held in place by strands of human hair or silk, the origin of modern screen printing was an American development. According to early pioneers such as Harry Leroy Hiett and Edward A. Owens, screen printing was done in the early part of the twentieth century (between 1901 and 1906). The first attempt at screen printing at this time was the production of felt pennants by Francis Willette of Detroit, Michigan.

In this fourth basic method of printing, a stencil bearing an image or design is attached to or processed on a screen made of nylon, polyester, silk, or metal cloth. When stock is placed directly under the screen bearing the stencil, screen printing ink or paint is forced through the open mesh of the screen with a squeegee by hand or mechanically. The parts of the stencil that cover up the little holes in the screen will not allow the pigment to be forced through and deposit itself on the stock. Those parts on the design that do not stop up the holes in the screen will allow the ink to penetrate through to the stock. See Figure 1. In other words, screen printing involves the principle of actually printing *through* a plate. It is more correct to call this process *screen printing** rather than *silk screen printing* or *serigraphy* because not only silk is used as the printing screen bearing cloth as is commonly assumed but also nylon, polyester fibers, organdy, cotton, stainless steel, copper, brass, and bronze.

A knowledge of equipment, supplies, processes, and techniques as they apply to this method of printing is a prerequisite for any worker in this field. The writer hopes that he will not insult the reader's intelligence by assuming that the reader knows nothing about screen printing.

* The term *mitography* (mi tog' ra fi) was coined by this writer during World War II with the intent of offering a term that is comprehensive, technically correct, concise, and easy to translate into other languages. The word was taken from the Greek prefix *mitos* meaning "threads or fibers" and the suffix *graphein* meaning "to write or print." *Photomitography* refers to the photographic processes of screen printing.

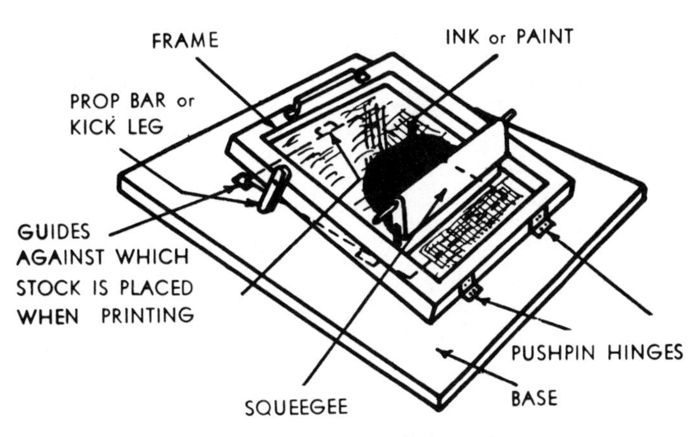

Figure 1. A screen printing unit.

This assumption only serves as a motivation for a simpler and more complete treatment of the subject.

The Frame

The frame is that part of a screen, often made of wood, to which the stencil cloth is attached. Frames for screen printing units are made of wood, metal, or both. Although many screens are ready-made by screen printing firms who cater to the printer, every screen operator should know how to make his own frames. The type and shape of frame used in controlled by the job that is to be printed. In making process equipment, it is most practical to use the simplest and the best materials available.

The most common frame is the flat frame which is used to print on flat surfaces. Most screen printers use kiln-dried white pine or basswood that is free of knots and other imperfections for the frame. It is advisable to buy lumber that is planed on all four sides, as this eliminates planing and squaring-up the wood. For screens up to about 36 inches x 36 inches (81cm x 81cm) in size, the size of the wood stock for the sides of the frame should be about 2 inches thick and 2 inches wide (5cm x 5cm). For bigger screens, the sides may be proportionately thicker and wider, since frames that are too thin have a tendency to warp more on bigger screens than on smaller screens due to usage, storage, and pull of the stencil cloth. Although white pine is the most used for screen frames, screen printers also use mahogany, spruce, hemlock, and boxwood for frames.

Figure 2 shows the three most common methods used by screen printers for assembling frames. Each method will serve its purpose if care is used in making the frame. All corners should be fastened together with nails and glue or screws and glue, excess glue being wiped

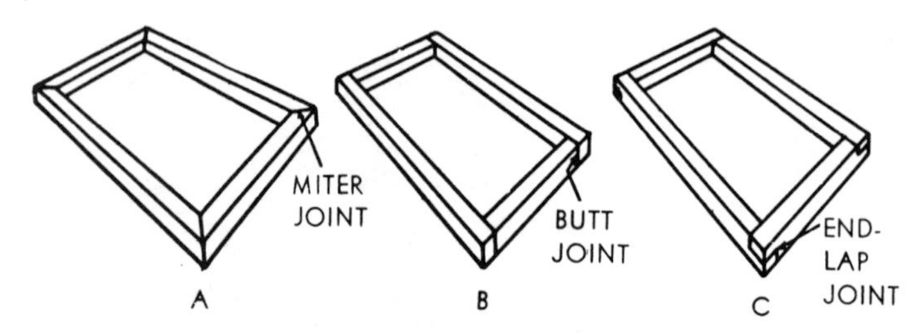

Figure 2. Three commonly used screen printing frames.

off immediately with a damp cloth after gluing. Finishing nails should be used and they should be set down about a little below the surface of the wood with a nail so that there would be no chance of a nail cutting the stencil fabric. Regardless of which method of assembly is used for the frame, the corners should be reinforced with angle plates, corner plates or angle irons, as frames do get much rough usage. All corners should be slightly rounded with sandpaper and the wood must be well sandpapered to remove all rough spots that may tear the stencil cloth if they are left on. The wood may be given a coat of shellac or rubbed down with a coat of boiled linseed oil, if desired, before attaching the stencil fabric to the frame.

There are four common methods in use for attaching screen fabric to screen printing frames. They are using tacks, the groove and cleat method, automatic stapler, and commercial patented techniques and frames for attaching and stretching screen fabrics.

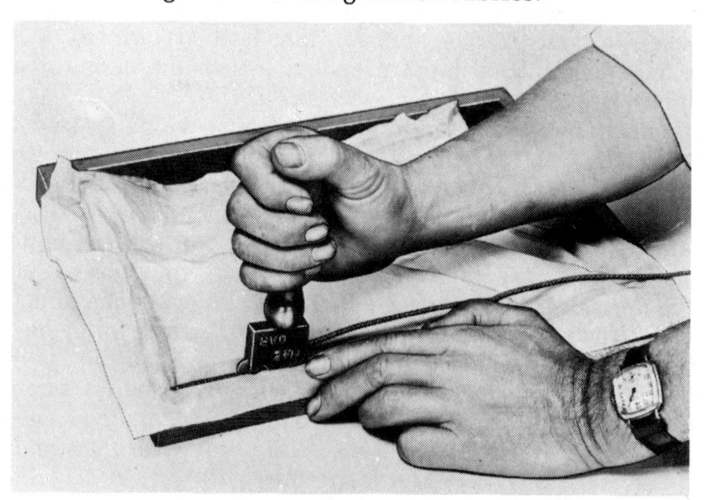

Figure 3. A special simple tool (The E-Z Stretch Method) used in the groove-and-cord method of stretching and attaching screen fabric to frame sides. Tool presses cord down over screen fabric into groove in sides of frame. **(Courtesy of Naz-Dar Company, Chicago, Illinois).**

Attaching Screen Fabric to the Frame

In tacking cloth to a frame, flat head carpet tacks about ½" (1.2cm) long are used. Attach the cloth so that the direction of the selvage (the length of the bolt) is in the direction of the longer side of the frame. Most stencil cloths are stronger in this direction; therefore, the cloth should run in the direction in which the squeegee is pulled. Arrange the fabric so that the threads in it are pulled parallel with the sides of the frame. Start tacking the cloth down in the center on one side of the frame and keep the tacks about ⅜" (.95cm) from edges of frame, keeping tacks about ¾ to 1 inch (1.9 to 2.54cm) apart. Drive in one row of tacks on one side, stretching the cloth by hand in the direction that the tacks are driven. The outside row of tacks are driven first, driving the tacks just hard enough to make the flat heads flush with the wood. After the cloth is tacked onto one side, then tacks are driven into the opposite side of the frame, stretching the cloth at the same time. In a similar manner, the tacks are hammered down on the other two sides, making sure that the stencil cloth is stretched tight. The inside rows are staggered as shown in Figure 4.

After the cloth is stretched and tacked on (if it is silk), it should be washed carefully with lukewarm or cool water or with water and soap to remove any sizing that may be present. This washing also aids in tightening the cloth. When the cloth is dry, see if the stretched fabric feels smooth in all spots on the screen. If certain spots are not stretched as tightly as others, then the few tacks may be removed carefully with a tool such as a screwdriver and replaced after correcting for stretching and smoothness. The cloth must be stretched perfectly

Figure 4. Staggering tacks or staples.

taut, otherwise it may be difficult to adhere screen printing films or to coat emulsions on it. Some screen printers gently roughen the fibers on such fabrics as nylon or polyester with a fine grade of pumice or paste available from screen printing suppliers, before applying a film or printing screen coating to fabric. One must be careful not to weaken the threads with the rubbing. As the novice screen printer works in the field, he will find that there are other more practical methods of cleaning and degreasing screen fabrics.

Some screen printers brush the bottom of the frame, in which the tacks are driven, with a coat of shellac. This aids in sealing the fabric to the frame and also may prevent leakage of ink between fabric and screen frame.

In the grooved-cleat frame, a groove is cut on the bottom side of the frame. See Figure 5. This groove may be made on a circular saw, with a grooving tool made especially for this purpose, with a wood chisel, or on a drill press. The depth of the groove should be slightly greater than the thickness of the cleat. If the cleat is made of stock that is of harder wood such as maple or birch, it will last longer and may be used over and over. About ⅜" (.93cm) square stock is a good size for the cleat. It may be a square sectioned one or a round dowel rod that fits snugly in the groove.

The screen fabric is forced into the groove with the cleat and held permanently in place. The edges of the groove and of the cleat where the cloth comes in contact with them should be rounded slightly with sandpaper so as not to cut the cloth. Use Number 4 or Number 5 flat-head wood screws that are about ¾" (1.9cm) long. The screw holes in the cleats should be countersunk so that the screw head will fit flush with the surface of the cleat. Keep screw holes about two to four inches apart.

In attaching the cloth, first press in one cleat and fasten the screws down but not completely. The cleat on the opposite side is then fastened

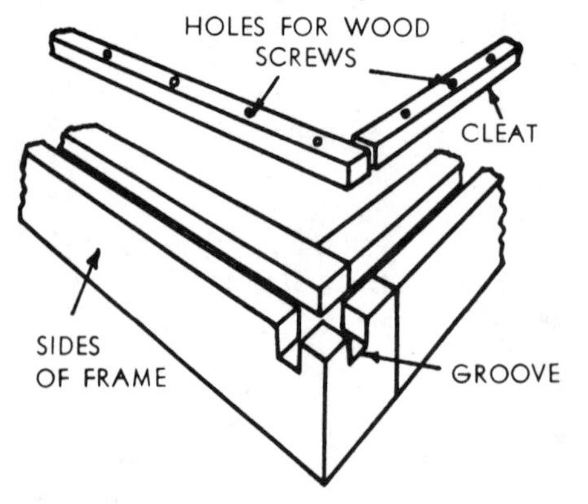

Figure 5. Construction of a practical grooved-cleat frame.

Figure 5A. The Key Line, a screen making and frame system, consisting of an independently made screen and a modular self-stretching aluminum master frame which permits installing, stretching, removing, and replacing the screen to, from, and back to the frame. Any screen fabric may be used, and after printing, the screen can be removed, stored and replaced in perfect register for reruns, eliminating the need for costly and wooden frame storage. **(Courtesy of Key Line, San Diego, California)**

down in a similar manner, stretching the cloth as much as possible. It does not matter if a slight tear should occur at a corner at the end of a cleat. The other two cleats are then driven down. After all the cleats are in place, finish tightening the screws, tightening them a little at a time so as to obtain the same amount of stretching on the screen fabric in all spots.

Screen fabric attached to a frame with an automatic tacking stapler and staples offers a very quick and easy method, providing the staples are driven in diagonally to the weave of the cloth. Staples driven in parallel with the cloth or the way the fibers run will tear the fabric. Staples should be driven in similarly to tacks and in approximately the same locations. It is practical to place strips of cardboard over the fabric and drive staples into the cardboard and not directly into the screen fabric. The staples can then be removed more easily by pulling on the cardboard strips.

Figure 3 presents a simple commercial method of stretching and attaching screen fabric that the beginner and advanced screen printer may use. With this method, the printer may employ varied size screens in which the frame sides have had grooves cut on the underside of the frame. Then the screen fabric is laid on top of the grooves, and a specially prepared cord about $\frac{1}{8}''$ to $\frac{3}{16}''$ (.31cm to .47cm) in diameter, depending on the groove, is forced over the cloth with a special tool, forcing the cloth into the groove. The cord may be reused for several stretchings; and when the cloth has to be tightened any time during its life, the groove may be cut a little bit deeper and the fabric may be reinserted with the same cord.

Figure 5A presents a very interesting and practical screen making and frame system for the screen printing shop or for an in-plant operation. The system features an independently made screen which may be installed in a self-stretching aluminum frame. The frame stretches the screen to the desired tension; and after printing, the screen may be removed, rolled up, to be inserted again into the frame for reuse.

Regardless of what method of stretching and attaching the fabric on a screen the printer may use, there are varied commercial frames made especially for producing printing screens quickly. However, where a patented screen frame is employed and designed for a specific purpose such as electronic circuit printing or chemical machining or for a specific screen printing machine, the printing screen must be used as specified by the manufacturer.

Chapter 2

SCREEN PRINTING FABRICS

The screen printing emulsion or coating, photosensitive resist, or screen printing film which produces the required image for screen printing must be adhered or processed on a special cloth or screen fabric. The screen fabric used is dependent upon the type of printing desired, quality of printing, type of stencil or masking medium that is to be adhered to the fabric, detail to be printed, and the surface upon which the printing is to be done. The fabric, regardless of what material it is, must have the right tensile strength so that it can be stretched taut without tearing; it must have clear tracing visibility at least equal to that of tracing cloth used by draftsmen; the mesh or openings enclosed by the threads of the cloth must be of uniform size; the threads must not unravel and must keep their woven position; the fabric must resist all paints, inks, solvents, cleaning solutions, masking mediums, stretching, squeegeeing, atmospheric conditions in storage, the vibration and pressure of screen printing machines, and other normal wear in its use in printing. In other words, much is required of a screen printing fabric.

The screen fabrics used in the United States and abroad are silk, nylon, polyester, metalized polyester, stainless steel, phosphor bronze, organdy, cotton, and on rare occasions bridal net, and some cheesecloth. The fibers for the fabric may be made of animal, plant, mineral, synthetic, and a combination of the above materials. Since the introduction of screen printing, usage and availability have proved certain screen fabrics superior to others.

Silk

The advances in the development of screen fabrics, especially since 1945, have aided in producing sophisticated screen printing applications such as very fine detail printing, circuit printing, and the like, and in refining screen printing production.

Of all the varied fabrics tried by the early screen printers, silk had been found to be satisfactory for general use. Because of the chemical and physical properties of silk and of the fact that it is a multifilament, screen printing film (indirect films) and emulsion coatings adhere best to it. Although, today, silk is not used as much as nylon and polyester because the latter are precisely woven and make fine detail printing more possible. However, silk has been used as a standard in relation to numbering of screen fabrics. It was no accident that screen printing was originally and is still known as "silk screen printing." The grade of silk used is known as *silk bolting cloth.* The silk originally was developed in Holland, Switzerland, and France in the nineteenth century for sifting flour. Most of our silk for process work is still imported from abroad, specifically, from Switzerland. Silk is the strongest of all natural fibers and better grades of silk will stand wear of 25,000 impressions and up. Screen printing silk is classified according to (a) weave; (b) number, representing mesh or openings per lineal inch or centimeter; and (c) strength quality.

In the weave classification, there are basically two types gauze weave and plain weave. See Figures 6, 7, and 8. The gauze weave produces a light weight, strong fabric with an open mesh. It does not get its name from the cheap type of materials, since most of those are woven with the plain weave. In the gauze weave, the warp consists of two threads which are twisted about each other and encircle the woof. This keeps the threads from slipping and makes for uniform mesh. The warp yarns are the lengthwise yarns in a fabric, and the woof or filling yarns run crosswise. In a good stencil cloth, both yarns should have the same possible strength and thickness.

The leno weave shown in Figure 7 is a variation of the gauze weave and gets its name from the fact that it is made on a leno loom. Both the gauze and the leno weave produce strong cloth.

The plain weave illustrated in Figure 8 is sometimes referred to as the taffeta weave. Taffeta silk is of this weave. In the plain weave, the fabric will wear well when the yarns are close together.

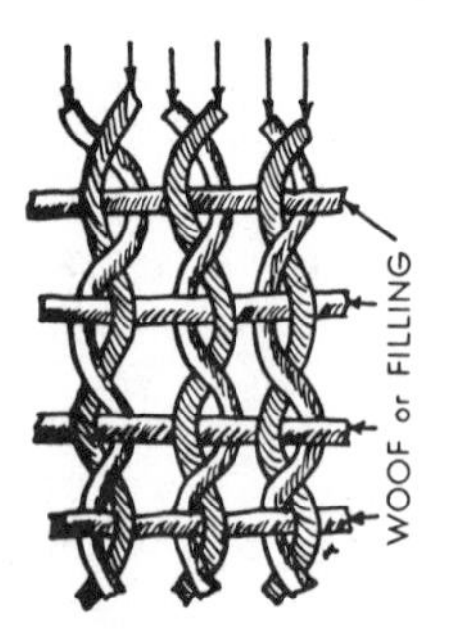

Figure 6.
Gauze weave.

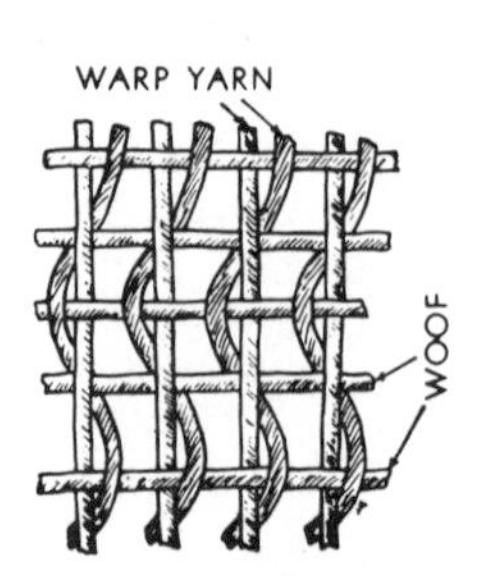

Figure 7.
Leno weave.

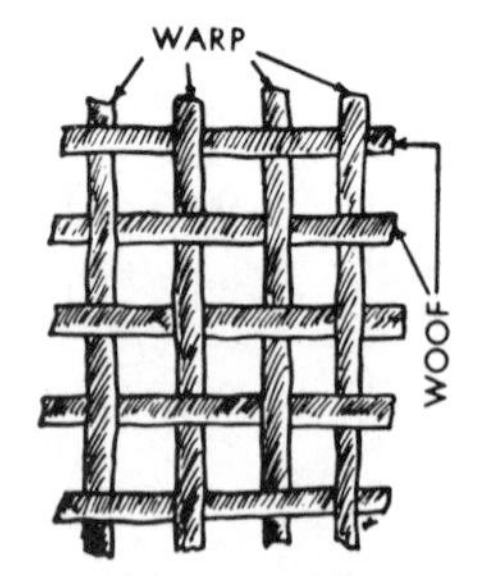

Figure 8.
Plain weave.

Warp threads run lengthwise and make up the main structure of the cloth.

As far as its number classification is concerned, standard bolting cloth ranges from No. 0000 to Number 25, Number 0000 being the coarsest and Number 25 being the finest. The higher the number, the smaller are the openings in the silk. For example, No. 2 bolting cloth, which is the coarsest generally used in screen printing work, has about 53 mesh or 53 openings per lineal inch; No. 25 has 200 mesh per lineal inch. Number 10, 12, 14, and 16 are the numbers most frequently used by screen printers with No. 12 suiting most purposes. Stencil cloths that do not use this numbering system still have to supply the mesh count information before it can be used in the screen printing industry.

To designate quality, the numbered silk has an "X," "XX," or "XXX" after it. The X or X's after a number indicate a stronger weave. According to quality, the silk is available in plain numbers (as No. 12, No. 14, etc.); in numbers with a single X after them (as No. 12X, No. 14X, etc.); in double X (as No. 12XX, No. 14XX, etc.); and in triple X (as in No. 12XXX, No. 14XXX, etc.). The double X quality is the one that is usually employed in screen printing and is the one shown in Table I. In the triple X quality, the mesh is counted one number coarser than in the other grades to allow for the thickness of the threads.

			STENCIL MEDIUM THAT MAY BE USED								
PHOTO (DETAIL)	PHOTO	PAPER	FILM	MESH	PHOTO (FINE DETAIL)	RESIST	APERTURE	NO. OF SILK	BLOCK-OUT	CELLULOID & CELLOPHANE	TYPEWRITER
5 and 6	.0115 .0101	66 74	x	x							
7 to 10	.0088 to .0057	88 to 109	x	x							x
11 and 12	.0055 .0053	120 125	x	x	x				x	x	x
13 to 16	.0040 to .0039	129 to 152			x	x		x	x	x	
17 and 18	.0032	164 170					x	x	x	x	

Table 1. Meshes and some stencil media that may be used with the mesh.

Double-X multifilament polyester is replacing Triple-X silk where more impressions and more wear are necessary in printing such as in thick deposits of textile inks. Silk screen fabrics are available in widths up to 60 inches (152cm) and in varied bolt lengths. The market fluctuations for silk and other screen fabrics are governed by shipments, imports, and general world conditions.

Taffeta silk is available in a range from No. 6XX (74 mesh per inch, 29 mesh per cm) to 16XX (157 mesh per inch, 62 mesh per cm), in bolts up to about 60 inches (152cm) wide and in varied lengths.

Generally, the finer the detail to be printed, the higher the number or the finer the mesh. However, if too fine a silk is used, the screen may clog; and it will be more difficult for the ink to pass through. Many screen printers use a mesh that is as coarse as possible, as open as possible, and as fine as is necessary to hold well the specific stencil medium to it.

Table I presents different numbers of silk used, aperture or opening size of mesh in inches, mesh count in inches and stencil types that may be used with the given silk number.*

Synthetic Screen Fabrics

Synthetic screen fabrics or cloths are woven from man-made fabrics. The most commonly used ones are nylon (polyamide) and polyester—available under varied trade-names. These fibers have a high resistance to abrasion, a high tensile strength, and elasticity; therefore, they fit well as screen fabrics. The uniform threads of synthetic cloths, especially the monofilament thread, produces square apertures in the cloth. Silk and polyester are available as multifilaments, that is the threads are made from more than one filament; nylon, polyester, and metal screen fabrics are woven from monofilaments, each thread consisting of one filament.

Screen printing suppliers sell polyesters in numbers from 6XX to 21XX (multifilaments) from about 65 to 300 openings per inch (25 to 118 openings per cm). Nylon is available in numbers equivalent to silk from about 6XX to 25XX, in meshes from about 30 to about 460 openings per lineal inch (12 to 181 per cm). Widths of synthetic cloths are available up to 120 inches (305 cm).

Organdy

Organdy is a cotton weave and comes in many grades. It should be used where small runs are desired because it is not as durable as silk. Knife-cut stencils and photographic plates may be applied to it.

* Generally, suppliers make charts available giving data on screen fabrics in the English and metric systems.

Cleaning it injures the threads; therefore, where accuracy is required, most screen printing workers do not reclaim it for reuse. Its use consumes more ink than silk and after continued use organdy, unlike silk or nylon, becomes flabby and loose. It is available in widths from about 37 to 60 inches (95 to 152cm). There are domestic and imported organdies.

Ovo or Organdy Voile

Organdy voile or ovo cloth is made of cotton and linen threads. It is a coarse cloth that is equal in mesh to about a No. 4 or 5 silk bolting cloth. It is used in printing on any surface where knife-cut stencils are attached to the cloth. It can be used for long runs ranging between 5,000 and 10,000 impressions. It is cheaper than silk and comes in about the same widths as silk.

Bridal Net

Bridal net is a cloth that may be used for roller printing in the screen printing industry. Although it is used abroad mostly, it is a good idea to have some knowledge of it. There are a few grades of this cloth in cotton and silk. Both may be used. It is the cheapest of the stencil cloths sold and cannot be reused. It is equal to about a No. 20 mesh and is only used with paper stencils which are glued or pasted to it.

Before the bridal net is attached on the underside of the frame with strips of gummed paper tape, it should first be dipped in water, wrung out, and then adhered. The net tears easily and is flimsy. However, once the stencil is adhered to it, the cloth is reinforced. The ink used may be regular screen printing ink thinned out to screen printing consistency or regular screen printing ink of the very cheap variety. The ink is applied to the required spots on paper or cardboard through the screen with a brayer or printing roller. A squeegee cannot be used, as it would tear the cloth.

There are other fabrics that perhaps could be used as screen printing frame cloth. However, before being accepted by the industry, they would have to withstand much experimentation under average conditions in screen printing.

Since one number of screen fabric is difficult to distinguish from another number just by ordinary inspection, it is suggested that the number of the fabric be marked on the screen frame in some permanent fashion. Some screen printers have a color code for the several fabric numbers that they use and paint each screen having the same fabric number attached to it with the same color. The screen printer should know at all times which of his screens are coarse and which are fine.

Chapter 3

NYLON AND POLYESTER SCREEN FABRIC

The use of synthetic fabrics has grown since World War II. The employment of these fabrics, including nylon, was motivated in the early 1940s when a shortage of silk developed because of war conditions. Its use and quality has increased, and it is finding more and more applications as a screen fabric in the industry in the United States and in other parts of the world. Nylon is a thermoplastic fiber which belongs to the polyamides group. Its thread is a monofilament as compared to the silk thread which is a multifilament (consisting of more than one filament to the thread). Yarn for monofilament fiber is made as individual threads; multifilament yarn consists of individual fibers twisted together to form weaving yarn. Generally, multifilaments such as silk and cotton have more "tooth" for adhering screen printing films. Monofilament fabrics have smoother surfaces which make adhesion of films to them more difficult.

Today, nylon is made especially for the screen printing trade and is woven mostly in the taffeta (plain) weave. It is also available in

Figure 9. Half-gauze (half-leno) weave nylon screen fabric.

the half-leno weave. See Figure 9. Nylon is and has been used for almost every type of printing in the industry. It may be employed in the preparation of most types of printing screens using screen printing films and coatings. It is practical for printing with ceramic inks, textile inks, for electronic circuit printing, for printing water-soluble inks, and all inks generally used in the industry. The screen printer is using nylon fabric by itself and to supplement the use of other fabrics.

Since nylon is a thermoplastic, it will melt if enough heat is applied to it. Its thermoplastic point is from about 455 to 482 degrees Fahrenheit (235 to 250 degrees Centigrade). In other words, when the printer has to adhere iron-on knife-cut films or stencils, he must use caution in the amount of heat applied. Also, care should be employed if thermoplastic adhesives are being employed to fasten the nylon fabric to the screen frame.

Nylon has high tensile strength, abrasion resistance, and durability. Thousands of impressions may be printed from a nylon screen which has been prepared correctly. Manufacturers maintain that 100,000 impressions may be printed from a well-prepared direct-type screen. A direct screen is one in which the sensitized emulsion or coating is applied directly to the screen fabric. Nylon, like silk, has resiliency and is not subject to becoming dented. Neither is it affected by alkalines, acids of low concentration, or most organic solvents. These are some of the reasons for its being used in dye textile printing. However, it is attacked by acetic acid and formic acid and is dissolved by phenol, cresylic acid, and methacresol.

The high tensile strength of the filament allows threads of relatively thin diameter to be used in the manufacture of the fabric. This results in a fabric with a large percentage of open area and better ink passage through the fabric. Thin diameter nylon threads allow for the manufacture of fabrics with a very high mesh count. Nylon is woven from about 16 to 465 threads to the lineal inch (6 to 183 per cm) and up to 80 inch (203 cm) width rolls. It is generally available in white, yellow, and red colors. Since monofilament threads do not soak up ink in the printing operation, nylon screens have less tendency to clog and are easier to clean. Ink deposit is equal to the thickness of the thread and the film or coating; consequently, because nylon is thinner, less ink is deposited on the printed surface. Also thinner ink deposits dry faster. It makes the printing of finer detail and halftones more practical, as finer meshes hold detail better. For example, No. 196 mesh nylon (77 mesh per cm) has as many adhering points for photographic film as No. 25XX silk, yet ink flow through the nylon will equal that of the openings in about a No. 10XX silk. This implies that when a printer is replacing a particular mesh of silk, he should choose a finer nylon mesh count. Nylon fabric is ideal for direct screens or those screens which are processed by applying emulsion directly onto the fabric.

Figure 10. Cincinnati True-Tension Chase, a commercial type of screen frame for stretching and attaching any type of screen fabric. The chase, which is available in varied sizes, has adjustment screws on all four sides to produce drum tight tension on fabric. **(Courtesy of Cincinnati Printing and Drying Systems, Inc., Cincinnati, Ohio)**

Stretching Nylon

Nylon may be stretched onto wooden frames, metal frames, floating-bar frames, commercial frames such as those illustrated in Figures 10 and 11, and on special jigs and stretching devices manufactured especially for this type of work. Generally, nylon should be stretched wet and as tightly as possible. Poor stretching of any fabric reduces film durability, causes bad register and offset marks on the printed surface, and will not allow screen to release correctly from the printing surface in off-contact printing. Nylon should be stretched from 3 to 7 per cent in both directions (in direction of warp threads and weft or woof threads), finer weaves being stretched slightly more than coarser weaves. Manufacturers recommend that mechanical and pneumatic stretching devices be used. See Figures 12 and 13. In attaching and

Figure 11. The Newman Roller Frame, a light weight precision fabric tensioning and printing screen for screen sizes of about 10″ (25.4cm) to 14 feet (4.27m), designed to stretch any fabric quickly and accurately to a tolerance of plus or minus ½ Newton/cm, allows for fabric adjustment at all times, and is designed for fabric removal for reuse from the frame. May also be bolted into all types of automatic presses or hand tables. **(Courtesy of Stretch Devices, Inc., Philadelphia, PA)**

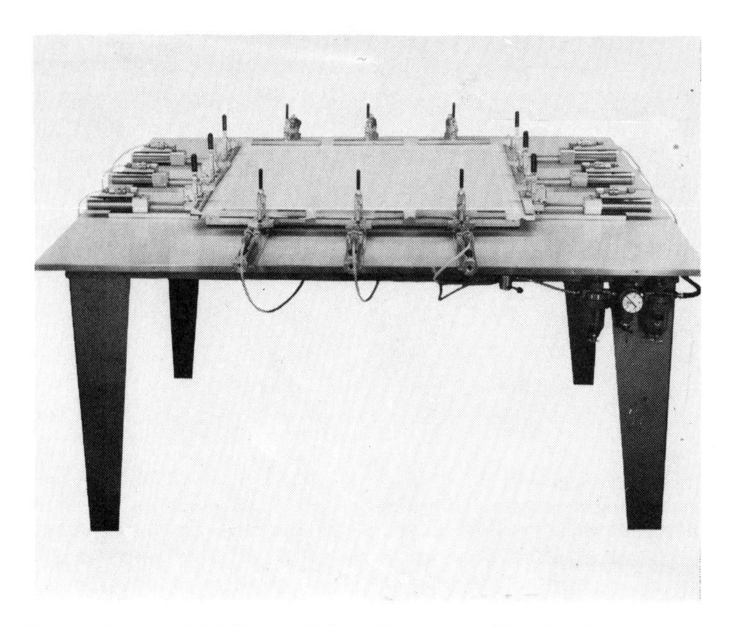

Figure 12. M and M Screen Fabric Tensioning Machine for accurate stretching any type of screen fabric on any size screen. Screen frame is placed on table with fabric on top of frame. Clamps are fastened to four sides of fabric and fabric is stretched to desired tautness with an air valve device. Fabric is then fastened to screen frame with an adhesive or other method. **(Courtesy of M and M Research Engineering Co., Oshkosh, Wisconsin)**

stretching, the threads should be parallel to the four sides of the frame. While special stretching frames with tension gauges are available from suppliers for doing scientific jobs of stretching, the following method may be used in stretching nylon. First, pre-stretch the nylon assuring that wrinkles and slackness are eliminated. Then, mark obvious pencil lines, parallel to the frame sides, on the nylon, about three inches from the frame sides. Keep distances between pencil lines in units of tens so that it will be easier to figure percentage of stretch. Measure these distances before and after stretching. For example, if the width distance between the two parallel lines is 20 inches (51cm) and the length distance between the other two lines is 30 inches (76cm) and the stretch required is 5 per cent, then the width and length distances after stretching should be 21 and 31½ inches (53 and 80cm) respectively. The nylon should be moistened with water after stretching and drawing of guidelines. Stretching at the screen corners may be decreased slightly to prevent tearing of fabric in these spots. The overtension in the corner areas may be prevented by laying the fabric slightly looser near the corners.

Figure 13. Illustration of a screen fabric stretching unit and use of unit in stretching and attaching any screen fabric onto any size frame. **(Courtesy of Photo Process Screen Mfg., Philadelphia, Pennsylvania)**

While nylon may be stretched either wet or dry, and natural silk must be wetted, polyester gauze does not require wetting.

It must be stressed that the correct stretching and adhering of fabric to screen frames is of utmost importance in producing a durable printing screen and good printing quality.

Cleaning Synthetic Fabrics

Assuming that the screen fabric is correctly stretched, the fabric must be cleaned and degreased perfectly in order that films and coatings adhere well to them. This is especially true of synthetic fabrics such as nylon and polyester. Often the manufacturer and supplier of screen printing films and coatings will specify the method of preparing these fabrics for better adhering of film or coating. Although nylon is supplied as clean as possible, it is necessary to clean new nylon before it is used to increase its adhering qualities. Cleaning and degreasing of the nylon is done after the fabric has been mounted and stretched on the screen frame. There are varied methods which may be employed for degreasing and cleaning the fiber so that it will have "tooth" or adhering qualities for films. The following cleaning and degreasing methods for nylon are used by screen printers in the United States and Europe and have been recommended by firms who weave and supply nylon for the trade and also by manufacturers of screen printing films and coatings which are adhered or coated directly on the nylon.*

* 1. Colonial Printing Ink Company, East Rutherford, N.J.; 2. Swiss Bolting Cloth Mfg. Co., Ltd., (St. Gall), Switzerland; 3. Tetco, Inc., Elmsford, N.Y.; 4. Tripette and Renaud, Paris, France; 5. Zurich Bolting Cloth Mfg. Co., Zurich, Switzerland.

Caustic Soda and Scouring Powder Treatment

Although this method appears complicated it is actually simple. A 20 per cent caustic soda (sodium hydroxide) solution is applied to both sides of the well-stretched new nylon screen with a medium hard nylon brush or a sponge. The solution is left on the fabric to react for 15 to 30 minutes. Because of the relatively high concentration of the caustic soda solution, it is suggested that a brush with a long handle or rubber or plastic gloves be employed to apply the solution, being careful not to splash the liquid in the eyes. It is a safe and practical method always for the printer to wear rubber gloves when cleaning or scouring a screen, regardless of the solution being used. After the 15 to 30 minute period, the nylon fabric should be remoistened with water, and sufficient kitchen cleanser should be poured and scrubbed on both sides of screen using a brush or sponge. The printer may also add a paste or microscopic powder available for this purpose to the cleanser for scrubbing both sides. Coarser nylon grades will withstand more scouring. Grades finer than about 225 threads to the inch should be scrubbed with great care, since these threads may lose much of their strength in the process. Any brand of kitchen cleanser which contains an active alkaline degreasing ingredient may be employed.

After the scouring, the fabric is given a thorough hosing on both sides with water to make sure that all traces of the caustic soda and powder have been completely removed, paying special attention to the frame corners and frame to prevent the hidden chemicals from leaking out on the screen later.

After the screen has been thoroughly washed with water, the screen is neutralized by giving the nylon a final rubdown with plain white household vinegar (5 to 6 per cent acetic acid solution). This will remove any microscopic remains of caustic soda or particles which may cause pin-holing during exposure to strong light and during regular printing. The fabric should be given a final spray with clean water after the vinegar treatment. A different brush, piece of cotton or cloth should be used to apply the vinegar; do not employ the same brush which was used to apply the soda.

Nylon which has been reclaimed or decoated after it has been used for printing is cleaned and degreased differently. The 20 per cent caustic soda solution should be left on the fabric for only 5 to 10 minutes; then, the fabric should be washed with a strong spray of water, neutralized with vinegar, and finally, washed off perfectly with water. It is not necessary to repeat the roughening of the fabric, since used nylon will have good adhesion for films and coatings.

Tri-Sodium Phosphate and Scouring Powder

This method is recommended before adhering photographic screen printing transfer-type film. The stretched nylon is scrubbed thoroughly with a stiff brush and a detergent containing a fine scouring powder. The detergent is then washed out with clean water. Then, tri-sodium phosphate powder is sprinkled on a cloth and is rubbed into the mesh until all powder is dissolved. Do this on both sides of the fabric with a sponge. After powder treatment, the powder should be washed out of cloth with water. The cloth is then rinsed with a 2 per cent solution of muriatic acid (hydrochloric acid). The screen should be allowed to stand for several minutes and then rinsed well with water. When the fabric is dry, it is ready for adhering of film.

Cresylic Acid Treatment

In this method, the nylon is first scrubbed with a detergent containing a fine scouring powder; and then, the detergent is washed out thoroughly with water. Then, a solution made up of one part cresylic acid and 9 parts methanol is sprinkled on the fabric and rubbed into mesh until fabric is covered with solution. The screen should be allowed to stand until fabric is dry. It should not be washed with water. When the nylon is dry, screen printing film may be adhered to it.

Another cresylic acid treatment consists of applying a 5 per cent solution of the acid with a piece of cotton to the center of the dry screen for 1 to 2 minutes, the solution being several inches from the frame edges. The acid should then be rinsed off well with water and fabric dried before using.

It must be noted that care should be employed in using cresylic acid, as stronger cresylic acid solutions will destroy the nylon or weaken it.

Abrasive Detergent

For adhering some screen printing films and coatings, just sprinkling an abrasive kitchen cleanser or detergent on both sides of the nylon will do the job. The cleanser is rubbed over the nylon with a sponge until the surface is cleaned and slightly roughened. The fabric is then rinsed thoroughly with water to assure that all particles of abrasives are removed. When the fabric is dry, film may be adhered. Here, again, nylon should not be abraded more than once.

Bleach

An 8 to 10 per cent sodium hypochlorite water solution can be applied to nylon for about 5 to 20 minutes. After the nylon is rinsed with water (to remove bleach) and is dried, it may be used for films and coatings. However, long and repeated use of bleach on the nylon will reduce the strength of the fabric.

Other Cleaning Techniques

A solution consisting of 5 per cent caustic soda and a liquid detergent applied over the fabric is suitable for degreasing nylon. It should be washed off well with water and dried before applying film or coating.

A cleaning technique employed in Europe for textile screen printing consists of using a solution of 5 cubic centimeters of sulphuric acid (66°Be), one-half gram of sodium or potassium bichromate dissolved in one liter of water. The solution is applied to the fabric and allowed to react for about 10 minutes. It is rinsed off thoroughly with water and allowed to dry before using nylon for preparation of printing screen.

Some screen printers have used ordinary detergents not containing abrasive particles and have applied the detergent solution to the nylon with a sponge. This may clean the fabric so that adhering of film or coating will take place. However, the detergent must be rinsed off perfectly before using fabric.

Polyester Screen Fabric

There is no one universal screen fabric, and each fabric has advantages and disadvantages. In similar fashion to nylon, polyester is a synthetic fabric, is evenly woven in varied mesh counts, possesses friction and abrasion resistance, will withstand stresses in stretching, is resistant to chemicals used in screen printing, and offers good adhesion to emulsion coatings and films, if cleaned and degreased. For some work, polyester may be used instead of metal cloths. The fabric is obtainable in monofilament weaves and in multifilament threads. It is available under varied tradenames, in white, in anti-halo red and orange colors.

Although synthetic fabrics may be stapled to screen frames, one must use care in stapling to prevent staples from tearing the fabric. Where the printer makes stapling a practice, it is suggested that he staple the fabric over the frame by fastening a cardboard strip between the fabric and the staples. It is more practical to employ adhesives developed for this purpose. While the correct adhesive is a compromise, lacquers, epoxies (generally a two-component formulation), and adhesives suggested by manufacturers may be used. Polyester may be stretched about 2 to 3½ per cent during the adhering and stretching operation.

Both mechanical and chemical methods may be used for producing a surface on the very smooth threads to which films and coatings may adhere best. In using any of the cleaning methods suggested for nylon, the printer must make sure that the threads are not weakened or damaged on the polyester. Silicon carbide microscopic powders or pastes or scouring powders, available from suppliers, may be used on new screens. The powder is applied on both sides of screen by rubbing lightly with a sponge. This should be followed by a thorough rinsing with water to assure that the wet applied powder or paste is completely removed. Manufacturers and suppliers of emulsions and films do offer specific suggestions in treating fabric or offer proprietary products for this purpose.

Metalized Polyester Screen Fabric

Metalized monofilament polyester fabric was developed by the Zurich Bolting Cloth Mfg. Co., Ltd., in the 1970's for close tolerance printing. It has an abrasion resistant metal coating embedded in the entire fabric. Direct, indirect, or direct-indirect printing screens may be adhered to it. It has good dimensional stability, if used according to the supplied directions. The fabric has good abrasion resistance and may be employed for printing thermoplastic inks which have to be printed in a liquid heated state and cool instantly on touching the surface. It may be used for printing where the electrostatic charge of nylon or polyester may lead to problems in printing.

While it is generally resistant to most inks, degreasing and cleaning agents, it may not be resistant to such solutions as sodium hypochlorite, acids and concentrated lye solutions. Therefore, in its use, the printer must follow specifically the directions of the supplier in such procedures as stretching of fabric, reclaiming and other steps. It is suggested that in using this fabric, as in many other procedures, the beginner test the fabric completely for the job.

In summary, use the simplest method that will work. The basic prerequisites for using nylon, polyester, or other fabrics are to make sure that the fabric is stretched tightly and correctly, that it is cleaned and degreased, and roughened very slightly so that no loss of fabric strength occurs. Some screen films just require a perfectly clean fabric and very little roughening. Solutions must be washed off thoroughly with water before applying film or coating to fabric. This is especially essential when decoating agents, enzymes, and reclaiming solutions are used for reclaiming fabrics. Any trace of these left on the threads will prevent film from adhering. Finally, the printer must follow the specific directions of the film manufacturer when applying or adhering a specific film or coating to the fabric.

Chapter 4

METAL SCREEN FABRICS FOR PRINTING SCREENS

The versatility of screen printing has brought about the use of varied types of screen fabrics for printing screens or screen printing plates. These fabrics were either adapted from other industries (as in the case of bolting silk from the flour sifting industry) or were used because the fabric answered an immediate and practical need.

While various non-metallic cloths such as silk, nylon or polyester are being employed for screen printing, these cannot be used for all printing. Where it is essential that a fabric withstand constant chemical deterioration of inks and solvents as in some dye printing or ceramic printing, where it is necessary for a screen to withstand constant abrasion, where a screen is to be reclaimed almost indefinitely, and generally, where a permanently long lasting durable screen is required, then the printer must use metal cloth fabrics or as it is termed in the trade, "wire gauze."

Because of the uniformty of the diameter of the wire used for weaving the cloth and the fine thickness of the wire available, it is possible to print the most detailed designs with uniformity. The open area in the metal fabric is uniform and greater than that of other screen fabrics. Unlike non-metal cloths, wire mesh or metal fabrics do not absorb inks or solvents and produce a more even color deposit. Frequent change of films does not damage the metal cloth. The inks slide through the metal easily, and metal screen fabrics are especially practical where ceramic inks, frit ink, flaky bronze powder inks, dye inks are used, and generally where precision work such as in fine dials is essential. A heavier ink deposit or thicker coat is obtained with metal screen fabrics. The printing screen is rigid and holds close registration. The metal fabrics may be employed for machine, semi-automatic, and hand printing. In the past, metal fabric was only used on small screens because it was not possible to stretch the metal correctly and because non-metal cloth was and is less costly. However, metal cloth is being used more and more on medium-sized screens and on some large screens. Although metal cloth is more costly and is not as resilient as silk, the constant and indefinite reuse of a metal screen lowers the cost; and the correct stretching and printing techniques can eliminate the second hazard. Screen printers, generally, must learn to handle not only metal fabric screens but other screens with the same care that any precision instrument requires, since precision printing is required of these screens.

Metal cloth employed for printing screens is of two weaves, plain weave and twill weave. The plain weave is generally used; the twill weave is occasionally used in the very fine weaves. As illustrated in Figures 14 and 15, the plain weave is woven so that the individual wire is over one wire and under another; the twill weave is woven over two and under two wires. In both weaves, the openings are square. Twilled weaves are woven of slightly thicker wires.

Like other screen fabrics, metal cloth is classified by number, the number denoting the mesh. Only square mesh (not rectangular mesh) is used for screen printing. Square mesh has the same mesh count or the same size openings both parallel to the length of the cloth and at right angles to the length of the cloth. The mesh or number of openings per lineal inch or centimeter is measured from the center of any given wire to a point 1 inch away from the wire. For example, Number 80 square mesh cloth would have 80 x 80 openings per square inch or 6,400 openings per square inch; while Number 300 metal cloth would have 300 x 300 or 90,000 uniform openings per square inch. Metal cloth is designated just as "Number 80" or "80 x 80," "Number 165" or "165 x 165", etc. Generally, varied meshes are available from about 80 per inch (31 per cm) to about 635 per inch (250 per cm). However, coarser cloths are also available. The lower the number of metal cloth, the larger the openings; the higher the number, the smaller the openings in the screen fabric. For screen printing, the diameter of the wire in the cloth may be given in parts of an inch or parts of a millimeter

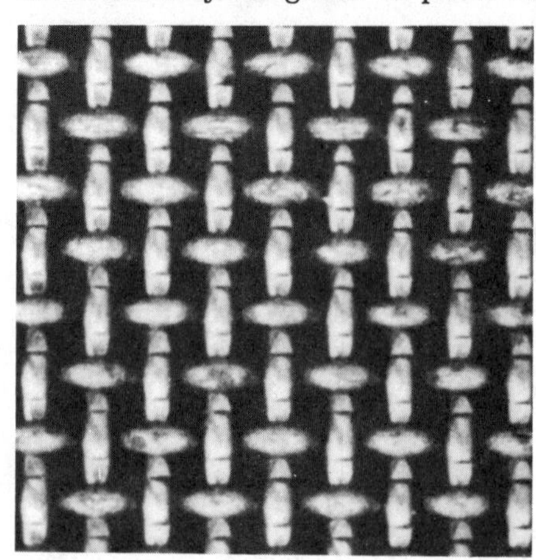

Figure 14. Plain weave. In this weave, each shute wire passes over and under the successive rows of warp wires. Warp wires are those running parallel to the length of cloth; shute wires or fill wires are the wires running directly across cloth. **(Courtesy of Newark Wire Cloth Company, Newark, N.J.)**

Figure 15. Twill weave. Each shute wire passes successively over and under two warp wires; each warp wire passes over and under two shute wires. **(Courtesy of Newark Wire Cloth Company, Newark, N.J.)**

instead of using gauge numbers, as is common with wires. See Figure 16.

The choice of the mesh is dependent on the deisgn to be reproduced, on the type of ink to be reproduced, and on the surface to be printed. The cloth may be purchased from screen printing suppliers in sizes from one square foot (.09 sq. meter) up to any size. Wire cloth is available in widths from 36" (91cm) to about 79" (200.7cm), and in any desired length.

	Mesh	Wire Diameter	Size of Opening	Approximate Percentage of Open Area	Silk Equivalent X, XX, XXX	
Stainless Steel Wire Cloth—Plain Weave	145 x 145	.00215"	.00475"	47.33%	12	—
	150 x 150	.0026"	.0041"	37.4%	—	—
	165 x 165	.0020"	.0041"	45.7%	17	—
	180 x 180	.0018"	.0038"	45.68%	—	—
	200 x 200	.0016"	.0034"	46.2%	—	—
	230 x 230	.0014"	.0030	47.6%	19	—
	250 x 250	.0016"	.0024"	36%	—	—
Phosphor Bronze Wire Cloth—Plain Weave	80 x 80	.0035"	.009"	51%	7	8
	100 x 100	.0032"	.007"	47%	9	10
	120 x 120	.0027"	.0056"	45.6%	11	12
	130 x 130	.0023"	.0054"	49.3%	12–13	—
	140 x 140	.0023"	.0048"	45.9%	—	—
	150 x 150	.0026"	.0041"	37.4%	—	—

Figure 16. Technical data of some wire cloths used for screen printing with some equivalent silk fabric numbers. **(Courtesy of Factory Enterprises, Inc., Pittsburgh, Pennsylvania)**

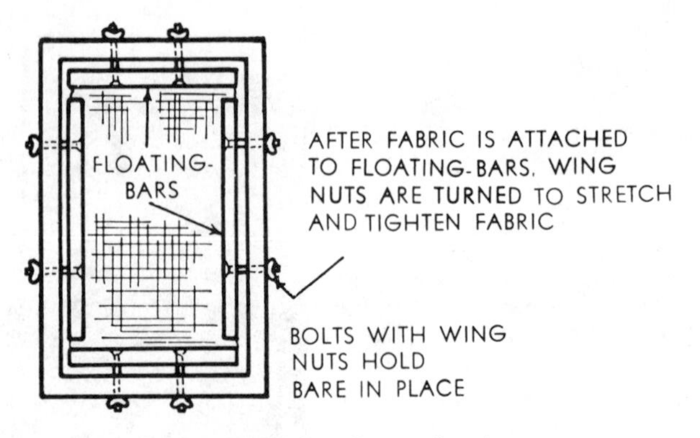

Figure 17. A four floating-bar frame.

Stretching Metal Screen Fabrics

Although metal screen fabrics are not as easy to stretch and attach to frames as non-metal fabrics, this should not present a problem to the printer. The metal fabric may be tacked or stapled to wooden frames, attached and stretched on floating-bar frames (see Figure 17), soldered and cemented to metal frames, and attached to special frames for hand and machine printing.

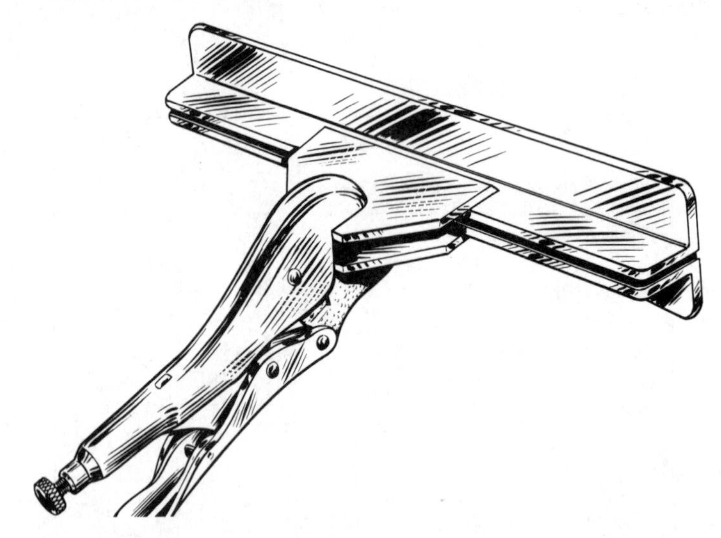

Figure 18. A tool made especially for easy and uniform stretching of all screen fabrics; rubber grip prevents slippage and tool allows for tension adjustment by turning knurled knob and for releasing jaws by flipping bottom lever. **(Courtesy of Silk Screen Supplies, Inc., Brooklyn, N.Y.)**

Suppliers and manufacturers recommend that metal gauze intended for precision work be attached to metal frames, since metal frames are not subject to any distortion. Aluminum, iron, and other metal may be used for the frame. Light-weight tubular frames are practical to use.

If wood is employed for the frame, it should be a strong type. The writer has had practical results with wood floating-bar frames that have been finished by soaking the frame and floating-bars with linseed oil. In attaching the metal fabric to the wood, the cloth is tacked or stapled first on the long side of the frame, then on one of the short sides of the frame, then on the opposite long side, and finally, on the second short side of the frame. In attaching the cloth, the cloth may be stretched with a seamer or stretching pliers which have a wide grip and which do not tear the cloth as shown in Figure 18. These stretching tools are available from suppliers and do aid in obtaining a greater pull on the cloth during the stretching operation. The stapling of the cloth is done through two or three layers of the fabric or, as illustrated in Figure 19, by using paper fiber about $\frac{1}{64}''$ (.398mm) in thickness.

Perhaps, the practical way for the beginner to attach wire gauze and stretch it well is to employ the floating-bar frame. For metal fabrics, three or four bars are used. It is suggested that the bars be the same dimensions as the sides of the frame. Also, it is advisable that a close-grained tough wood be used and that the wood be finished by rubbing well with linseed oil. Since metal printing screens are used for long periods of time, it is well to use care in the finishing operation. The metal fabric may be tacked or stapled to the floating-bars. Enough pressure is then put on the bolts to stretch and tighten the cloth for the printing job at hand. Care should be used in the handling of the screen so that no objects are dropped on the fabric parts, since kinking, indentations, or sag may result. Kinks cannot be removed, therefore carelessness must be avoided.

If a commercial stretching unit is available of the type illustrated in Figure 12, it may be used to stretch metal fabric onto the screen. Practical frames for metal screen fabrics are commercial frames built especially for hand, semi-automatic, and machine printing. These stretch metal fabrics easily and quickly onto the frame.

Sensitized photographic coatings such as polyvinyl alcohol, polyvi-

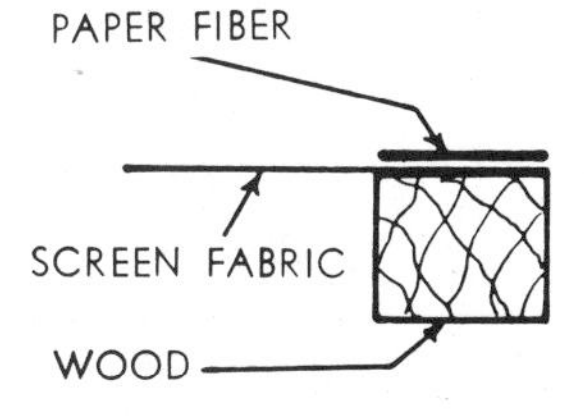

Figure 19. Tacking or stapling metal screen fabric to underside of frame.

nyl acetate, modified plastics, commercial screen printing emulsion coatings, gelatinous coatings, transfer-type sensitized screen printing films, direct-indirect screen printing films, and knife-cut films may be attached to metal screen fabrics, providing the screen fabric is prepared correctly.

The important step in the preparation of the fabric when making a printing screen is to ensure that the metal fabric is cleaned perfectly. Since metal is non-absorbent, it is essential that the fabric be clean and devoid of oil, grease, reclaiming solutions, and finger marks, in order that the emulsion, film, or coating used to make up the printing screen adhere well to the wire gauze. Most metal screen fabrics have a protective oily coating on the threads and also handling marks. These must all be removed completely and the metal must be immaculately clean before attaching the emulsion, coating, or film.

The metal fabric may be cleaned in the following ways: (1) The screen fabric may be cleaned with a 5 to 10 per cent glacial acetic acid solution for about 5 minutes and then rinsed well with hot water; (2) The fabric may be held and moved directly over a gas flame or Bunsen burner and then scrubbed with a clean brush to prepare the fabric for receiving films or coatings. However, one must be careful not to hold the metal too long over the flame. (3) Any mild caustic may be employed to wash the fabric and then a hot water rinse used to remove the caustic solution. (4) An older method of cleaning wire gauze is to insert a block the same thickness as the screen frame under the wire. The wire may be scrubbed with a coarse cloth that has been dipped in pumice and naptha or pumice and lacquer thinner. After the fabric is rinsed well in hot water, the film or coating will adhere to the wire. (5) A 10 per cent alkali solution or a 20 per cent ammonia solution may be used to clean or degrease the wire cloth. (6) Also, commercial cleaning solvents may be obtained from screen printing suppliers for this purpose. Finger marks must be kept off the cloth after the fabric is cleaned.

Care must be employed in the storage of metal fabric screens that no objects fall or are dropped onto the fabric.

Chapter 5

SCREEN PRINTING INKS

Color is part of nature's plan. Man cannot avoid it, since colors influence the nervous system of any person with normal eyesight. Basically, colors are used because they make graphic arts presentation more natural and lifelike and because they afford a medium for reproducing the environment or that to which we respond. Because of its unusual graphic color presentation, screen printing has made great impact in graphic communications.

The screen printing industry began to show growing pains only when colored inks were developed that could be used directly from the container and under normal conditions. Although at present, on occasion, the term "paints" is used in place of "inks," the term "paints" was used originally when the industry was developing. It was felt that "paints" had a better connotation as far as general qualities for a printing medium were concerned than "poster colors" (another term used in the early days of screen printing). However, the medium used in screen printing is ink, since its results are the same as those produced by inks in the other graphic arts and its application is done by squeegee, rollers, and vacuum, while paints are brushed, sprayed, or rolled onto a surface.

Plus all the qualities of ink generally used, screen printing inks must meet other prerequisites. The ink must be deposited by squeegeeing through the cloth bearing the design onto stock placed under the screen. In doing this, there must be no sluggishness under the squeegee, regardless of method, whether done by hand or mechanically. The inks must not clog or stop up the mesh or openings in the cloth; they must not cut and wear the cloth; they must not dissolve or destroy the printing screen being used. They should print a clean edge and not one that is ragged, crawling, or creeping. Generally, these inks must dry either through oxidation, evaporation, polymerization, fusion, or combinations of these methods, yet not so fast that they clog the screen. However, the newer UV (ultraviolet) curing inks dry almost instantly when exposed to ultraviolet energy; yet they do not clog the screen. Where necessary, they must be deposited thick and leave an embossed effect, sometimes about twenty per cent heavier than that done by ordinary relief printing. Where not necessary, as in printing halftones and in dye printing on textiles, they should leave no embossed effect.

Screen printing inks must adhere to the following surfaces: paper, cardboard, wood, metal, plastics, rubber, textiles, glass, ceramic products, leather, cork, plaster, and combinations of the above materials. Also, the color and ink should not rub off or chip off the material upon which it is printed. Most important, screen printing inks must not interfere with the printing operations in any phase of the printing cycle.

Inks should stand some "doctoring up" by the printer. However, this should be done according to the manufacturer's specifications, since too often the user will cheapen and spoil a product, after the manufacturer's chemists have spent years developing an excellent ink worked out under given conditions according to a specified formula. The pigment in the ink must have an enduring and changeless quality as far as color is concerned. We see then that inks are as changeable as the wind as far as their properties are concerned. The industry may well take pride in the fact that such requirements have been met. In fact, there are some inks (such as fluorescent inks) whose most practical method of application is by means of screen printing.

Not only are there different requirements for inks in the industry but their classifications vary. While classification of screen printing inks is a difficult task, they may be grouped according to (a) surface upon which they are applied; (b) as natural or synthetic; (c) as opaque, transparent, semi-transparent (translucent); (d) as flat, semi-gloss, gloss, and luminescent; (e) according to vehicle used; (f) according to their method of drying; and (g) specialized inks. When the screen printer understands the classifications, he will understand generally the subject of screen printing ink. The varied classification is the result of borrowing and adapting from related industries in the early stages of screen printing and the developing of products particularly suited for screen printing in the later stages and stages pending. Although, only that was borrowed which was necessary to give it birth, the resulting industry is one with products and techniques that supplement graphic arts and enhance the value and appearance of products in other industries.

According to the surface upon which inks are applied, inks are known as "vinylite inks," "glass inks," "glass etching inks," "textile inks," "porcelain inks," etc. Natural inks are those made from substances found directly or indirectly in nature, while synthetic inks are all or partly man-made and are the result of chemical research.

Opaque inks have the ability of hiding the surfaces completely over which they are printed and also do not permit light to pass through. Obviously, transparent inks permit light and vision to pass through. In this class are also included those inks that can be used directly to print over other shades producing one or more different colors. In using opaque inks, two or more colors may be mixed before printing to produce a third color but the ink will not print over another color and produce a third color as a result of printing. Semi-transparent or transluscent inks have a transparency that is between opacity and transparency.

In the fourth classification, flat inks, are included those that dry with a non-glossy finish. The gloss and semi-gloss are inks of different degrees of shiny finish depending upon whether there is a "long oil varnish" or a "short oil varnish" in them. Varnishes are designated as long oil, medium oil, and short oil. This classification is dependent on the number of gallons of oil there is per 100 pounds of gum or resin. For example, long oil varnish usually contains about 25 to 50 gallons of oil per 100 pounds of gum or resin, while short oil varnish contains about 5 gallons to 100 pounds of gum. Long oil inks have gloss, are usually sold as enamels, and are made by grinding pigment in natural or synthetic resin oils and drying agents. Luminescent inks are of three types: fluorescent inks, daylight fluorescent inks, and phosphorescent. Fluorescent inks glow under ultra violet light or black light. Daylight fluorescent inks glow or emit light in the daylight when exposed to daylight (not direct sunlight, however, as this limits their use). The phosphorescent inks continue to glow or emit light after the charging light is removed.

The vehicle classification is a very practical and informative one. A *vehicle* is a liquid or substance with which very finely ground pigments and other materials are mixed, dissolved, or suspended. Generally, the vehicle is made up of solvent and binder. The binder serves to bind the parts of the ink together and aids in the application of the ink; the solvent makes the ink fluid so that the ink can be printed. Vehicles that are used in screen printing are definitely dependent on other products that go into the ink and are not necessarily made up of one substance. They and the related substances that go into the ink determine the compatibility of the ink or pigment. A pigment is said to be compatible when it is capable chemically of existing in an ink or paint mixture without harmfully reacting to itself or other parts of the mixture. It is interesting to note that while UV inks generally consist of pigment, vehicle, and a reactive agent or sensitizer known as a "photoinitiator," the vehicle is 100 per cent solids.

In the vehicle classification, inks may be known as oil inks, synthetic inks, oil and water inks (emulsions), and water inks. Oil inks are made of pigments or oil-soluble dyes that are ground or mixed in natural or synthetic oils. Pigments are usually powdered forms of coloring matter; dyes are generally coloring matter dissolved in a liquid.

Oil inks dry by oxidation. This means that the oil combines with the oxygen which burns the oil slowly and hardens the film. Drying oils used are such oils as linseed oil, soy bean oil, tung oil, or perilla.

Because these oils, which are in liquid or paste form, dry slowly, certain driers made up of salts of metals are added to the inks to hasten the drying. Cobalt, T japan, lead, manganese, and others are added to hasten drying.

Synthetic vehicle inks contain resins or oils which are formed by chemically controlled reactions and generally use plastic types of materials as part of the ink composition. The pigment, which may be man-made or a natural one, is mixed with the vehicle and other parts in such a way that the resulting ink be of squeegee consistency and its drying controlled.

A resin is a natural or synthetic solid or semi-solid organic material obtained by means of chemical reaction. As part of an ink, it may approximate natural resins in varied properties. When the resins are dissolved to the liquid state and suspended in a vehicle, on drying, they produce an ink or coating forming a hard, solid, and resistant surface. Synthetic resins such as alkyds, ureas, phenolics, modified phenolics, and others differ from natural resins in chemical construction and in their behavior with reagents.

The vehicles in lacquer and lacquer enamels, which are also synthetics, are usually mixtures of resin, plasticizers, cellulose nitrate, or other cellulose derivatives. Plasticizers or softeners aid in obtaining a thoroughly mixed homogeneous product and give desirable properties. The vehicle is combined with drying oils, metallic driers, and solvents which are the evaporating agents.

Synthetic inks dry by evaporation, polymerization, or both. In evaporation, the volatile substances evaporate and leave a film consisting of gums, resins, and pigments. Polymerization is a chemical reaction in which single minute particles of matter (molecules) link and form larger molecules without any change in atom ratios. With synthetic inks, drying must occur normally and must exclude low temperature, high humidity, and excessive thickness of film. Synthetic inks are made so that they may air dry or may be baked according to given temperatures and time to hasten drying and improve the film.

Table II shows some materials and inks that may be applied to the materials.

Solvents for varying conditions in working with synthetic inks differ depending upon the given ink and manufacturer. It is obvious, therefore, that since these inks are complex chemicals, they cannot be mixed readily by the average person; and any variation in their composition must be done specifically according to the manufacturer's directions.

Where it is necessary to do constant mixing of inks, mechanical mixers of the type illustrated in Figure 20 may be used.

Since some solvents and inks may be flammable, they should be used with care and not exposed to open flames, sparks of electricity, and lit cigarettes. Where a shop may have many different inks and

MATERIAL	TYPE OF INK					
	OIL	SYNTHETIC	WATER	DYE	PORCELAIN ENAMEL	*LUMINESCENT
CARDBOARD	x	x	x	x		x
CERAMIC PRODUCTS	x	x			x	
DECALCOMANIA		x				
GLASS	x	x				
LEATHER	x	x		x		
METAL	x	x			x	
PAPER	x	x	x	x		x
PLASTICS	x	x				
RUBBER	x	x		x		
TEXTILES	x	x		x		
WOOD	x	x	x	x		

* May be applied to other materials if correct undercoat is used.

Table II. Different materials and inks that may be printed on these materials.

solvents in storage, they generally are stored in explosion-proof rooms. Also, if certain solvents are toxic or health hazards, their inhaling and coming in direct contact with a worker's skin should be avoided.

In oil and water vehicle inks, the smaller proportion of the vehicle is oil and serves to give better qualities to the ink. Water inks are made of such pigments as earth colors and artificially prepared mineral pigments which are mixed with such water soluble gums or binders as gum arabic, dextrine, glue, casein, or water glass. Those used for screen printing work are the finest ground artist's color mixed generally in water, glue, and glycerine.

A distinction must be made between gums and resins used in screen printing inks, even though they both produce the same result.

Figure 20. "E-Z" paint and ink mixer for mechanical mixing of screen printing inks, stiff viscous paints, and thin liquids. Mixer uses five gallon, two gallon, and one gallon pails as the mixing container. **(Courtesy of Naz-Dar Company, Chicago, IL)**

A gum is a substance that dissolves or swells in water and is compounded by nature. A resin usually doesn't dissolve in water and may be found in nature or may be man-made.

There are three sources for color used in screen printing inks: earth, chemical, and lake. Earth colors are found naturally and are collected and refined for specific purposes. Chemical colors, which are being used more and more, are obtained by chemical reaction between different compounds and elements, and are as complex as the field of chemistry. Lake colors are a special type of organic (animal and plant) coloring matter made with inert substances such as alumina or whiting. They can be combined with a transparent or semi-transparent base of squeegee consistency, and they do have pronounced transparency when made into an oil ink. The latter colors must not be mixed with the other colors, unless so specified, as harmful reactions to the color will occur.

Dyes in the form of inks in the screen printing industry are of three types: direct; those that require mordants; and special dyes*. A direct dye is used to print on textiles and is applied to the cloth directly without any mordants (agents which penetrate the fiber to be colored and aid the dyestuff in forming a compound that is insoluble upon the fiber). Those that require mordants may be printed directly on cloth after a mordant has been mixed into the ink, or the cloth may have to be treated before being printed. Special dye inks are prepared chemicals for given textiles and are applied under specific conditions. Generally, they require some method of curing or finishing with heat or steam so that the dye will be fast.

There are definite times when the printer has to change the qualities of the ink he is using such as to retard drying, to hasten drying, to use extenders, etc. Of course, in using any of these compounds, he must follow the manufacturer's directions. A *retarder* is a solution such as lithol varnish or lithol oil which slows drying and improves screening qualities. Varnishes used in graphic arts are classified according to consistency ranging in numbers from No. 00000 to No. 8, No. 00000 being the thinnest in consistency and No. 8 being the heaviest. Numbers 1, 2, and 3 are generally recommended for screen printing work.

An *extender* is a product that "extends the ink used" and reduces the cost of printing. They are substances that add more bulk and hardness to the ink and, of course, increase area coverage. They should not change the color tone and quality of the ink. There is a limit to how much extender can be used, since it reduces the opacity of the ink in relation to the amount of extender used.

A *transparent* base is a clear, neutral colored substance of buttery consistency which may be used to (a) thicken inks that are too thin; (b) prevent creeping, blurring, and ragged edges in inks that have too much flow; and (c) to obtain transparent inks by mixing the base with concentrated colors that are not meant to be used by themselves because of their great color strength. These bases consist of such metallic soaps as aluminum stearate or aluminum hydrate mixed with a vehicle.

A *reducer* reduces the length of drying time for ink. Here again, the reducer must not change the color or alter the working qualities of the ink. *Driers* that are added to ink to accelerate drying are governed by the type of ink and the compounds in the ink. The drier used is determined by the fact whether the ink dries by oxidation, etc. Each drier will react differently and should be used only as recommended.

* The following book treats the subject of textile screen printing and dyes more completely: Kosloff, Albert, *Textile/Garment Screen Printing*, ST Publications, Book Division, Cincinnati, Ohio.

Any of the inks and the compounds used to vary the qualities of the inks mentioned are obtainable in pint (.473 liter), quart (.946 liter), half gallon (1.89 kilogram), and gallon size (3.78 kilogram).

There are also additives which were developed specifically for screen printing: for example, anti-dry screen sprays and anti-static compounds. The anti-dry sprays are recommended for spraying the inside of printing screens for prevention of drying of inks in the screen and prevention of loss of time in washing screens. Anti-static compounds are added to the ink to prevent build-up of static electricity which induces clinging of sheets or material to printing screen and smearing of prints.

Since today's screen printing inks are chemicals formulated to produce specific results, before the screen printer selects an ink for a difficult material surface, he should check into the properties of the ink. Inks are manufactured for both general and specific work. For example, there are long-oil alkyd inks which are prepared for printing on paper, cardboard, foil, glass, wood, metal, felt, acetate, acrylics, treated polyethylene, butyrate, phenolics, polyesters, polystyrene, and as an adhesive for flocking. On the other hand, an acetate ink may be formulated specifically for use on acetate material, an acrylic ink for acrylic surfaces, and a specific vinyl ink may be recommended for vinyls and for vacuum forming work. Epoxy inks or catalytic inks were developed for adhesion to difficult surfaces such as glass, ceramics, ferrous and non-ferrous metals, and to thermoplastics and thermosetting plastics.

It must be evident to the screen printer that to develop one or two types of inks that would meet all screen printing requirements is a very difficult task. Therefore, the beginner should try out any ink first on a sample of the specific material that is to be printed before running the complete job. When mixing ink, he should mix it on the same color material that is to be printed, or better yet, on a glass placed over the colored material to be printed to obtain an impression of how the stock and color of ink will blend or contrast. When in doubt, the screen printer must work closely with the manufacturer of the ink.

In summary, the screen printer must realize that the whole purpose of graphic communication is to produce a specific image in the observer's or reader's mind. The correct use of design, color, and pretesting of ink all aid in this endeavor.

Chapter 6

FLUORESCENT SCREEN PRINTING INKS

The growth and history of the screen printing industry is punctuated by important developments which seem to stand out and which have contributed greatly to the industry. Some of these developments (which are interdependent) were the introduction of knife-cut film for the making of printing screens, the introduction of ready-to-use screen printing inks, the standardization of the preparation of photographic printing screens, the organization of the Screen Printing Association International, mechanization, the availability and dissemination of technical information to needy screen printers, and the development of fluorescent inks and colors.

Screen printing daylight fluorescent inks came into general use in about 1948 and made an impact on the whole graphic arts industry with their brilliance, dramatic vividness, eye-catching appeal, and their stress on the important message in both copy and art. Since they are best applied by means of screen printing, they are a common ink or color in the average screen printing shop. Screen printing is ideal for printing these colors, since a relatively thick uniform coating is required to insure full brightness, stability, and weatherability. Also, while the more recently developed and manufactured daylight fluorescent ink can be printed through finer screen fabric meshes, fluorescent pigments are somewhat coarser in particle size than conventional pigments. These daylight fluorescent inks are printed on thousands of window displays, decals, bumper strips, industrial safety applications, car cards, letterheads, posters, 24-sheet posters, blotters, pennants, magazine covers, greeting cards, outside cardboard, sign cloth, and numerous other items. Because of the striking difference between ordinary and daylight fluorescent colors, fluorescent inks play a very important role in screen printing for outdoor and indoor advertising.

Daylight fluorescent inks are luminescent materials. Luminescent materials are substances which give off or emit light. The light may come originally from the radiant energy of the sun which is absorbed by some substances when the energy attempts to pass through the substance. Since the absorbed energy cannot disappear, it may reappear in the form of heat, or it may produce photochemical action as light does on a photographic film, or the energy may just be emitted as visible light. The absorbed radiant energy is of shorter wave length than the energy or rays given off. The action of giving out light of one color by absorbing light of a different color is known as fluorescence. Phosphorescence is the emission in darkness of previously absorbed light. The difference between fluorescence and phosphorescence is that phosphorescent materials absorb both natural and artificial light and glow in darkness after the light source is removed. Fluorescent materials glow in daylight or as long as the activating or light source is present. These inks are also fluorescent under "black light" which is another name for ultra-violet light. These fluorescent colors are not luminous in darkness, that is, they do not glow in the dark unless exposed to black light. The inks not only have regular colors of their own but also possess the ability of absorbing daylight and changing the daylight into stronger color of the same hue or same color.

Ordinary ink or paint color is reflected light, and each ordinary color has a different wave length or output of energy. For example, red reflects its own color when light falls on it; the other colors are absorbed and dissipated as heat. A fluorescent red color owes part of its color also to reflected light. However, the fluorescent color converts the other colors (green, blue, and violet) to the wave length of red and emits them as red light. These colors glow as if lighted from within. It is this glowing property that has made this type of colors known as daylight fluorescent inks or colors. The fluorescent inks used by the average printer have up to four times the brightness and visibility of corresponding hues of conventional screen printing inks. Fluorescent inks appear to be very bright in dim light such as dusk or dawn and are very effective under black light.

For a diagramatic explanation of the reflection characteristics of ordinary colors, in terms of their respective wave lengths as measured in Angstrom units, see Figure 21. Figure 22 illustrates the addition of light by conversion of shorter wave lengths to the length reflected by the basic daylight fluorescent color. It is this conversion and addition to the basic wave length that gives daylight fluorescent colors the additional brilliance and visibility.

Originally, the daylight fluorescent colors were stable for about 30 days when activated or exposed directly to sunlight; now the light stability of these colors in outdoor exposure has improved greatly. The colors will last indefinitely indoors and may be employed in graphic arts where vividness and impact of color are essential. Although fluorescent inks available now are finer ground, quicker drying, and more easily applied in a thinner film, manufacturer's directions for their application must be followed in their use.

The pigments used in the inks are basically fluorescent dye-stuffs which are carefully and chemically compounded, milled, and mixed

Comparative Wave Lengths
Ordinary Colors

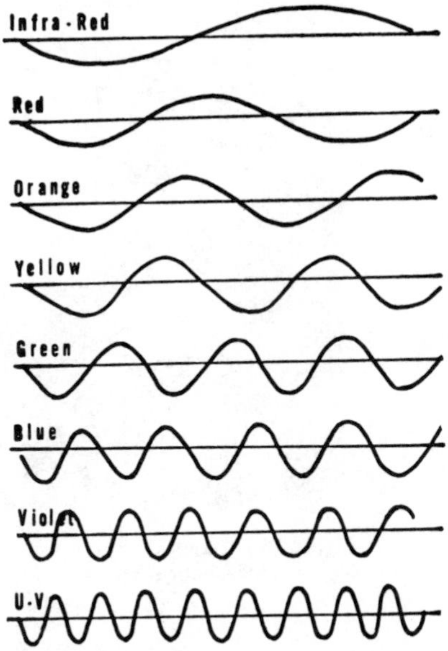

Infra-Red
Red
Orange
Yellow
Green
Blue
Violet
U-V

Figure 21. Ordinary colors reflect only their own wave lengths as shown in the chart above. Invisible infra-red has an ultra-long length not discernible to the eye. The shorter length of the red wave initiates the visible colors and each wave length grows progressively shorter as its color approaches the ultra-short, invisible ultra-violet band.

Comparative Wave Lengths
Daylight Fluorescent Colors

Infra-Red
Orange
Yellow
Green
Blue
Violet

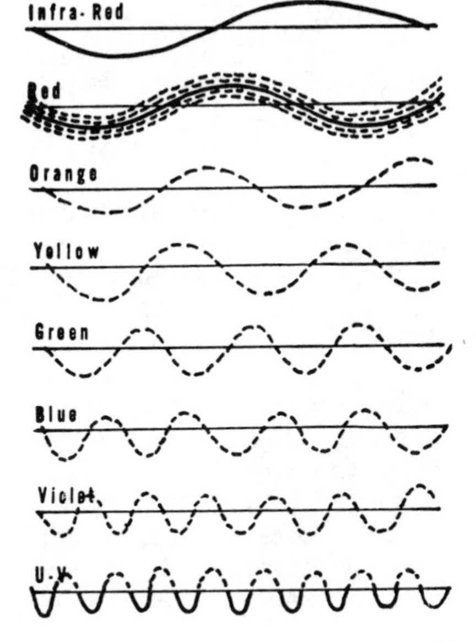

Figure 22. Note that basic wave lengths for each daylight fluorescent color correspond to those of the ordinary colors. However, red, for example, as shown, "borrows" from hues of shorter wave length, converting to the red wave length, thus adding strength both in brilliance and in visibility. Daylight fluorescent colors cannot convert the longer wave lengths, only the shorter ones; consequently the extra strength diminishes as the basic colors are lower in the spectrum, as, for example blue.

Figure 23. A research laboratory for the constant improving and developing of fluorescent inks and paints. **(Courtesy of Lawter Chemicals, Inc., Northbrook, Illinois)**

in a laboratory-controlled plastic resin. Daylight fluorescent colors are dyes trapped inside a colorless, transparent, insoluble resin. The resin is ground to a powder which is then mixed and milled into a carefully selected carrier. See Figures 23 and 24. The amount of dye held in each tiny part of the ground resin is small, and this necessitates putting an extraordinary amount of pigment or ground resin into each of the fluorescent colors to obtain practical maximum brightness.

Using Fluorescent Inks

Generally, there are two types of daylight fluorescent inks—the oil base and the fast-dry type. The inks are printed through standard printing screens used in the industry. However, the screen must resist the dissolving action of the inks. For example, a lacquer knife-cut film should not be used for printing fast-dry lacquer-type fluorescent inks. Here again, the manufacturer's directions must be followed specifically for best results. There are varied bright colors available from the manufacturers and suppliers. Each color should be mixed thoroughly before using. Thinners used with the color should be ones recommended by the manufacturer. Daylight fluorescent colors should not be mixed with other fluorescent colors or with other types of inks, since the mixture may not "fluoresce." The excessive use of thinners does reduce brightness and stability; therefore, they should be used with discretion. For

Figure 24. A paint mill grinding fluorescent materials. The mill exerts a rubbing or milling action on the pre-mixed ink or paint causing a breaking down of the pigment agglomerates. The finer the pigment particles, the smoother the ink or paint film. **(Courtesy of Lawter Chemicals, Inc., Northbrook, Illinois)**

indoor exposure where the ink is not subject to direct sunlight, the printed coat will remain effective for many months and the ink may be printed through a Number 12 or Number 14 screen fabric or its equivalent. However, where the printing is intended for longer outdoor exposure (such as on gasoline service promotions) a Number 8 or Number 10 silk or its equivalent should be used for printing. Most fluorescent inks are applied with one stroke of the squeegee, either in hand printing or in machine printing. Of course, a double stroke of the squeegee or less pressure on squeegee will produce a thicker film. The thicker the coating, the greater is its resistance to exposure. The printed inks may be dried naturally or may be force-dried on the various available drying machines.

Daylight fluorescent colors show off to greatest advantage when they are surrounded by dark, contrasting colors and are brightest when they are applied over a white surface. To achieve the most striking effects, fluorescent colors should not be used alone. They may be employed in spots to bring out important points. The fluorescent color may also be surrounded with about 50 per cent dark or contrasting color. They are not practical for fine halftone printing except where a black halftone illustration may be printed on a surface on which has been coated a solid film of fluorescent ink. Where lettering is printed with these inks, there should be plenty of space between the letters to make reading easier. The fluorescent ink should have a flat finish. Flat films absorb light; glossy films reflect light and do not allow light to activate the fluorescent ink.

Fluorescent and phosphorescent inks are not radioactive and are non-hazardous. However, it must be stressed that radioactive inks which are self-luminous are frequently applied by screen printing (for example, on watches and clock dials) and are hazardous to those unskilled in handling such materials.

Fast-Dry Daylight Fluorescent Inks

The fast-dry daylight fluorescent inks are daylight fluorescent pigments ground in a quick drying vehicle. These inks are bright, more flexible, and are practical for outdoor posters. They dry mostly by evaporation. They must be printed through lacquer-proof screens such as photographic types, water applied films, glue-tusche types, and knife-cut paper printing screens. Bleached resistant-type squeegees are recommended for printing fast-dry inks.

Where daylight fluorescent inks are being printed on a surface that is not white, the surface should be coated first with a flexible white undercoat. Daylight fluorescent fast-dry inks may be printed on the uncoated side of sign cloth, on plastics, on nylon, and on unfilled cotton. When in doubt as to adherence of ink to printing surface, a test printing should be made.

Daylight fluorescent displays are printed to be exhibited only for the useful life of the ink and not for the life of the display. If the fast-dry inks are protected from the direct sunlight, they will be effective for a long time. Daylight fluorescent printed displays may be stored under cover indefinitely without change similar to plain screen printing inks.

The fast-dry inks dry naturally in about 30 minutes and may be force-dried in 30 seconds to 2 minutes under standard driers when exposed to a heat ranging from about 180 to 250 degrees Fahrenheit (82 to 121 C).

A well ventilated area is essential for printing and drying. Drying process must be complete to prevent offsetting when the printed matter is stacked. One stroke of the squeegee may be used to apply a coat thickness of approximately 1.00 to 1.5 thousandths of an inch (.0025 to .0038cm). After printing, the screen may be cleaned with lacquer thinner, toluol, xylol, naphtha, or solvent recommended by manufacturer. Screen fabrics equivalent to Number 8XX to 14XX may be employed for indoor displays; screen fabrics equivalent to 8XX and 10XX may be used for outdoor displays.

After posting 24-sheet displays, it is recommended that the poster be washed with clear water, since paste absorbs ultraviolet and cuts down on brightness.

Oil-Base Daylight Fluorescent Inks

The oil base inks, if well printed, will hold their brightness for the same length of time as the fast-dry inks, about 3 to 6 months of outside exposure. The inks dry by means of an oxidation-polymerization process naturally in about 1 to 4 hours depending on the stock printed, thickness of coat, and other shop conditions. Heat from gas, infra-red, and jet-type driers may be used to force dry the inks. As much heat may be used for drying these inks as is employed for general drying of ordinary ink on screen printing stock. Oil base inks may be applied through most printing screens onto paper, wood, metal, glass, decal papers, and other surfaces having a flat white undercoat. The

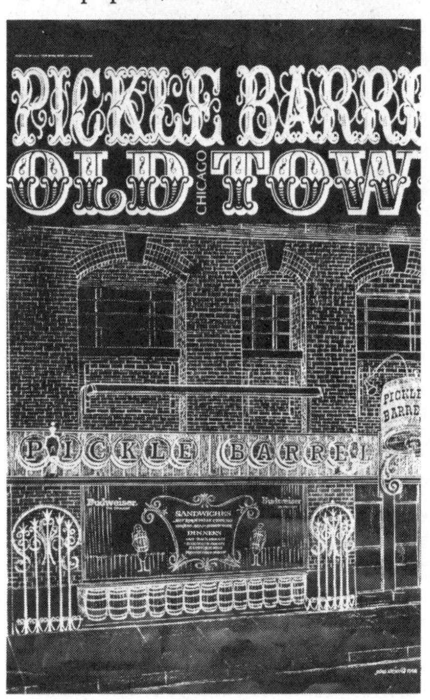

Figure 25. An attractive 21″ x 29″ (25.3cm x 73.7cm) multi-color poster printed in two impressions. Varied fluorescent colors were printed in one impression on a special multi-color press; the second impression printed black to stress all the colors printed in the first impression. **(Courtesy of Burke Communications Industries, Inc., Chicago, Illinois)**

inks may be printed through Number 8 up to Number 16 silk or equivalent screen fabric.

The inks may be thinned with mineral spirits or solvents recommended by the manufacturer. Lettering printed should be bold style and offer contrast to the rest of the copy. Overprint varnish should not be coated over the ink, since fluorescence may be decreased.

Oil base inks should not be mixed with fast-dry lacquer fluorescent inks. Similar to fast-dry inks, in wet posting of 24-sheet posters, the

Figure 26. A multi-color poster, printed for display in all parts of the world by means of fluorescent colors, beautifully interprets the sparkling mood of a large city. **(Courtesy of Switzer Brothers, Inc., Cleveland, Ohio)**

posting paste should be washed off with water from the fluorescent surface.

Figures 25 and 26 illustrate displays printed with daylight fluorescent inks.

Black-Light Fluorescent Colors

Black-light fluorescent colors are best applied by screen printing. Black-light fluorescent inks are activated by "black light" (see Chapter 5). Sometimes these colors are called "invisible" because they have neutral or near-white colors in daylight or under incandescent light. Most black-light inks appear like conventional colors in ordinary daylight. However, they do glow with amazing and brilliant effects when they are activated by a lamp or a source of near-ultraviolet light. The source may be a mercury vapor lamp or a black-light fluorescent lamp available for this purpose. The difference between black-light fluorescent inks and daylight fluorescent inks is that the latter inks are fluorescent under daylight and under black light; while black-light fluorescent inks are only activated by black light.

The printing of black-light colors is similar to screen printing daylight fluorescent inks. These colors do not mix like ordinary screen printing inks; since under black light, the results may not always be the same. The printer should follow specifically the directions of the manufacturer in their use.

Chapter 7

SOLVENTS USED IN SCREEN PRINTING

The ambition of developing a universal solvent that would be safe and practical to use for all purposes in screen printing may be compared to the development of a universal drug that could cure all illness. Humans vary and their illnesses vary. As long as the printer will print on every possible material and shape, he will have to learn to adjust to the use of existing solvents.

Many chemical solutions are employed in screen printing. These solutions are used to thin ink, retard and accelerate drying, extend the covering power of an ink or finish, clean screens after printing, remove film or emulsion from screen fabrics, clean screen fabrics before application of film or emulsions, and other uses. Simply defined, solutions are mixtures consisting of a solute and a solvent. The solute is the substance which is dissolved; it may be a solid, liquid, or a gaseous substance. The solvent is generally a liquid in which the solute dissolves. Often the solvent may be an organic solvent employed to dissolve solid materials such as resins. As far as the printer is concerned, solvents are compounds or substances which are used to dissolve other substances in order to form solutions that are essentially alike and to provide a means of transferring a solid substance (in the form of ink) from one place to another such as in printing, roller coating, and finishing. A solvent is really a processing agent which has been developed to be used under specific conditions.

Since the screen printer employs different types of inks, he will also use varied solvents. It is important, therefore, that he become familiar with those that he used frequently, with the classification of solvents generally, and with terms commonly employed to explain the properties of solvents. Solvents are almost as important as the ink that the printer uses. He employs solvents to change the viscosity of ink and to dissolve solids. He uses them as evaporating agents and as plasticizers. Used incorrectly, they are hazardous, costly, time consuming, produce printing difficulties, decrease efficiency, and lose customers. It is no accident that an ink manufacturer specifies types of solvents to use and often insists on the customer using the manufacturer's tailormade product. The printer must realize that a solvent which dissolves one ink easily may have absolutely no solvent power for another type of ink. Inks today are the result of laboratory experimentation and of chemical formulation. Formulations are changed either positively or negatively with the addition of solvents. For example, if the printer is printing with an acrylic ink, any of the following solvents such as ester, ketone, ether-alcohol, toluene, benzene, or ethylene chloride will affect the ink. However, only the manufacturer of the specific ink knows his formulation and can recommend the most practical solvent or combination of solvents for thinning or retarding drying. This example can be repeated for almost any screen printing ink. Also, since many inks and finishes are synthetic and are printed on varied materials, slightly different solvents may be used; although the solvents may belong to one classification. An example of the latter is adhering liquid used to partly dissolve or soften the knife-cut lacquer-type film in adhering film to screen fabric. The active solvent in most of the adhering liquids is of the ketone or ester type. These are modified with solvents and diluents by the manufacturer so that the liquid will not dissolve the film completely, so that the solvent will not be too toxic, so that it will be somewhat safer to use, and will not injure the skin when solvent is used repeatedly. It is obvious, therefore, that solvents manufactured for specific purposes must be used as per specifications.

The paint, varnish, lacquer, and ink industries use mostly the following types of solvents: turpentine, alcohols, esters, ketones, ether-alcohol, coal-tar and petroleum hydrocarbons, and plasticizers.

For the printer, the important solvents may be petroleum hydrocarbons. Hydrocarbons are chemical compounds composed of hydrogen and carbon. They are divided into two groups known as aliphatic and aromatic. The chemical difference between these two groups is in the structure or arrangement of the atoms of hydrogen and carbon within the molecule. However, from a practical point of view the distinguishing factor between these two groups is one of solvency.

Example of aliphatic solvents are mineral spirits, kerosene, naphtha, and benzene. Aliphatic solvents are generally characterized by low solvent power and a K.B. value of about 27 to 50. The K.B. value represents a standard in a range of solvency value derived from a test known as a Kauri-Butanol test. The Kauri-Butanol value is a measure of the solvent power of hydrocarbon solvents. Solvent power is a liquid's ability to dissolve certain substances. It causes a decrease in viscosity or an increase in the fluidity of a substance. Solvent power prevents precipitation or separation into solid form. For example, according to this test, toluol or toluene with a solvent power or value of 105 K.B. represents very high solvency while kerosene with a K.B. of about 29 represents low solvency value.

Aromatic solvents are characterized by medium to high solvent power and a K.B. value of about 60 to 90. Solvents such as toluol, benzol, and xylol have high solvent power and a K.G. value of about 80 to 115.

Besides the aliphatic and aromatic solvents (hydrocarbon solvents), the printer uses alcohols, ketones, esters, and chlorinated solvents. Examples of alcohols are methanol (methyl alcohol) and butyl alcohol; of esters are ethyl acetate, amyl acetate, and butyl acetate; of ketones are acetone, methyl ethyl ketone (MEK); and of chlorinated solvents are carbon tetrachloride, ethylene dichloride, and trichlorethylene.

The practical solvent needed by the printer is not different in quality than that required in other graphic arts. He prefers a solvent that has uniformity; one that will have the same working properties each time it is used under the same conditions. If possible, solvents should be odorless or have agreeable odors and not be toxic. They should have as high a flash point and as high a flammability rating as possible. They should have proper evaporation rate and should aid in holding resins, binders, or compounds in solution. They should help in keeping the ink from drying during the printing operation and also aid in penetration. Because it is difficult for the manufacturer to develop one universal solvent with all these qualities, the printer must know how to use varied solvents safely.

Solvents are chemicals and their correct use involves a knowledge of solvent power, type of solvent, boiling point, evaporating rate, flash point, flammability ratings, toxicity, etc. As far as evaporation is concerned, solvents are classed as fast evaporating, medium evaporating, slow evaporating, and extra slow evaporating. Acetone, ethyl-acetate, and benzene are fast evaporating; ethyl-alcohol and toluene are medium evaporating; amyl alcohol and butyl alcohol are slow evaporating; and ethyl lactate and "Butyl Cellosolve" are very slow evaporating. Generally, solvents with the fastest evaporation and lowest boiling point are the most flammable. The very fast drying inks used in screen printing are formulated to be fast evaporating and with as high a boiling point as possible. These inks are usually printed in areas with a planned drying and exhaust vent system. Evaporation rates of solvents are important, have been determined by research, and are supplied by the manufacturer. Vapors from solvents and inks should be carried away from the source of formation as rapidly as possible.

Toxicity

Since careless use of solvents is potentially dangerous, it is imperative that the user know as much as possible about each solvent. Solvents such as pentane, mineral spirits, ethyl alcohol, ethyl acetate, petroleum benzene, and heptane are relatively harmless. Toluene (toluol), xylene, amyl acetate, butyl alcohol, amyl alcohol, are more dangerous. While benzene, methyl alcohol, formaldehyde and carbon tetrachloride are definitely hazardous. Industrial solvents may have a physiological effect on humans and are toxic or poisonous to some extent when they are inhaled continually, especially at high concentrations. This toxicity will vary with the individual and with the type of solvent, ink, or solution contacted.

The safe use of industrial solvents includes counteracting the effects of inhalation of vapors, the effect on skin, the effect of taking a solution into the body, and the elimination of fire hazards. Industrial safety standards, state, federal and local codes, and manufacturers of solvents specify the conditions for working safely with solvents. The printer must follow these conditions.

To prevent inhalation of vapors, especially those that may be toxic, working areas in shops must have proper ventilation. Gloves should be worn to prevent prolonged or frequently repeated contact of some solvents with the skin, since these tend to de-fat and dehydrate the skin and cause skin irritation. Where very dangerous solvents are used on some jobs and inhaled as in the spraying of such solutions, it is suggested that a mask supplying fresh air be used. There is a maximum allowable concentration (MAC) of industrial solvents which can fill a given volume of air for safe breathing. This concentration is expressed in charts and tables in terms of parts by volume of solvent vapor per million parts of air (PPM). A solvent added to a solution may make the solution more toxic or destroy the desirable working properties of the original product.

Flammability ratings have been worked out in units on an arbitrary point scale in which the flammability of ethyl ether is 100 points and carbon tetrachloride at the low end of the scale is 0 points. The higher the flammability rating the more is the tendency for the solvent to burn. For example, kerosene has a flammability rating of 40; toluene 75 to 80; acetone 90; and benzene 95 to 100.

Most solvents are also supplied with information about their flash points. The flash point of a solvent is the lowest temperature at which it will ignite when the solvent or solvent vapors are exposed to an open flame momentarily. Generally, solvents with the fastest evaporation and lowest boiling point are the most flammable. This implies that if a low flash solvent is used in an enclosed shop area and the solvent vapors are not allowed to be exhausted and if the air is very heavily laden with vapors, the heat from a large electric bulb may ignite the vapors.

Flash points are as varied as the solvents. Some solvents will flash at 0 degrees Fahrenheit, another one may flash at 260 degrees Fahrenheit. See Figure 27.

Flammable solvents do not burn; it is the vapors of the solvents that explode or burn. A very important point to remember is that solvent

	Type of Solvent	Boiling Point Degrees F and C		Flash Point Degrees F and C		K.B. Value
I.	AROMATIC HYDROCARBON					
1.	Benzol	172–176F	(78–80C)	5F	(−15C)	110
2.	Toluol	230–231F	(110–111C)	35F	(2C)	105
3.	Xylol	260–318F	(127–159C)	74F	(23C)	97
II.	ALIPHATIC HYDROCARBON					
1.	Heptane	198–212F	(92–100C)	13F	(−11C)	36
2.	Hexane	150–160F	(66–71C)	−25F	(−32C)	30.5
3.	Kerosene	350–572F	(177–300C)	135F	(57C)	29.2
4.	Mineral Spirits	312–393F	(156–201C)	105F	(41C)	36
5.	Stodard Solvent	300–404F	(149–207C)	108F	(42C)	35.4
III.	KETONES					
1.	Acetone	131–134F	(55–57C)	−4F	(−20C)	
2.	Cyclohexanone	307–314F	(153–157C)	116F	(47C)	
3.	Methyl Ethyl Ketone (MEK)	174–177F	(79–81C)	34F	(1C)	
4.	Methyl Isobutyl Ketone	237–247F	(114–119C)	81F	(27C)	
IV.	ESTERS					
1.	Amyl Acetate	230–302F	(110–150C)	93F	(34C)	
2.	Ethyl Acetate	158–185F	(70–85C)	40F	(4C)	
3.	Isopropyl Acetate	183–194F	(84–90C)	54F	(12C)	
4.	Methyl Acetate	127–131F	(53–55C)	5F	(−15C)	
5.	Normal Butyl Acetate	244–262F	(118–128C)	90F	(32C)	
V.	GLYCOL-ETHER					
1.	"Cellosolve"	270–279F	(130–137C)	130F	(54C)	
2.	Ethylene Glycol	374–410F	(190–210C)	240F	(116C)	
3.	Methyl "Cellosolve"	255–257F	(124–125C)	115F	(46C)	
VI.	ALCOHOL					
1.	Isopropyl Alcohol	177–181F	(81–83C)	69F	(21C)	
2.	Methyl Alcohol (Methanol)	147–151F	(64–66C)	52F	(11C)	
3.	Normal Butyl Alcohol	240–246F	(116–119C)	111F	(44C)	
4.	N-Propyl Alcohol	204–208F	(96–98C)	90F	(32C)	

Figure 27. Some solvents used in screen printing, presenting the boiling points and flash points in degrees Fahrenheit and Celsius, and the Kauri-Butanol values of hydrocarbon solvents.

vapors being heavier than air seep to the lowest area in the shop. Where possible, exhausts should be placed as near to the floor as is practical and the vapors exhausted immediately. Screen printing shops generally control possible hazards connected with the use of flammable solvents by avoiding concentration of vapors.

Care and Use of Solvents

While solvents may differ, their safe care and use must be simplified and routinized in the shop. Even the most harmless solvents should be handled carefully. Each solvent, like each type of ink, should be kept in a safe container. Each container should be conspicuously labeled with the solvent name, directions for its use, and precautions in use. Containers should be stored out of the direct rays of the sun and away from any form of heat, with the opening caps or plugs upward. In removing the cap, the container should be opened away from one's face. Solvents such as acetone which have high volatility and a low flash point must be stored so accumulation of vapors of an explosive concentration is prevented. Where solvents are filled from a storage tank, the tank should be grounded to eliminate static electricity.

It is most practical to store solvents in areas away from working areas of a shop. The large screen printing shops which print all types of ink and use varied solvents, have special storage areas for solvents, inks, and finishes. These storage areas are fireproof quarters with adequate fire protection and vents for ventilation. The exhausts prevent vapor pressure from building up and tend to eliminate fire, explosion, and toxicity hazards.

Figure 27 presents data on some solvents used in screen printing.

Chapter 8

THE SQUEEGEE

The final results of any industry are the sum totals of the different techniques employed in that industry. Each tool, skill, adaptation, and each individual contributes to a final and interdependent industry. Even the humble squeegee, which at first glance seems to be a simple device, is yet the most used means of depositing screen printing ink by hand or machine.

There are other methods of forcing the ink through the printing screen such as employing a vacuum force to pull the ink through or using a roller technique for application. However, the squeegee is the device generally used to force the ink through the cloth bearing the design upon stock placed upon the screen. The squeegee consists of a grooved wooden board which serves as a handle, a rubber blade inserted and protruding from the groove, and a resting device. Figures 28 through 31 show sections of approximate sizes of squeegees used. Figures 29 and 31 are the most commonly used. Figures 29 and 31 are made of two boards. Figure 32 shows how a handle may be attached to different type squeegees for one-hand operation.

While aluminum is used occasionally for some handles of squeegees, most handles are made of wood. The grooved handles or boards may be made of hard or soft wood that is kiln dried, free of imperfections, and is straight grained. Soft wood such as white pine is used because it is strong enough and light enough to handle in big sizes. Since squeegees come in lengths up to about seventy-two inches (183cm), the weight of the squeegee is important. A lighter squeegee is less tiring to use.

The parts on the handle that come in contact with the worker's hands should have rounded edges to prevent callousing and blistering of the hands. The rubber blade must fit the groove in the handle perfectly. If the fit is a poor one, then different colored inks that may dry in the space between the blade and groove of the handle may affect the color of ink being printed. Some workers shellac the spots where the blade comes in contact with the grooved part of the handle, as this has a tendency to keep ink out and makes it easier to wash

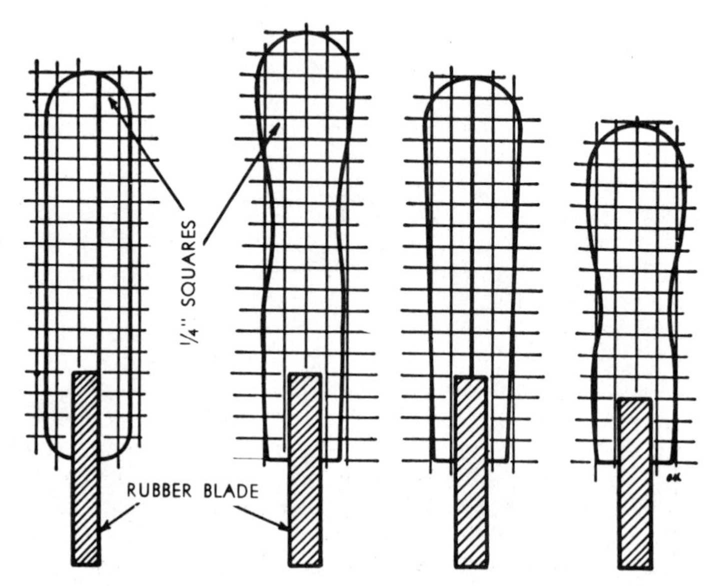

Figure 28 through 31. Cross section of most commonly used types of squeegees, showing two-piece construction in Figures 28 and 30. Squeegees illustrated in Figures 29 and 31 are most popular.

the squeegee. In the larger screen printing shops where three and four color halftones are printed, a different squeegee is used for each color; and each squeegee is cleaned after use and saved to print its given color. Wooden parts on the squeegee should be sandpapered so that there are no rough spots on them.

The rubber used for the blade may be a synthetic one such as polyurethane or another type that has good resistance to moisture, abrasion, and heat; it must resist animal, mineral, and vegetable oils and fats. It should resist the oxidizing effects of metallic ingredients used in screen printing inks; the rubber must not be affected by benzenes, alcohols, lacquers, enamels, screen cleaning and adhering solutions, etc. These man-made rubbers have good fire resistance and are generally better for screen printing than natural rubber, which does not last as long and is distorted and dissolved by the varying solvents, pastes, and solutions used in screen printing. The source of all these materials is the same as the source of all plastics and synthetics. Rubber

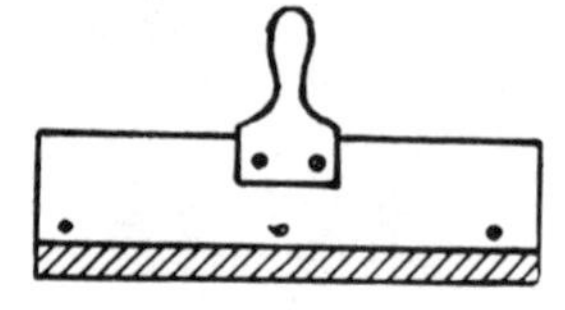

Figure 32. The squeegee illustrated above makes one-hand operation possible.

blades come in varied grades of hardness which, for screen printing, are measured in "Shore 'A' Hardness" scale or in "Durometers" ranging from about 45 to 80 durometers.
For example, an extra soft blade is 45 to 50 durometers, while a very hard blade is 75 to 80 durometers. Generally, most suppliers stock rubber blades in soft, medium and hard grades.

The printing edge of the blade governs the sharpness and deposit of ink, and the long edge of the blade must be perfectly parallel with the surface printed. Figure 33 presents profile shapes of commonly used blades.

The blade is fitted snugly into a groove or between two pieces of wood and is held in place by driving wood screws or telescopic bolts through the wood and rubber, the screws being placed about four inches apart, driven alternately, first into one side of the wood then into the other. The thickness of the blade may vary from about ¼″ to ½″ (.63cm to 1.27cm); the height may range from about 1½″ to 3″ (3.8cm to 7.6cm). The thickness, height, and length of the blade depend upon the size of the squeegee handle and the length of the squeegee. Although the printer who is handy with tools could easily make his own squeegee, it isn't practical. Excellent squeegees which will serve all purposes are sold cheaply enough by screen printing

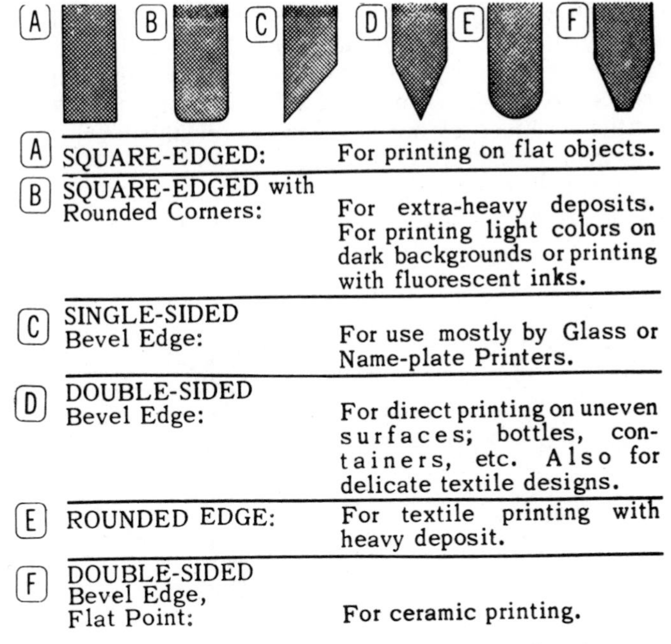

Figure 33. Squeegee blade profile shapes and suggested use in screen printing. **(Courtesy of Advance Process Supply Co., Chicago, Illinois)**

suppliers, the price depending on the lineal length of the squeegee in inches. The complete squeegee may be bought in any length, or the blade or handle may be bought separately.

The length of the squeegee used depends upon the job and the size of the frame in which printing is done. It is advisable to have a squeegee that is about 2 or 3 inches (5 to 7.6cm) shorter than the inside dimensions of the screen. It should be long enough to print a full impression in one stroke and long enough to cover completely the design being printed.

To keep the squeegee from falling into the ink between impressions and to allow the worker to rest it, it is essential that nails or dowel rods be driven or inserted in the ends as illustrated in Figure 34. Some printers drill holes through the handle and insert dowel rods at right angles to the handle to serve as rests as shown in Figure 35. The squeegee is generally held with two hands and rested between impressions. Where desired (where squeegee is small enough) a one-hand squeegee (see Figure 32) may be used, as it leaves the other hand free.

Like all tools, a squeegee requires a certain amount of care. Chief of these is making sure that the blade is sharp and true. A good ruler or yardstick may be used to test the straightness and sharpness of the blade. When the edges of the blade become dull, worn, and uneven, then it is essential that the blade be sharpened by the worker or by a screen printing supply firm. A squeegee that isn't sharp and true will deposit an unequal film or layer of ink, sometimes to the point where the inexperienced printer may believe that the fault lies with the ink or cloth in the screen or both. When printing on screen printing machines, the trueness of the squeegee blade must be examined at intervals to insure accurate deposit of ink.

A blade can easily be sharpened by anyone with the sharpening jig shown in Figure 36 or the machine illustrated in Figure 37. This

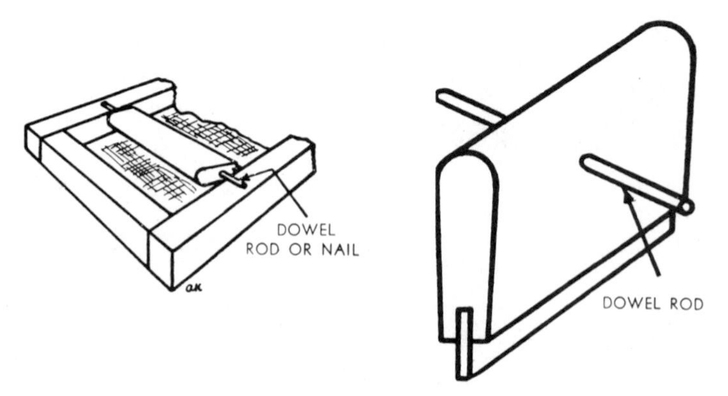

Figure 34, left and Figure 35, right. Two methods of preventing squeegee from falling into ink.

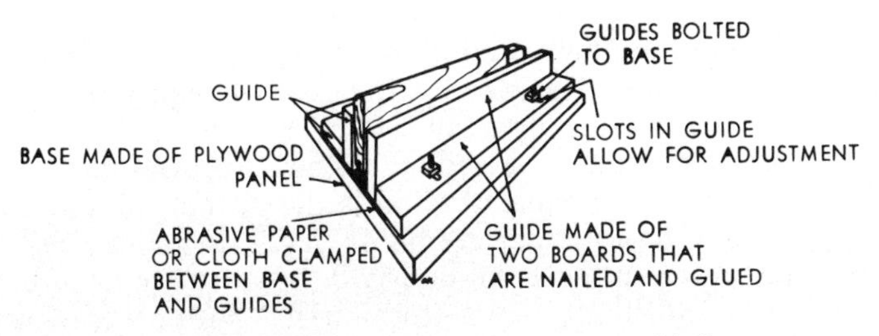

Figure 36. A jig for sharpening squeegee blades.

jig is easy to make and may be made of any wood. The length of the jig may vary from 1 to 3 feet (.305 to .914m). Use about a No. 0 sandpaper, garnet paper, or garnet cloth; 80 to 120 grit emery cloth; or new or used sandpaper belting as the abrading medium. Holding the squeegee in an upright position, move it back and forth over the abrasive material until a sharp smooth blade is obtained. If a belt sander or disc sander is available, it will save the printer work in sharpening the blade. The speed of the sander should range between 1000 and 1300 revolutions per minute. Faster speeds than these may melt the rubber, since

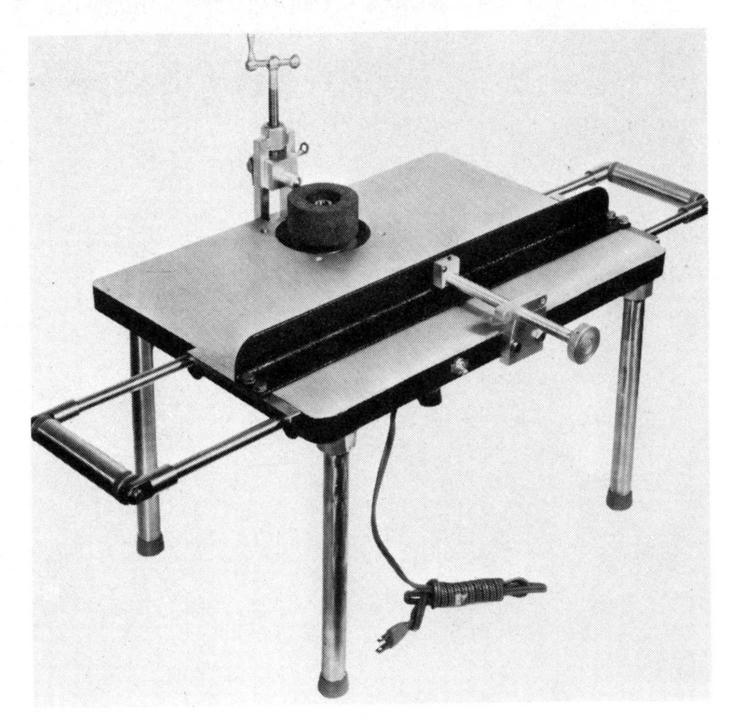

Figure 37. A machine for sharpening varied length squeegees. **(Courtesy of Naz-Dar Company, Chicago, Illinois)**

most of the synthetic rubbers are thermoplastics and become soft when heat is applied to them. Should this occur, then apply a little water as a coolant to prevent decomposition and softening. Also, press the rubber just lightly enough to abrade it without melting it.

Other ways of sharpening the blade are to cut off the dull part with a sharp knife, hand paper cutter, or machine paper cutter. If the knife blade or paper cutter is rubbed with a wet cloth, it will cut the rubber easier. If the blade is so worn that it cannot be sharpened, then a new blade can easily be fastened into the groove of the handle.

Squeegees must be kept clean and are cleaned with the same solvent or cleaning solution as is used to clean out the screen after the printing is completed. A squeegee that is left uncleaned will be impossible to clean once the ink dries on it. Also, the dried ink may interfere with future ink applications of different colors. After being wiped clean, the squeegee is stored for about two hours to allow for complete evaporation of solvents. It is advisable to cover the rubber blade with some French chalk when a squeegee is stored for a long time. For ordinary storing, the squeegee should be hung or laid on the handle with the blade up.

Figure 37 illustrates a machine for sharpening squeegees.

Chapter 9

REGISTER IN SCREEN PRINTING

Register in screen printing refers to controlling each impression so that all parts of the design will print in the exact desired areas and spots every time the stock or object is placed or fed under the hand-operated or machine-operated screen. Correct registration depends upon the care given to all the steps in the complete printing success. The printer will not have any difficulty if he uses care in doing the following: attaching the screen fabric as tightly as possible; preparing and adhering the printing plate; bringing the screen down upon the base exactly in the same location each time; feeding the stock in the same spot each time; and if possible, doing the printing under the same atmospheric conditions (should the printer be working with stock or material that may shrink or expand).

Different techniques and devices are employed in screen printing to assure that perfect register is obtained. For printing on paper, cardboard, and other thin stock, it is suggested that the base of the screen unit be built up with a sheet or two of strong wrapping paper, tympan paper, book paper, etc. The sheets may be attached to the base with masking tape, Scotch tape, gummed paper tape, or tacks. The makeready or preparation of the screen unit for proper impression is done on the paper. When printing a one-color job, all the printer has to do is draw lines on the makeready sheet, drawing a pencil line at the bottom and another line at one side. In printing, the stock is placed against the latter lines which serve as guides.

Register guides may be made or set on the base of the printing unit or on the makeready sheet so that generally stock may be registered against three register guides. Usually, the guides are placed so that stock will be registered against two guides at the bottom and against one either on the right or left side, as illustrated in Figure 40.

A simple guide that may be used for feeding thin stock is illustrated in Figure 38. This guide may be made by folding masking tape, plastic tape or gummed paper tape and fastening th tape guide in the required spots on the makeready sheet or on the base. A more accurate method of registering flat stock up to about ⅛" (.31cm) thick and one used by

Figure 38. A simple guide.

the writer is to cut V grooves in the top makeready sheet, then folding the cut groove back over the stock to form a register flap as illustrated in Figure 40. If these flaps are made longer where it is possible, they will serve as an aid in removing the printed stock from the screen, since the flaps will have a tendency to peel the stock off the screen.

Where stock is about 1⁄16″ (.16cm) thick or thicker, it is advisable to use guides made of metal, cardboard, paper fiber, or plastics. These guides may be made or may be bought from screen printing establishments. Pieces cut from angle irons, tee irons, and the flat pieces cut from hinges make ideal guides, since they already have countersunk holes in them. Figure 39 illustrates a common and simple guide that may be attached to the base with two small screws, usually fillister or flat head screws. After the guide is placed in the required spots, it is fastened to the base by tightening down the screws.

Most of the commercial guides are about 1⁄16″ (.16cm) thick or more. To use them in registering thinner stock, it is necessary to cover the screen base with cardboard and then cut out recesses for the guides in the cardboard. The top of the guides should be even with or slightly lower than the top surface of the stock being printed. Also, the guides should not have sharp points that may abrade or cut the screen fabric, should the fabric come in contact with the guide. Where it is necessary to protect the underside of the silk from a guide, it is advisable to tape masking tape on the spot of the screen fabric where the fabric comes in contact with the guide. This procedure should also be followed to protect the screen fabric or printing plate from sharp material like glass or metal when printing on the latter materials.

Where it is necessary to print on thick stock or very thick objects, the screen has to be adjusted permanently so that when it is in printing

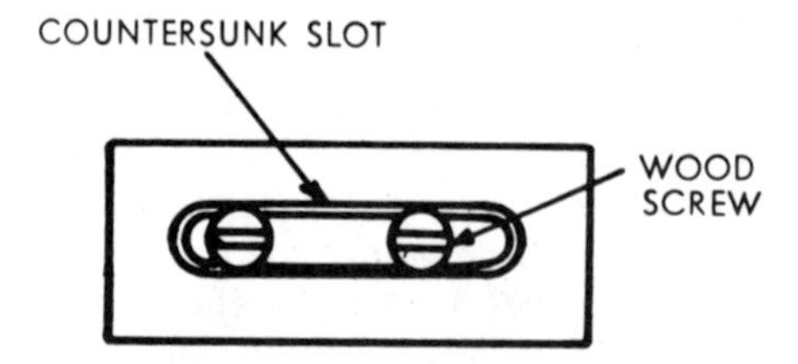

Figure 39. An adjustable guide.

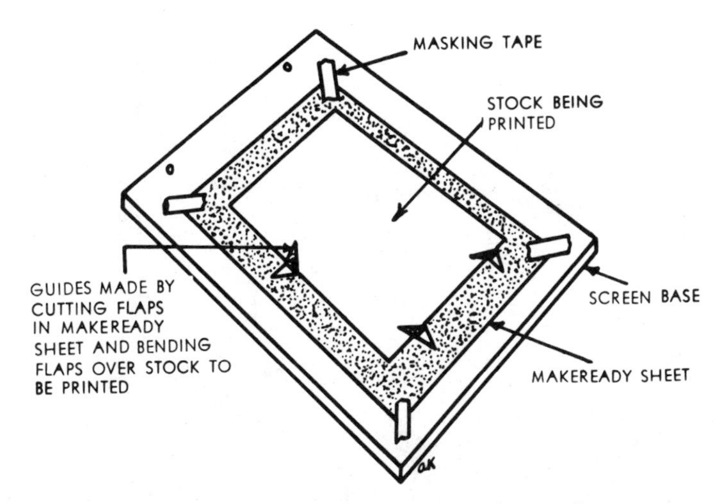

Figure 40. Registering paper, cardboard, plastics sheets, etc.

position the distance between the screen and the base will approximate the thickness of the object being printed. Two methods that may be employed to register thick objects for printing are illustrated in Figures 41 and 42. Another method used to vary the distance between the screen and the base is to insert springs between the hinge bar or screen and the base. The nuts on top of the hinge bar may be tightened down to adjust for thickness of stock. If springs are not available, then a piece of the same material or the same thickness as the stock that is being printed is cut, drilled, and placed over the bolt between the hinge bar and the base. See Figure 43. Of course, the front part of the screen would have to be built up to the same height to prevent the front of the screen from dropping too low. This may be done by fastening small blocks to the underside in each corner of the front part of the screen frame or by attaching the blocks to the base.

Where necessary to print flexible and irregularly shaped material that is difficult to register such as pieces of fabrics, sport shirts in which it is not possible to insert solid forms, or print more than one color on the above types of jobs, the method illustrated in Figure 44 and 45 may be used. To register the above type of jobs, it is first necessary to tape or tack down a piece of transparent sheet such as a plastic sheet or draftsman tracing paper and then print an impression on the transparent sheet as shown in Figure 44. The stock to be printed is then placed or registered under the print on the transparent sheet (see Figure 45), and the transparent sheet is folded back. With the transparent sheet folded out of the way of the screen, the printing is done on the material in the exact spot in which the material was registered. This procedure is repeated every time an impression is made.

Figure 47 illustrates the use of side cleats. They are simple to

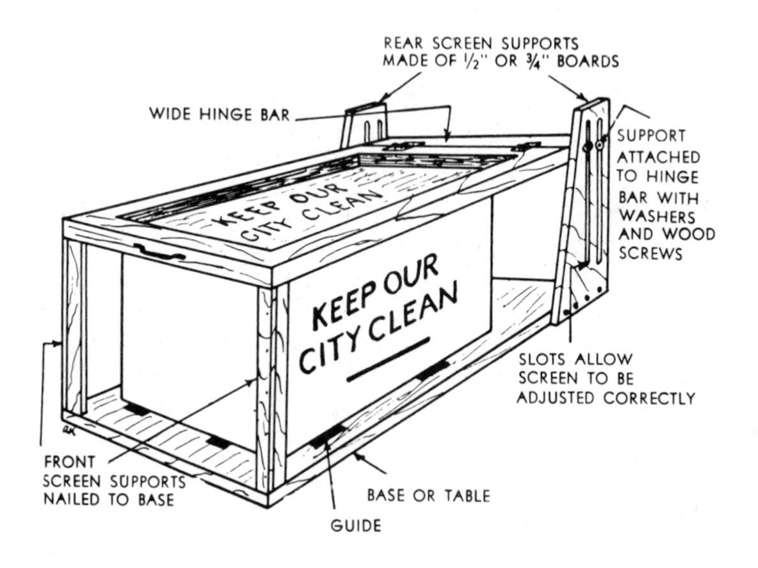

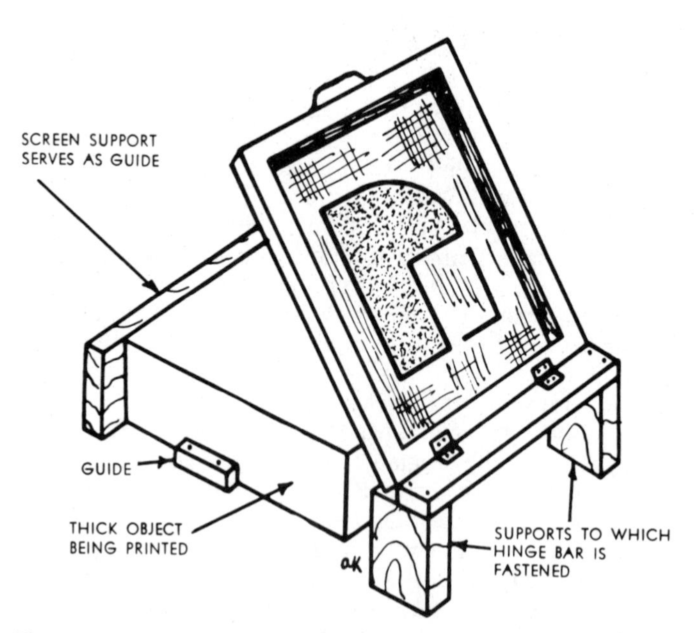

Figure 41, above, and Figure 42, below show methods of registering thick stock and large objects.

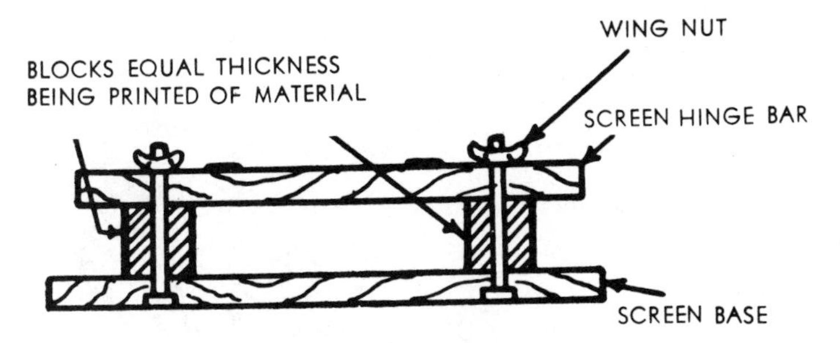

Figure 43. Adjusting for thickness of stock.

Figure 44, top, 45, center, and 46, bottom. Registering irregularly shaped or flexible material.

attach and to remove and may be used when it is necessary to print very many impressions and when the hinges may get too much wear. They tend to eliminate side-play on the part of the screen because of loose hinges or other causes. Side cleats tend to keep a screen in the required spot on the base every time the screen is lowered and tend

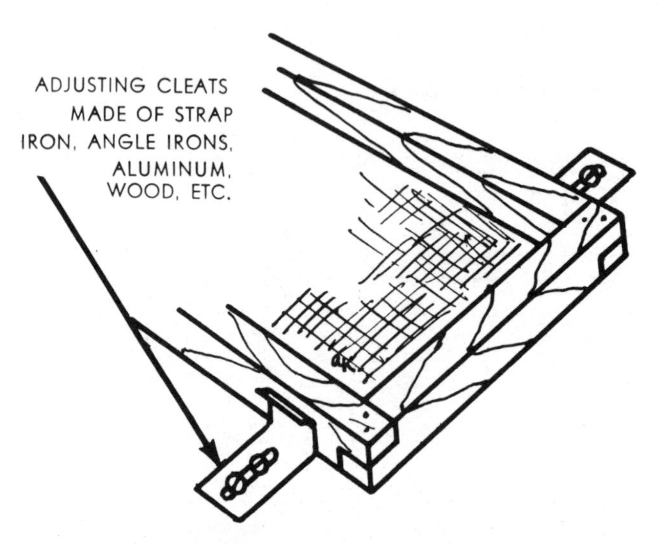

Figure 47. Cleats as an aid in registration.

to eliminate the moving of the screen under the squeegee pressure which sometimes produces smearing on the print. Another method to do away with side-play is to attach a ⅜″ (.95cm) dowel pin on the underside of the screen on the end of the frame in which there is the greatest sideplay. A hole the same size as the dowel rod is then drilled in the base so that when the screen (with the permanently attached dowel pin) is lowered, it will fit snugly into the drilled hole in the base.

Other examples of methods of registering are illustrated in Figures 157, 158, and 159 in Chapter 25 for printing varied colors on textile bolt material and other bolt material. While rotary and flat bed screen printing machines are used commercially for printing wallcoverings, wallpaper, and the like, the above registration techniques may be used by the beginner to print on bolt material. These units may be built by the beginning and advanced screen printer who is handy with tools using wood as the construction material.

In printing on glass or other very smooth stock, it is often necessary to keep the screen slightly off-contact during the printing operation, contact between printing plate and stock only occurring under the squeegee when squeegee is pulled and pressed over the screen fabric. A slight off-contact screen may be obtained by taping enough masking tape on the underside of the screen frame to obtain the desired results.

Printing in more than one color (multi-color printing) requires accurate and precise registration, especially in doing photographic work and reproducing designs by means of the halftone process. With the latter, the slightest distortion in one plate or color will spoil the final appearance of the printing. It is more difficult to adjust for register when doing this type of printing with hand-operated screens than when printing on screen printing machines, as the machines have automatic adjustments.

Carefully checking each color before running it with the original full size design and the colors already run will aid registering. It is a good idea to print proofs on transparent paper and to use the proofs to test for register. By holding transparent proofs over a light or window, the test can be made for either exact register or for minute overlapping of color where the latter is desired.

Chapter 10

PRINTING SCREENS
Knife-Cut Film Printing Screens

The stencil consisting of a prepared sheet in which a design is cut is at least as old as the Egyptian culture. Remains of this art which reproduced designs by placing a stencil over a surface and brushing or forcing pigments through the cut away spaces have been found dating back to about the time of the twelfth Egyptian dynasty (about 2300 B.C.).

It was this type of stencil that was first tried immediately before World War I in screen printing work to print on felt, which presented difficulties in printing with other methods. However, to say that the technique used for printing in screen printing is stenciling is similar to saying that photoengraving is stenciling. Printing plates in the screen printing industry are comparable to printing plates used in the other graphic arts. They can print thousands of impressions; they may be made by hand, etched, or produced by the action of light and chemicals; they can be made so that they print large areas or fine detail. They can print solid lines or halftones. Printing screens can be used for hand screening or for machine printing. These printing plates can print at hand-operated speeds or when necessary, as in screen printing machine printing, up to about 5,000 impressions an hour.

There are about forty different types of printing plates used in screen printing but all of them may be classified either as hand-prepared or photographic. Hand-made printing screens may be classed as direct or those prepared directly on the screen fabric (such as tusche-glue or resist) and indirect hand-made screens exemplified by the knife-cut film screen which is prepared away from the fabric and is adhered to the fabric before printing. Generally, screens that are hand-prepared fall under the following three classes: knife-cut, block-out, and wash-out or resist. Photographic printing screens are prepared photo-chemically with the aid of light and chemicals and are of three types: (1) direct photographic, that is, emulsions which are prepared directly on the fabric of the printing screen; (2) direct-indirect types or products consisting of films and emulsions which are also prepared directly on the screen fabric; and (3) indirect or transfer-type photographic screens which are first prepared on a temporary surface and then transferred to the screen fabric. The photographic screens and the knife-cut film screens are the most used today. Because the commercial knife-cut film is very practical and the one generally tried by the beginner, we shall deal with it first. In subsequent chapters, the writer will deal with other printing screens.

In the knife-cut printing screen, the areas that are to be printed are cut away; what is left over is made to adhere to the fabric on the screen. The printing screen consists of what has been adhered to the screen fabric and the fabric. Ink will be forced through only those areas that are cut away in the film; those parts of the stencil that are not cut out will keep the ink from being deposited onto stock under the screen. Knife-cut printing screens all have the same thing in common; they are all cut with knives and other sharp cutting tools. In this group are included the plain paper cut stencil, shellacked paper, lacquered paper, lacquer-coated decal paper, shellac-coated decal paper, thin plastic sheet, and commercial screen printing film.

Commercial Knife-Cut Film Printing Screens

The commercial knife-cut film printing screen consists of a transparent or translucent thin transparent plastics sheet or paper to which a specially prepared film is cemented semi-permanently. Generally, the film is made by applying a cement to the backing plastic sheet or paper and then spraying several coats of lacquer, shellac, or a specially prepared film over the cement-covered sheet. Commercial film has three to eight coats accurately applied under controlled conditions. The specially prepared cement on the paper or plastics sheet holds the film to the sheet until it is necessary to peel the film off or to adhere to the film to the printing screen. Areas and spots of the film may be cut and then stripped or peeled away, leaving the backing sheet intact.

The film that is attached to the backing sheet comes in different transparent colors, in varied film thicknesses, and in matte or gloss finish. The colors of the film are generally amber, green, gray-blue, and ruby. Transparent colors for films are chosen usually because they show other colors in their true cast. This makes it easy to tell colors apart without outlining the separate color in a design when the design is placed under the film paper. The film which has the plastic backing sheet is more transparent film than the film with the paper backing sheet, thus making detail in a design more visible. Unlike the paper backing, the plastic backing sheet does not absorb moisture. This lack of moisture is a great aid in cutting very big printing screens which are subject to shrinkage or expansion before the film is applied to the screen.

The films available today are tough enough to stand normal wear, flexible, easily cut, easily peeled, easily adhered to the screen, simple to remove from the screen, and are capable of being stored in normal atmospheric conditions for long periods. As a matter of fact, when these requirements were met by manufacturers of films, the development of screen printing became a reality because it has almost eliminated tedious early methods of preparing screens.

The film coating on the backing sheet comes in thin, medium, thick, and extra thick grades, each grade used when necessary and the medium grade being used for general work. In printing areas or lines up to about a half inch wide, the thinner the film coating, the thinner the coat of ink deposited; the thicker the film, the thicker the coat of ink deposited. However, the thickness of the ink deposited is also dependent on the thickness of the screen fabric. Thin coats are necessary when there is an overlap of one color over another when applying transparent inks. Also, when it is necessary to save ink. The thick film is good for stressing main colors; for lettering outline; printing on felt and other such materials; for use on coarse meshes of silk or wire cloth; is used for heavier deposits of ink on metal, wood, glass, for flocking, etc.; and where it is necessary to stress slight variation in color. The films are made so that they can be used for printing with oil inks, water inks, and lacquer inks.

Preparation of Film Screens

In using film screens, the sheet film is taped or tacked over the design, film side up, and the parts that are to be printed are cut away by hand with sharp instruments, being careful to cut the film without cutting the backing sheet. Although the process is simple, there are certain basic techniques that will aid the printer. The most important, perhaps, is to choose good sharp tools. It is possible to cut a good printing screen just with a sharp knife, just as it is possible to make a good mechanical drawing with just a pencil and ruler. However, for the average printer it is advisable to invest in the following: a knife, a good ruler made of metal or glass, a 30–60 degree triangle and a 45 degree triangle (each about eight inches high), French curve, circle cutter, adjustable bicutter, a compass cutter, a swivel cutter, and an Arkansas slip stone to whet and hone the blades on the cutting instruments.

Although the cutters shown in Figure 48 may be made easily of parts of drawing instruments or darning needles, etc., it is suggested that they be bought. The commercial ones are inexpensive and are made of surgical steel, are razor sharp, and will stay sharp for a long time. When they begin to get dull, they may be sharpened either on a slip stone or at the establishment where they were procured originally. Bi-cutters illustrated in Figures 49 and 50 come fixed and adjustable.

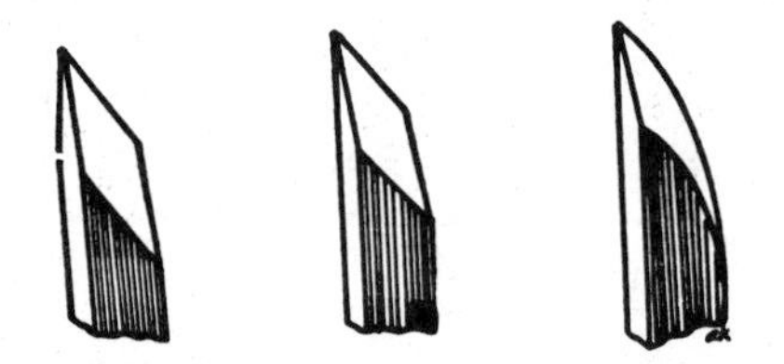

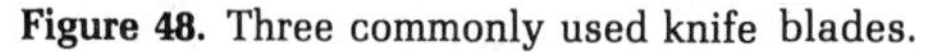

Figure 48. Three commonly used knife blades.

Figure 49. Bicutter head.

They are used for cutting straight and curved parallel lines. The cutting heads on the fixed bi-cutters come in sizes ranging in widths from about $\frac{1}{32}$" to about $\frac{1}{2}$" (.08cm to 1.27cm). The heads may be removed easily, and different size cutters may be fastened to the handle when necessary. Handles on all cutting tools are about the same size as penholders. The adjustable bi-cutters consist of one cutting head on which the cutters may be adjusted to cut parallel lines ranging from about $\frac{1}{16}$" to $\frac{3}{4}$" (.16cm to 1.87cm).

The circle cutter shown in Figure 51 is designed to cut circles from about $\frac{1}{16}$" (.16cm) to about 4" (10.2cm) in diameter with a cutting blade sharpened on both edges, permitting cutting to the right and left in a circle or arc. The compass cutter in Figure 52 will cut circles ranging from about $\frac{3}{4}$" to about 27" (1.87cm to 68.58cm) in diameter. Both the circle cutter and the compass cutter will cut single and double lines, depending on the type of cutting head used.

Besides the above cutters, the film cutter should also have a swivel cutter. A swivel cutter has a revolving blade for cutting curves. When cutting, the blade may be revolved freely or can be clamped in a fixed position. All the above cutting tools may also be used to cut paper, cellophane, and celluloid plates.

The printer must make sure that the film he uses has not been

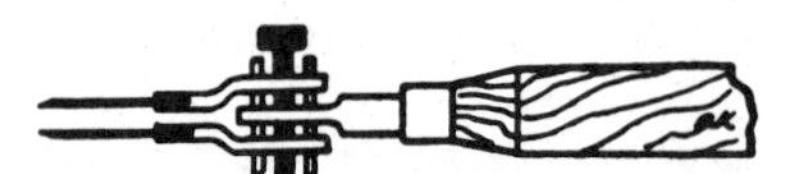

Figure 50. Adjustable bi-cutter.

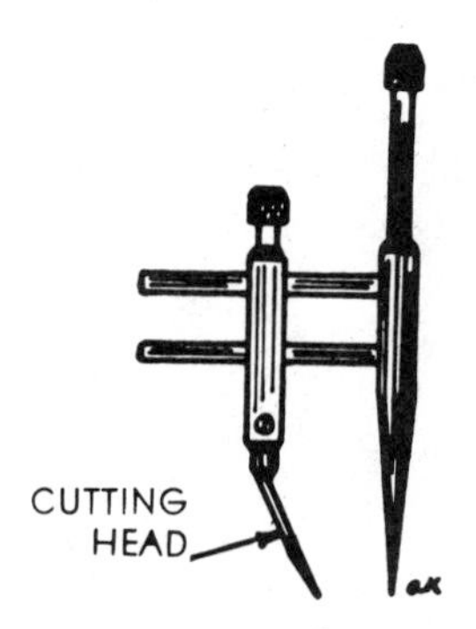

Figure 51. A circle cutter.

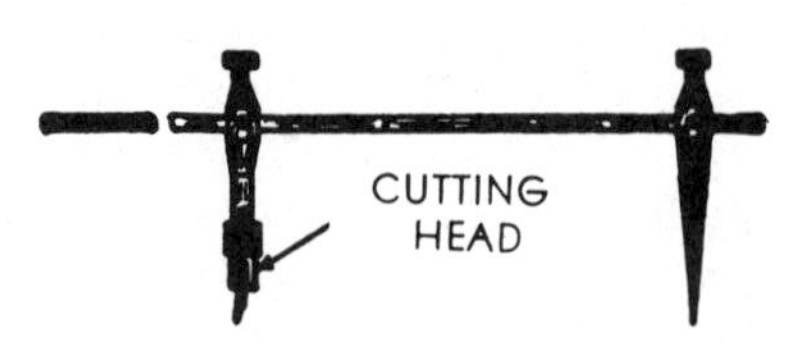

Figure 52. Beam compass cutter.

stored too long. Old film is difficult to cut, has a darker color, and will cause trouble when it is adhered to the screen. Although, the better films manufactred may be stored in standard atmospheric conditions for about a year and still produce good printing plates. In storing film, keep it in places that are not too humid and not too hot or too cold. Any film paper left over should be kept in its original tube (film paper is usually sold in tubes), and the film sheet should be rolled with the film side out to keep the film from separating from the paper or plastic backing sheet.

Experts in the film cutting field unroll the film the night before they are to do the cutting. This gives the film a chance to adjust to atmospheric conditions of the room.

In preparing film, fasten the design to a drawing table, drawing board, or any smooth surface board. Cut a piece of the film sheet two to four inches larger in each direction than the design and tape it over the design. Start cutting, in tracing fashion, being very careful to cut only through the film but NOT through the backing sheet, as this may make it difficult to adhere the film to the screen fabric. Make sure that the cutting tools are sharp and use very light pressure in cutting. It is advisable that the beginner do some practice cutting of straight lines, curved lines, and circles before actually starting on a regular job. A simple design should be used for the first trial.

Where the printer is to do fine detail cutting, it is suggested that he use a magnifying glass as an aid in seeing and cutting. These are not costly and come with a swivel joint which allows the lens to be placed at any desired angle or position, leaving both hands free. See Figure 53. Those who cut detail in film constantly are advised to have an optometrist or an oculist prescribe magnifying glasses that may be worn in the same fashion as oridnary glasses or over one's glasses. Any magnifying glasses should magnify detail two or three times. Where it is necessary to use a light to see the work better, it is suggested that the light be placed forward of the work about six inches (15.2cm)

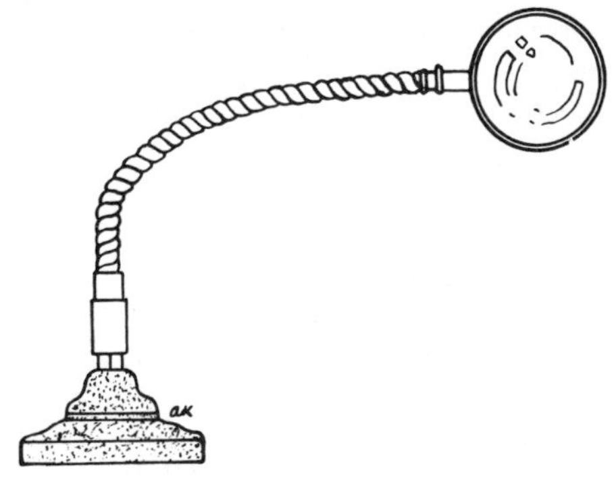

Figure 53. Adjustable magnifying glass.

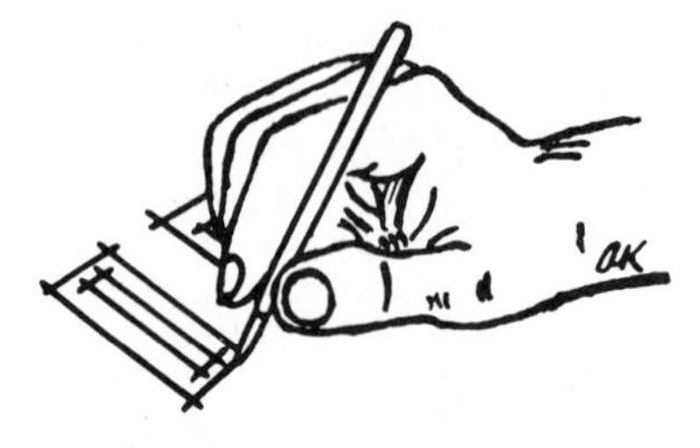

Figure 54. Knife cuts extend past corners.

to one foot (30.5cm) above the work. This produces less glare from the film and makes it easier to see cut lines.

In cutting the film, continue the cut a little past the corners, as illustrated in Figure 54, otherwise the film will not peel right. After cutting is completed, strip off the film until the whole design is peeled. See Figure 55. If there are large areas from which film has been peeled, it is a good idea to cut slits through the backing paper. This will aid in attaching the film to the screen and will keep the paper from buckling during the adhering operation.

When it is necessary to do a rush job, especially where a design is too large for one individual to cut, some film cutters cut clear through the film, backing paper and design, cutting through the whole unit, the cut being made uneven, so that the two halves can then be fitted together when it is necessary to attach the film to the screen.

Adhering Film to Screen Fabric

Generally, there are two types of film—lacquer film or film that is softened or dissolved by lacquer type solvents, and water-soluble film or film that is dissolved by water alone or water plus another solvent.

There are two methods of adhering film to the screen: the solvent method and the thermo (heat) method. The solvent method is the most frequently used. In this method, the film is dampened just enough to soften it so that it will adhere to the screen fabric. In the thermo method (which is used mostly on shellac film paper and shellacked paper), the film is applied to the screen cloth with a warm pressing iron.

Figure 55. Peeling film.

Before adhering the film to the screen, make sure that the screen cloth is clean. If the fabric used is new silk, it is advisable to wash it with water or water and a good face soap after the silk has been stretched on the frame. This will remove any sizing that may be in the cloth. Nylon, polyester, or metal cloth may be washed and degreased in a manner recommended by the supplier of the screen fabric. The fabric is then dampened with a cloth with adhering liquid or a lacquer thinner to remove any additional dust and other minute particles that may interfere with adhering.

Before starting the adhering operation, build up a layer under the film to make the film come in perfect contact with the screen cloth. The layer may be one of cardboard, pressed wood, plastic sheet, or a piece of glass about a half inch smaller in length and width than the inside dimensions of the screen. Place the layer on the base of the screen and center the prepared and cut film, film side up, on the layer. Close screen over film, making sure that there is perfect contact between screen and film. Place weights over the frame of screen to keep the screen cloth in contact with the film or use C-clamps to hold the screen down to base and start attaching film to screen.

An adhering liquid used must be one that is recommended by the maker of the film used to make the printing screen. Usually, adhering liquids used are lacquer thinners, amyl acetate and solvent naphtha, acetones, acetone and amyl acetate, alcohol, and commercial adhering solvents. Using the wrong adhering liquid will prevent proper adhesion, will produce ragged edges when printing, and may even dissolve the film. A good way to test adhering liquid is to dip one's finger inthe liquid and touch a piece of the film with the finger. The film should stick to the finger upon touching film. Good adhering liquids must stick to film quickly and must evaporate quickly. Acetones should not be used as adhering liquid for film with a plastic backing sheet. Generally, water or water and isoproyl alcohol are used as adhering liquids for adhering water-soluble film. Water-soluble film is used much for printing lacquer inks.

To adhere film, obtain two soft clean cloths of the underwear variety. Hold one small cloth in one hand and the other in the other hand. Wet one cloth well with the adhering liquid; and after squeezing out excess liquid into the container, wet a small area of screen, starting in one corner over film, wetting about a 6″ by 6″ (15.2cm by 15.2cm) area at a time, and dry immediately with the dry cloth, rubbing lightly just enough to remove excess liquid. Although it is not essential, an ordinary electric fan blowing on the film as it is being wiped will aid in producing excellent adhesion especially when preparing large screens. The wetting and drying operation should take about five to ten seconds. Wetting a larger area may require a longer time to wipe dry, consequently employing too much liquid. Using too much liquid may produce ragged or serrated edges in printing. Continue wetting the screen and rubbing it dry, adhering in the same direction to prevent wrinkling, until the whole film is adhered to the screen fabric.

A two inch camel hair brush may be used to apply liquid instead of a small cloth. If brush is used, pour liquid into a small open dish, dip brush into dish, wipe excess liquid on the sides of the dish, apply liquid by brushing it on a small area, and wipe brushed spot lightly and immediately with a soft cloth. In any of the adhering methods, after the film is adhered, allow it about 10 to 15 minutes to dry.

When film is dry, peel backing sheet off, starting the peeling in any of the four corners. If the adhering operation has been done correctly, the backing sheet will peel off easily. However, if for any reason any part of the film is not adhered right, the film and the backing sheet may peel away from the screen. Should this occur then turn the screen down and wet and dry the film again. When film is dry, finish the peeling operation. Should there be some spots where the film is not attached to the screen, turn the screen, film side up, and dampen the part not adhered from the underside of the screen, patting down on the film side with the hand to complete adhesion.

Usually, no trouble in peeling is encountered. However, if the backing sheet will not come off, especially during the summer months when it is damp and humid, place screen over a light box. The heat from the fluorescent tubes or electric bulbs in the box will dry the moisture out in the paper backing sheet and permit peeling. Generally, film with a plastics backing sheet does not give this trouble. If a light box is not available, an ordinary flat metal plate that has been heated to about 95 to 100 degrees Fahrenheit (35 to 38 degrees Celsius) may be placed against screen for about five minutes.

After the film is attached to the fabric, the open borders around the film in the screen are filled in with such block-out materials as lacquer, varnish shellac, tape, paper, or commercial block-out substances. A knife-cut film plate that has been correctly cut, prepared, and adhered should last easily for about 5,000 to 10,000 impressions.

It is suggested that after the film is adhered, the screen be thoroughly bathed with a slow-drying solution of whatever reducer is used with the ink that is being printed. For example, if an oil-vehicle ink is employed, oleum may be used; if lacquer, then a slow-drying thinner, etc. This wiping of the screen will saturate the silk fibers and will eliminate the clogging of the ink during the run of the job. It is also a good practice to bathe the screen similarly whenever the printing operation is interrupted. This operation will save the screen, and may even prevent a stain of the design on the fabric after the film is removed.

Removing Film from Screen

When printing is completed, the ink is washed off the screen and printing plate with the solution recommended for the type of ink being used. If the film is not needed any more, the screen can be reclaimed by cleaning the film off of the screen fabric in the following manner. Lay some newsprint or plain newspaper on the base of the screen, making sure that there is perfect contact between the screen cloth and paper. It is a good idea to use the same layer of cardboard for this operation to obtain contact as was used to adhere the film. Saturate

Figure 56. A 39″ x 25″ (99cm x 63.5cm) six-color poster, machine screen printed with flat oil-vehicle ink using printing screens prepared with knife-cut film. **(Courtesy of Litho Paint Poster Company, Chicago, Illinois)**

a cloth with cleaning solvent, a good grade lacquer thinner, or acetone and rub over the film parts of the screen fabric. After the film has been soaked for a few minutes, raise the screen and pull the paper away quickly. The paper will pull away all of the film. Then finish cleaning both sides of the fabric with a clean rag dipped in the cleaning solution, and the screen is ready for the next job.

Figure 56 presents a multi-color large poster printed on a screen printing machine from hand-made knife-cut film printing screens.

Chapter 11

KNIFE-CUT HAND-MADE PRINTING SCREENS

The idea of permanence does not appeal to the human mind. Man strives constantly to change himself, his environment, or both. In this change process, he must sift and accumulate knowledge which will enable him to understand his own sciences, his own arts, and his industries and techniques. Although the commercial knife-cut film printing screen is the most used of the knife-cut screens today, it is to the printer's advantage to have a knowledge of the preparation of the following hand-made knife-cut screens: (1) plain paper-cut printing screen, (2) shellacked paper, (3) lacquered paper, (4) thin plastic sheet, (5) shellac film paper, and (6) lacquer film paper printing screen. These were some of the earliest hand-prepared screens used and may still be employed for some printing jobs. Plain paper, shellacked paper, lacquered paper, and very thin plastic sheet may be attached directly to the screen fabric. The shellac film paper and lacquer film paper have a cement between the shellac film or lacquer film and the paper which holds the film to the paper temporarily. The film papers are attached similarly to the commercial knife-cut film, that is, the backing paper is peeled away, leaving the shellac or lacquer film on the screen. Although shellac film paper and lacquer film paper were hand made by the pioneer screen printer, they are not made as much today, because of the simplicity of preparation, cutting, sharpness in printing, ease of makeready and registration in printing of commercial film, even though commercial film does cost slightly more than the hand-made. Therefore, in this chapter, we shall deal only with plain paper printing screens, shellacked paper, lacquered paper, and thin plastics sheet. These types of hand-prepared screens may be used for printing large outdoor signs and posters.

In preparing and cutting any of the above screens, the same cutting tools are employed as are used to cut commercial knife-cut film printing screens. However, to prepare the knife-cut hand-prepared screens, a hard smooth cutting support is necessary on which to cut the stencil. The support may be made of wood, glass, or metal; cardboard or plastics surfaces may also be used as supports. However, the cutting marks left on them may interfere with future cutting.

The best wooden cutting surface is one that consists of end grain blocks of hard wood (such as maple) glued carefully together and surfaced smooth. Cutting on wood that has the grain parallel to the cut has a tendency to lead the knife away from the line. Although glass dulls knives more quickly, glass is easily obtained and makes the best support as it produces a sharp cut line. The knives, however, can easily be sharpened at shorter intervals than for cutting film. Also, the glass may be used as a contact support under the cut plate when attaching the plate to the screen to make it come in perfect contact with the screen fabric.

In preparing transparent or translucent stencils such as vellum paper, the paper may be cemented or carefully taped over the design to be reproduced. In preparing a knife-cut stencil which is not transparent, such as plain paper, the design may be drawn directly on the coated paper, or the paper may be cut first and then coated with shellac or lacquer. However, if the stencil to be cut is first cemented with an adhesive, wax, or clear rubber cement to a cutting base such as a cardboard, the stencil will be easier to cut and the smallest parts and the details will remain in place on the cardboard support until it is necessary to attach the paper to the screen fabric. The cement or adhesive may be obtained from screen printing suppliers. After the stencil is adhered to the screen fabric, the cardboard cutting support is just peeled off, and the paper will remain on the screen.

Generally, the knife-cut plates presented in this chapter would not be used to produce fine detail. They are used to reproduce larger printing areas when it is necessary to prepare stencils in a hurry on not too accurate jobs. These printing screens are prepared with coarse screen fabrics ranging from about 52 to 110 mesh per inch (about 20 to 43 mesh per cm). Almost any screen fabric may be used, depending on the conditions and wear in printing that the screen is to be given.

Paper Printing Screen

The paper screen, perhaps the easiest to cut, ordinarily used for quick and short runs of about 100 impressions, is just held to the screen by the adhesiveness of the screen printing ink when printing. In making a knife-cut paper stencil, almost any paper may be used. However, a regular transparent paper that lies flat during cutting, and that may be used for multi-color work is sold by most reliable screen printing establishments for paper-cut screens.

If a thick deposit of ink is desired, a thicker paper is employed and a coarse, thick screen fabric is used, as the screen is composed of the paper and the fabric. Any of the papers that are tough and not too fibrous, so that the paper may be cut without tearing or leaving minute fibers on the cut edges, and transparent (where it is necessary to lay paper over a design) may be used. Where a water color ink is to be used, it is a good idea to employ a waterproof paper or one that is oil treated. Any of the following papers may be used: regular transparent stencil paper; vellum tracing paper; 25 pound wrapping paper; poster paper; glassine paper; or any thin strong paper.

It is advisable to make the paper the same size as the inside dimensions of the screen. This will eliminate filling in open borders in the screen. After the design is drawn on the paper, it is carefully cut out and attached to the face side or underside of the screen. Masking tape, gummed paper tape, or plastic tape may be used to hold it to the frame on the screen so that the cut paper will not move from its fixed position on the screen. Screens may be reclaimed easily by just peeling off the cut paper and cleaning the screen with a suitable cleaner depending on the type of ink used.

When there are loose centers in a design or in such letters as "O," "D," etc., that may have a tendency to slip, it is advisable that the printer dab the middle of the loose pieces with glue or lacquer and then place them in the correct spots on the screen to secure them better.

Shellacked Paper Screen

The shellacked paper screen consists of a transparent paper that is covered with a white or orange shellac to aid in attaching it to the screen. It is obviously better than plain paper, since it can be attached more permanently to the screen fabric and, therefore, will produce better detail in printing and will last for longer runs. The shellac may be applied by brushing or spraying. Where much of this paper is to be used it is advisable to spray the coats on, as a more uniform coating is applied. The type of shellac used may be any four pound-cut to eight pound-cut shellac. Four pound-cut shellac is that which has four pounds of gum shellac dissolved in a gallon of shellac solvent which is usually denatured alcohol; five pound-cut shellac is five pounds of gum to a gallon of solvent, etc. About two coats of shellac should be applied to the paper allowing enough time for complete drying between coats.

After the shellac is applied to the paper, the paper is laid over the design and the design is cut out, cutting through the shellac and the paper. The paper may then be adhered to the screen in the following manner: place the shellacked and cut paper under the screen in perfect contact with the fabric. If necessary, place a layer of cardboard or glass under the cut and shellacked paper to make it contact perfectly the underside of the screen fabric. Then lay a piece of any paper or a smooth soft cloth over the screen fabric and press over the paper or cloth with a moderately warm pressing iron. Since shellac is a thermo-plastic, that is, it melts when heat is applied to it, the heat of the iron will soften the shellac enough to make the shellacked paper stick to the underside of the silk. Care must be exercised in pressing not to get the iron too hot. It is advisable that the novice try out a piece of shellacked paper that is uncut or that part which makes up the border of the screen to see how the paper will adhere and approximately how much heat and pressure are necessary.

Some printers do not use the thermo or heat method to attach shellacked paper to the screen but adhere it with a commercial solvent or denatured alcohol in a similar fashion to that of the commercial knife-cut film.

After attaching the shellacked paper, the small open areas bordering the paper are then sealed with shellac, or a lacquer filler, or with tape, and the screen is ready for printing. If the screen fabric is to be reused, the paper and the shellac is removed from the screen with a solvent such as denatured alcohol, paint remover, or a commercial solvent recommended by the screen printing supplier. The shellacked paper stencil may be removed in similar fashion to removing commercial knife-cut film as explained in Chapter 10.

Lacquered Paper Screen

The lacquered paper screen is similiar to the shellacked paper screen, except that the finished paper is adhered to the screen with a solvent in the same manner as the commercial prepared knife-cut film sheets. The lacquer used to coat the paper should be one sold by the trade for that purpose or it may be a good spraying type lacquer that is applied rather thick. It is best to spray the lacquer on, spraying on about two coats, as a more uniform film is obtained. The lacquer also may be brushed on carefully, if spraying equipment is not available. The solvent or liquid used to adhere the cut lacquered paper to the screen may be a good grade lacquer thinner or any preparation that is recommended by the maker of the lacquer used to coat the paper. The lacquered paper may be removed from the screen with a good thinner, acetone, or a solvent that may be bought from any screen printing supplier.

Plastic Film Stencils

The toughest and most permanent of the knife-cut stencils was made and is made of plastic sheet film about .001″ to .005″ thick (.0254mm to .127mm). Although some screen printers maintain that plastic sheet such as cellulose nitrate or other plastics are difficult to cut, the cutting can be mastered with practice. These stencils which were used by the early printers may be used for printing on felt, canvas, leather, ceramic products, rough surfaces, wrinkle finished surfaces, and are practical for long runs. Commercial solvents and cements may be used to adhere the stencil to the fabric. The printer may also employ epoxy cements or epoxy inks to adhere the cut plastic sheet to the screen fabric.

In adhering the celluloid or plastic film, place it in perfect contact with the underside of the screen fabric and start attaching it to the screen cloth. Use a cloth pad or a pad made of layers of felt or silk that can be held conveniently in one hand. Soak the pad, allowing the excess liquid to drain off, and go over the inside of the silk right over the stencil, starting in one corner and working out from the other. Continue attaching a small area at a time until the cut plastic sheet is attached to the underside of the screen fabric. Here again it is advisable that the beginner try out adhering a piece of the stencil first, before starting to adhere a regular job. In attaching the stencil, the printer must make sure that all edges of the plastic sheet are adhered perfectly to the screen fabric before filling in the screen borders.

Some printers use the very thinnest plastic sheet obtainable and give the sheet a couple coats of shellac before cutting and preparing the stencil. The cut sheet is then attached to the screen with a warm iron in the same manner as shellacked paper.

This type of stencil is generally difficult to remove from the screen fabric. However, the reclaiming of the screen depends on the type of cement used to adhere the plastic film to the fabric.

There are other mediums such as decal paper, glue covered paper and pressure-sensitive materials that may be used to make hand-cut stencils. Although they do not offer any special advantages, they do give the printer other mediums with which to work in emergencies. Their preparation is smiliar to those explained above.

Chapter 12

BLOCK-OUT PRINTING SCREENS

In tracing the development of screen printing we find that there is a certain heritage in this field that is similar to other industries. We have inherited methods in screen printing that basically have resisted change and still have industrial and avocational usefulness. One of these developments is the block-out printing screen. Block-out printing screens are made by blocking out or filing in the openings in the screen fabric with masking mediums in those areas on the screen cloth through which the ink is not to be squeegeed. Those areas on the screen fabric through which the ink is to be forced or squeegeed are left open.

Masking mediums which are used as fillers for block-out printing plates are lacquer, glue, shellac, varnish, collodion, paper, and commercially prepared fillers. The last are best. There are lacquer-resistant, water-resistant, and oil-resistant fillers. The most commonly used fillers are lacquer and water-soluble fillers.

Water-soluble block-out medium is usually pigmented and is resistant to oil inks, lacquers, and enamels. It can be removed from the screen with cold, warm or hot water when necessary. It may be painted on with a brush on the inside of the screen; or, if the area is large, a piece of cardboard may be used to apply the filler in squeegee fashion. Where necessary a second coat may be applied. When this type of block-out jells, it may be warmed slightly in a double boiler. If too thick, it may be thinned down with warm water.

Lacquer type fillers usually are made from substances that have a lacquer base and are applied with a brush or with a piece of cardboard in a similar fashion to water-soluble fillers. They are durable and wear well. They can be removed completely with a commercial filler remover that is supplied for a given filler by a manufacturer or with lacquer thinner or acetone. The solvent that is supplied for removing the filler in many cases can be used also for thinning the filler so that it can be brushed more easily.

A good filler is one that flows readily and brushes easily. It should dry in about fifteen to thirty minutes and when dry should show no minute holes or pin-holes. The filler should be flexible and not crack or chip under the pressure of the squeegee. The filler should be one that may be washed off when desired or after printing. Fillers come in dark blue, green, red, and white colors so that if pin-holes do occur in brushing or application they will be seen easily.

Most screen fabrics ranging from about Number 10 to Number 18 (106 to 171 mesh per inch or 42 to 67 mesh per centimeter) may be used for the preparation of the screen. With coarser fabrics the fillers may have a tendency to seep through after application to screen cloth or during the drying stage and cause pin-holes. Generally, fillers are applied by brushing on to the design areas of the cloth. Where it is necessary to fill in the areas between the design and the frame, it is advisable to squeegee it on with a piece of cardboard. Some printers spray on block-out mediums, then print through the dried and sprayed portions of the screen to obtain perfect reproduction of spraying effects. Lacquer block-out medium is more practical for spraying. Here again, the beginner should first make a trial printing screen before starting on a regular job. Fillers generally are applied to the screen with the screen in a horizontal position to keep the filler from running. Should the filler run or drip with the screen in a horizontal position it would indicate that the block-out medium is too thin.

Block-out printing screens may be used for single color or multi-color printing. It is a quickly prepared and inexpensive printing screen and is especially good for short runs of about 100 to 500 impressions. This screen is usually employed for reproducing large printed areas and where sharp detail is not essential. However, the sharpness of detail in preparing this screen is dependent upon the skill of the printer in applying the filler with the brush and the quality of the filler. Although the printer should know how to make his own block-out mediums in an emergency, with the superior commercial fillers available it is not practical for him to give up his time to preparation of fillers.

Preparation of Block-Out Printing Screen

The procedure in preparing this printing screen is determined by the number of colors to be printed. In preparing a printing screen that will print a single color, the original design is drawn full size directly on the screen fabric with pencil or waterproof ink (usually black) or the original may be copied on the screen cloth by placing the design under the screen in the desired location. The traced or drawn lines may be permanent and serve to outline the design on the screen fabric. This method is ideal for the artist, especially for reproducing fine art subjects, since he can do his drawing directly by blocking out on the fabric. After the filler is dry, the inside and outside of the screen near the frame are sealed with masking tape, gummed paper tape, or plastic tape, depending on the type of ink used in printing.

Preparation of Block-out Printing Screen for Multi-Color Work

If it is desired to print a multi-color job, then the printing screen preparation procedure differs. A single screen may be used to print all the colors or a separate screen can be used for color. In using a single screen the design is traced or drawn on the screen cloth. The portion of the screen that is to print the lighter or first color is left open and the rest of the screen is filled. After printing, the filler is washed off and the screen is blocked out, leaving open only those parts of screen that are to print the second color. The rest of the colors are applied similarly. The original design is used under the screen in obtaining registration for printing.

If more than one screen is used, then the screens are each placed over the original design and only that part of the design is traced on each screen that is to print a given color. Everything else on the screen fabric is filled in except that area through which the ink is to be squeegeed. The printing procedure depends on the order in which the colors are to be printed and the printer may print as many colors as he desires. A practical way to prepare one screen for multi-color work is to plan the printing so that the masking medium need not be washed off after a color is printed, but more of the screen is filled in for each successive color until only that part of the screen is left open which is needed for the final printing.

Another method that is used by printers to prepare a block-out screen is known as the divisional line, key-line, or marginal line method. This method is really a modification of the single screen multi-color block-out screen. In this screen the divisional lines or parting lines show where different colors divide. These divisional lines are filled in on the screen fabric with one type of filler. The lines remain permanent for the printing of all the colors. The thickness of these lines on the cloth will vary depending upon the type and size of job that is to be reproduced.

Then everything on the screen, except the areas that are to print the first color, is filled in with another filler. The solvent for cleaning off this filler must not dissolve the filler used for the divisional lines. Usually a water-soluble filler may be used for blocking out the lines and a lacquer type filler is used for filling in the rest of the screen to print the different color.

After the first printing, everything on the screen is blocked out except the areas that are to print the second color. When the second color is printed the filler for the second color is washed off the screen and the screen is prepared similarly for the third color, fourth color, etc. Those printers who use this type printing screen maintain that it prevents an embossed effect where one color overlaps another color, the overlapping occurring on the unprinted space left open by the divisional lines. Also, these lines aid in registering the stock for printing.

Both opaque and transparent inks may be used with the above type of screen and with any of the printing block-out screens explained in this chapter.

Screen Sealing with Fillers

Fillers are also used for general screen sealing such as covering up pin-holes and spots that may open up during printing to make sure that ink will seep through only those parts in a design that are to be printed. Fillers are used to block out the areas on a screen between the design part of a printing screen and the screen frame. The type of filler used would be governed by the ink that is to be employed in printing. Any filler applied to the screen must not be dissolved by the ink. However, when the area between the frame and design is large, then it is advisable to use paper to block out this part of the screen as illustrated in Figures 57 and 58. Any good grade of stencil paper, vellum paper, or any strong translucent paper may be used. Ordinary butcher wrapping paper may be employed as a block-out medium for runs up to about 500 impressions.

To use paper for blocking out, cut a piece of paper about ⅛″ to ¼″ (.32 cm to .64 cm) smaller than the inside dimensions of the screen. Then cut out in the center of the paper an area slightly larger than the design and shaped the same as the design. The block-out paper is then attached to the underside or face side of the screen with masking tape, plastic tape, or gummed paper tape so that tape overlaps paper and part of design and paper and frame as illustrated in Figure 58, being careful not to cover up any part of the design that is to be printed. After printing, the block-out paper may be removed easily by simply peeling off the tape.

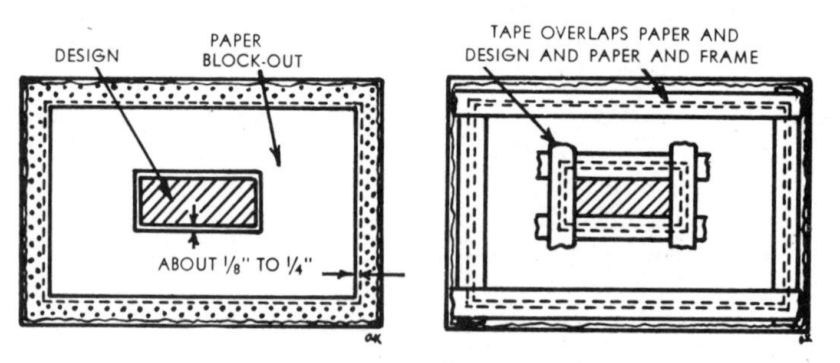

Figure 57, left, and Figure 58, right. Blocking-out screen with paper and tape.

Chapter 13

TUSCHE OR WASHOUT PRINTING SCREEN

A young industry is like a child in infancy; the qualities that predetermine its future are acquired in the early years. In an infant these qualities are taught, learned, and imitated; in a new industry they are borrowed, adapted, and created. The wash out printing screen is one of the creations of the industry. It is one of the early hand-prepared screens and was developed by Franz Weiss of Chicago in about 1931 (U.S. Patent 1959992). Weiss produced such excellence with this screen that it motivated the use of the method by artists and screen printers on federal projects of the Works Progress Administration (WPA) in the 1930's. Weiss originated the method of producing shading effects and copying embossed patterns such as wood grains, sandpaper, wire mesh, and the like which he placed directly under and in contact with the screen fabric. He then transferred the pattern to the screen by rubbing with a "tusche" or wax crayon over the fabric in contact with the pattern. The tusche or washout screen gave the printer who did not have cameras and photographic equipment a method of producing shading and even halftone effects. The screen may be used in combination with knife-cut film screens and other printing screens.

The washout screen also known as the resist, etched, or tusche-glue method of screen preparation is a favorite of artists and is quite often employed in printing on textiles. However, it may be employed to print on other surfaces. In this screen the screen fabric is covered with two masking mediums, one just covering the parts of the screen through which the ink is to pass. The other blocking-out medium covers the whole screen including the first masking medium. The first masking medium covering the parts to be printed are then washed out, or etched or eaten out with a solvent; the second masking medium unaffected by the solvent used or the ink to be employed in printing, remains on the screen and covers those areas in the screen through which the ink is NOT to be squeegeed. See Figures 59, 60, and 61.

Generally, tusche is used for the masking medium to cover the design parts on the screen and water-soluble glue is used as the second masking medium or filler to cover the rest of the screen. Because tusche

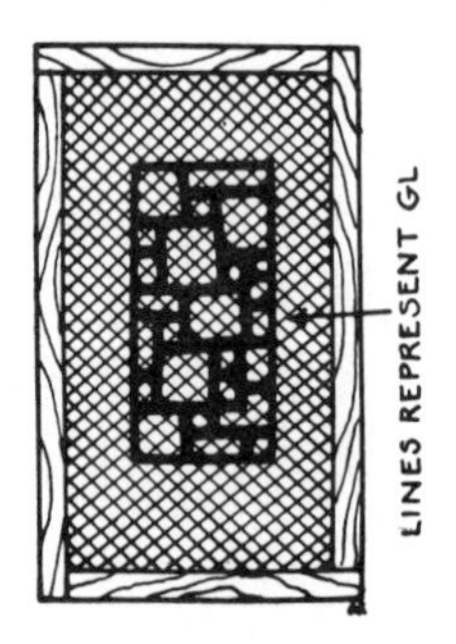

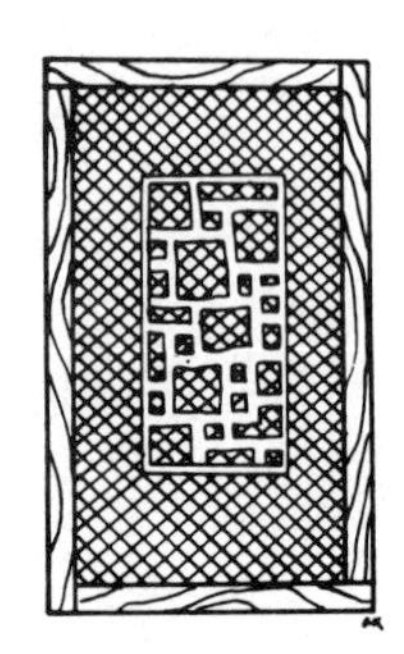

Figure 59, left. Design is brushed on with tusche on top of screen fabric. Figure 60, center. Whole top of screen is covered with glue. Figure 61, right. Tusche and glue are washed out in design areas of screen fabric.

and glue are the most commonly used fillers for this plate, this process is often referred to as the tusche-glue method. The reason that tusche is used in combination with a filler rather than just using a filler such as glue alone as a blocking-out agent on the fabric is that more detail and better shading effects can be obtained by brushing on tusche than by brushing a filler such as glue alone. Also, the design is obtained by applying tusche directly in the design areas on the screen fabric. While in the block-out method the design is obtained by blocking out around the design. Lacquer, oil, and synthetic type screen printing inks may be used with the tusche glue method.

There are other combinations of fillers that may be employed for the washout plate. Some of these combinations are tusche and lacquer; tusche and shellac; glue and lacquer; glue and shellac; asphaltum and glue; and the combination of liquid glue, a drop or two of show card color, and a drop of glycerine to serve as the first masking medium with lacquer being used as the second masking medium. The combination of masking medium used is governed by the type of ink to be printed and the ease of preparation of screen. Because the tusche-glue method is the easiest for beginners, we shall deal with it. The other combinations of masking mediums would be prepared similarly, except that different solvents would be employed for washing out and for cleaning the screen.

The tusche generally used is known as lithographer's liquid tusche. Tusche is an inky, black, and slightly greasy liquid resembling India ink and is generally composed of steric acid, lampblack, shellac, and a wax substance such as tallow or soap. Tusche is soluble in water before drying. When dry it is soluble in kerosene, naptha, benzene, turpentine, toluol, lacquer thinners, and commercial solvents supplied by manufacturers. The solvent used should be the one that is recommended by the manufacturer of the tusche. Tusche is supplied ready to use and may be thinned to brushing consistency with commercial mineral spirit base, naphtha, kerosene, benzene, or water. A good grade of tusche is one in which the ingredients do not interfere in any way with the functioning of the complete tusche process. It may be bought in liquid form in varied size containers or in solid shapes in the form of lithograph crayons or lithograph pencils. For screen printing work Numbers 1, 2, and 3 crayons or pencils are used, Number 1 being the softest and Number 3 the hardest.

The glue used is a good grade liquid glue and one that can be washed off with cold water. To toughen the glue and to give it body some printers add white show card color to the glue. The little bit of show card color that is added also makes it easier to detect pinholes in the screen fabric after the fabric is masked in the required areas. However, because some show card colors may have ingredients in them that may tend to change the chemical composition of the glue, it is advisable that the processor make a trial screen before doing the regular work.

Any screen fabric ranging from about a Number 12 to a Number 18 silk or equivalent screen fabric may be used in the preparation of this screen. Number 200 to 250 synthetic or metal cloths are recommended. The finer the cloth the sharper the edge or line that can be printed. The skill of the printer or artist and the use of a finer woven cloth will tend to eliminate serrated or ragged edges in printing. If coarser meshes are used the fillers may have a tendency to seep through when being coated creating pinholes.

The design may be drawn directly on the fabric with a pencil or it may be traced from the original design placed under the screen. Although it is not necessary if good products are used, some printers cover the bottom or underside of the screen with a sizing made of about two teaspoons of plain cornstarch dissolved in a glass of cool water. The sizing dries quickly (in about 15 to 20 minutes) and aids in temporarily clogging the mesh, makes traced lines more visible against the white background of the cornstarch, and prevents the tusche and glue from seeping through the silk. Then the design is brushed on with tusche on top of the screen fabric up to the edges of the design using a sable show card brush or a similar brush in the same fashion as making a drawing. Allow tusche to dry well. A fan may be used to hasten drying. After about one-half hour when the tusche feels dry to a light touch of the finger, brush a second coat over the first dried coat. When dry the tusche should be opaque black. Although some experienced printers do not use the second coat of tusche, it is advisable that the beginner use two coats. The tusche must cover the design areas well in order to prevent the glue or filler coat from covering permanently the design spots in the screen.

When the second coat of tusche is dry, pour in a small amount of the liquid glue at one end on the inside of the screen. Spread the glue evenly over the whole screen fabric with a piece of cardboard in squeegee fashion also covering the tusche parts. If a thin coat of glue is used, then a second coat should be applied after the first coat has dried completely. Two thin coats are preferred to one thick coat. If the printer is not able to obtain glue that he may use directly for a tusche-glue screen, then he may prepare glue by mixing one part liquid glue and one part water and adding a tablespoon of glycerine to each glass and one-half of the glue-water mixture. The glycerine makes the glue mixture more flexible and has a tendency to prevent the glue from cracking once it dries on the screen.

After the glue is dry, the tusche parts on the screen are washed away carefully on the bottom side of the screen with a soft cloth saturated in a solvent recommended by the manufacturer of the tusche or by using turpentine, naphtha, kerosene, or benzene. If a cornstarch sizing has been used, the saturated cloth will remove the tusche and the sizing. The washing out is completed carefully on top on the inside of the screen, placing newspapers between base and screen to absorb excess solvent. Any particles of glue that may remain around the washed out edges may be very carefully brushed off with any small hard-bristled brush. When the design areas are completely open, the inside and the outside borders of the screen are blocked out or taped and the screen is ready for printing.

The tusche-glue method lends itself to single color and multi-color printing. However, the printer must be aware of the fact that on dry days when the glue dries on the screen fabric there is a tendency for the prepared printing screen to shrink slightly. This shrinking is unnoticeable when printing one or two colors. When printing more colors the shrinking may prevent perfect registration of colors. Printers may overcome this difficulty by allowing for this slight shrinkage or by blending in the lighter colors by printing the darkest color last.

When the printer has developed the technique of preparing this screen, then he can try using lithograph tusche crayons or pencils in combination with liquid tusche to obtain varied shaded effects. The liquid tusche may be used to obtain solid areas in printing in combination with the pencils or crayons. The stick or solid form of tusche is used similarly to ordinary crayon and is washed away with the same type of solvents as liquid tusche.

Another and more modern technique of preparing a washout screen, employed by this writer, uses a pressure-sensitive paper or material as the temporary resist and glue or mucilage as the more permanent filler. However, the permanent filler employed would depend on the type of screen printing to be printed. The procedure for preparing the screen involves making cutouts of pressure-sensitive paper of the design or areas which are to be printed and then pressing the cutouts onto the underside of the screen fabric. Pressure-sensitive paper consists of an adhesive sandwiched between two layers—one layer, the base having the adhesive on it, and the other layer known as the release paper covering the adhesive. When the release paper is peeled off, a tacky surface is exposed which can be adhered semi-permanently to another surface. Pressure-sensitive materials may be purchased from screen printing suppliers, paper merchants, and from art shops.

The procedure for making the temporary cutout resist involves tracing the design onto the release paper and cutting through the release paper, adhesive, and base paper with a sharp film-cutting or stencil knife. When the design is completely cut, the release paper is removed from the design cutouts and the design parts are pressed lightly to the desired areas of the underside of the fabric. When the cutouts are all in place, the screen is placed onto a flat surface, a sheet of clean newsprint paper is laid on top of the silk over the design areas, and a soft cloth is pressed lightly over the paper on top of the cutouts to make them adhere firmly in place. After the design parts have all been pressed semipermanently in place, the printer may then squeegee a coat of glue or mucilage across the underside of the screen fabric, covering the fabric and the pressure-sensitive paper. After the first coat dries, a second coat may be applied at right angles to the first coating. When filler coats have dried, the pressure-sensitive cutouts may be peeled off leaving the design areas open for printing.

Other interesting and practical combinations of resists and blockouts are the use of liquid rubber-based products and photographic emulsions as the temporary resist, and lacquer, enamel, glue, or shellac as the more permanent blockout or filler. The blockout or filler employed depends on the type of screen printing ink or dye to be printed.

Liquid latex or rubber-based products, which can be purchased in art shops or from screen printing suppliers, do not require a solvent for their removal from the screen. They may be applied with a brush, pen, or cardboard in similar fashion to tusche in the design areas on the inside of the screen fabric. After the design is dry (these rubber type liquids dry quickly), any of the above permanent blockouts may be applied over the design and the rest of the inside of the screen. When the blockout has dried, the rubber resist may be removed by rubbing with an art gum, a soft pencil eraser, or with one's fingers. Removing the resist will also remove the blockout coating on the resist, leaving design areas open in the screen.

In employing a photographic emulsion or gelatin with lacquer or another blockout, two coats of unsensitized photographic emulsion are squeegeed on the inside of the screen, allowing each coat to dry well. The design is then painted on the underside of the screen fabric with a black or red lacquer. When the lacquer is dry, the sensitizer for the particular emulsion is brushed quickly on the outside of the screen only, being careful not to allow any of the sensitizer to coat any part of the inside of the screen. The screen may be coated and brushed under ordinary light. However, once the screen is brushed with the sensitizer, it should dry in the dark. After the sensitizer and emulsion

Figure 62. An original five-color, flat oil color print, printed with tusche-glue printing screens on 17" x 22" (43cm by 56cm) stock. **(By Maurice Yochim, Chicago, Illinois)**

are dry, the screen is exposed for about 6 minutes to strong sunlight or to any exposing type of light used in screen printing shops, if these are available. After exposing, the screen is washed out gently in water that is about 100 to 120 degrees Fahrenheit (38 to 49 degrees Celsius). The emulsion under the lacquer which was not exposed to light and is soft will dissolve and wash away, taking the lacquer covering with it. Those parts of the screen emulsion which were exposed will not dissolve and serve as the blockout for the printing screen.

Photographic unsensitized emulsions and sensitizers are available from any reliable screen printing supplier. Chapters 14 through 16 deal more specifically with photographic emulsions.

Figure 62 shows a five-color, flat oil-vehicle ink print produced with tusche-glue printing screens.

In summary, while the average shop today generally employs varied types of photographic printing screens for most of its printing, the hand-prepared screens presented in Chapters 10 through 13 have served and still serve the printer in producing printing to answer his individual needs. They are especially practical for the beginner, the shop which may not have the required photographic equipment, and for teaching purposes in schools.

Chapter 14

PHOTOGRAPHIC PRINTING SCREENS

Photographic science is as important to screen printing as it is to the rest of the graphic communications. The photographic principles first developed in England to print on textiles and wallpaper by Mongo Ponton, Sir Joseph W. Swan, and others from about 1840 to 1875 were the background for the development of photographic printing screens in this country. Experimentation in the screen printing field in the United States by T. V. Cook, Roy C. Beck, Al Imelli, Charles Peters, A. Mario Gomez, Harry L. Hiett, etc., since about 1914 with hand-prepared and photographic printing screens and the adaption of techniques from related fields had produced many different types of photographic screens. It is interesting to note that since the early screen printer felt the need for photographic screens, they tended to develop at the same time as hand-prepared screens. Photographic screens are used in almost every shop because they are accurate, tough, durable, dependable, print the finest detail, simple to make, can print up to about 10,000 impressions, print on any surface, and may be cleaned and stored away after printing. Few of the screen printing pioneers deserve more recognition than Harry L. Hiett, who experimented, developed, and has given to the world his successful photographic and hand methods of screen printing techniques.

The trend since World War II has been toward more delicate and fine detailed printing and it has brought an increase in printing on such products as radio dials, instrument panels, decalcomanias, textiles, glass containers, thermometers, and the like.

The principle of photographic printing screens which is similar to that of all photography is based on the fact that certain substances or chemicals will change their properties or characteristics after being exposed to light. The substance that changes chemically when exposed to light is commonly known in photography as a sensitizer. There are sensitizers in liquid form and sensitizers in emulsion form. The emulsion usually consists of a light-sensitive salt and a colloid.

If certain glue-like substances such as gelatin, albumen (the white of an egg), glue, collodion, etc., are dissolved with a salt such as potassium bichromate or ammonium bichromate, the dissolved substances will become hard after being exposed to light. These gelatinous or glue-like substances are known as colloids. Scientifically, a colloid is a substance that is midway between a solution and a suspension. A solution is a mixture which the dissolved particles are very small; a suspension is a mixture in which the solid particles are relatively small and will settle out after standing. In a colloid the dissolved particles are intermediate in size. When in this finely divided condition colloids have characteristics that are made use of in screen printing work.

The colloid gelatin alone or in combination with another colloid is used extensively for making emulsions and sensitizers. When mixed in exact proportions in water with certain types of glue, bichromate salts, and exposed to light, a very tough and lasting film for photographic screens may be made.

The classification of photographic printing screens are varied but generally they are classified (1) according to method of application of sensitized emulsion or film to screen, and (2) according to trade names. In the first classification sensitized screens are known as (a) direct, (b) direct-indirect, (c) indirect or transfer, and (d) completed screen. In the direct method the sensitized liquid emulsion is applied or coated directly on the screen fabric, and processed on the fabric. The direct-indirect screen is produced by placing an unsensitized screen printing film in direct contact with the underside of the screen. The film, which is semipermanently coated on a support sheet, is adhered to the screen fabric with a liquid sensitizer and the processing of this film is completed on the fabric. In the transfer or indirect method the emulsion or film is first prepared on a temporary support such as a thin transparent plastic and then transferred and attached to the underside of the screen fabric. The completed method is one in which the screen is finished completely first on such material as yoshino paper, uncoated typewriter stencil paper, mousseline de soie, or any screen fabric and the completed photographic plate is attached to a screen or is filed away in an envelope for future use. The latter method is not used much but is practical for mailing and storing finished photographic printing screens.*

In the material classification, printing screens are known as polyvinyl alcohol and ammonium bichromate screens, gelatin screens, carbon tissue, etc. In the trade name classification are practical screens that give good results if directions of the manufacturer are followed accurately. The trade name classification really consists of the first three main classifications but is a commercial way of protecting techniques and formulas worked out by establishments for successful reproduction of printing screens.

* The following book deals more specifically with photographic screens: Kosloff, Albert. *Photographic Screen Printing*, ST Publications, Book Division, Cincinnati, Ohio.

Generally, the steps in preparing photographic screens are: (1) preparation of positives or original design, (2) preparation of sensitizer, (3) application of sensitizer or sensitized emulsion to screen fabric or to film on a support, (4) exposing, (5) developing, and (6) actual screen printing. Basically, the photographic process consists of placing a positive or negative against a sensitized surface in a photographic contact frame or in an exposing frame and exposing the whole unit to a strong light. The parts on the sensitized surface that are exposed to the light will harden so that they cannot be dissolved in warm water; while those lines or areas of the sensitized film which were covered by the black or red opaque ink will remain soft and will be washed away with hot, warm, or cold water. These washed-away areas on the film are the parts through which the ink will be squeegeed when the film is attached to the screen fabric on the hand screen or printing machine screen.

Preparation of Positive

A positive is exactly the opposite of an ordinary film negative. What is black on the negative will be clear or white in the positive; what is white or clear on the negative will be black on the positive. Generally, it is first necessary to make a negative and then make the positve from the negative. Every spot that is filled in with opaque ink on the positive will be open on the completed printing screen.

Although the camera method of making positives is preferred, positives may also be made by hand. In making positives by hand the printer must use negative opaque ink which is an ink similar to India ink but more opaque. Negative opaque ink comes in black and red colors and is used to make drawings for negatives and positives and also for retouching negatives and positives. A good opaque ink is one that flows freely from pen or brush; may be used on film, celluloid, paper, or glass; dries fast; does not build up to a thick layer; does not chip off; and one that absolutely does not allow light through the inked spots. Opaque inks may be obtained at screen printing suppliers, photographic supply houses, photoengraving suppliers, or at art shops and may be thinned when necessary. India ink may be employed in an emergency on transparent paper but the printer must make sure that there is definitely no light passing through the inked lines and areas, as this may cause trouble in the correct completion of the screen.

Hand positives may be made on celluloid, on specially prepared mat-finished transparent plastics negative sheet, on strong transparent photographic tracing paper, or any good transparent paper that will not buckle when the ink is applied to it. The drawing may be done directly on the sheet or the sheet may be placed over the design and the design copied. Transparent plastics sheets for positives and negatives come in thicknesses from about .003″ to about .010″ 0.0762 mm to 0.254 mm. For small lettering on such jobs as dials, bottle printing, and the like, it is suggested that the letters be set in regular type, printed on transparent sheets, and dusted with a bronze or similar powder while the ink is still damp or wet. The powder on top of the ink will insure perfect opacity.

One of the common methods that the screen printer employs for making positives is to use commercially printed letters and designs and paste these on transparent sheets for reproduction purposes. These types, numerals and designs are available in many font assortments designed for making up positives and copy. The characters are printed in opaque ink on self-adhering transparent sheets. To prepare the positive the printer loosens the characters from the backing sheet and places the self-aligning characters, tacky side down, in the desired spot on a thin transparent plastic or paper sheet. There are also sheets and material known as "paste-up" copy which are printed in an opaque color on white paper. The paste-up letters may be pasted on regular card stock or may be composed in special composing sticks and used for copy to be photographed as negatives. The positives are made from the negatives.

There are also film sheets or photographic masking sheets for making or aiding in the completion of hand positives or negatives. These are very transparent, usually deep red or dark amber color, in which the design is cut with film cutting knives. The film which has a translucent plastic or paper backing sheet is placed or taped over the original and cutting is done in tracing fashion similar to that of hand-cut film printing plates. After cutting, the cut film portions are stripped away, leaving the image or the design on the transparent backing sheet. When the prepared film is placed in contact with a sensitized emulsion, light will pass only through the cut portions which have been peeled away but not through the masking film left on the backing sheet. This screen is exceptionally good where a photographic screen is needed for a job on which detail is not too intricate. It may be used to mask out certain unwanted parts of a photographic screen and may be employed over Ben Day sheets (which are sheets having various designs such as dots, half-tone effects, cross hatches, etc.) as illustrated in Figure 63. Photographic masking sheets eliminate hand brushing with opaquing substances and produce sharp edges in printing.

The best copy to use for making photographic printing screens are positives made by a camera. Camera positives are made on transparent plastics or on glass. Both are good. In exposing very large plastics or film type positives there may be a tendency for the positive to buckle, if the frame used for exposing is not of a vacuum type.

The positives or negatives for screen printing stencils may be made from hand drawings, done in black on white, shading effects, photographs, from air-brushed drawings, oil color paintings, etchings, water color paintings, halftone photo positives, and from the object itself.

Figure 63. Using photographic masking sheets to obtain desired effect.

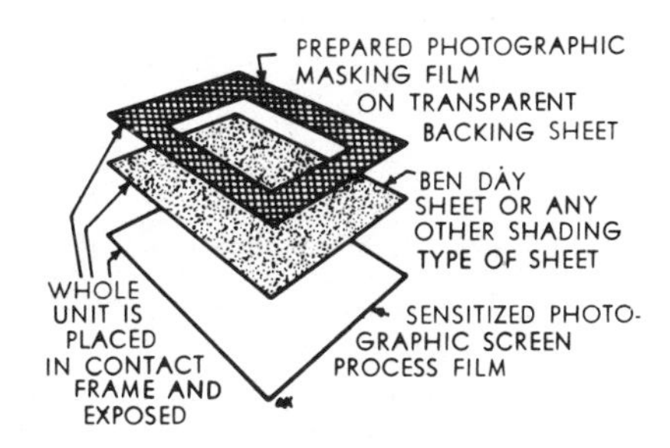

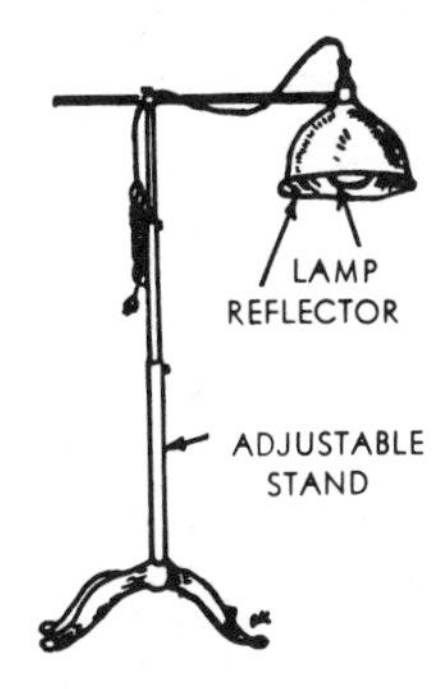

Figure 64. Photo-flood light unit.

Figure 65. Reflector with clamp.

The original used should be the actual size or larger. However, best results are obtained when the original is made larger and then reduced. A good original is essential to the making of a good printing screen and a good screen can ordinarily be made from a positive that is absolutely opaque.

Screen printing shops also prepare copy and photographic positives mechanically. For producing copy, patented letters and designs of varied size are pasted onto special layout sheets; lettering templates for titles and display are used; self-adhesive type and designs are adhered to transparent films producing a positive directly; and devices of the type illustrated in Figure 66 and 67 are employed.

PREPARATION OF SENSITIZER

Many screen printers have their photographic screens made by establishments which cater specifically to the trade. However, every screen printer should know how to prepare a photographic screen in an emergency and be familiar with the photographic process, materials, and equipment used, since the preparation of the photographic screen is not any more difficult than the preparation of the screens described in the previous chapters.

A novice starting in this type of work must observe the rules of mixing chemicals. Chemical cleanliness is the first prerequisite. Where

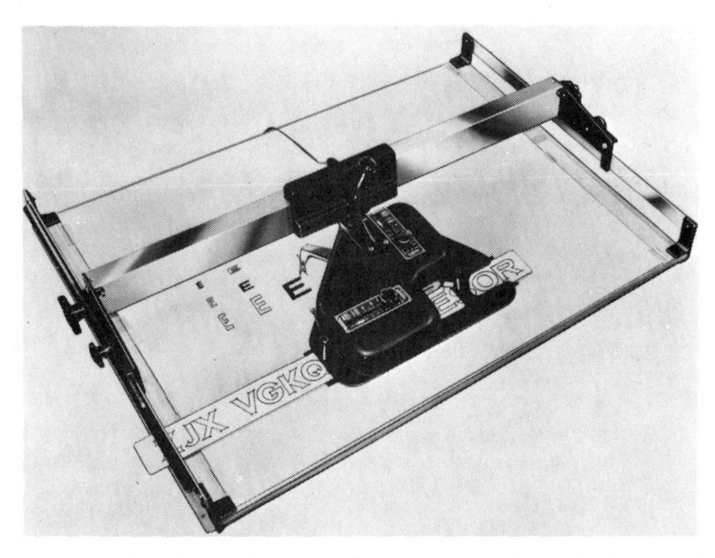

Figure 66. The "Varigraph," a non-photographic unit for producing varied styles of vertical, slanted, italic, condensed, and extended alphabets in different sizes, and for cutting of film in the preparation of printing screens. **(Courtesy of Varigraph, Inc., Madison, Wisconsin)**

necessary, distilled water should be used for the making of the different solutions. If distilled water is not available, filtered rain water, or boiled water that has been filtered through a wad of sterilized white cotton (that may be obtained in any drugstore) may be used. Ordinary tap water may be used only upon the recommendation of the manufacturer of the materials. All chemicals should be dissolved in the order prescribed by the manufacturer or by the formula. Do not add a chemical until the previous one is completely dissolved. Warm water will hasten dissolving but boiling water or too much heat may cause reactions to occur that may destroy the value of the solution and what the printer is trying to accomplish. Also, the printer must realize that some of

Figure 67. Stripprinter Photo Composing Headline Machine designed for producing varied sizes and styles of type from 6-point to 3 inches (7.6cm) high direct from film alphabets onto photographic paper or film. Unit prints positives, reverses, patterns and brush styles, has automatically time exposures, does not require darkroom or permanent installation. **(Courtesy of Stripprinter, Oklahoma City, Oklahoma)**

these light-sensitive salts may be poisonous or injurious slightly to the skin; therefore, care must be taken by the person handling them. Glass or polyethylene utensils should be used, if possible. Sensitizers should be kept in corked dark brown bottles. When melting gelatins and other substances a double glass boiler or a porcelain finished one should be employed. Because they may be washed easily, pyrex type glass bowls, are ideal for this. Metal trays should not be used, especially for holding sensitizers, as the metal will react with the sensitizer and spoil it. However, stainless steel type trays may be used with most sensitizers.

It is suggested that the printer who does not use photographic screens often buy small quantities of solutions, since each batch is fresh when used and it is not necessary then to save any solutions in the interest of economy. The cost of materials is a small part of the total printing job, therefore, the best and most reliable materials should be used.

Generally, the sensitizer may be in liquid solution or in emulsion form. It may consist either of a colloid such as gelatin applied on a surface over which a liquid sensitizer is brushed or the sensitizer may be composed of a colloid and a light-sensitive salt. The salts that are affected by light and generally used are potassium bichromate or ammonium bichromate. Since the 1960's diazo sensitizers have been employed as sensitizers and as part of a presensitized product.

Some of the early printers applied the sensitized emulsion directly to the screen fabric or to a waxed and polished temporary support such as the ferrotype plate or transparent plastic sheet, exposed the emulsion, and then transferred the exposed and developed emulsion to the underside of the screen fabric. In experimenting with coating, either the temporary support or the screen may have the colloid alone applied to it and stored away until it can be used. Before exposure the colloid covered screen or support may then be sensitized by immersion or brushing the sensitizer on with brushes that are two or three inches wide and will not shed the hair. Usually, photographic safety lights are used while sensitizing to prevent spoilage of the film.

The formulas for sensitizers vary and are carefully compounded but ordinarily the most used ones may contain accurate proportions of the following: ammonium bichromate, or potassium bichromate, ammonium hydroxide, glycerine solution, and distilled water. Of course, a diazo sensitized emulsion would contain diazo compounds. In using the sensitizer or the sensitizing bath, the printer must make sure that the temperature of the sensitizer is 60 degrees Fahrenheit (16 degrees Celsius) or lower for good results. If the sensitizing bath is too warm it may melt the film, especially if the film is made up of gelatin compounds. While gelatins are insoluble and swell in cold water, they do dissolve in hot water. Where it is necessary to dry film an electric fan may be used for this purpose. The drying takes about five to ten minutes. For best results sensitized film is used as soon as it is dry. Dry sensitized film must be kept in the dark.

Exposing the Sensitized Film

The sensitized film may be exposed either dry or damp depending on the type of screen that is being prepared. The length of exposure may be determined by experimentation but may vary from about 2 to 25 minutes, depending on different factors. In exposing, the positive is usually placed against the sensitized film so that the positive is in reverse, that is, it reads backwards. In exposing a hand-drawn positive which is drawn on translucent material the exposure time is increased about one-third.

The type of light employed for exposing is very important. The light used must be uniform in actinic intensity. That is, the light energy should produce uniform chemical change in all areas during all the time that the light is on. Light energy for exposing sensitized films, printing screens, and other photographic products may be supplied by such lamps as metal halide, carbon arcs, mercury vapor, blacklight fluorescent units, and photo-flood lamps. See Figure 68 through 71. Historically, arc lamps have proven practical because they produce a uniform quantity of light in a given time, produce high ultraviolet light, are free of flickering, and may have reflectors to aid in producing even and brilliant coverage. Because of the efficiency of other lamp sources, carbon arcs are not used as much as they were originally. Regardless of the type of lamp used in exposing, the screen printer must standardize exposing procedure.

However, the beginner may employ the plain Number 2 photo-flood lamp for some plates. The lamp may be used singly, or where more light is required, two may be connected with or without reflectors. Photo-flood lamps are similar to ordinary electric incandescent lamps and are cheap. The life of this lamp varies from about five to six burning hours. The Number 2 photo-flood uses about twice the wattage that a Number 1 photo-flood uses, and therefore, gives approximately twice the light intensity of a Number 1. The reflectors for photo-flood lamps are generally attached to stands that may be adjusted horizontally and vertically to almost any position. The lamps are more effective when mounted in reflectors.

A satisfactory reflector is the common clamp-on type available from electrical and photographic supply houses. These reflectors are available with reflecting bowls of various diameters. Be sure that the reflector used is large enough to permit free circulation of air around the photo-flood lamp to aid in dissipating the heat generated by the lamp, which is considerable. A reflector at least ten inches in diameter

Figure 68. nuArc carbon arc printing lamp for all types of screen printing exposure; this 75-amperes lamp has motor driven mechanism for assuring constant light source with 110 amperes current through arc, and has a color temperature of 7000 degrees Kelvin. **(Courtesy of nuArc Company, Inc., Chicago, Illinois)**

is sufficient to prevent the lamp exploding from its own heat build-up, and usually costs no more than the smaller sizes.

All of the above lights are made so that they can be used on regular light circuits. The lamps vary in price according to light output and are designed to be standard equipment in any well equipped shop. The photo-flood lamps with reflectors also vary in price. Lamps may have automatic switches which enable the printer to set the exposure

Figure 69. The Akulite, a 3KW metal halide lamp, designed for exposing diazo emulsions in sizes ranging from 20″ x 20″ to 68″ x 68″ (50.8cm by 50.8cm to 127.7cm by 172.7cm). Lamp is designed for exposing direct and direct-indirect emulsion coated screens which may require light frequency of about 4,000 angstrom units (400 nanometers). **(Courtesy of Majestic Bolting Cloth Corp., Somers, New York)**

Figure 70. Day Star II, a portable metal halide exposing unit, has a scientifically designed reflector, and is a practical light source, especially for the small shop or beginner, who exposes small and medium size screen printing films and screens. Unit is connected in regular 110 volt circuit. **(Courtesy of Naz-Dar Company, Chicago, Illinois)**

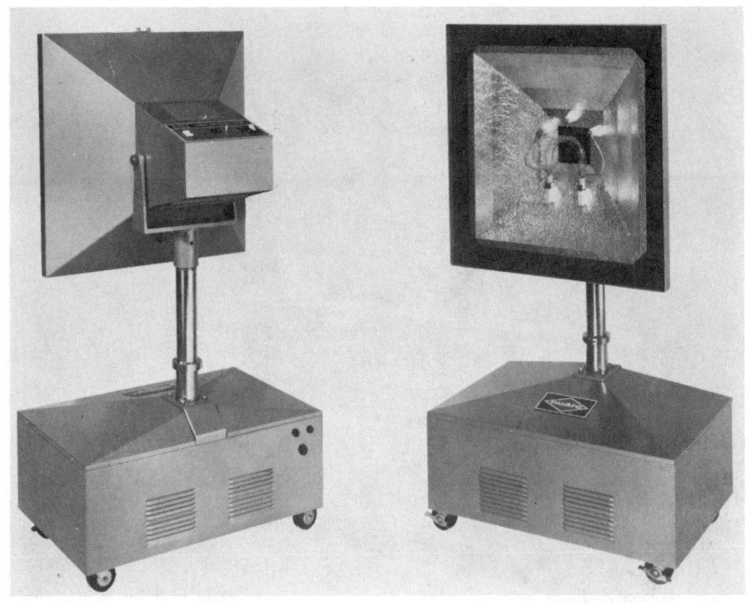

Figure 71. Instant start, 4000 watt metal halide lamp for exposing varied photographically sensitized materials, is equipped with metal halide lamp as standard, but is available with an interchangeable mercury vapor lamp as an accessory for other exposing work. **(Courtesy of nuArc Company, Inc., Chicago, Illinois)**

to desired time and when the end of exposure time is reached the lights switch off automatically. Photographic processes must be carried out with proper equipment.

In order to prevent light seepage in exposing and to assure reproduction of every detail of the positive or negative, it is necessary to have perfect contact between sensitized film and positive. To obtain such contact photographic contact frames or tables should be used for exposing. These may be home-made but it is advisable to buy them. Vacuum contact tables are available in standard sizes. These may also be used as light tables for preparation of drawings, positives, etc. See Figure 72. They are suitable for exposing the film and a positive from small to very large sizes, and for exposing direct screens. These may be made to order for specific conditions.

Developing

After the sensitized screen or film is exposed, it is developed or washed out. In washing out or developing, the exposed screen or film is washed out in water that generally is about 95 to 115 degrees Fahrenheit (35 to 46 degrees Celsius) until the desired image or pattern appears

Figure 72. Polycop direct contact vacuum frame for exposing varied size direct screens in perfect contact with film positive or negative. Unit is available in sizes with inside dimensions from 24″ x 30″ to 80″ x 110″ (61cm x 76cm to 203cm x 279cm), and can be used to expose screen printing film, presensitized films, and direct-indirect films. **(Courtesy of American Screen Printing Equipment Co., Chicago, IL)**

in the film or screen. Developing or washing out is a very important part of the photographic process. It is generally done by placing the screen printing film in a tray made of polyethylene, glass, stainless steel, or one that is porcelain finished. A good sink may also be used for this purpose. The film may be rocked gently back and forth, forcing the water to flow over the film and dissolve out the unexposed parts.

In washing out an exposed screen, the screen is wetted on both sides and a gentle water spray is used to develop out the unexposed parts until the image appears sharp and clear. Developing or washing out is generally done with the lights on, since once the exposed sensitized surface is placed in water, it may no longer be light-sensitive. If all the steps are done correctly, the screen printer will encounter no difficulty in washing out.

Printing

After the washed out film has been adhered to the screen fabric or after the screen has been washed out, the screen is blocked out with the correct blockout material outside the image area for printing. Screens which may be water soluble must be reinforced, if they are to print water soluble inks or dyes. While there are emulsions which are resistant to water soluble inks and dyes, brushing or squeegeeing a coat of synthetic varnish or enamel over the inside of the screen will make the screen resistant. An air gun may then be used to blow open portions of the design. This allows the design to be printed, after the reinforcing is dry, without deteriorating the stencil film.

In textile decorating plants where a large volume of this type of screen printing is done, the "blowing" is done by sliding the wet screen over the polished edge of a steel triangular tube connected to an air compressor. The polished edge is provided with tin slits which tend to spread the compressed air evenly over the screen.

All inks except water soluble ones may be used with most photographic plates. Ink with the finest ground pigments available should be employed. In ordering ink it is suggested that the printer specify to the supply house the quality of the ink that is necessary since most establishments have inks for printing through photographic screens and for photographic halftones.

Reclaiming Photographic Screens

Reclaiming screens involves cleaning off the ink completely and thoroughly immediately after printing, and removing emulsions, films, or coatings from the screen fabric without injury to the fabric. Nonmetal and metal fabric screens intended for long runs and meant to be stored for reuse may not be reclaimed. Generally, nylon, polyester, and metal fabrics may be reclaimed. However, reclaiming solutions which will remove very resistant gelatin and nongelatin emulsions and films may damage silk. Often directions for reclaiming of screen fabric are included with directions for processing of screen. If the printer decides to use a new technique or product for reclaiming, he should test the method on a small screen before reclaiming a large one.

There are varied methods and formulations for reclaiming screens, depending on the type of photographic emulsion and on type of screen fabric. Gelatinous films and coatings may be removed from fabrics, including silk, by soaking screen in scalding hot water for about 10 minutes and then removing film by scrubbing carefully with an ordinary stiff bristle brush. Enzyme type solutions and other products available from screen printing suppliers may be employed. These are not injurious to hands and fabrics and are used as specified in directions for removal of gelatin films and emulsions. However, enzyme solutions must be rinsed off perfectly with water to assure that microscopic particles of solution are not left on the fabric which may interfere with future applications of emulsions.

Bleach (sodium hypochlorite), 1 part bleach to 10 parts water, may be used on gelatin and non-gelatin direct and indirect screens and on bichromate and diazo sensitized screens. Generally in using any reclaiming solution, the screen is first soaked in hot water and the solution is swabbed on liberally with a bristle brush on both sides of the fabric. After the bleach solution is allowed to remain on for about 5 to 10 minutes, the emulsion and screen are rinsed off thoroughly with water. Since the sodium hypochlorite solution is a bleaching agent, caution must be used in applying it.

Big screens which have a very good grade of silk and are meant to be saved for future use should be reconditioned with a silk reconditioner before applying a photographic film to silk. Washing silk two or three times with a bleaching solution without using reconditioner may destroy the fabric.

Figure 73 illustrates an emulsion and film remover unit for cleaning and reclaiming screen fabrics. These types of units employ warm tap water under great pressure applied with a hose and spray gun for washing away direct coatings on fabric, photographic films, blockout coatings, and water soluble films. For removal of some direct coatings it is suggested that a household bleach solution be brushed over the coating and solution be allowed to remain on for about three minutes. Then spray is used to clean off coating. Some gelatinous films and stubborn carbon tissue may require an enzyme type solution application

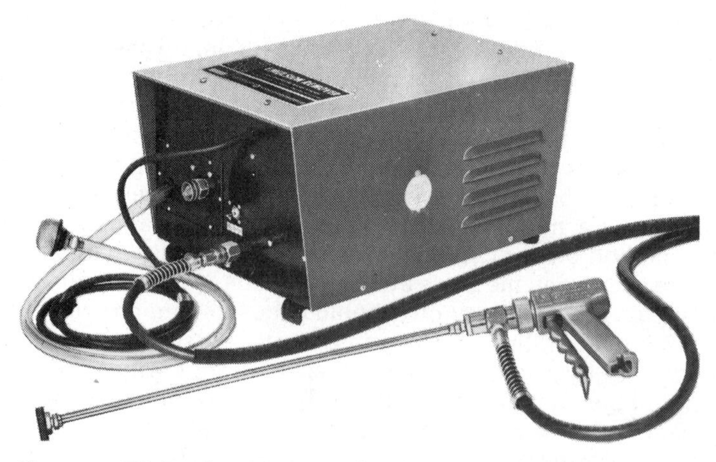

Figure 73. KO Emulsion Remover for cleaning and reclaiming screen fabrics. **(Courtesy of American Screen Printing Equipment Company, Chicago, Illinois)**

before using water spray. These solutions also must be rinsed off thoroughly, since particles drying on the fabric may interfere with adhering of future films or coatings.

Screen printing shops which reclaim many printing screens daily use a reclaiming system which employs tanks and screen washing machines. These systems generally use safe chemical reclaiming solutions which eliminate flammable solvents, toxic odors, are non-corrosive, and save on cleaning time and rags. There are units designed to clean any size wooden or metal screen and removes films, diazo and bichromate emulsions, and all inks (except dried-in epoxy inks). It eliminates the need for cleaning and degreasing prior to application of stencils. The chemical solutions used in the tank are heated to about 160°F to 200°F (71°C to 93°C). The screen is immersed in the warmed solution in the tank for about 5 to 10 minutes and is then removed and rinsed with water or with a pressure washer of the type illustrated in Figure 73. An automatic screen wash system is shown in Figure 74 for cleaning and washing varied types and different size screens.

There are also other completely automatic machines available in

Figure 74. Wash-Aire Screen Wash System for automatically washing and cleaning small and very large screens with solvents that are compatible with inks being removed from screens. As screens move on a heavy duty chain conveyor they are cleaned and at end of cycle screen shuts down the machine and stops conveyor. Machine is easy to operate and conveyor units may be added at either end of machine; unit has filter for screening and removing solids. **(Courtesy of M & M Research and Printing Aids, Oshkosh, Wisconsin)**

multi-units, which wash and reclaim any size screen without stopping to open or close doors. To operate, the operator simply sets screen on track, pushes control button, and screen travels to washing chamber, pump is turned on and off when finished, screen is then carried out of machine, and machine stops.

Chapter 15

PHOTOGRAPHIC SCREEN PRINTING FILMS

Screen printing photographic films consisting of emulsions on plastics or paper backing sheets have been used in this country since the 1920's for making photographic printing screens. They are sold so that they do not have to be sensitized before exposing and are also available unsensitized. Most of the commercially prepared films available from screen printing suppliers, photographic supply houses, and art shops are usually free of burdensome technical complications. However, their use requires that the printer become familiar with all of their characteristics. Manufacturer's directions must be followed accurately. The manufacturer has simplified the chemical formula usually in easy-to-follow steps and assumes that the user will not overlook the "human formula". If one simple step is overlooked in the procedure, the printing screen will present difficulties either in its completion or in printing.

Although originally the beginner was forced to prepare his own screen printing films by coating a base with some photographic gelatin, all types of screen printing films today are available internationally. Those films that are purchased sensitized must be kept away from any type of actinic light until the film is being exposed or developed. Those films that are manufactured with an unsensitized emulsion may be handled in the light. However, once this film is sensitized it must be kept away from light until it is exposed and then placed in the developing bath immediately. Generally, photographic safety lights may be used when handling sensitized films.

A common film paper used in screen printing and still used by the beginner and for teaching purposes is what is known as carbon tissue or pigment paper. Carbon tissue originated in England and was developed in the United States for screen printing work after the first World War. Originally, carbon tissue consisted of a paper which was coated or impregnated with a gelatinous emulsion in which finely ground particles were suspended. The carbon tissue used in screen printing work still consists of a backing sheet (generally paper) onto which a coating made up of a colloid such as gelatin and iron oxide or jeweler's rouge and pigments or dyes for color are applied. The iron oxide, pigments, etc., used give the tissue strength, aid in obtaining sharpness of detail when the tissue is developed, are a coloring agent, have binding qualities under light, help in locating imperfections in the developing, and aid in releasing the plate from temporary support. These carbon tissue sheets are available in about thirty different colors. The most common colors of carbon tissue are red, brown, black, and purple. In using any carbon tissue the manufacturer's specifications for storage and care must be followed. These products may be used for reproducing line and halftone positives.

Some of the commercially prepared screen printing films may not be sensitive to light when bought and must be sensitized before the tissue can be exposed to light. Prepared films may be obtained in any size from a small sheet to rolls about 40 inches wide and 12 feet long (101.6cm wide and about 3.96m long). Since carbon tissue is an available photographic screen printing film product that is inexpensive and may be used by the beginner, it is practical to deal with its properties and preparation. Also, after working with carbon tissue, the beginner will find that it is easier to use commercial screen printing films or "indirect" films.

There are two general methods of preparing carbon tissue, the dry and the wet method. With the dry method the tissue is sensitized, squeegeed upon a temporary support, allowed to dry, and then exposed. In the wet method the tissue is sensitized, attached to a temporary support, and exposed when the tissue is wet or in a damp condition. Although both methods have advantages and disadvantages, the wet method is used by most printers because it eliminates the slight and minute distortion which may occur sometimes when the film dries before it is exposed. However, exposing a wet film requires a little more time. Either method may be used for single color printing, multi-color work, or for printing with other types of screen printing plates.

The printer will have an accurate method of screen printing at his disposal if he learns the simple techniques of carbon tissue or pigment paper screens. These photographic films have been used for accurate printing on such jobs as instrument dials where a tolerance of plus or minus three to four thousandths of an inch was necessary. The film can be transferred to ordinary screen frames and to floating-bar frames; it lends itself perfectly for printing presses. The floating-bar frames illustrated in Figure 75 are used for stretching metal and other fabrics. Generally, the fabric is stretched first by attaching the cloth to the frame. Then the fabric is attached to the floating bars. The floating bars offer a means of obtaining very tight large screens, especially where metal fabrics are used. The tightening of the cloth is accomplished by tightening the wing nuts. For this type of plate the best grades of screen cloth to use are good qualities of silks about 12XX to 18XX in number and quality and metal cloth equivalent to

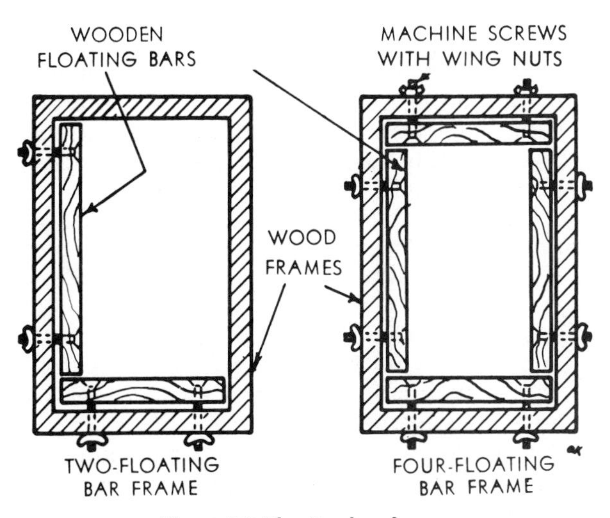

Figure 75. Floating-bar frames.

these numbers or in meshes from about 120 to 300 mesh per inch or about 50 to 118 mesh per centimeter.

In preparing a printing screen by the wet carbon tissue method the following general procedure is used: (1) preparation of temporary support; (2) sensitizing of film or carbon tissue; (3) exposing; (4) developing or washing out; (5) transferring tissue or image to screen; and (6) screen printing. If supplies and equipment are available, it should take from 30 to 45 minutes to prepare the printing screen. It is advisable to have the following material and equipment before starting: (1) carbon tissue or another type of photographic film; (2) temporary support; (3) trays for sensitizing and developing; (4) sensitizing solution; (5) a source of actinic or exposing light such as carbon arc, mercury vapor, No. 2 photo-flood lamp, etc.; (6) photographic contact frame or vacuum printing frame; (7) a squeegee or hand roller; (8) newspaper; (9) thermometer having a scale of about 40 to 125 degrees Fahrenheit (4 to 52 degrees Celsius); (10) a plain electric fan; and (11) a photographic ruby lamp or safety lamp.

For a first trial it is advisable that the printer choose a simple subject and make a small printing screen for the first attempt.

Preparation of Temporary Support

The temporary support is used to hold the carbon tissue, pigment paper or film until it is ready to be transferred to the underside of the screen fabric on the screen. The support may be a transparent sheet of polyester, vinyl, acetate, or acrylic plastic sheet about .003″

to .005″ (.001 to .002cm) thick, or stainless steel. *If polyester is used as the support,* it does not have to be waxed and polished perfectly to assure a smooth surface so that the film will release easily from the support when necessary. Any good floor or furniture wax, that has a higher melting point may be employed. When the applied wax is dry, the surface is polished with a soft cloth until all traces of the wax are removed. The surface should be polished and waxed twice. The waxing and polishing operations must be properly performed, otherwise the support may not peel away from the film when the tissue is applied to the screen.

It is possible to use the film or glass positive or negative directly without employing any other support by applying a transparent and clear protective coating over the glass or film on emulsion side. The coating may be a solution of vinyl lacquer, a vinyl acetate solution (dissolved with a solvent recommended by the manufacturer), or clear spraying lacquer. The coating may be applied by dipping the negative into the vinyl acetate solution, by pouring the solution over the film, or by spraying the clear lacquer onto the film or glass. The film should be taped down around the edges onto a solid support to keep it from buckling when the coating dries on the film negative or positive. After the clear coating is dry and hardened, the coating is waxed similarly to the temporary support.

After cleaning and polishing, it is suggested that the temporary support be kept in an envelope which may be made of wrapping paper or kraft paper. This envelope will keep the support generally clean and polished and will prevent dust and other particles from collecting on the surface.

Sensitizing

After the temporary support is prepared the required piece of carbon tissue or film is cut to a size that is about two inches longer in length and width than the positive, negative, or hand-made original being used. Make sure that the carbon tissue or film used is not very old, as old photographic film will not expose right and will resist developing action of the water. The manufacturer of the film will advise the user on storing and care of tissue, especially in the very humid sections of the country and during humid seasons, and even on what type of sensitizer to use, if the manufacturer does not supply the sensitizer.

In sensitizing the carbon tissue it is important to watch that the correct sensitizing solution and the proper strength is used. Bichromate salts are employed generally for the sensitizer and if too much salt is used the tissue will become brittle soon after it is dried on the screen fabric. These salts come in crystal and granulated form and it is advisable to use the best grades as they do not contain impurities. The pure granulated grade, the chemically pure (C. P.) grade, and the analytical reagent type are all acceptable. Bichromate salts are obtainable in any photographic supply house. The difference between a screen that will print 2,000 impressions and one that will print 10,000 impressions is dependent on the sensitizer and its correct preparation.

The formulas for sensitizers are about as varied as the types of carbon tissue or films used and different printers have found success with varied mixtures. It does not make any difference whether the formula is (A) two and one-half ounces of potassium bichromate to one gallon of water (70.87 grams of bichromate in 3.78 liters of water); (B) three and one-half ounces of potassium bichromate, one-half ounce of acetic acid to one gallon of water (99.22 grams of bichromate, 14.2 grams of acetic acid to 3.78 liters of water); or (C) two ounces of potassium bichromate to 100 ounces of water (56.70 grams of bichromate to 2.96 liters of water). Regardless of whether the formula contains ammonium bichromate, potassium bichromate, ammonium hydroxide, glycerine solution, and water, the important point is that the ingredients are dissolved according to directions. Varied sensitizers may work but the best sensitizer is one that produces a film that remains elastic, tough, one that provides for minimum exposure time, does not produce fog or a thin hardened layer on the film, and one that works under most climatic conditions. Chemicals must be fresh and should be kept in glass, pyrex, or plastic containers.

Harry L. Hiett* found that better results are obtained by using a sensitizing solution that has become slightly acid and recommends that the sensitizing solution be used after it is two days old. He used two and one-half ounces of potassium bichromate (70.87 grams) to one gallon of water (3.78 liters) for the wet tissue method, and one and one-half ounces of potassium bichromate (42.52 grams) to one gallon of water (3.78 liters) for the dry method.

The temperature of the water used for the sensitizing solution should be 60 degrees Fahrenheit (15.6 Celsius) or less, preferably less. It is a good idea to test the water with a thermometer until the printer can definitely tell by touch, although the touch method is not an accurate procedure. It is suggested that the solution be chilled prior to using. This may be done by running cold water from a faucet over the container or by keeping the sensitizer in a refrigerator. The solution should be stored in a dark corked bottle in a dark cool place. It is not wise to use the sensitizer after it has been kept in liquid form for two weeks, although these chemicals may be kept in the dry state almost indefinitely.

When the sensitizing solution is correctly mixed, place carbon tissue in solution, being careful to prevent formation of air bubbles. The

* H. L. Hiett, "Photo Stencil Screen Work," *Signs of the Times*, Vol. 124 (April, 1950) pp. 58, 96–97.

tissue must be kept immersed, emulsion side down, for about three to ten minutes or until two ends of the tissue start to curl.

After the tissue has been sensitized, take the temporary support and place the tissue, film side or emulsion side down, on the cleaned and polished surface. Press a squeegee or roller gently over the tissue backing sheet, working from the center outward. Continue flattening out tissue on the support until you are sure that there are no air bubbles between tissue and support. The handling of the tissue must be done in the dark or under a photographic safety light. Then place a clean piece of newsprint or newspaper over the tissue and cover the sheet of newspaper with a piece of cardboard, placing a very light flat weight over the cardboard to keep everything in contact. Keep tissue covered and in the dark until it is ready to be exposed. It is wise to use the sensitized film when it is still wet or in a damp condition.

Exposing

In the wet method it is necessary to expose the sensitized film so that light passes first through both the positive and the transparent support. Exposing is done in a photographic contact frame or vacuum frame or table. The contact frame illustrated in Figure 76 which may be made by the printer will work well when the parts are arranged and assembled as shown.

When the contact frame is locked a *safe edge* or soluble edge is made on all four edges of the tissue. This safe edge protects the outer parts of the tissue from exposure to light and the edge is used later for handling the film. It aids in removing the backing sheet during development. It also keeps the tissue from sliding off the temporary support while the film is in the developing bath. It is made by applying negative opaque ink, black tape, masking tape, or any opaque masking medium over the glass of the contact frame about one half inch over

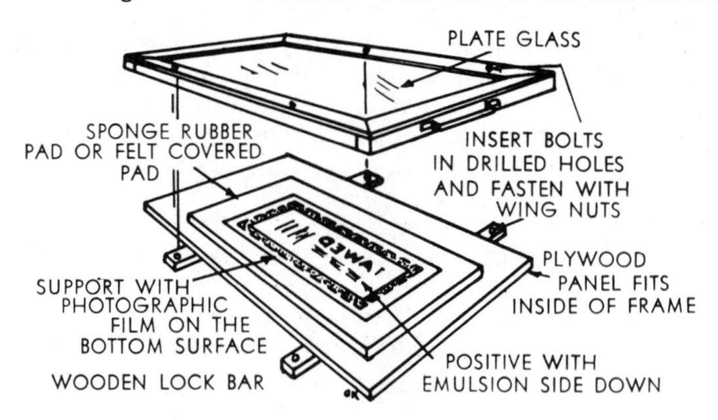

Figure 76. Photographic contact unit.

each edge of the tissue. If a black opaque edge is included on the positive containing the design to be reproduced, it may not be necessary to make an opaque edge on the contact frame glass.

The time of exposure will vary depending on the type of photographic film, sensitizer, light source used, type of positive used, and distance of exposing contact frame from light. The distance of the light from the frame varies from about eighteen inches (45.72cm) to four feet (1.22 meters). The time of exposure may vary from about one minute to thirty minutes. Arc lights make possible the minimum time of exposure; Number 2 photo-flood lamps take a longer time. When the distance from the lamp to the plate is doubled, everything else being equal, the exposure is approximately four times as long; when the distance is tripled, exposure time is approximately nine times as long, etc. As a photo-flood lamp ages the time of exposure should increase slightly to make up for loss of light intensity.

The length of exposure time may be established easily by the printer in the following manner: After the film and positive are locked in the exposing frame, fourteen strips of opaque masking tape or any opaque paper are taped over the exposing frame glass covering the film, leaving about one inch of the top of the tissue uncovered. Start exposing the whole unit at about two and one-half feet (.762 meters) away from the light source. At the end of two minutes remove the top strip; after four minutes remove the second strip immediately next to the exposed area; after six minutes remove the third strip; etc. At the end of one complete exposure or at the end of thirty minutes all of the strips covering the tissue will be removed and the printer will have a series of exposures timed at intervals two minutes apart and the whole film exposed in a time range from two to thirty minutes. If the printer desires he may change the interval to one minute and use more strips of narrower paper. When the film is developed, attached to the screen, and printed, the results of the exposure will be revealed and the printer will find the range of the best time exposure for a given type of tissue or film being used. Of course, the time will be objective only if the distance of the light from the film is always the same and if the same source of light is used.

Correct exposure time is important. If the film is underexposed, there will be loss of detail and a thin, weak film may be produced. Overexposing a film hardens the sensitized emulsion too much, and makes it difficult and often impossible to adhere the film to the screen fabric. Also, there is difficulty in stripping the backing sheet from the emulsion.

Regardless of what type of light is being used, the film must be kept from overheating. Since most carbon tissues are gelatin compounds, they will melt at anywhere from about 80 degrees Fahrenheit (27 degrees Celsius) and up when the tissue is damp or wet. The melting of the film can be prevented by placing a fan between the light and the contact frame and having the fan blow on the contact frame, by placing a plate glass between the light source and the exposing frame, or by doing both.

Developing or Washing Out

After the tissue has been exposed it is developed by placing the support bearing the tissue in a tray of water, the temperature of which must be kept between 100 and 110 degrees Fahrenheit (38 and 43 degrees Celsius). The temperature should be kept within this range. The thermometer may be used to check the water temperature. Allow the support and the film to remain immersed in the water until the unexposed film or gelatin compound begins to come out between the backing sheet and support. Then carefully pick up a corner of the backing sheet and peel away the sheet. If the backing sheet does not come off easily and clean, let it remain in the water a little longer.

When the backing sheet is removed the completion of development is carried out by rocking the support very gently, thus washing and removing all soluble parts. One of the common troubles of carbon tissue failures is insufficient development. Do not hasten development by rubbing film with a cloth or hands, as this may destroy the design or image. The water will dissolve away all the unexposed parts. When it is obvious that all the unexposed parts have dissolved, immerse the support and film in another bath of clean water, the temperature of which is about 100 degrees Fahrenheit (38 degrees Celsius). Continue washing and developing until the water appears clear. Finally, immerse support in a tray of water that is about 70 degrees Fahrenheit (21 degrees Celsius) or less and allow it to remain in this bath for about two minutes before mounting film on screen fabric.

Mounting Developed Image on Screen

The screen fabric must be cleaned before the film is mounted on it. It is advisable to wash silk with hot water to remove foreign particles and sizing on silk. Perfect adhesion of film to fabric is essential and any foreign particles on silk will prevent this adhesion. If wire cloth is used, the very thin protective coating of oil or grease must be removed, as these coats will prevent the film from adhering. Weak acid solutions or a weak ammonia solution may be applied to both sides of the wire cloth. The cleaning solutions are washed off first with hot water and then with cold water. Rubber gloves should be worn in handling these solutions, as even the weakest solutions of some acids will injure the hands. Allow screen to dry with the aid of a fan to preshrink it as much as possible.

Synthetic cloths such as nylon or polyester may be cleaned with commercial cleaning liquids or agents and then washed and rinsed thoroughly with hot water. Some printers use trisodium phosphate solutions which they scrub over the fabric and then rinse the solutions off thoroughly with hot water to clean and degrease these fabrics.*

Before mounting tissue on screen, it is suggested that a raised cardboard surface, about an inch or two smaller in length and width than the inside dimensions of the screen, be made. The raised surface serves to make better contact between screen and film. Then center and place the temporary support, film side up, over the raised surface. Be very careful not to move the screen once it is placed on the film, as the image or design may be distorted or spoiled. When the fabric is in contact with the film, blot gently on the inside of the screen with newspaper. Blotting removes excess moisture and assures contact. Blot well a second and third time, if necessary. Place weights on the frame part of the screen to keep fabric in perfect contact with film. Allow tissue to air-dry naturally. Although a fan may be used to hasten drying at this stage, it is not advisable. A film that dries naturally is tougher and prints more impressions.

If the support does not come off easily, then the film is still damp and the screen must dry longer. Once the support is removed, the borders on the screen are filled in with a filler or masking medium and the screen is ready for printing.

It is not necessary to use hardening agents for most screens, as bichromate salts naturally harden themselves. However, where the printer has to print with some luminescent, phosphorescent, ceramic, and other inks of this type, it is sometimes necessary to harden the film by immersing it in a hardening agent before attaching it to screen. This must be done carefully, as some hardening agents will interfere with the adhesion of the film to the screen fabric. Also, a hardening solution coated on the screen may make it more difficult or impossible to reclaim a screen.

Figure 77 illustrates a typical job printed on transparent acetate thin sheet in three colors with photographic screen printing films.

In summary, practical printing screens may be produced by hand or by photographic means. However, regardless of the method of producing screens, the final screen, which is a negative image, prints a positive image. While the discussion in this chapter deals mostly with carbon tissue because it stresses practical principles, there are varied transfer or indirect type printing screens used today. They are known as *indirect* screens because the processing of the film or image is *not done directly* on the screen fabric but is transferred to the fabric after processing. While carbon tissue type screens may employ a temporary support for processing, most indirect or transfer type products, whether presensitized or unsensitized, consisting of an emulsion on a base or

* The following book deals more completely with preparation of photographic printing screens: Kosloff, Albert, *Photographic Screen Printing*, Signs of the Times Publishing Company, Cincinnati, Ohio.

Figure 77. A "gang-up" job or more than one design was screen printed in reverse on the back of acetate sheet in red, blue, and yellow colors, employing three photographic screens for printing. The blue and red colors were printed first and yellow was printed over the two colors. (Courtesy of Superior Silk Screen Industries, Inc., Chicago, Illinois)

support sheet, are processed on the support sheet. Ordinarily, the specific directions for processing are supplied by the manufacturer. Directions are not difficult to follow and the steps generally consist of exposing a positive in perfect contact with the sensitized film, washing out in warm water after exposure, mounting washed out images on screen fabric, and removing support sheet after correctly drying of film.

However, since commercial indirect films are intended for more specific precision printing, the following steps must be stressed again to obtain correct processing: 1. Proper fabric stretching is very important. 2. Make sure that screen fabric, especially synthetic and metal fabrics, are degreased to remove residues and dirt with a commercial grit paste or degreasing liquid available for this purpose. 3. Definitely standardize exposures using a step wedge or series of exposures to arrive at best exposure. 4. Use a buildup layer on which washed out film is placed when adhering film. 5. Allow film to dry completely before removing backing sheet.

Chapter 16

Direct and Direct-Indirect Photographic Printing Screens

In spite of the fact that the screen printer's use of the indirect or transfer type screen may be satisfactory, today's printer must have knowledge of and be able to use *direct* printing screens and *direct-indirect* screens or *direct-film* screens. Direct screens are much used and the screen printer employs these where a more durable screen is needed. In a direct screen the photographic emulsion or direct-film is applied and processed directly on the screen fabric, as compared with an indirect or transfer type in which the film is first processed on a temporary support and then transferred to the screen fabric. Today's direct screen emulsions, both the diazo and bichromate sensitized products, do not produce serrated or ragged edges in detail printing, if products are processed correctly. A correctly prepared direct screen, especially one made on wire cloth, is very durable since the fabric is impregnated with the emulsion coating or direct-film and the toughness obtained is similar to that obtained in impregnated plastics. Direct emulsions adhere to all screen fabrics and are easy to prepare.

There are two general types of direct screens: (1) direct-emulsion coated screens and (2) direct-indirect or direct-film screens. As has been mentioned, the first type is processed by coating an emulsion (generally presensitized) on the screen fabric before completing the rest of the steps in the preparation of the screen.

The direct-indirect screen processed with a direct-film is prepared directly on the screen; however, after screen preparation, the film or emulsion carrying the image is left on the screen fabric and the emulsion support is removed before exposing screen. This type of screen is tough, easy to prepare and is very versatile.

Direct printing screens may be coated with natural type emulsions or with synthetic emulsions. The gelatin emulsion is the natural type. The synthetic type of screen was developed simultaneously both in this country and abroad during World War II. In the latter type are included such screens as the polyvinyl alcohol, polyvinyl acetate, polyvinyl chloride, polyvinyl alcohol-polyvinyl acetate screen, and the varied commercial products. The synthetic and the commercial direct emulsions are used more, especially on jobs where the solvents in inks will attack a gelatinous type screen and where a tough inert screen is needed. Today's screen printer may obtain an emulsion for printing with any screen printing ink. While commercial synthetic emulsions are used more often than gelatinous formulations, gelatinous emulsions are still used in varied parts of the world. They do offer another type of direct screen to use in an emergency and gelatinous screens may be made resistant to chemicals in inks by brushing or coating the photographic area on the screen with certain lacquers, enamels, or solutions obtainable from screen printing suppliers. While there are varied types of commercial products and different types of direct screens, after the emulsion is coated or applied to the screen fabric, the processing steps are similar. Therefore, we shall explain the more common method—that of preparing a direct-emulsion coated screen. The emulsion used for direct screens may be applied in the light-sensitive state or it may be applied to the fabric unsensitized and a sensitizing solution brushed over the emulsion.

Preparation of Direct Screen

For direct screens, the screen fabric must be stretched very tightly on the frame. For large screens where close registration is required and for wire screens, printers may use floating-bar screens, commercial screen frames, or stretching units. If silk is being used, a good quality of Numbers 14 through 18 may be employed to obtain ease in application of emulsion. Meshes of 125 to 300 per inch (50 to 118 per cm) may be used for synthetic fabrics and wire cloth. Coarser weaves may require more of the emulsion and may be more susceptible to development of imperfections. However, direct-indirect screens or direct-films are easily processed on coarser fabrics.

If silk is new, it should be washed well. The oil or grease coating on wire cloth must be cleaned off. The treatment of nylon screen fabric is covered in Chapter 3. Wire screens will last indefinitely, if care is given them. An important precaution in their use is to place them down in such a way so as to avoid denting the screen. A dent, especially if it is in the image area, necessitates the removal of the wire cloth from the screen.

Preparation of Emulsion and Sensitizer

If the sensitizer is commercially prepared, full directions are usually given for its preparation. If the sensitizer is to be prepared by the printer, then the same care and cleanliness in its preparation must be observed as in the preparation of photographic film screens. It is best to use distilled water for all solutions. Whether a sensitizer is prepared from powders or liquids, the final sensitizing solution should be strained through filter paper or through a clean piece of silk or wire cloth that has been folded over two or three times.

Some of the older practical formulations for sensitizers and emulsions may suggest heating the ingredients in order to dissolve them. The beginner or student should use a glass or porcelain finished double boiler for this purpose. Pyrex glass dishes or glass baking dishes may also be used. Water is boiled in one container and the other container with the dissolved ingredients in it is placed in the boiling water. The ingredients in the upper container should be dissolved completely without boiling.

If the printer desires to prepare an emulsion from gelatin in similar fashion to the pioneer screen printer, then it is advisable that the photographic gelatin be allowed to soak in the required amount of water (preferably distilled) for about thirty minutes to two hours, depending on the gelatin or formula. Where a color is specified in a formula, a water soluble aniline dye or a stamp pad ink which will not affect chemically the other ingredients in the sensitizer should be added to the solution when the emulsion is being prepared. Colors of dyes generally used are purple, red, and green. Very little color is added to the sensitizer to aid the printer in application and in detecting pinholes and other imperfections, should they develop. With some formulations the coloring matter is applied on top of the emulsions after it has dried on the screen. However, it is not essential to add coloring matter to the formulation.

The formulas for direct screens are similar to film or transfer screens. Most of the colloid ones contain (besides gelatin, which may be originally in sheet, grain or powder form) exact proportions of glue; potassium bichromate (which is usually dissolved in distilled water); glycerine solution; a neutralizer such as carbonate of magnesia or borax; and more distilled water to make enough solution. While bichromate salts may be listed as the sensitizing agent in the formulation, since about 1965 diazo powders or solutions have also been employed as sensitizers. The following are varied examples of formulas and proportions used: (A) one-half ounce (14.4 grams) of a good grade gelatin or photographic gelatin dissolved in four ounces (120ml) of distilled water, one-half ounce (14.4 grams) of granulated potassium bichromate, and one-fourth ounce (7ml) of aniline dye; (B) screen covered with photographic gelatin, dried and brushed with a sensitizer made by dissolving one-half ounce (14.4 grams) of potassium bichromate in a pint (.47 liter) of distilled water; (C) a formula using a synthetic emulsion recommended by Du Pont which employs a polyvinyl alcohol (11.5 per cent by weight), a saturated solution of potassium bichromate (5 per cent by weight), distilled water colored with a blue pigment (83.5 per cent by weight); polyvinyl alcohol is sold as a powder that is soluble in water; (D) a liquid formula made of 19 parts of a solution which is prepared by dissolving one-half pound (.23kg) of polyvinyl chloride in three quarts (2.85 liters) of distilled water, and one part of a solution composed of one ounce (28.8 grams) of ammonium bichromate dissolved in three quarts (2.85 liters) of water.

While any of the above formulas will work, the beginner is advised to purchase commercial products or emulsions from screen printing suppliers. For a first trial it is suggested that a small screen be attempted.

Application of Emulsion and Sensitizer

There are different methods of preparing direct screens. The common method, whether the emulsion is lightsensitive or not, is to apply the emulsion in liquid form and allow it to dry on the screen fabric. Commercial emulsions are applied by pouring some of the solution onto the fabric and squeegeeing the emulsion back and forth several times until a uniform even coating is obtained. Some screens are covered with a gelatin sheet which is soaked in water. Then the gelatin is sensitized after the sheet is adhered to the screen and dried. If the photographic design is to cover the whole screen (these screens may be used in combination with hand-prepared screens), then the emulsion should cover the whole fabric.

The sensitized emulsion may be applied in the dark, in subdued light, under photographic safe-lights, or in ordinary daylight, depending on the type of sensitizer. However, after the emulsion is applied to the screen, the sensitized emulsion covered screen must dry in complete darkness. If the printer is in doubt as to the amount or safety of light that a safe-light gives off then he should test it before using it in his shop or darkroom.

Any safe-light or the ordinary ruby light used should not affect the photographic sensitized screen in any way. A simple way to test light for safety is to allow a small area of a sensitized screen or film to be exposed to the safe-light, the rest of the screen or film being covered with opaque tape or paper. If at the end of the testing period there is no difference between the exposed and covered-up part of the film or screen, then the safe-light may be used. If the printer is forced to use a safe-light that may affect the sensitized screen or film, then he should move the light farther away from the sensitized screen or change the bulb for a smaller size or wattage.

The drying of the screen may be hastened with a fan, heat, or both. Generally, heat is not specified for drying commercial emulsions. Where heat is used, it should not be too close to the emulsion, as too much heat may cause blistering or cracking. It is a good idea to keep the screen about two or three feet away from source of heat. It is not advisable to use a source of heat which gives off light energy at the same time that heat is given off.

Generally, commercial emulsions are applied by squeegeeing a little of it onto the fabric with a squeegee, sharp edge of a piece of cardboard, or with special coaters. The emulsion may also be applied with a camel hair brush; it may be flowed onto the fabric with a cup, keeping the screen in a vertical position and allowing emulsion to cover the underside of the fabric; or the solution may be poured into a shallow tray and the clean screen dipped into the solution so that the entire underside is coated. Some shops place the coated screen on a whirler, with the coated side of the screen up, and whirl the screen until the solution is distributed evenly and uniformly over the surface.

Stainless steel mesh is coated in the same fashion as other fabrics. The sensitized emulsion is applied first on one side of the screen (underside) and then on the other side (inside), allowing the first application to dry completely in the dark before the second application is made. This impregnates the wire cloth with two coatings and the tendency of the emulsion to lift is prevented during development or washout. Other coats may be applied on the underside, if there is a need to produce a very tough screen.

There are methods of applying direct emulsions to the fabric that tend to eliminate ragged or serrated edges in printing. These devices do not require placing the coated screen on a whirler. The tendency in the application of the direct emulsion to the screen fabric is to coat the underside of the screen using some device such as the coaters illustrated in Figures 78, 79, and 80. These devices for application tend to apply the coat so that when the screen is etched out, the detail is sharper than with brushing or squeegeeing the coating onto the fabric.

Where a formula specifies that the emulsion be applied on the underside of the screen or where a coarse screen fabric is used, it is suggested that after the first coat is applied, the screen be turned end for end and the second coat applied after the first one has dried.

Where sensitized gelatin solutions become lumpy due to standing, they may be reheated within a week or ten day period. They should not be used after that period. Sensitizing solutions or sensitized emulsions must be kept in dark brown glass or polyethylene containers during this period. Generally, suppliers specify length of time emulsions may be stored.

There are products which will resist most solvents and inks. However, if for some reason it is necessary to make photographic screens

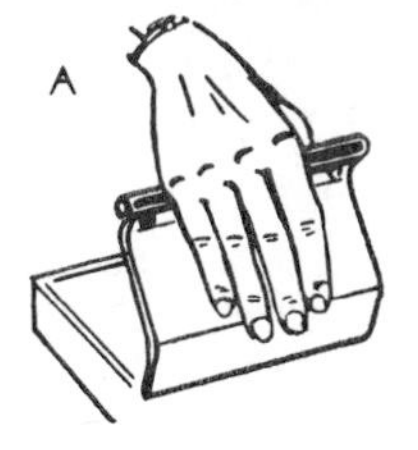

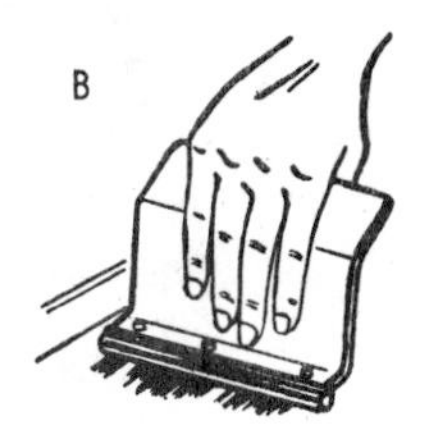

Figure 78. A direct emulsion coater for applying photographic emulsions and other coatings directly onto screen fabrics. **(Courtesy of Precision Screen Machines Company, Hawthorne, N.J.)**

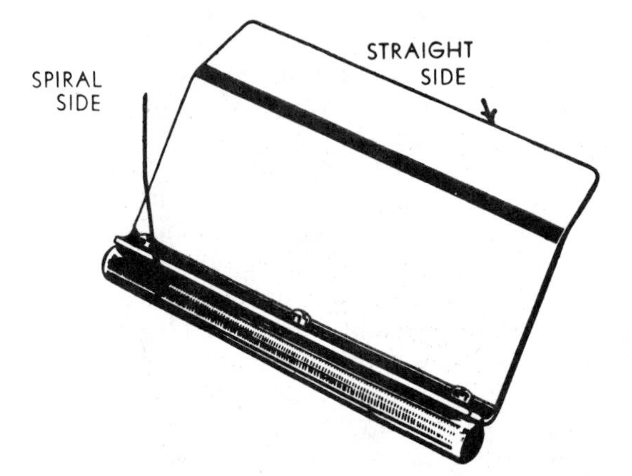

Figure 79. Straight side of coater is used to apply first emulsion coat. When first coat is dry, the second coat is applied with spiral side of coater. **(Courtesy of Precision Screen Machines Company, Hawthorne, N.J.)**

more resistant to wear and to solvents in inks, hardening agents or solutions are employed. These solutions which are easy to prepare and to use may consist of solutions in which there are very small parts of glycerine and formaldehyde, or three parts of formaldehyde and one part of butylaldehyde. The mixing and weighing of formulas is specified both in the metric units and in English units. More practical hardening agents are available commercially.

Exposing

Generally, when making direct screens the prepared screen should be exposed and developed as soon as possible. Screens coated with some commercial emulsions may be kept longer before exposing. How-

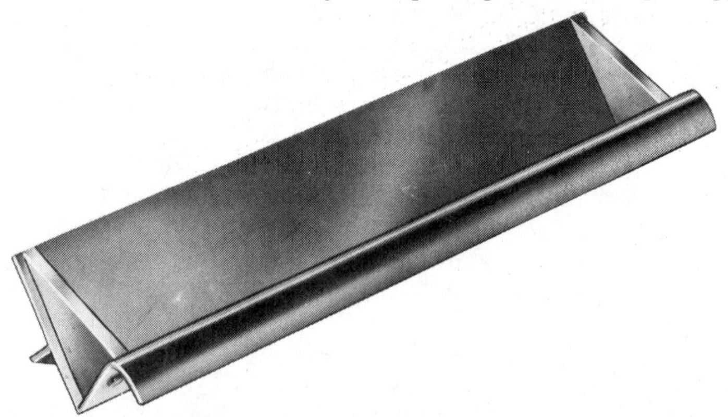

Figure 80. Direct-Emulsion Scoop Coater for applying emulsion onto fabric. In coating, emulsion is poured into coater and coater is pulled up and tilted slightly against fabric. **(Courtesy of Advance Process Supply Company, Chicago, Illinois)**

ever, this should be specified in the directions for the preparation of the emulsion. Exposing of direct screens is done in contact vacuum tables, in contact frames, or in units of the type shown in Figure 81, which may be made in any size by the printer. To produce better contact between positive and screen in Figure 81, it is suggested that foam rubber about ½″ to 1″ thick (1.27cm to 2.54cm) be placed between contact block and screen. If exposing units are not available, then cut a piece of black painted plywood panel or black cardboard so that it fits snugly on the inside of the screen frame against the screen fabric. Tape it or fasten it with brads to the frame so that the board makes perfect contact with the fabric and so that it will not move. Then turn screen over and center positive with the drawing or design side in contact with fabric. There must be perfect contact between positive and sensitized fabric, otherwise light will seep between positive and fabric and will distort detail when design is reproduced on printing plate. Then place a piece of plate glass over positive so that glass covers all of screen and expose.

Another practical and simple technique for exposing film positives and coated screens is the "cementing method" of exposure. This procedure may be used for exposing any size direct screen. A good quality rubber cement is used for cementing the positive to the coated screen fabric. The cement should be thinned with cement solvent or benzol, one part cement and one part solvent. As rubber cement dries quickly, cement mixture should be kept covered so that it does not evaporate when not in use. If some evaporation takes place, more solvent may be added to the mixture.

In the cementing method of exposure the positive is placed right side up, on a clean flat surface and the whole positive surface is coated with rubber cement, brushing the cement on uniformly with a clean brush. The underside of the screen fabric where the positive is to con-

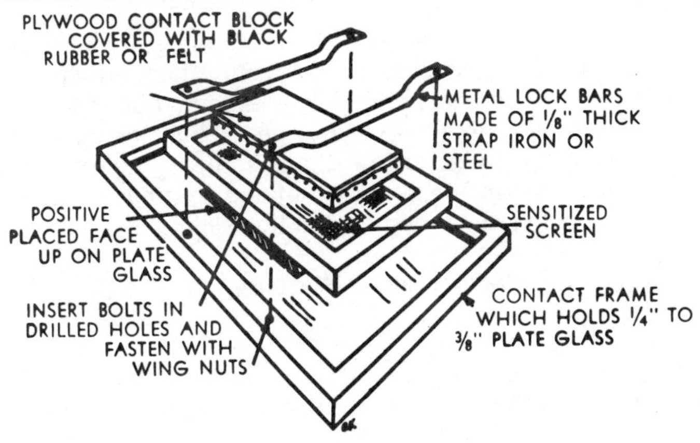

Figure 81. Photographic contact unit for direct screen.

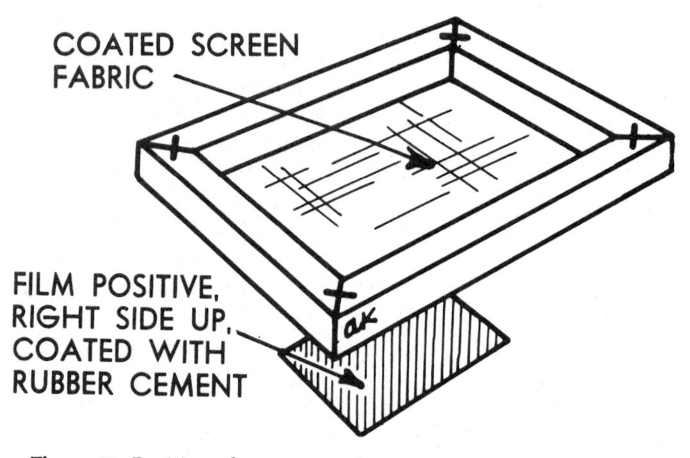

Figure 82. Position of screen in relation to positive for exposing.

tact is also coated with cement. See Figure 82. Both surfaces must be coated well and must dry before contacting for exposure. As soon as surfaces are dry, place screen over positive, and place two sheets of newsprint paper on inside of screen over positive area. Then rub over paper with a piece of soft cloth or cotton, making sure that perfect contact is obtained between whole positive and fabric. Contact may also be obtained by simply using a roller or brayer and rolling over screen fabric pressing down on fabric. The cement will hold the positive in perfect contact with fabric. After screen is exposed, the positive is peeled off, and the spots of rubber cement remaining on the fabric are cleaned off by rubbing with the finger or with a cloth that is dampened but not saturated with solvent, rubbing the cloth over the cemented fabric. The screen is then ready for developing or washing out in water.

Exposing procedure is similar to that of photographic transfer film. Exposing time for direct screens varies from about 1½ minutes to 30 minutes; distance of screen from light source is about 4 inches to 4 feet (10cm to 1.22cm), depending on type of light being used. If not enough time is given to exposing direct screens imperfections such as pinholes may develop, since the sensitized coating or emulsion may not have been hardened enough by the light energy.

Developing or Washing Out

After exposing, the screen may be developed or washed out by placing it in a sink or container which is filled with water the temperature of which is 110 to 115 degrees Fahrenheit (43 to 46 degrees Celsius). The water should not be allowed to go above 115 degrees (46C), as water that is too hot may melt away some of the image detail. Some direct screens made with commercial emulsions may be developed in cold water. The water is applied to both sides of screen with a hose or glass. The light should not be turned on until all of the screen is completely wet. Continue applying water until all the details appear clearly and distinctly. With some gelatinous screens and with most synthetic screens a gentle spray of water may be applied to wash away the unexposed parts. Then finish developing by applying cold water to stop developing and remove the rest of the minute particles clinging to the screen. After cold water is applied, place the screen on two or three thicknesses of newspaper or on a soft smooth cloth so that the underside of the screen is in contact with the paper or cloth. Then blot carefully on the inside of the screen with newspaper pressing at the same time to remove excess moisture. After excess moisture is removed place screen in a vertical position and allow it to dry with the aid of a fan. If the screen is prepared correctly, there should be no imperfections. However, should there be an occasional pinhole in the areas where detail will not be spoiled, it may be blocked out with a masking medium. When screen is completely dry it may be taped or blocked out around the edges and the screen is ready for printing.

Direct-Indirect or Direct-Film Printing Screens

Direct-indirect or direct-film printing screens are available as unsensitized products which have to be sensitized by the printer or as presensitized products which do not have to be sensitized. The direct-film consists of a predetermined emulsion thickness on a support or base. Although the direct-indirect product is prepared on the screen fabric, it eliminates coating the screen fabric.

These screens have advantages* and may be used for printing very fine detail and large area printing, produce very many impressions, have good fabric adhesion, since the film bridges and encapsulates the mesh. During exposure the film is in direct and perfect contact with the positive. Also, some of the unsensitized type of products may be adhered to screens days before sensitizing and exposing screen and film.

The simple processing of the screen involves (1) preparation of sensitizing emulsion, (2) adhering and sensitizing film, (3) drying adhered film, (4) exposing film, and (5) washing out. Standard fine or coarse monofilament or multifilament screen fabric may be employed. However, it is best to see that the fabric is stretched correctly and is cleaned and degreased.

Sensitizing and adhering of film may be done in one step after sensitizer or sensitized emulsion is prepared. It is best to process screen

* Kosloff, Albert, "The Ins And Outs of Direct/Indirects," Screen Printing Magazine, Vol. 66, No. 7 (July, 1976) pp. 32–33, 55.

under subdued light; however, after film is adhered to screen fabric, the screen should dry in the dark. To adhere film to screen, the film is placed, film side up, on a smooth flat surface such as glass, plastic, or cardboard which is smaller than the inside dimensions of the screen frame. Then the sensitizer, usually supplied with the film, is poured in at one end on the inside of the screen, and the sensitizer is stroked slowly back and forth with a soft squeegee, assuring that there is perfect adhesion between direct-film and screen fabric. This simple application sensitizes and adheres film to fabric and screen is allowed to dry in a horizontal position.

The same type of actinic light sources may be employed to expose direct-indirect screens as are used to expose other screens. *The film support or base is removed before exposing.* In exposing, the emulsion side of positive is placed in direct contact with the dry film or underside of screen. Here again, the exposure will vary depending on the type of light, strength of light, distance of screen from light, and type of copy being reproduced. It is suggested that the beginner make a trial exposure as a first attempt.

After exposure, the direct-indirect screen is washed out by wetting both sides of screen with water that is about 95 to 110 degrees Fahrenheit (35 to 43 degrees Celsius), spraying water first on the underside of screen than on the inside. The gentle spraying is continued until the screen is clean and sharp, and perfectly open in the design areas. The screen may then be blotted gently with newsprint paper and screen is allowed to dry, blocked out in the borders, and made ready for printing.

Reclaiming Metal Fabric Screens

Generally, the printer will save photographic screens for a given length of time. However, where it is necessary to reclaim a screen it may be done as explained in Chapter 14.

Screen printing inks do adhere to metal, therefore, it is essential that the screen, like non-metal fabric screens, be cleaned perfectly immediately after the printing is completed, since once the ink dries the coating will be more difficult to remove. The same solutions that are used for reclaiming other screens or for removing photographic and other coatings may be used for reclaiming metal fabrics. Also, stronger solvents that normally would corrode or eat up silk and organdy may be used on metal cloth. Where a screen cannot be reclaimed with solvents or cleaning or reclaiming solutions, and this situation is rarer than with non-metal cloths, then the coating on the wire gauze may be burned off by passing the screen back and forth uniformly in the required areas over a direct flame. This should be carefully done, since excessive heat or flame may distort, stretch, or contract the threads so that there may be difficulty in reusing the fabric. Although

Figure 83. Illustration of a five color screen printed window shade designed for a child's room. Direct printing screens were used to print vinyl inks on the shade material. **(Courtesy of Viola Studios, Chicago, Illinois)**

solvents should be used first to remove coatings from metal fabric, since there are solvents that will remove almost any coating from a metal that normally will eat up a non-metal screen fabric, burning a metal screen to clean or reclaim it should be a last resort. After the coating is removed, the particles should be brushed off and the screen washed perfectly with hot water and allowed to dry.

Figure 83 shows an illustration of a window shade screen printed with direct photographic printing screens.

Chapter 17

A BLACK LIGHT FLUORESCENT EXPOSING UNIT

As has been mentioned before, all photographic printing screens must be exposed to a source of actinic light at one stage of their processing. This type of light produces photochemical effects on sensitized emulsions or coatings. The first source of light used for exposing photographic screen printing plates, which were direct screens, was sunlight. While sunlight served as an exposing light, it was not possible to control it, to standardize it, and to use sunlight when necessary. Necessity and research produce multiple outcomes. As a result, the light sources employed for exposing sensitized screen printing films and direct screens are carbon arc lamps, pulsed xenon arc lamps, black light fluorescent lamps, mercury vapor lamps, quartz iodine lamps, photoflood lamps, sunlight type lamps, insect bulbs, and high wattage incandescent lamps. The commonly used light sources are carbon arc lamps, black light fluorescent lamps or tubes, and pulsed xenon lamps.

Black light is a common name for certain types of ultraviolet rays having a wave length between 3200 Angstrom* units and 4000 Angstrom units. Black light lamps are a form of fluorescent lamps. They may be mounted in the same type sockets as ordinary fluorescent tubes of the same dimensions. Black light lamps differ from ordinary fluorescent tubes in the chemical composition coated on the inside of the tube. The coating fluoresces or glows when it is exposed to ultra-violet light which is produced when the current is turned on. The coating or material is known as a phosphor and the composition of the phosphor varies depending on the color of light to be produced by the fluorescent lamp.

There are positive reasons for using black light as an exposing light. Black light lamps provide a cool light source so that the sensitized film may be brought almost in contact with the lighted tubes. This does away with the need for cooling most gelatinous films during exposure. Also, since the light is the same strength over all the areas of

* The Angstrom is a unit which is used to measure the wave length of rays and is equal to one hundred-millionth of a centimeter.

the length of the tubes, the exposing unit offers equal light distribution over the whole area of a film or screen.

There are different types of black light lamps. Those used for exposing printing screens range from about 6 to 60 inches (15.24 to 152.4cm) in length, from ⅝ to 2⅛ inches (1.588 to 5.397cm) in diameter, and from 4 to 90 watts in electric power. The most common lamp lengths for screen printing exposing units are 12 inches (30.5cm), 8 watts; 18 inches (45.72cm), 15 watts; 24 inches (60.96cm), 20 watts; 36 inches (91.44cm), 30 watts; and 48 inches (121.92cm), 40 watts. It must be noted that generally the manufacturer's published length of tubes also includes the sockets at both ends of the tube, since in constructing any unit and in fitting tubes in desired areas it is more practical to include the sockets as part of the complete dimension. Actually, the length of the lighted tube may be 2 to 3 inches (5.08 to 7.62cm) less, depending on the manufacturer's length of tube. However, the length for the tubes illustrated in Figure 85 is minus the socket length.

Before constructing any unit, it is suggested that the printer draw or lay out the whole unit to full scale on paper and use this layout for reference. The layout may show position of ballasts, starters, where holes are to be drilled for attachment of parts, and indicate wiring and other data that the printer will need. Although the actual construction is simple, everything must be planned before starting. Wood screws, machine screws with nuts, or binding posts may be used to fasten parts to the upright pieces and to plywood base. See Figure 84. Lamps, sockets, ballasts, starters, and hardware parts may be obtained from local electrical equipment suppliers, from hardware stores, or direct from manufacturers of such equipment. The number of parts is dependent on the number of lamps to be used. In order to make assembling of parts easier, it is suggested that the parts be numbered and that their location on the master drawing be numbered also.

Black light fluorescent units require that proper ballasting devices and starters be used in their construction. A ballast is a device which develops a high voltage surge or push needed to start the lamp safely and efficiently. It also limits the flow of current through the lamp so as not to burn out the lamp. The ballast and starter used with the lamp must be recommended by the manufacturer or supplier of the lamps. Expensive ballasts are not needed, since the lamps are not on for long periods of time during operation.

The illustrations show a unit built by the writer for experimental and research purposes and for exposing varied screen printing sensitized films and coatings. Although twelve 15-watt (18 inches or 45.72cm long) black light fluorescent tubes were employed for this unit, the same method of assembly and wiring may be used for larger units. Here again, the printer should work with and receive advice from the manufacturer or supplier of the parts. The unit may be used with any standard 110 volt circuit.

Although the unit is inexpensive to build, the cost would vary, depending on size of exposing unit desired, size of lamps, ballasts, starters, etc., and on locality in which material is purchased.

In summary, the general procedure for making the unit is:

(1) Make a master or full-scale drawing.

(2) Make upright pieces of dry ¾-inch (1.9cm) thick white pine. The height of the upright pieces may be about 6 inches (15.24cm); the length depends on the number of sockets and the distance the sockets are placed from one another. This should be figured out on the master drawing before starting. The sockets are attached to the upright pieces so that sockets are near one another and face opposite one another on the two upright pieces. The lamp should fit snugly between the two facing sockets. For the size lamp described in this chapter it is suggested that the distance between center to center of lamp not exceed approximately 3 inches (7.62cm).

(3) After sockets are fastened to the two upright pieces, attach upright pieces to base with wood screws so that the lamp will fit well and can be taken out and inserted easily. (See Figure 84).

(4) Attach ballasts and starters to base, using wood screws or machine screws and nuts to fasten parts to base.

(5) Wire all connections as per Figures 85 and 86. Connections should be soldered neatly. Make sure that wires connect where they should and that all connections are insulated. Wire may be any standard single wire that can be used on a 110 volt circuit.

(6) When parts are attached and connections made, insert a lamp in each opposing pair of sockets to test connections and parts. After each lamp has been tested individually, insert all lamps and test complete unit. Any standard switch that may be used in a 110 volt circuit can be employed for this unit.

(7) A thin sheet of aluminum or sheet tin is cut and inserted under the lamps to serve as a reflection sheet as illustrated in Figure 87. The sheet may be attached at each corner with wood screws to the upright pieces. A sheet of fiber paper that has been painted white may also be used as a reflection sheet instead of the aluminum.

(8) A box of ¼ inch (.64cm) plywood may be made to fit around

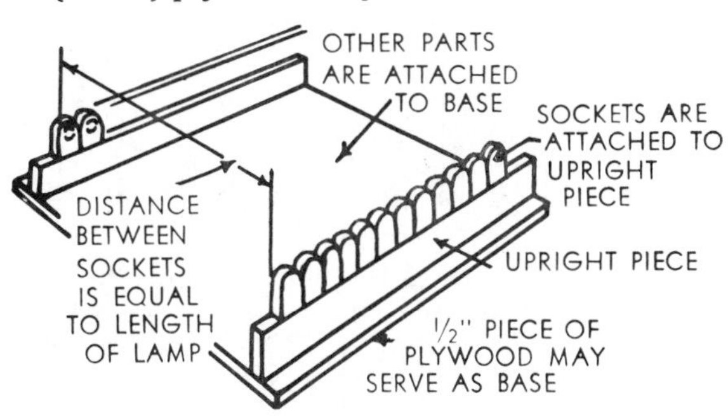

Figure 84. Method of attaching sockets on edges of uprights mounted on plywood base.

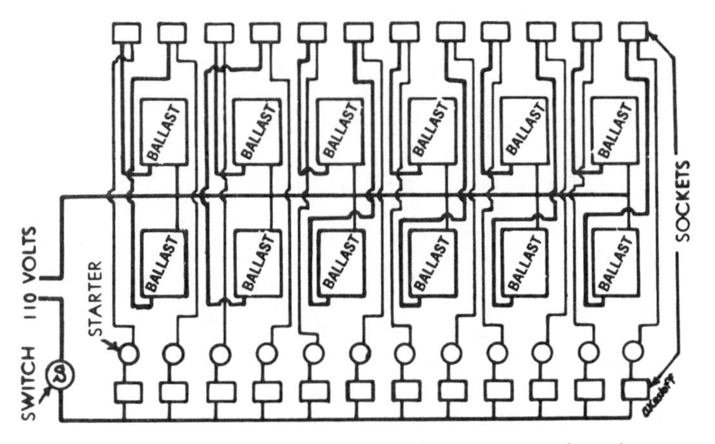

Figure 85. Wiring of starters, ballasts, sockets, and switch is shown in this diagram. Lines of various thicknesses are used to make tracing of wires to various parts easier.

the unit for protection of parts and for carrying the unit. The base board of the unit may be bolted with machine screws to the bottom of the box. If the unit is a large one employing large lamps so that it cannot be carried easily, then casters may be attached to the box in order to allow it to be moved into desired working areas.

(9) In the event that portability is not desired, as may be the case with larger units, the outer case design may be modified for mounting

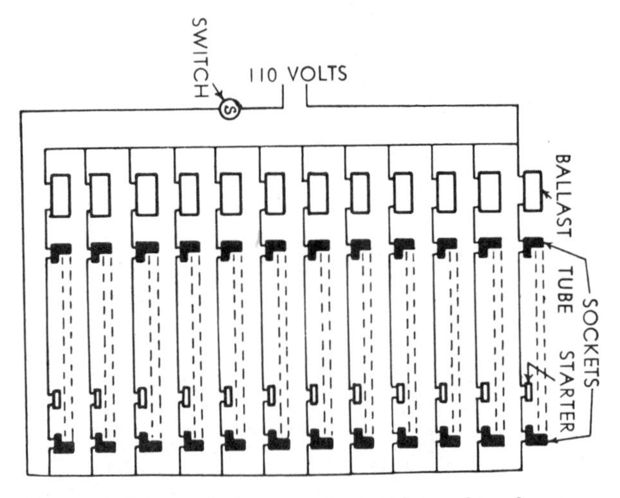

Figure 86. Schematic diagram shows relationship of various components when wired as in Figure 85. This diagram indicates sequence of ballasts, starters, sockets, and switch in relation to 110 volt supply, but does not indicate placement or arrangement of parts on plywood base.

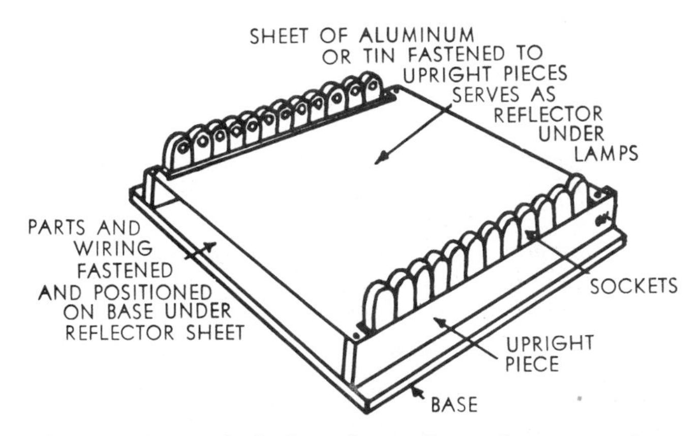

Figure 87. One method of attaching reflector sheet to uprights so that it will be properly positioned under lamps when they are in place.

Figure 88. Completed black light fluorescent exposing unit, showing compact arrangement and hinged cover on which metal hooks have been installed to hold supply cord when unit is not in use. Unit may be used for vertical or horizontal exposing.

under a table covered with a plate glass which may be set in a wooden framework. Compression springs and bars may be attached to the wooden framework in such a manner that they will hold positive and film or even positive and a screen in contact during exposure. In this manner the table top may comprise the exposing frame and the exposing unit underneath the plate glass will furnish a non-variable light source for exposures.

(10) A by-product of building this exposure unit for table mounting would be its adaptability to use for visual inspection, retouching, opaquing, and other operations requiring transmitted rather than reflected light. A piece of tracing paper laid on the glass surface will give adequate diffusion of the light for this type of work.

Since dust will cut down on the efficiency of light, it is suggested that the lamps be kept clean and dust free. Also, during exposure, there must be perfect contact between the positive and film or screen.

Figure 88 illustrates the complete unit with carrying case.

Figure 89 shows the black light fluorescent unit in use.

Figure 89. A film positive which has been cemented with rubber cement to a direct screen being exposed with the unit described in this chapter. The unit is completely portable and may be used anywhere that a source of electric power of standard 110 volts A.C. current is available.

Chapter 18

SCREEN PRINTING WITH TYPEWRITER STENCILS

The writer's desire to reproduce his collection of gypsy music without employing photographic printing screens led to the simplification of the process described in this chapter. After reproducing some pages of music, he experimented more by printing other subjects and was impressed by the distinctiveness of the printing produced with this medium. Figure 90 shows some jobs that have been processed by the author during a time of about ten years using ordinary typewriter stencils as printing plates.

Printing with typewriter stencils in screen printing work is similar to printing with other printing plates. Because of the simplicity of preparation of the stencil and the results obtained, it offers many advantages to the beginning and advanced operator. It presents to the printer another type of printing screen for reproducing detail such as typed matter, illustrations, and written matter. It may be used in combination with other printing. It is possible to obtain from about 1,000 to about 3,000 impressions from one typewriter stencil, depending on the quality of the stencil and the care practiced in printing. It supplements ordinary typewriting because with it one can print with the beautiful oil-vehicle inks that are available in the industry. One, two, three or more typewriter stencils can be printed at one time. Different colored inks may be used and the inks employed are more durable and better than that used in ordinary duplicating machines, thus making it possible to print with this medium on paper, cardboard, wood, metal fabrics, etc. When desired, an embossed effect may be produced in printing. This printing screen is practical for printing letters and also for printing on screen printing presses.

A prepared stencil is already a printing plate consisting of a paper fiber and a coating and is similar to a screen fabric with an adhered coating forming a printing plate. These stencils and the materials necessary for preparing them may be obtained in any stationery store. Typewriter stencil sheets consist of a very fine tissue paper of the yoshino tissue paper quality covered with a waterproof coating through which

Figure 90. The author used typewriter stencils to produce the above printed work. Left, letterhead, paper store time of opening notice, sheet music; center, handkerchief and announcement; right, wooden store time of opening notice and felt belt.

most inks will not pass. The tissue paper used is one that has thin long fibers, good tensile strength, and high porosity. The coating applied to the paper is usually dark blue in color and its composition varies depending upon the manufacturer. After the tissue paper is covered with the composition or coating it becomes more durable and keeps its shape.

When drawing, writing, or typing on the stencil, the coating is forced aside by the typewriter keys or a simple tool and the very porous paper is exposed. The exposed spots or areas on the paper allow inks to pass through.

Preparation of the Stencil

Since typewriter stencils are inexpensive, it is advisable that the best ones be used. The preparation of the stencil is simple. Any stenographer who knows how to type a stencil may prepare it. However, it is not necessary to send out to have a typewriter stencil prepared, as the printer can easily do this himself. Stencils for screen printing require more care in their preparation than those prepared for ordinary duplicating. When typewriting, the speed of typing should not exceed about thirty words per minute. A little heavier pressure should be used than for ordinary typing. The completed stencil must be perfectly translucent or transparent in the typed spots and where lines have been written or drawn.

If possible, avoid making corrections on these stencils, as the error will show up more in screen printing because the ink deposited is thicker and more concentrated. In ordinary stencil typing a correction fluid is applied over the spot to seal the coating where an error was made on the stencil. Where it is absolutely necessary to make a correction on a stencil it is first necessary to use a rounded small glass rod to press and smooth down the coating before applying correction fluid. The glass rod is supplied with the bought fluid. In using the glass rod to smooth down the coating, the best procedure is to work from the outside of the error toward the center. Most correction fluids may be used also as a cement for cementing one stencil to another. When typing capital letters and such letters as *w* and *m* it is necessary to strike these keys harder than when typing such letters as *e*, *o*, and *c*.

For making lines, drawings, signatures, writing, and accurate lettering on these stencils a stylus and a lettering guide is used. A stylus is a tool similar in shape to a penholder but supplied with different points or heads. The most common styli used for stencils are the ball point, wire loop, wire points bent at an angle, and the wheel stylus. See Figures 91 through 94. Any stylus used must be free of burrs so that it will not tear the stencil. Lettering guides are made of thin transparent plastic similar to lettering guides used by draftsmen and used in a similar fashion. The letters on these lettering guides for stencils

Figure 91. Ball-point.
Figure 92. Wire loop.
Figure 93. Wire point.
Figure 94. Wheel stylus.

come in sizes from one-eighth of an inch (.328cm) in height to one inch (2.54cm) and in varied sizes and styles of alphabets and numerals. If used correctly, it is very easy to make the line drawings and letters so that reproductions in printing are clean cut and have no ragged edges.

In doing lettering with a guide and a stylus use little pressure on the first stroke when executing each letter. Go back and forth over the original stroke until all of the coating has been pushed away. Be careful not to use too much pressure or the paper in the stencil may be cut or torn. After making a few letters, the printer will find that the work is not difficult. For ease in drawing or writing on stencils, it is suggested that a portable illuminated drawing unit be used. A light box or illuminated table of the type found in screen printing shops will serve the purpose. Or, the printer may make one as illustrated in Figure 95.

In is necessary to place a writing plate under the stencil when making drawings, writing, reproducing illustrations, signatures, etc., on the stencil. These writing plates are generally made of frosted translucent thin celluloid sheets with at least one side roughened. In using the plate place the rough side of the plate up directly beneath the stencil. Place design on illuminated board and writing plate over the design. It is a good idea to make the design or "dummy" on a transparent

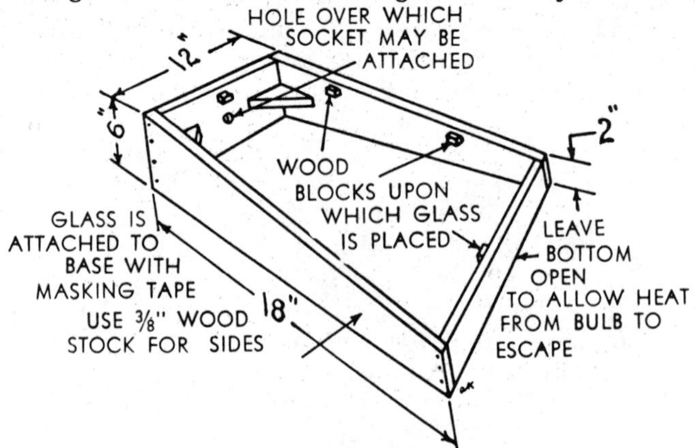

Figure 95. Portable illuminated unit.

paper. The stencil is taped over the writing plate and the work is done on the illuminated unit so that inspection of the work can proceed as the work proceeds. In making signatures and writing use a little more pressure than that used for ordinary writing. When writing or illustrating do not allow the stencil to wrinkle. Hold stencil down with one hand near the spot where the writing is being done, exerting little pressure, and write with the other hand. There are also sensitized and unsensitized photographic typewriter stencils sold by some firms. However, this writer has made photographic typewriter stencils by making regular direct photographic screens, cutting out the required stencil to fit the typewriter duplicator, and printing the stencil. This type of stencil is very tough, will print thousands of impressions, reproduces fine detail and illustrations, and can be easily cleaned for reuse.

Generally, follow the manufacturer's directions in working with these stencils and very little difficulty will be encountered. As the work on these stencils progresses a technique is developed which will make this plate comparable (where it has to be used) to other screen printing plates.

The newer type "thermal" stencils are also practical for screen printing and are easy to prepare. These are specially prepared typewriter stencils which are "cut" or made on a thermocopy machine; although they may also be prepared on a typewriter. The stencil will reproduce drawings, newspaper and magazine articles, and the like. They are simply prepared by placing copy, face up, on the stencil backing sheet, between backing sheet and stencil, and running stencil and copy through a thermocopy machine.

Attaching Stencil and Printing

The stencil can be attached to any screen fabric from a very coarse quality to about a Number 12. Silk, silk-organdy, or organdy may be used. This plate may be used for hand printing and for machine printing, especially for reproducing very legible letters.

In attaching stencil to fabric turn frame so that the fabric side is up and center prepared stencil on it with the illustrated, typed, or positive side of the stencil down and in contact with the fabric. Attach it to the screen with masking tape. See Figures 96 and 97. In attaching, tape stencil on one side to the fabric or frame so that tape overlaps stencil about one-half inch. This overlapping is essential in preventing any of the ink being squeegeed through at the stencil edges. Pull gently on the stencil so that it does not wrinkle and attach it on the opposite side. In a similar manner attach the third and fourth side of the stencil. Press tape down lightly on top of stencil to make sure that tape holds stencil well in place. The tacky quality of the ink used in printing will hold the rest of the stencil in perfect contact with the fabric when the ink is forced through with the squeegee.

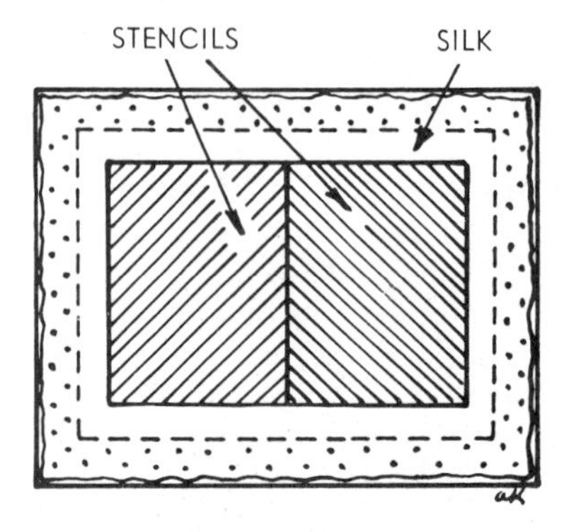

Figure 96. Centering two stencils on underside of screen fabric.

Best inks to use with this type of printing plate are oil-vehicle types and enamels. Lacquers and some synthetic inks may dissolve most typewriter stencils during printing and the coating will be destroyed or pinholes will be formed. The ink used should be slightly thinner than that used for other screen printing, as in this case the ink has to go through openings in the fabric and openings in the paper fiber in the stencil. Also, it is not necessary to have as much ink in the screen as for printing with other printing screens, as little ink is used up in each impression. Although to the beginner this stencil may not appear as strong as other printing screens, it will last and can be cleaned and stored away for future use.

After printing, the excess ink is removed, and the screen is cleaned by placing two or three pieces of newspaper between the screen and base, and pouring in enough cleaning fluid to just cover the fabric. Hold screen down and work the cleaning fluid back and forth over the screen with the squeegee. After the ink has been dissolved, soak up the mixture of ink and fluid with a soft cloth. Then turn screen up and very carefully remove tape and peel off stencil. The same type

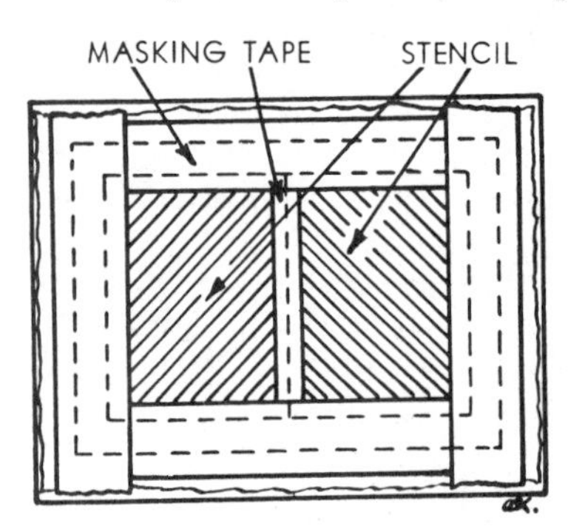

Figure 97. Stencils attached to underside of screen with masking tape.

of cleaning fluids are used for cleaning this screen as are used to clean other oil-vehicle inks.

After the screen is completely cleaned, place stencil on a sheet or two of newspaper, soak a small piece of soft cloth in kerosene and rub the soaked cloth very gently over the whole stencil, first on one side and then on the other side. Hold stencil up to the light to inspect effects of cleaning. Lettering and design parts in stencil must be perfectly transparent. The writer has found that the best cleaner for typewriter stencils through which oil-vehicle inks have been printed is a good grade of kerosene or commercial stencil cleaning fluid. Kerosene cleans them well and also seems to strengthen the stencil for its next use. When the stencil is clean place it between two pieces of newspaper and blot away excess liquid. Allow stencil to dry so that it can be stored and used again when necessary.

Chapter 19

DRYING SCREEN PRINTED MATTER

The beginning screen printer today may attempt to dry his printed matter in similar fashion to the early pioneer printer by placing the prints on home made racks. However, with the introduction of drying equipment, drying systems, special inks, and technical aid and knowledge, the industry is in a position where the beginner may receive much help in drying printed products. Because heavy deposits of ink are screen printed on every type of material with so many varied inks, drying may become a problem, if the beginner does not plan for practical drying.

Drying of screen printed matter is dependent on the rest of the steps in this phase of printing. The final success of screen printing is dependent upon the complete drying of the printed matter. The ultimate test in any printing must determine the following: whether the print is dry; whether the ink will not post-heat or heat up after the printed sheets are stacked or packed; that the ink will adhere to the material or stock permanently; whether the dry ink will be the desired color; and generally whether the ink will dry quickly and practically. Therefore, the printer, to turn out a successful job, must be aware of all steps in printing, including correct procedures in drying. With the exception of the newer ultraviolet (UV) curing inks, which dry almost instantly, most drying of screen printed matter takes from about 15 seconds to 24 hours depending on the surface printed. Drying may be classified as natural or air drying and as forced or accelerated drying. Or we may classify drying according to what happens to the ink chemically.

Drying on racks or with machines and choosing a drying machine involves knowing what type of printing one is planning to do, the maximum size of stock or material to be printed, the types of inks and coats one is planning to print, the maximum number of impressions per hour needed, on what type of stock or material the printer will print, and whether gas, electricity, or air will be used as the source of power.

The drying of inks on a surface involves changing a liquid into a solid coating or film without destroying or distorting the surface. Drying of screen printing inks deals with a system consisting of ink, substrate printed on, drying or curing equipment, and method of drying. Usually screen printing inks dry by means of oxidation, evaporation, absorption or penetration, combination of these processes, and by means of ultraviolet (UV) curing. The choice or design of drying equipment must take into account all of the involved factors.

Although absorption does take place as in printing with dyes and textiles, screen printing inks (unlike newsprint ink) do not dry by absorption. In the case of the dye, the ink or dye has to go through fixation, that is, it has to be fixed or cured before it is completely fast and dry.

Most inks contain some thinners or solvents. Evaporation of these results in drying or curing. In evaporation the solvents or diluents in the ink pass into the air as a vapor or gas. In oxidation some ingredient or ingredients in the ink combine with the oxygen in the air and as a result of this oxidation, which is a chemical process, different compounds are obtained after the ink has dried. Fusing is a finishing process in which vitreous enamels, ceramic inks, and other similar inks are applied to articles and a complete union of the ink and the article is obtained through melting or fusing the ink into the pores of the material being printed. These inks fuse and melt at high temperatures and at the same time must burn out the carrying vehicle without leaving any carbon or deposit that will dull, darken, or destroy the color or affect the final finish in any way. In polymerization the ink undergoes a chemical action while it is drying when the molecules or single minute particles in the ink form larger molecules without changing the chemical composition of the ink.

Lacquers, synthetic lacquers, lacquer enamels, and synthetic inks dry by evaporation; oil-vehicle inks dry mostly through oxidation. The latter may be dried naturally. The former inks, textile inks, ceramic inks, vitreous enamels, and plastisol opaque type inks usually have to be exposed to some form of heat to complete the drying and finishing process.

Since most screen printed work takes time to dry, the screen printer cannot usually stack the printed job immediately after printing and must plan for adequate equipment to aid in drying. Also, wherever possible and where machine printing is done he must try to cut down on drying time. Any drying equipment used must be sturdy and simple, must allow for circulation of air, and must be portable, preferably on wheels or casters, so that it can be moved out of the way when necessary. Contrary to opinion the simpler equipment has given the best results. The racks used should not spoil the printed surface and should allow for easy placing and easy removal of matter after it is dry.

Regardless of what style of drying rack is employed, the design should allow the circulation of air, or heat where necessary, around the printed matter. If printed material is stacked one on top of another and air is not allowed to circulate normally, drying is interfered with, and in some cases the printed matter will become warm and may even catch on fire due to the excessive oxidation and spontaneous combustion that may take place. Also, in the drying process the screen printer must make sure that the evaporating solvents and ink exhausts do not add to the polluting of the air.

Figure 98 through 103 show suggested and exaggerated views of drying racks and techniques that may be made by the printer and which may be used successfully for racking. In an emergency, signs, cardboard, fiber board, etc., that have been printed may be clipped with common clips shown in Figure 103 to wires or clothes line cord that has been stretched across a room. When drying printed glass it is suggested that the glass be stored vertically or diagonally. There are also commercial drying units on the market which cater specifically to screen printing shops, each unit having from about fifty to one hundred racks on it and each rack varying in size, as illustrated in Figure 104.

Forced Drying

Originally and traditionally drying racks were used and are still being employed where it is necessary to dry printed matter. However, where it became necessary to do more printing in a given time and in a given area and as screen printing became more mechanized, accelerated methods of drying began to develop. The development is constantly going on, since the versatility of screen printing and the other variables in the drying process demand constant research. Therefore, the machines employed for drying screen printed matter and for accelerating or racking drying work cannot be put into one universal classification. Neither can one type of machine answer the drying needs of all general printing. The machines have much in common only when the printing is done on paper ad cardboard and similar stocks or on materials having similar properties and being printed with similar inks. Where printing is done on textiles, ceramics, glass, wood, cork, decalcomania papers, and many other materials, the drying equipment is forced to take on specialized specifications.

However, the manufacturers of drying equipment do attempt to meet requirements. The conventional machines have allowed and do allow for some method of removal of solvent laden air to recirculate air in some fashion preventing fire hazards. Most dryers correlate the speed of the drying process to the speed of the printing machine or hand printing. Drying machines are safe, easy to operate, and are trouble free during operation. They are designed to dry the common inks used in screen printing. Also, the machines attempt to eliminate distortion of stock during the drying process. Their maintenance is simple,

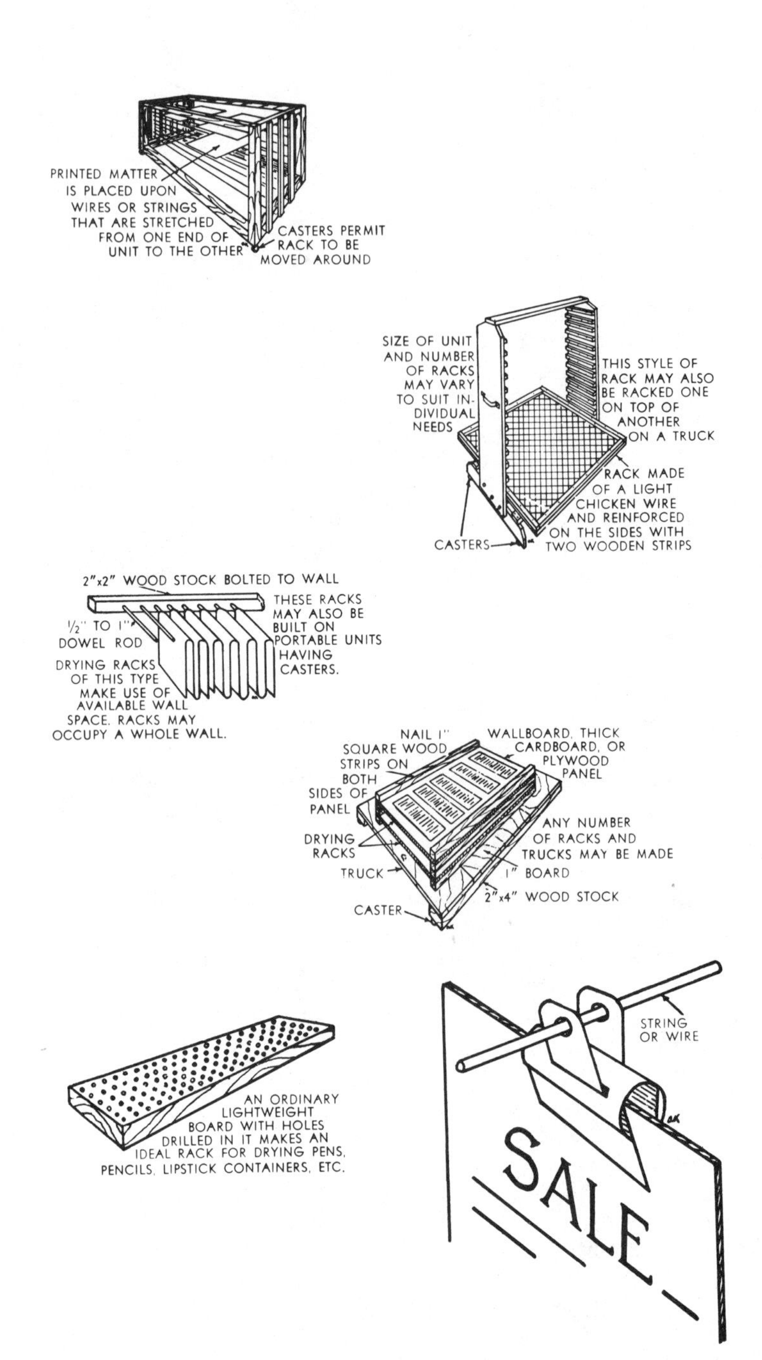

Figure 98, top left; Figure 99, top, right; Figure 100, center, left; Figure 101, center, right; Figure 102, bottom, left; Figure 103, bottom, right. Drying racks and techniques used in screen printing.

Figure 104. Atlas Multi-Rack with 50 trays varying in size from 32″ x 48″ (81cm x 122cm) to 52″ x 69″ (132cm x 175cm) for drying screen printed materials of different size and thickness. **(Courtesy of Atlas Silk Screen Supply Company, Chicago, Illinois)**

their cost of operation is relatively economical, and the machines occupy less space than would a number of conventional, flat racks necessary to hold an equivalent number of prints for drying. They have variable speed controls which allow for automatic, semi-automatic, and hand printing.

Generally, drying machines or drying units fall into three types—those that dry printed matter normally or naturally, those that employ heat energy and air to aid and accelerate drying, and ultraviolet drying or curing units which employ ultraviolet energy for almost instant drying. Racks of all types and many wicket conveyors dry printed matter

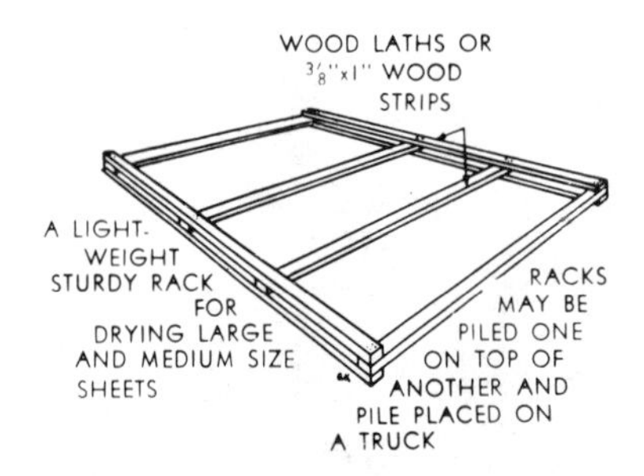

Figure 105. A practical racking shelf.

naturally. Most other machines, with the exception of ultraviolet curing units, use heat to aid drying.

The wicket type natural air dryer is one of the most common drying machines found in screen printing shops. It is a conveyor device designed to handle freshly printed sheets up to about ½″ (.64cm) in thickness during the drying process. It may be termed a conveyor racking device. Generally, wicket type conveyors dry sheets naturally and do not employ heat forcing or accelerating drying. However, the reader must not confuse this type of dryer with the large type ovens used in screen printing of large metal signs which do employ wicket conveyors enclosed in an oven. On wicket units the sheets are picked or placed manually or mechanically on each wicket or wire or tubular shelf. The sheet is placed on edge and travels slowly in upright or semivertical position. The design of the wickets prevents the sheets from touching each other. The upright position of the sheets allows the solvents to leave quicker. Where the wickets or shelves travel in a vertical direction rather than in the common horizontal direction, a fan must be used to draw fumes away into an exhaust system.

It is possible for a shop to have as many wickets or shelves on the dryer as is practical. Also, the wicket conveyor may be connected to the screen printing machine and thus eliminate the cost of operation of the conveyor. The speed of the conveyor may be adjusted to correspond to the drying cycle of sheets and the speed of the press. The dried and printed stock may be removed manually or piled automatically at the end of the dryer or the sheets may continue back on the underside or undertrack of the machine for more drying and airing. Since generally no heat is applied to the wicket type dryer, the machine will not distort paper or cardboard stock in the drying operation or tend to create difficulties in register. Fans may be employed to aid in the circulation of the air as an aid in drying. The drying cycle depends on the job, on the type of ink printed, and on the number of impressions desired per hour.

The drying machines employing heat energy to accelerate drying use direct or indirect heat obtained from electricity, from infra-red lamps, from quartz lamps, and from hot air jets. Regardless of the source of heat, the machines employ a moving conveyor which travels under the heat area or through a heat chamber. The printed work is dried by being placed on the moving conveyor and by being exposed to the heat. The drying cycle depends upon the type of ink printed, the type of heat, the material being dried, the length of time the printed object is exposed, and the cooling of the object before it is taken off the conveyor.

Many methods have been tried to hasten drying and to apply heat to the screen printed matter. Generally, the heat is transferred to the heating chamber or heat area by means of convection, radiation, conduction, or a combination of these methods. Figure 106 shows a convection drying unit which has been used successfully to dry printing. Convection involves the transfer of heat through fluids such as air currents, steam currents, water currents, and other liquid currents. This method is employed in ordinary drying, steaming of textiles, in convection ovens, in ordinary gas ovens, etc. In radiation, heat is transmitted directly through penetrating rays from its source to the surface of object being heated or dried. Infra-red rays which are given off by infra-red amps are a form of electromagnetic waves and travel through the atmosphere with great speed. When the rays strike an object they are absorbed and the radiant energy is changed to heat energy. Other industries used radiation for surface finishing before screen printing adopted it. In radiation the surrounding air does not serve as a medium of transfer and this does away with expensive insulated equipment and ovens. The standard scale for measuring infra-red and light rays is known as the Angstrom scale. The rays used for drying, baking, and heating in process work are between 6,500 and 14,000 on the Angstrom scale.

The machines used in screen printing shops may employ the following principles of drying: the jet principle, infra-red energy, a combination of first exposing the printed matter to convection currents and finish the drying by means of infra-red, ultraviolet curing, and zone oven type drying.

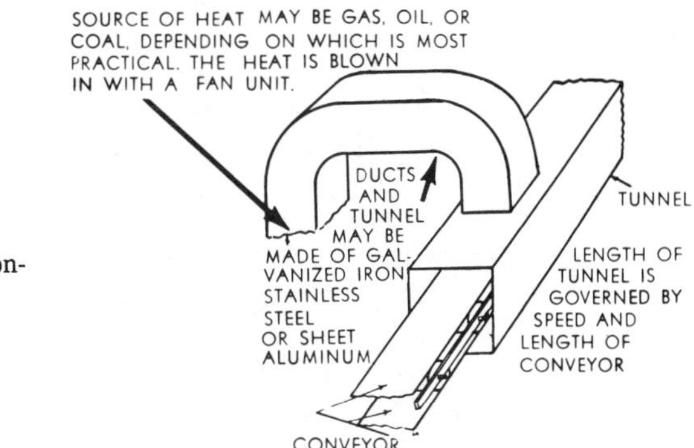

Figure 106. Main parts of a convection drying unit.

The machines employing the jet principle of drying screen printed matter employ both heat and a blast of air for quick drying. These machines are high speed drying units used for varied evaporation type drying. The conveyor carrying the printed work, generally sheets, travels below the heating unit. Heat energy may be obtained from gas, electricity, or oil. At the same time warm air is blasted at high velocity through a perforated sheet and blows away the solvent vapors being removed by the higher temperature. The blasting of the air jets accelerates the evaporation process so that the printed sheets may dry in seconds. The air blast holds the sheet flat against the conveyor belt and produces drying by preventing solvent laden air from forming. In this type of drying principle the temperature is lower than in other heat machines and prevents distortion of stock. Drying is controlled by speed of conveyor. The machine may have a cool air blower installed on the delivery end in order to reduce temperature of stock. The hot air may be reclaimed and reused. In these machines temperatures can be varied up to about 250 degrees Fahrenheit (121 degrees Celsius).

Machines employing radiant energy stress the fact that the drying takes place from inside out, as the heat rays penetrate the finish, which in turn heats and dries the inner layers of finish and then the outer layer. Any ink whose drying is hastened by application of heat may be dried with infra-red. In spite of its many advantages the printer must realize that not all inks and finishes may be dried with this form of energy and that individual experimentation is necessary. For most drying (not fusing) the temperature varies from about 150 to 350 degrees Fahrenheit (66 to 177 degrees Celsius). Too high a temperature and incorrect time of drying may change the value of a color and may even scorch the material. Usually the higher the temperature the less is the drying time. With drying textiles the printer must realize that the temperature will vary somewhat and that the amount of heat required is governed by the thickness, weight, and the type of fiber in the textile. The printer may obtain temperature variations by varying the distance of the lamp from the printed or finished matter, by using lamps of different wattage, by changing arrangements of lamps, and most important, by simply experimenting.

Infra-red lamps are similar to electric light bulbs but are designed to give little visible light as compared with ordinary electric light bulbs and more infra-red energy. The lamps which may be used on standard power outlets are obtainable in the following wattages: 250, 375, 500, 750, 1000, 1250, 1500, 2000, 2500, and 3000. The temperature ranges of infra-red equipment will vary depending upon the number of lamps, the size of the lamps used, and the distance of the lamps from the printed matter. Infra-red lamps with individual gold plated reflectors seem to give practical results.

Some infra-red machines offer dual belt conveyors; each may be run alone or in opposite directions or both may be run at the same speed in the same direction.

When installing infra-red equipment it is advisable to consult reliable manufacturers of such machines or lighting engineers. It is necessary to experiment with conditions that will approximate conditions of the work being printed. The supplier of the ink or finish can furnish drying time and other information that will aid the printer.

The equipment may be easily installed on portable drying units over conveyors, near screen printing presses, or connected to the presses. The portable units may be tilted to any desired angle. In any portable drying unit it is suggested that there be installation of switches at both ends of the conveyor if the conveyor is longer than about 8 feet (2.4m). As is true of other types of drying machines, the conveyor and infra-red heat source should be connected so that if the conveyor ceases to function, the lamps or infra-red panels will shut off automatically.

Infra-red drying machines are available completely constructed or the printer may obtain basic component parts and build his own drying machine.

Conveyor speeds used in screen printing vary from about 1 to 10 feet (.3 to 3.0 meters). However, the conveyor should be designed so that it has variable speed. The conveyor or oven should make allowance for a cool-down area so that the operator may remove the printed matter without burning his hands. The cooling chamber may consist of fans. A slight circulation of air (but not a draft) is desirable to drive off the volatile substances. Where infra-red lamps are used over a conveyor, the lamps should be spaced about 6 to 18 inches (15.24 to 45.72cm) from center to center of lamp. For most efficient application of heat the lamps may be staggered as illustrated in Figure 107. Lamps or panels should never touch actual work.

Besides using infra-red lamps as a source of heat, printers have and are employing flat radiant panels or infra-red panels, metal resistance elements, and quartz lamps.

Although infra-red ovens are used, zone type ovens are greatly used for drying screen printed matter. In the zone type oven the conveyor travels through the oven or drying machine. These are very long machines. The machine consists of a large oven which provides a means

Figure 107. Illustrates staggering of lamps.

of controlling the baking or drying cycle, heat distribution, ventilation, recirculation of air and recuperative cooling. In this type of oven one or two zones or sections of the oven are used to bring the printed matter up to baking or drying temperature and to exhaust the volatiles. The next two zones hold the printed matter at drying temperatures. The last or fifth zone containing no heating unit is used for recuperative cooling. In this zone the heat from the conveyor and from the work is transferred with a fresh air supply to the first zone to start over the cycle of drying for the new printed material. This type oven may be designed to have high temperatures. Common temperatures range from about 75 to 400 degrees Fahrenheit (24 to 204 degrees Celsius). In other words, the work may enter the oven at temperatures of 75 degrees Fahrenheit (24 Celsius) and the temperature brought up to 400 degrees Fahrenheit (204 Celsius) as it travels through the heat zones and back to a temperature at the unloading zone so that the work may be handled at a comfortable temperature. These ovens are large, long, and efficient, but are used mostly by the screen printing specialist who prints on metals and metal sheets. The conveyor is generally a wicket type, the wickets being made of light strong tubular material.

Figures 108 through 116 present varied types of drying machines used in screen printing. The comments under each illustration are not complete but do illustrate specifications that are common in screen printing.

Figure 108. General Enclosed Chamber Wicket Dryer for drying screen printed sheets up to 52" x 76" (132cm x 183cm) in size. Drying may be accomplished with high volume forced air at room temperature, or with controlled elevated temperature plus high volume forced air. **(Courtesy of General Research, Inc., Sparta, Michigan)**

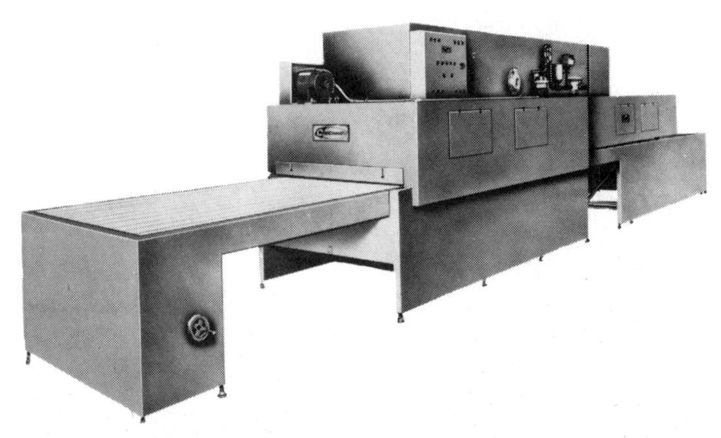

Figure 109. Cincinnati Super-Jet III Dryer, designed for drying varied types of screen printed material and for delivery from almost every type of press. Unit is adjustable to automatic, semiautomatic, and manual speeds, available in varied conveyor width and speeds, and introduces fresh air into dryer and removes solvent laden air, thus producing a minimum of upset in air conditioned shops. **(Courtesy of Cincinnati Printing and Drying Systems, Inc., Cincinnati, Ohio)**

Figure 110. A detailed view of an infra-red oven 14 feet 8 inches (4.27m 20cm) long, employed to dry screen printed designs on metal signs and roller-coated applications. The machine dries average size signs, 20 x 30 inches (50.8 x 76cm), in 2½ to 6 minutes. The oven uses banks of infrared lamps, each 375 or 500 watts. A two elevation, 20-foot (6.1m) long conveyor carries the work through the oven then transfers work to lower level where signs travel back to starting end of oven and cool at the same time. **(Courtesy of Fostoria Industries, Inc., Fostoria, Ohio, and Moore Signs, Detroit, Michigan)**

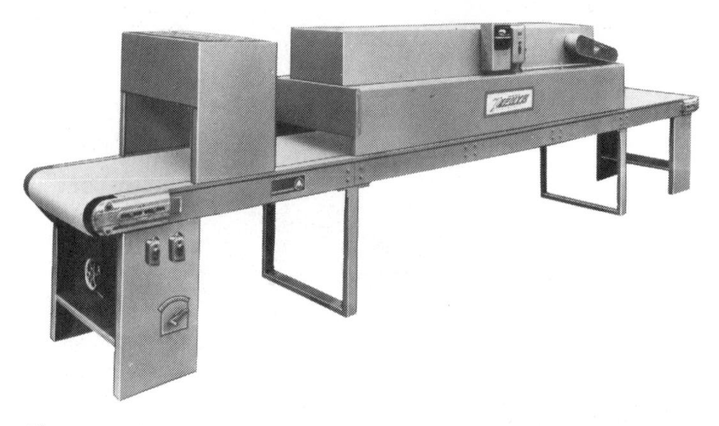

Figure 111. American Zephyr, a container and parts drying system for drying varied sizes and shapes of screen printed plastic containers. Temperature of unit ranges from 80 to 180 degrees Fahrenheit (27 to 82 degrees Celsius) with a conveyor speed varying from 1 to 7 feet (.305 to 2.134m) per minute; adjustable entrance and exit panels permit containers up to 14 inches (35.56cm) in height to be dried. **(Courtesy of American Screen Printing Equipment Co., Chicago, Illinois)**

Figure 112. A mechanized screen printing plant showing screen printing presses which print sheets up to 52″ x 80″ (132cm x 203cm) in size. Printed sheets are fed automatically into wickets of chambered wicket dryer which can dry printed matter at room temperature, at elevated temperature, or at elevated temperature plus high volume forced air. **(Courtesy of General Research, Inc., Grand Rapids, Michigan)**

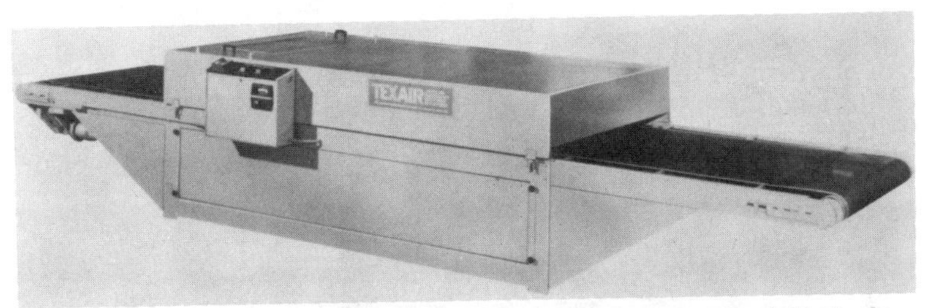

Figure 113. American Texair Dryer, a textile cure-dry system, available in three standard belt widths of 30″, 48″, and 60″ (76cm, 122cm, and 152cm), designed for drying and curing scorch-free high speed drying of textiles screen printed with solvent-based, water-based, or plastisol inks. The ink is first dried by subjecting the imprinted stock to high velocity jets of temperature controlled heated air until the solvent is substantially removed; while the material is still warm, it is automatically moved to another position where it is further heated by radiant heat for a sufficient time to cure the ink. **(Courtesy of American Screen Printing Equipment Co., Chicago, Illinois)**

Ultraviolet Curing or Drying

As has been implied, various methods of drying were developed during the past such as evaporation of inks, oxidation, penetration or absorption, polymerization, changing a liquid to a solid as in hot-melt ceramic printing, and combination of methods. Regardless of the principle employed in drying, each method consists of a system dealing with inks printed, substrates printed on, and the use of some form of energy or unit to change the liquid coating to a solid dry coating.

Research in drying also has motivated exposing coatings to non-conventional forms of energy such as microwave, macrowave (radio-

Figure 114. Precision Combo Dryer, an infrared and hot air system with variable speed belt control, individually controlled temperature zones, and allowance for modular construction for future expansion. Unit uses radiant energy for raising temperature of the fabric and ink, and controls fabric entrance into hot air chamber where the necessary cure time is maintained. **(Courtesy of Precision Screen Machines, Inc., Hawthorne, N.J.)**

Figure 115. The Linde Photocure System, designed for high speed low temperature curing of UV activated chemical coatings and screen printing inks; has an infeed conveyor length of 53″ to 73″ (135cm to 185cm); will cure substrate widths of 24″ to 73″ (61cm to 185cm); is safe, clean, and water cooled; will print matte and glossy finish on the same material, and multicolor printing curing. **(Courtesy of Linde Photocure System, Union Carbide Corp., Indianapolis, Indiana)**

frequency), laser energy, and one of the latest methods known as ultraviolet (UV) curing. Although the principle of ultraviolet curing has been known since about 1944, it took until 1967 before it became a production process.

UV curing is part of radiation, that is, it involves radiant energy. UV energy between 2000 and 3700 Angstrom units has proved most practical for curing or drying ultraviolet curable inks. This type of drying or curing deals with a revolutionary and evolutionary system in which a coating, ink, or adhesive in semiliquid state is converted almost in-

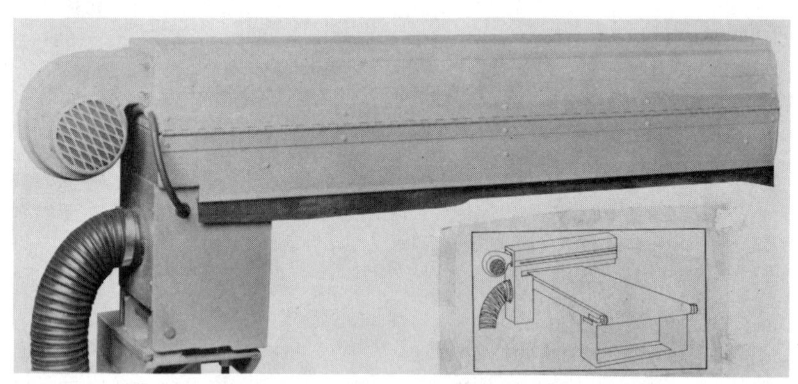

Figure 116. The Magnum UV Curing System Module for UV curing of screen printed products. The module is a complete safe unit that can be mounted on an existing conveyor so that the printed stock can be transported underneath or through the module. The module is available in 24″, 36″, and 48″ size (60.96cm, 91.44cm, and 121.92cm). As many modules as necessary may be used to achieve curing. **(Courtesy of American Screen Printing Equipment Co., Chicago, Illinois)**

stantly by exposing the printed ink to UV energy. In this type of drying the energy is selectively absorbed by the special inks. The UV inks do not dry by means of typical air drying, heat, or heat and air supplied in some form. The ultraviolet curable inks dry or cure by exposure to UV light (not to heat) and drying is brought about by photochemical reaction. Generally, the inks dry when allowed to pass on a conveyor under a curing machine. See Figure 115–116. It is interesting to note that the very quick drying is due to the fact that UV curable inks do not contain solvents, as compared with conventional inks which may contain about 25 to 50 per cent hydrocarbons.

UV curable inks are specifically and chemically formulated and generally consist of substances known as (1) photoinitiators or photosensitizable monomers, oligomers, and polymers; (2) inhibitors; and (3) pigments or dyes.* A monomer is a single unit (molecule) which joins with other monomers to form a polymer, producing polymerization. In polymerization, two or more small molecules (monomers) form larger molecules of the same composition percentage as the small molecules. Thus, when the photosensitive monomers are exposed to UV light, this conversion of monomers to polymers produces an almost instant dry film in seconds.

The inhibitor in the ink makes it possible for the ink to remain stable in storage. The pigment part of the ink is chosen so that it does not absorb UV energy.

Standard printing screens are employed for printing the available UV ink colors, which may include clear, color extenders, modifiers, and halftone colors for application on different substrates.

An advantage claimed for this process is reduction of air pollution, since the curable materials are almost all solid systems and polymerize completely, they do not contain any solvent which is discharged into the atmosphere. Compared to conventional drying systems, there is a saving of plant working space, labor, and, of course, drying time. Curing may be done under controlled temperatures which make possible the control of heat for substrates which are sensitive to heat. Since UV energy is necessary for curing, inks do not dry in the screen and may be left there for long periods; also finer meshes may be used for printing.

In summary, there is no one universal printing screen, nor is there one type of ink which may be printed on all materials, or one type of drying or curing system which will answer all the screen printing needs for the printer. Regardless of what type of drying or equipment the printer will use, it must be stressed that each important process must be put in proper relation to the total interdependent processes in the shop. The printer should choose any process only after objective experimentation and trials.

* Kosloff, Albert, "Ultraviolet Curing or Drying," *Technical Guidebook of the Screen Printing Industry,* Screen Printing ASsociation International, 1975, 4 pages.

Chapter 20

SCREEN PRINTING MACHINES

The screen printing industry finds itself under the inescapable necessity of working in close relation with many other industries. Because we live in a mechanical age, every growing industry ultimately develops machines that are peculiar to it. This development is brought about usually by demands within the industry and by outside industries. Since the early part of the 1930's it became evident that phases of screen printing would become mechanized and there resulted even then home-made jigs, machines, and much experimentation. All the efforts down to the present time, many of which were costly and unsuccessful, added and contributed to the industry.

In order to understand the advantages and disadvantages of screen printing machines, one must comprehend generally the possibilities and limitations of screen printing. Machine printing eliminates tedious hand squeegeeing, racking, reracking and drying; it reduces fatigue by doing away with stooping, lifting, juggling, and produces enthusiasm on the part of the workers. It increases production from about five to nine times as compared with manual printing and at the same time cuts down on about fifty per cent of the effort. Where a drying unit is designed with machine printing (with most machine printing such a unit is necessary), there is a saving of over three-fourths of floor space which is ordinarily required for racking and re-racking. Screen printing machines may be obtained for printing and coating small jobs, for printing on conical, cylindrical, and spherical shapes, and for printing and coating flat materials on such sizes as 14″ x 22″ (35.6cm x 55.9cm), 14″ x 28″ (35.6cm x 71.1cm), 22″ x 28″ (55.9cm x 71.1cm), 22″ x 44″ (55.9cm x 111.8cm), 32″ x 44″ (81.3cm x 111.8cm), etc., up to sizes about 98″ (2.49 meters) long by any practical width. The squeegee pressure at any point on a stroke may be controlled. Machine printing makes screen printing adaptable to many jobs that cannot be done by other methods. Also, machines produce work that is better and more uniform in quality, since the short contact of screen and printing surface and the lack of play in the screen tends to prevent slurring and other imperfections.

Often in the progressive plants, which have thousands of impressions to do daily, the plant is forced to develop its own machinery or jigs or to buy such machines as presses, coating machines, drying equipment and conveyors, projection enlarging machines, cameras, dye steaming equipment, die cutting machines, etc. Machine printing is not apart from screen printing; it is the most practical way of doing printing in the big shops.

This does not mean that the day of the small screen printing shop which produces excellent work with its manual and semi-automatic output is gone. In many cases work has to be done by hand, especially where printing requires special jigs, where the surface printed has complex curves, where the number of impressions may be too few for machine printing, and for dozens of other reasons that keep the smaller shops busy.

Because of the nature of screen printing, most of machine printing work caters only to certain phases of the printing in the field. Generally, the machines manufactured may be divided into the following five classes: (1) machines that print on flat surfaces of most common materials; (2) machines that print on cylindrical and spherical objects and partly cylindrical and spherical objects of varied materials; (3) textile printing machines and jigs; (4) machines for printing electronic circuits; and (5) coating machines. While it may be impossible to mention the very many past developments of printing units, one must include such units as the one-man squeegee (see Figure 117) which answered and still answers needs for the printer; the various hand printing units built or purchased by the beginner; the cylinder and automatic screen printing rotary machines employed for printing on all types of bolt materials; and the many electronic circuit printing machines designed and built in the captive shops.

The dream of every printer is to own one machine that would do the complete work of the above five types. However, it is just as impractical for manufacturers and designers to produce a machine that will answer all the requirements for the screen printing shop and still be cheap enough, as it is to produce one printing press that will do linotyping, bookbinding, and intaglio, letterpress, and offset printing.

The specifications for screen printing machines are as varied as the field itself. However, any press used has to be flexible to a certain degree because of the flexibility and variation of the work done in the industry. In other words, a screen printing machine must lend itself to do several jobs. Unlike printing in other phases of the graphic arts, screen printing machines must print on flat surfaced stock such as paper, cardboard, wood, metal, plastics, leather, textiles, ceramic materials, decalcomania paper, etc. A machine that prints on flat surfaced stock should be able to print on material from paper thickness to stock that is about one inch thick, and should hold a screen that is large enough for most jobs in the industry. It should print ceramic inks, vitreous enamels, thermosetting enamels, textile dyes, electronic circuit inks, etc. In actual printing the ink must not drip through the screen but should be forced through only by squeegeeing or other method used in ink application.

Whether the screen printing press is to print one prototype or mass-produce thousands of impressions, generally the press may have the following basic elements: (1) a platen or base with a vacuum or other hold down system to keep material being printed in place; (2) a frame to hold printing screen; (3) a squeegee; (4) a method of registering material; and (5) a method of adjusting screen height from base allowing for accurate breakaway for producing off-contact and full-contact printing.

The press should print at speeds from about 750 impressions per hour and up and have registration that is perfect. The material being printed should be held in place and should be released immediately after printing, regardless of the thickness of the stock. There are machines that do excellent printing on thicker stock but when thin material such as paper or cellophane is printed and when the design covers the entire screen or material, then the printed stock adheres to the underside of the screen after each impression. The result is that the press has to be stopped after every impression and the stock has to be peeled off before the next sheet is fed. This difficulty may be eliminated by using a vacuum base or table and placing thin stock on vacuum base. Most screen printing presses do come equipped with vacuum tables.

Because many impressions are produced per hour, machines must be built so that they can be combined with a drying unit, since quick printing necessitates quicker drying. Operation on machines should be safe and simple and should not require too much experience and practice. Makeready should not take longer than in hand operated set-ups. Any machine should guard against feeding errors and spoilage, since spoilage with large area impressions and objects is costly. Of course, the printing machine should be able to use the regular printing screens used commonly in the industry. The machine should lend itself to print with screens that are stretched with varied fabrics. There should be a system of guides for registration that can be changed for different size jobs and the guides should not cut or destroy the plate or fabric in the screen. Screens should be clamped easily in printing position and removed easily when necessary. Also, it should not take too long to clean up the press after printing. The press should be sturdy so that parts will not be worn out too quickly because of vibration and other stresses.

While the above specifications may seem immense and challenging, it is interesting to note that most of the requirements have been met in the design of the machines. There are presses today that print flat stock that is up to about one-half inch thick and range anywhere from 450 to about 3000 impressions per hour. Although most presses employ hand feeding, mechanical feeding devices may be had, since there are machines that are semi-automatic and completely automatic. There is perfect register and the registering may be done automatically. Adjustments for registration are made either by means of hand wheels, by mechanical stops set by screws, or by pushing buttons on control panels. The better presses can even be adjusted for register while the press is running. The screens are interchangeable and are varied in size. Standard shop screens may be used on most presses.

Most printing machines employ the squeegee principle for depositing the ink onto the stock. Presses are available that will print on the forward stroke of the squeegee, backward stroke, both, or double-print where it is necessary to have more ink deposited as in printing on textiles, felt, in some decalcomania jobs, etc. The squeegee can be stopped at any point on the screen either automatically or by some such arrangement as a foot pedal. On some presses the squeegee is stationary and the screen moves back and forth; while in other designs the screen is stationary and the squeegee moves back and forth. The squeegee can be adjusted for pressure or angle at which it will print best with a given ink or on a particular screen fabric or stock. On some presses the screen is in a horizontal position while in one press the screen is almost vertical with the squeegee moving up and down over the screen. Most machines have a fountain or reservoir for holding the inks which are fed to the screen or onto the squeegee, the quantity of ink being regulated easily. As has been mentioned, there are also automatically operated vacuum units that hold the stock to the printing base and prevent stock from adhering to the bottom of the screen.

While the squeegee principle of ink application through the printing screen is used on most screen printing machines, the screen printer should be cognizant of the vacuum or suction principle of applying screen printing inks onto materials. This principle of the suction or vacuum apparatus (Patent No. 3,172,358) was developed by Franz Weiss of Park Ridge, Illinois in 1965. On this type of press, air is evacuated from below the material being printed and the pressure of the air above pushes the ink through the screen onto the printing surface. This machine developed by Weiss, is a multicolor printing machine. However, it is able to print an unlimited number of colors in a single impression through one screen in register. The colors may be any number of combinations of inks and fluorescent inks. The printer must follow specifically the directions of the manufacturer of the machine in the use of the special ink, makeready of screen, and in the simple preparation of the artwork.

Because of the general, specialized, and varied screen printing machines, the printer must be objective in choosing a press and take into consideration the specifications for which a certain machine has been designed. Figures 117 through 135 show different screen printing

Figure 117. The General Cylinder screen printing press, one of the first successful presses of this type, for printing on flexible and semi-rigid stock such as foil, plastic sheet, decals, posters, and the like. Machine prints fine line, halftone copy, and other copy with fine registration at high speeds. Press has automatic feeder, automatic ink distribution and may be synchronized with UV and other driers. Press has a vacuum printing cylinder which causes substrate to hug curvature of cylinder, and sheet is printed and peeled immediately from screen. **(Courtesy of General Research, Inc., Sparta, Michigan)**

machines. Figure 132 presents a completely automatic and specialized screen printing machine which uses all metal seamless cylindrical screens manufactured for printing varied types of textiles, transfer paper, floor covering, halftone, leather, etc. While the screens generally are prepared by the machine manufacturer, the printer in the local

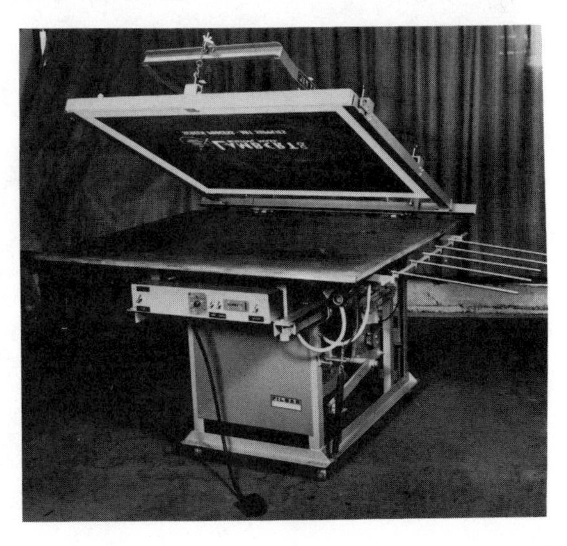

Figure 118. Filbar Screen Printing Press designed for printing on varied materials from 22″ x 30″ to 44″ x 64″ (55.9cm x 76.2cm to 111.7cm x 162.6cm), has automatic take-off, is practical for long and short runs, has a variable speed up to 900 impressions per hour, with foot operated electric brake. Press uses varied size frames. **(Courtesy of Graphic Equipment of Boston, Inc., Boston, Massachusetts)**

Figure 119. M & M Medalist Husky self-adjusting screen printing machine with gripper fingers for printing any material .003″ to ¼″ (.0762mm x .635cm) thick, with or without automatic take-off, comes in sizes which can print areas of 25″ x 38″ to 60″ x 90″ (63.5cm x 96.5cm to 152.4cm x 228.6cm). Unit has variable squeegee stroke and angle adjustment, flood coater adjustment, and may be adjusted to any conveyor. **(Courtesy of M & M Research and Printing Aids, Oshkosh, Wisconsin)**

Figure 121. The Autoroll Model M-20GA3 Universal Automatic Screen Printer developed for high speed printing and decorating of cylinders, ovals, flat, and conical shaped parts varying in size from a fraction of an ounce up to gallon size containers. Machine is designed to receive, print any type of ink, and deliver printed ware to synchronized drying equipment. **(Courtesy of The Autoroll Machine Corporation, Salem, Massachusetts)**

shop may be supplied equipment and technological information for the production of his screens. While conventional screens may be produced in the local shop, the preparation of specialized rotary screens may require special equipment such as film copying machines, coating equipment, exposure machines, screen developing tanks, degreasing tanks, photosensitive lacquers, and stripping tanks in which the rotary screens may be reclaimed for future use.

Another interesting development of a web-fed screen printing press was that developed in 1964 (Patent No. 3,155,034) by George W. Reinke. This machine also has a rigid cylindrical printing screen made into a self-supporting drum with a stationary squeegee inside the cylindrical

---

Figure 120. The Argon Hydra, precision hydraulically driven screen printing machine, with uniform squeegee stroke even at very low speeds; press guarantees constant ink distribution, printing definition, allows for squeegee pressure, flood bar pressure, correct squeegee printing angle, and for mounting different screen frames. Units are available for printing areas of 15⅜ x 20″ (39 x 51cm) to 30 x 40$\frac{3}{16}$″ (76 x 102cm) with maximum substrate thickness up to 1½″ (4cm). **(Courtesy of Cincinnati Printing and Drying Systems, Cincinnati, Ohio, and Argon Service Ltd., Milano, Italy)**

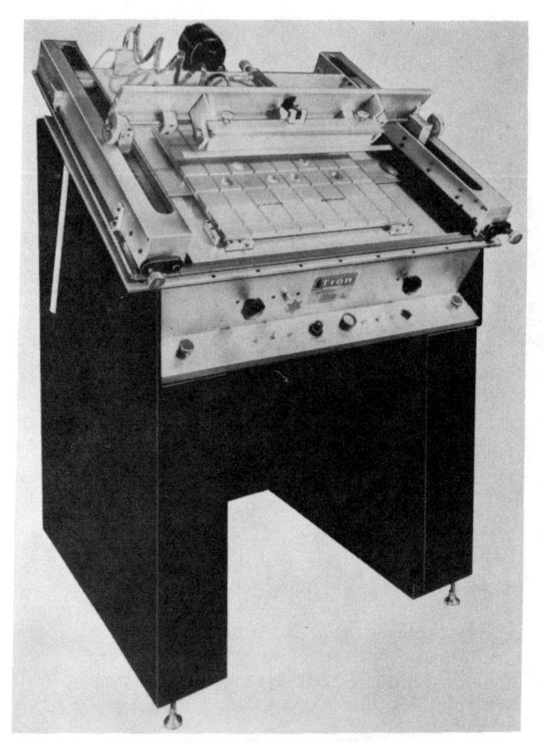

Figure 122. UniTron Screen Printing Unit for precise screen printing of electronic circuits consists of three components:a. a pre-registration system; b. a specially designed chase 30″ x 36″ (762mm x 914mm); and c. an automatic screen printing cycling system. Machine has a print area of 18″ x 24″ (457mm x 610mm), a slanted platen for easy inspection and feeding, a quick change squeegee, a drawer slot for insertion of chase, and is designed for easy conversion from hand to mechanized printing. **(Courtesy of Chemcut Corporation, State College, Pennsylvania)**

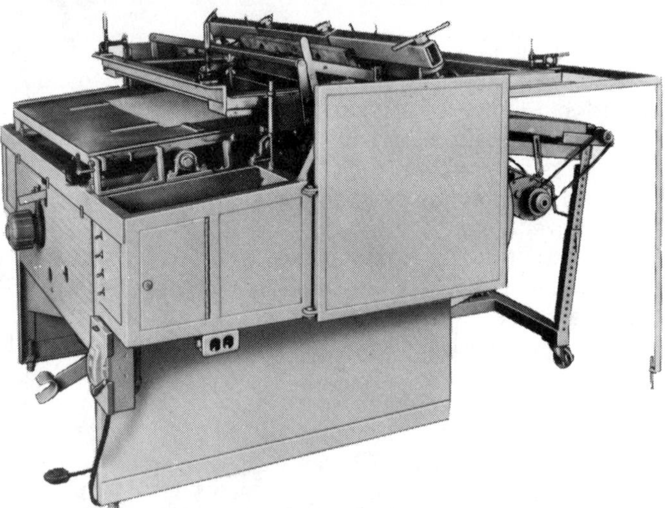

Figure 123. The Lawson Aladdin Cylinder screen printing press produces speeds up to 2000 impressions per hour, prints on all weight paper, cardboard, decals, vinyls, corrugated cardboard, light gauge metal, and prints all types of inks. Press is available in sizes which print from 24″ x 34″ to 45″ x 65″ (61cm x 86.4cm to 114cm x 165cm). **(Courtesy of Lawson Printing and Drying Machine Co., St. Louis, Missouri)**

Figure 124. The Rolaprint 3-D screen printing press, all mechanical from feed to delivery into a UV dryer on the left, for printing on cylindrical containers from 2 ounce to one gallon (56.8cc to 4.55 liters). The two units may produce from 300 to 3500 pieces per hour, depending on filling the ramp with parts and size of container. **(Courtesy of American Screen Printing Equipment Co., Chicago, Illinois)**

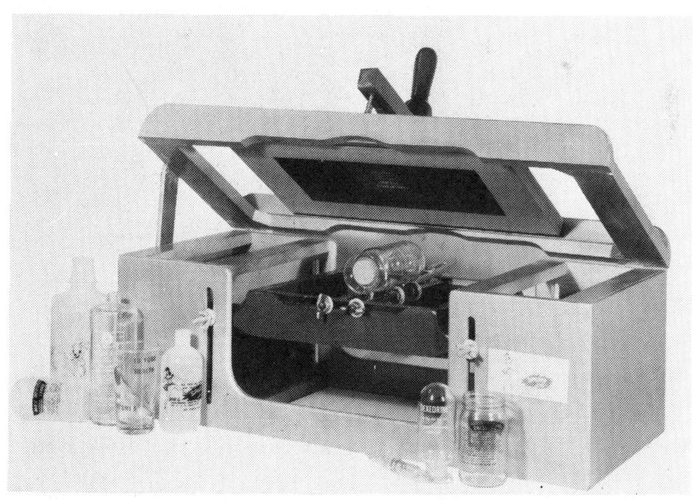

Figure 125. Sparky Jig, a semi-mechanized unit for screen printing on bottles, lamp bases, tumblers, and all types of cylindrical objects. Printer is available in varied size units so that printing may be done on objects from ½″ (1.27cm) in diameter to 55 gallon (208.175 liters) drums. **(Courtesy of Photo Process Screen Mfg. Co., Philadelphia, Pennsylvania)**

Figure 126. The Autoroll Slideflex Screen Printer, a flat bed machine, designed for close tolerance screen printing of electronic circuits and chemical machining. Machine has a work table which rolls up precision rails from load position to the print position where it accepts its impression, then returns to load position, automatically ejecting the printed part for inspection. Machine accepts screens up to 40″ x 54″ (101.6cm x 137cm) and has a speed of 700 impressions per hour. **(Courtesy of Autoroll Machine Corporation, Salem, MA)**

Figure 127. Cincinnati Powered Poster Printer, a semi-automatic machine, capable of screen printing 400 large posters or banners 44″ x 64″ (112cm x 163cm) sheets per hour. The unit may be built up to 18 feet (5.486 meters) in length for printing on any material including pressure-sensitive and reflective stock. **(Courtesy of Cincinnati Printing and Drying Systems, Inc., Cincinnati, Ohio)**

Figure 128. Precision Giant Plastic Printer, a hydraulic powered machine which can accommodate printing areas from 8 feet (2.438 meters) to 30 feet (9.144 meters), long plastic signs and can also be used to print on large sheets of glass, steel, or wood. The illustrated printer has a printing area of 100″ x 135″ (254cm x 342.9cm) and a 14 second printing cycle. It has a squeegee that can be adjusted independent of printing cycle and sheets are front fed and ejected at rear. **(Courtesy of Precision Screen Machines, Inc., Hawthorne, New Jersey)**

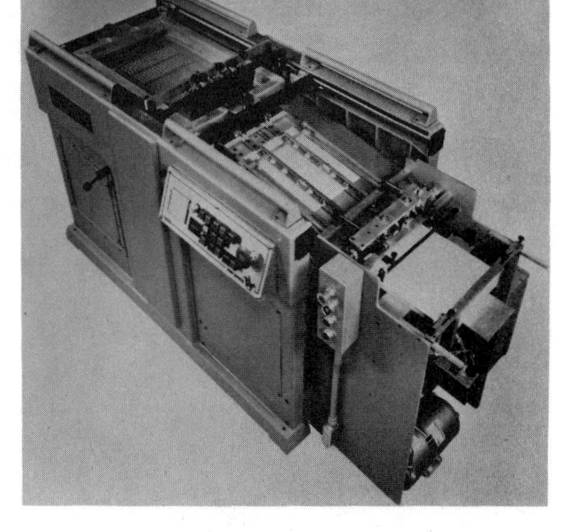

Figure 129. Pony Express screen printing machine designed for printing heat transfers, decals, greeting cards, application of adhesives for flock, glitter, beading, etc., prints sheet sizes up to 11″ x 17″ (27.9cm x 43.2cm) at speeds varying up to 4,000 impressions per hour, and guide controls while press is running. **(Courtesy of General Research, Inc., Sparta, Michigan)**

Figure 130. The Pace Screen Printing Machine designed for accurate registration to produce 400 to 1000 impressions per hour. It prints on varied stock up to 1½ inch (3.8cm) in thickness and up to 35 x 45 inches (88.9 x 114.3cm) in size. Three-fifths of its printing cycle is open for feeding. **(Courtesy of Atlas Silk Screen Supply Co., Chicago, Illinois)**

Figure 131. Vastex Textile Printer, manually operated unit for printing garments and textile materials, uses standard textile inks and printing screens, snaps cloth taut and uniformly for single or multi-color printing, and centers garment automatically for register in printing position. **(Courtesy of Vastex Machine Company, Roselle, New Jersey)**

Figure 132. The Stork Rotary, a completely automatic screen printing machine, using rotary cylindrical screens, prints on all types of textiles from fine synthetics to needlefelt carpetings, wallcoverings, transfer paper, and the like. The machine is synchronized with a drier consisting of 1 to 5 sections, has an infeed device, is easy to operate, and is designed for the possibility of printing cloth on both sides. The printing width may vary from about 1620 to 3200mm (63.8 to 126″), printing 8 to 20 colors of repeat designs from 640 to 1018mm (25.2 to 40″) in size, at a speed of 4 to 80 meters (13.12 to 262.4 feet) per minute. **(Courtesy of Stork Brabant, Boxmeer, Holland)**

Figure 133. A new version of the Buser Flatbed Screen Printing Machine which has been manufactured since 1948, available in five printing widths varying from 64″ (164mm) to 126″ (3200mm); prints repeat patterns 16″ (400mm) to 118″ (3000mm); set by pushbutton operation, and will print up to 21 colors with a production speed of 32.81 feet (10 meters) per minute. The continuous run of the printing belt on the underside of the machine advances the printing of repeat patterns on natural or synthetic fibers, as well as transfer paper. **(Courtesy of Fritz Buser Ltd., Wiler, Switzerland)**

Figure 134. The Auto-Pak All-purpose Screen Printer has an optical patented registration system for the precise printing of such items as clinical thermometers, flow meters, and other such items; unit prints from a minimum 1/16″ up to a 10″ stroke (.156cm to 25.4cm), with a squeegee stroke that may travel from slow to fast; machine has a single and automatic printing cycle and register marks on items printed project onto optical systems for check on exact registration. **(Courtesy of Joseph E. Podgor Co., Inc., Philadelphia, PA)**

screen making contact with the material being printed with precision up to 5,000 impressions per hour.

Since it is not possible to present all data about each machine, the specifications under each illustration stress generally the versatility of screen printing machines. Also, since it is not possible to present the very many machines available today internationally, it is hoped that the sampling available in this chapter will be of help to the reader.

Figure 135. A floor model Walco Roller Coater machine for applying screen printing inks, adhesives, and other coatings to varied materials from 1⅝″ (4.13cm) thick to 48″ (122cm) wide. Coaters are available for coating one or both sides of materials and also in larger sizes. **(Courtesy of L. R. Wallace Co., Pasadena, California)**

Chapter 21

SCREEN PRINTING OF DECALS

There are millions of decalcomanias produced in this country for advertising, decorative, and identification purposes. The consumer is interested in them because of their economic and colorful message. They are a practical method of advertising, because they can be produced in varied style designs in different colors, can be applied easily to any surface, are durable; do a job which is comparable to many hours of work of a highly paid artist, and may be used on complex curved surfaces which cannot be printed with the aid of jigs or in a press.

The use of decals is greatly varied. They have been applied to store windows, toys, furniture, trucks, buses, street cars, boxes, clocks; they have been used as name plates, instruction panels, for imitating fine leathers, wood grains, and grain of stone; they have been applied to glass, ceramic materials, porcelain enameled surfaces, and have found many other uses too numerous to mention. The size of a decal may vary from agate size type to a size about four feet by four feet.

The term "decal" has come to denote any communicative message which is processed prior to application such as pressure-sensitive label, transfer, heat transfer, die-cut label, dry transfer, etc. Generally, decalcomania printing is a process of printing designs, pictures, and type matter in the form of transferable film on specially prepared decal paper or backing sheet for later transferring to surfaces of different materials and varied shapes. Decal paper consists of a sheet, a starch layer and top layer of water-activated gum. The desired design or colors are printed directly on the gum surface. The paper must handle well, be porous enough, and have good wet strength. The decal gum must provide a good printing surface. The ink making up the print must be flexible, tough, and must retain all its properties after the paper is removed. The decal printing had its beginning after the discovery of lithography. The word "decalcomania" which made its appearance in the latter part of the 18th century and which comes from the Greek was motivated by the "decalcomaniacs" or enthusiasts of this art in France and England who found in this art an expressive hobby. The decalcomania process took root in the United States in the 1890's and about ten years later was an accepted and controlled phase of the graphic arts.

Decal printing is done today by lithography, letterpress, intaglio, and screen printing. There are advantages in producing decals by screen printing. The major advantage is that a heavier deposit of ink or color and more flexible film may be applied. Small quantities may be printed economically. It gives the printer another medium with which to work. Any size decal can be printed by this process. Where decals are large they may be printed singly; where small, more than one may be ganged up on one screen to save effort and to produce more copies in one impression. Screen printing machines may be used to produce them. Just as many decals in the screen printing industry are printed on machines as are printed manually. In fact, an incentive for developing screen printing machines was the need of a quicker method for printing decals in the industry.

Decalcomanias are printed on special decal paper which is available from screen printing suppliers, lithography suppliers, paper suppliers, and graphic arts distributors. The paper on which the printing is done generally is of uniform smooth finish and is usually a light creamy or natural color. There are two types of decal papers available: simplex or single paper and duplex or double paper. The simplex paper is coated with a decal solution on which the design or transfer is printed. The duplex paper consists of a heavy backing paper on which a tissue paper is attached semipermanently. The decal solution which receives the printed impression or design is coated on the tissue paper. Both papers are used but the simplex is employed more. Simplex paper is used generally for slide-off decals and this paper may be obtained with a clear lacquer coat or a white lacquer coat already applied. The latter paper with the applied lacquer coat usually is die-cut to the approximate shape of the decal before printing on it. The duplex paper is used for fine lettering, for printing heavy ink deposits, for large decals, for making varnish-on or cement type of transfers, and generally for outdoor applications. Decals made on duplex paper do not slide off the paper but are applied in a different manner. Decal papers vary in size and are obtainable in sizes up to about 44″ by 64″ (111.76cm x 162.56cm). There are different types of simplex paper. Some can be used under ordinary atmospheric conditions and other papers have to be used under controlled atmospheric conditions. To prevent the paper stock from shrinking or expanding under working conditions, it is a good idea to sore or lay out the paper in the same room twelve to twenty-four hours prior to working, since shrinking and expanding of larger sheets (which is governed by temperature and humidity) will interfere with perfect registration in printing. The larger plants are air conditioned both as to humidity and temperature.

Although in the earlier days of screen printing, the printer may have prepared his own decal paper and in an emergency the printer may do likewise by coating it with exact proportions of a solution of starch and gum arabic, it is not advisable and practical to coat paper, since bought papers are better. If possible, coated papers should not be handled too much, as finger marks on the coated surface will mar it and interfere with printing.

Usually, the colored inks in a decal are printed between clear lacquer inks, one clear coat directly upon the decal paper and a final clear coat applied over the design after the design has been printed on top of the first lacquer coat. The clear coats aid in tieing in the details in the design. The clear lacquer which is printed as a solid area is the same general shape as the finished colored design and is about $\frac{1}{16}$" (.157cm) to $\frac{1}{8}$" (.217cm) larger around the design. See Figures 136 and 137. As it is hard to distinguish where the first clear lacquer coat is printed on the paper because of the transparency of the lacquer, it is suggested that the paper be marked in some fashion so that it be fed and registered correctly for the other colors that are to be printed on top of the first clear lacquer coat. The prepared screen that is used for printing the first clear coat is saved and used to print the top clear coat. Of course, the printing screen used will have to be one that resists the action of the ink.

Synthetic inks, lacquers, and enamels may be used for printing

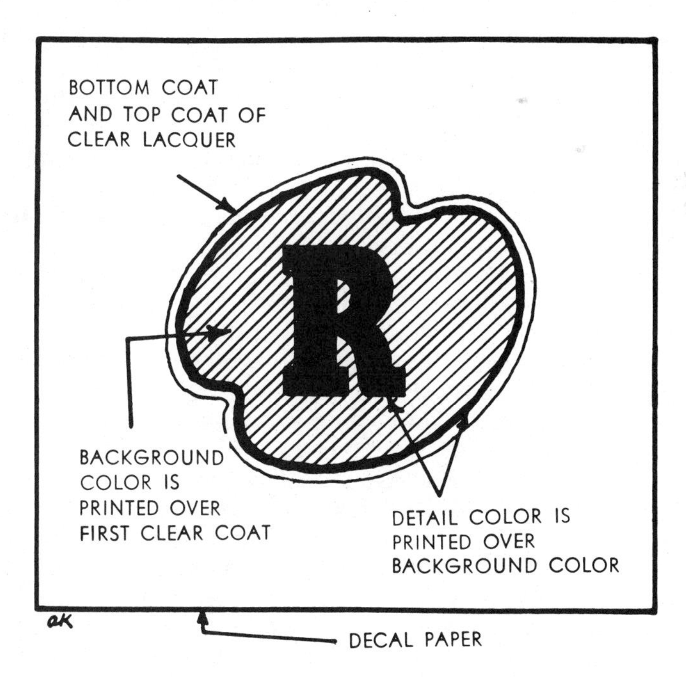

Figure 136. Description of slide-off decal.

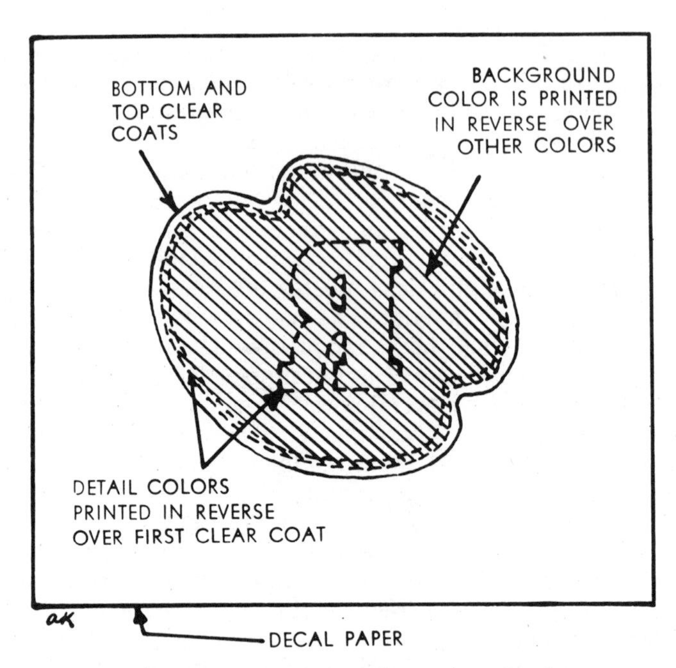

Figure 137. Description of varnish-on decal.

decals, with lacquers and synthetic ink preferred because enamels have a tendency to stiffen quicker, are not as durable, and take longer to dry. In printing ceramic or vitrifiable decals, which are employed for indirect decorating as compared with direct screen printing, the decals are used for decorating such products as floor and wall tiles, glassware, cookware, dishes, for porcelain enameled surfaces, and the like. The decal or transfer has special inorganic or ceramic inks printed on it, which, after application and drying on the ceramic surface, has to be fired or fused at temperatures up to about 1650 degrees Fahrenheit (899 degrees Celsius), depending upon the ink printed.

Many of the inks employed by the printer for screen printing of decals are actually plastics and synthetics which are applied by means of printing. When these plastics and synthetics go through the drying process, which may involve any of the drying methods or all drying processes, the inks take on the qualities of plastics.

Two words which are greatly used and misused in screen printing are "lacquers" and "synthetics." Strictly speaking the word "synthetic" has reference to anything that has been synthesized or put together by man from man-made raw-materials. When using the term synthetic in relation to an ink or finish we usually mean an ink in which the vehicle is predominantly a solution of synthetic resins and which are not combined with cellulose derivatives or products. The resin vehicle used for inks and finishes is changed by the addition of various oils and resins to produce an ink of almost any desired quality. The use of synthetics is not only a matter of substitution or necessity, but is an outcome of a desire to carefully control the materials used in the ink to produce desired properties.

Lacquers are also man-made but their composition is not as varied as synthetic inks. They were brought about by a desire for a quicker drying finish. Generally, lacquers may consist of vehicles which are mixtures of resin with plasticizers and *cellulose derivatives.* Ordinarily, lacquers consist of the film forming material of cellulose ester; a plasticizer; a solvent for dissolving the cellulose product; and the pigment, if the lacquer is not a clear type. Although originally cellulose nitrate (which is made by treating cotton fibers with mixtures of acid such as nitric and sulphuric) was used for lacquers, other cellulose materials are also employed.

Further confusion arises when the printer uses the term "enamel." Ordinarily, enamel refers to a pigmented ink made from natural coloring matter, varnish which usually is made from linseed oil or another natural product, and other natural substances found in nature and compounded by man. Popularly, an enamel, whether natural or synthetic, is a gloss color. Thus, the printer must designate whether he wants an ordinary enamel, synthetic enamel, or a lacquer when referring to ink for decal printing. Regardless of type of ink, any ink used for decal printing must have flexibility and elasticity and at the same time be durable enough to withstand the atmospheric elements and other conditions.

Because synthetic enamels retain durability, gloss, flexibility, color, and are not subject to alligatoring, cracking, etc., manufacturers of inks generally recommend their being used for exterior decals. However, lacquers have a more permanent flexibility. Synthetic enamels are practical for large decals and those which do not have very fine detail in them. They have better adhering qualities. Synthetics have good weatherability because as a rule they give a heavier film deposit. They have been used in the past because they do not dissolve lacquer printing screens as lacquers are subject to do. However, with the present water soluble film that is available and the photographic printing screens, lacquers can be printed as practically as enamels. Synthetic enamel printed decals are generally slip-sheeted to prevent their sticking to one another when they are stacked in piles.

Lacquers may also be employed for interior and exterior decals. They are better for instances where extreme detail is of great importance and where very extreme durability is not required; therefore, they have been used for many types of decals designed for interior use. Lacquers are especially good for printing decals which are to be adhered to the inside of glass. The great advantage of lacquers is their reduced drying time, and since decals often are not heat dried, especially between coats because of expansion and contraction and curling of the decal paper, this is an advantage. Lacquers, as a rule, do not have to be slip-sheeted. They do have slightly more odor than synthetic enamels.

It is suggested that neither lacquer nor synthetic enamel decals should be heat-dried or force-dried as the decal paper will curl and may contract too much in relation to the decal causing trouble in registering the different colors in multiple-color printing. Decals should dry naturally (especially large decals) when several decals are ganged up on one screen and when multi-color work is being done. Any of the inks may be printed on both the simplex and duplex decal paper.

It is advised that the printer make use of the best properties of both lacquer and synthetic inks in printing. For example, in printing decals the base or background coat may be a clear synthetic enamel with lacquers being printed on top of the enamel to represent the design, especially if the design has fine detail in it. After the design is printed, a top coat of clear synthetic enamel printed over the lacquers will provide durability, enough flexibility, and adhering qualities. Lacquers and simplex paper may be used for the smaller types of decals of the slide-off type; a combination of synthetic inks and lacquers printed on duplex paper may be employed for larger decals and for decals subject to outside exposure.

Although there are other combinations and other inks, the printer has three practical combinations for printing decals: the all lacquer printed decal; the all synthetic ink decal; and the lacquer and synthetic enamel combination decal. Also, before generalizing about enamels, lacquers, or any combination, the printer should make trial prints to investigate the working qualities of inks.

Decals usually are classified according to their method of application such as slide-off, face-down, and varnish-on decal. In the slide-off type shown in the illustration in Figure 136, the decal is applied to the required surface by being saturated with water for a specific short time at room temperature, slipped or pulled a little over the edge of the decal paper, the exposed edge placed in position on the surface, and the backing paper gently withdrawn from underneath the printed design. Where slide-off decals are to be applied to opaque surfaces, the colors are printed as for ordinary jobs, that is, the background color is printed first and the rest of the colors are printed over it in their right order. In the latter case it is not necessary to print or apply an adhesive coat over the design as the transfer already has its adhesive between the paper and the design.

Where slide-off decals are to be applied on the inside or back of transparent surfaces such as glass or plastics, and where the decal is to be observed by one facing the transfer attached under the transparent surface, it is necessary to screen an adhesive over the entire surface of the design. To apply this type of transfer moisten the decal in water, apply decal face-down to required cleaned spot, and squeegee or roll down backing paper with a squeegee or roller. After about twenty minutes the backing paper is soaked off with water and removed carefully without lifting the transfer from the surface. Dab the transfer carefully with a soft cloth and wipe away excess water.

Another method of printing decals that are to be applied to the back of glass is to print the design in reverse directly on top of the decal paper, printing the colors in reverse order, then applying them as simple slide-off decals. Figure 137 shows a reverse decal.

Decal adhesives are generally water soluble and will adhere to glass, painted metal, lacquered surfaces, etc. Printing screens which are water soluble should not be used to apply this adhesive. Decal adhesives come prepared to be used directly from the container or simple specific directions for their mixing are supplied by the manufacturer.

In the varnish-on or cement type illustrated in Figure 137 the decal is placed directly on top and in contact with the applied surface so that the design is between the backing paper and the applying surface, and the backing paper is removed from the transfer, leaving the decal exposed, face up, and attached to the surface. Duplex paper is used ordinarily in making varnish-on decals. The first impression, which is clear lacquer ink, is printed on top of the tissue paper in reverse and then the rest of the design is printed in reverse. For example, if a two color decal is to be printed consisting of a background in one color and the detail in another color, the detail color would be printed first in reverse on top of the clear coat and the background color printed next in reverse over the detail. Over this would be printed another clear lacquer coat. Regardless of the number of colors in this decal, all of them would be printed in reverse order. Each color must be perfectly dry before the next one is applied.

In applying the varnish-on decal, the backing paper and the tissue are separated slightly at one corner or along one edge to make the final peeling of the backing paper easier before applying adhering varnish and before placing the decal in the required spot. After the decal is pressed into the required place, the backing paper is removed by peeling it off carefully and then the tissue paper may be removed by soaking it off with water.

In attaching a varnish-on decal, the adhering varnish or cement is applied directly to the face side of the decal with a brush or a piece of soft cloth, applying a thin coat of cement. Then the decal is placed face down over the cleaned and desired spot, and the backing paper is smoothed out with the aid of a roller, squeegee, sponge, or soft cloth before the varnish or adhesive is completely set to prevent formation of air bubbles between the surface and decal. In removing the backing paper, especially where the decal is not small, try to peel it off in narrow strips, peeling the strips horizontally or vertically instead of peeling the paper off in one piece. This will make it easier to keep the transfer in place and prevent it from wrinkling. When the backing paper is removed the surplus varnish may be cleaned away carefully with a mineral type of cleaner such as turpentine or benzene and the transfer left alone.

The varnish-on decal may also be attached to a surface by applying the cement to the surface instead of the face side of the decal.

The application of decals is an important part of decal work, especially varnish-on decals, and should be taken care of by simple specific directions on the part of the printer. Printing of directions for transferring and storage usually done on the back of the backing paper or on the decal envelope is part of the printing job, since the finest printed decals may be spoiled in incorrect application or in storage. Surfaces should always be cleaned well before applying decals to them. In applying the mounting varnish or cement, a fast-setting varnish, obtainable from screen printing suppliers, should be used. It should be pliable, have plenty of adhesion, applied thin, and dry to tack in about five minutes. While some pressure sensitive or pressure adhered transfers and labels are not permanent, an applied decal is intended for permanent use and not for removal.

Correct storing of printed and water applied decals is important. Shops specializing in screen printed decals generally seal the decals in thin transparent plastic film to insure their staying moistureproof and dustproof. It is suggested that these types of decals be stored in a cool dry area off the floor, avoiding excessive heat from steam pipes, radiators, and sunlight. Neither should decals be stored in damp basements or near open windows. A practical temperature for storage is between 60 and 80 degrees Fahrenheit (16 and 27 degrees Celsius).

While any artwork that can be drawn, photographed, or printed can be produced by screen printing decals, successful registration of each color and detail is essential. Each color is printed separately and after printing the colors should be checked against the colors in the original artwork. Also, ceramic decals should be test fired on the substrate or ojbect to which they are to be applied before doing a production run.

Chapter 22

SCREEN PRINTING ON PRESSURE-SENSITIVE MATERIALS

The increased use of pressure-sensitive or pressure-adhesive products since World War II emphasizes the need for clarifying some differences between decalcomanias and pressure-sensitive or self-adhering labels. Today's printer who prints on decalcomania papers may also produce printed matter on pressure-sensitive material. While the two products may appear to be the same and produce the same end results, they do differ in composition, processing, and application. As has been implied in the previous chapter, a decal is a design in film form or a transferable printed film which has been printed upon a temporary support sheet (decal paper). The film, at the time of application to the receiving surface, may be released from the support sheet with water which transfers the film from the support. A decal usually exhibits a small transparent sealing edge around the design film. Also, a decal is intended for permanent use and not for removal.

A pressure-sensitive label or pressure-adhering or self-adhering label may be employed for permanent or temporary use, depending on the ingredients in the label and on the end use of the product. Basically, pressure-sensitive stock may consist of three parts—(1) a base material, bodystock, of face stock having a printed message on it; (2) a tacky adhesive coating on the bodystock; and (3) a liner, backing, or release paper covering the adhesive coated side of the bodystock. See Figures 138 and 139.

The adhesive is sandwiched in between the bodystock and release backing paper. Although pressure-adhesive labels are also called dry-release or dry decals, they are not true decalcomanias, since the release paper does not have to be wetted for removal. However, they do serve the purpose of transfers, since they may be transferred and adhered to varied surfaces. Unlike decal paper, bodystock must be dense, nonabsorbent and should allow adhesive to stick to it. The bodystock may be treated with a coating to better anchor the adhesive and aid in producing a better bond with the adhesive which is applied over the bodystock. Generally, screen printing is done on the bodystock,

Figure 138. Removing a three-color, reflective, pressure-sensitive emblem from a screen table which uses a one-arm squeegee for printing. The protective paper backing is peeled off before applying emblem to surface **(Courtesy of Decal Products Co., Newark, New Jersey; and Minnesota Mining and Manufacturing Co., St. Paul, Minnesota)**

but sometimes also on the release paper. The printing may be done on the back of the bodystock and also on the side facing the release paper and the adhesive applied over the printed message. Bodystock may be paper or any of the following materials: white tag stock, litho stock, plastic impregnated stock, vellum, latex impregnated papers, fluorescent stock, pyroxylin metallics, reflective materials, very thin metal foils laminated to a heavy base paper; transparent, translucent, and opaque thin plastic sheets such as mylar, vinyl, and acetate. The bodystocks most often used for screen printing are paper, vinyl, mylar, acetate, mylar faced vinyl, and aluminum foil. There are double-sign

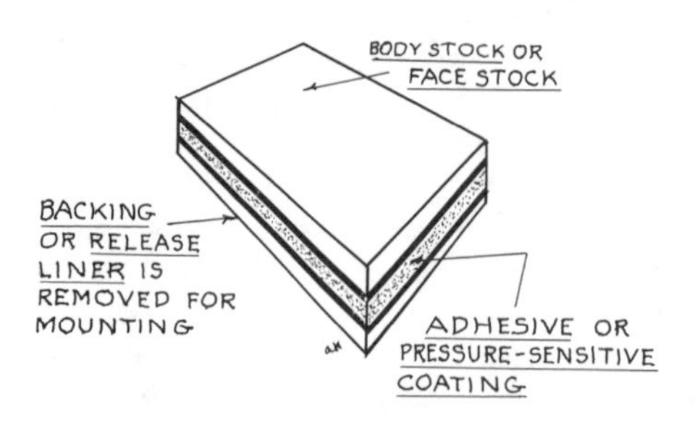

Figure 139. Cross section of pressure-sensitive stock.

stocks designed for two messages on one label. With the stock the second message is printed in reverse on clear film and the first message is printed on top of the release paper. The type of surfaces being printed indicates that much of the work is best done with screen printing. This implies that the printer must use care in selecting his inks for printing. Where he is not sure of what ink to print on a surface, it is suggested that he consult with his ink supplier or bodystock supplier.

The release paper serves two purposes—it must protect the adhesive (and also the message, depending on the method of printing) and it must be removed easily when desired. When the release sheet is removed, the bodystock with the message on it may be pressed down onto the desired surface, generally using just hand or finger pressure. Ordinarily, silicone compounds are used as release coatings. The coating is an insoluble and an incompatible substance. Since speed of label application is desirable, easy release is essential. The release paper must repel adhesion without destroying tack. Generally release papers are made of glassine, parchment, and kraft papers. The degree of release and finish may be governed by the manufacturer at the request of the printer. Where needed different degrees of release levels on opposite sides of sheet may be produced.

Pressure-sensitive labels may be applied to almost any surface without application of heat, moisture, or paste. Pressure-sensitive material is available in any width size and in large rolls so that the screen printer may screen print any size message or label. While most pressure-sensitive labels are intended for permanent use, some types provide for easy removal.

These labels have grown in use because they are easy to adhere for permanent or temporary application to varied surfaces and materials where exceptional resistance is needed to exposure, moisture, heat, cold, electricity, abrasion, and the like. The temporary labels can be peeled off the surface without leaving any adhesive on the surface. The temporary labels may remain removable for an extended period of time (often years) and not mar or etch finishes. A permanent pressure-sensitive label is one that cannot be removed without destroying the surface to which it is attached or without destroying the label. In both of these types the adhesive ans surface are brought into contact with pressure generally at room temperature.

Although the printer constantly discovers new uses for these products, he may print different colors and inks on the varied bodystock surfaces for producing large truck and gasoline station signs, bumper strips, window displays, to the very small schematic drawings applied to machines. Packaging and point-of-purchase displays have been greatly affected by pressure-sensitive materials. Mistakes in printing on large and on small surfaces may be corrected by printing on pressure-sensitive material and applying material over the mistake area.

A very good adhesive must have both tack and adhesion. Tack

is the property which makes a material stick to a surface and also resists immediate removal. Adhesion refers to the strength of the bond. A pressure-adhesive paper generally is one that is permanently tacky at room temperature. The formulation of the adhesive consists of latex or synthetic rubber compounds. According to manufacturers, the adhesion is due to polar bonding rather than chemical or mechanical bonding. There are many types of adhesives; one will adhere to nearly every surface. Usually the process employs three types of adhesive material: (1) an adhesive backed material ready to be printed; (2) liquid adhesives; and (3) transfer tape supplied in rolls. Tape adhesives are coated on release paper that may be easily applied to any material which the printer may use either before or after printing. The adhesive is transferable to the stock. Liquid adhesives may be roller-coated onto bodystock or applied through a coarse printing screen (No. 6XX or 8XX silk or equivalent fabric) onto the stock. The printer must not attempt to modify adhesives, since this may spoil purpose of the adhesive.

In working with pressure-sensitive materials, the printer should try out every step relating to the printing process to determine the suitability of the material for printing and for the end use. Pressure-sensitive materials require care in handling. The material should remain wrapped and in the original carton until it is ready to be used. The paper should be stored in a cool dry place away from hot pipes and other sources of heat and not stacked too high. Generally, these materials have a certain shelf life and it is not practical to print on the materials after they have been stored too long. When choosing a screen printing ink, the printer must use one that will adhere best on the surface of the bodystock. Since bodystocks are not only papers, but may be of varied plastics or metal foil surfaces, the ink chosen should be one that will adhere best to the type of bodystock being printed.

While the novice may find the cutting of the stock more of a problem than ordinary paper or cardboard because of the adhesive between the two layers, the cutting may be done if the following is observed. It is suggested that packs of about 100 to 200 sheets, depending on the thickness, be cut at one time, employing a guillotine cutter having a razor sharp blade. The blade should be dusted with powdered zinc stearate, talcum powder, or cornstarch to prevent the material from adhering to the blade surface and dulling the blade. Some operators apply a silicone spray on the blade to prevent accumulation of adhesive. If there is evidence of the adhesive being pressed out on the cut stock, the adhesive may be removed with a rubber squeegee or by working with a latex glove and rubbing the cut edges with the glove. The cut edges may also be brushed over with a bag containing zinc stearate powder. It is recommended that stock not be trimmed before printing except where stock is to be cut to a smaller size for the screen printing

Figure 140. Four color pressure-sensitive seal printed on .004″ (.102mm) thick vinyl sheet material with vinyl inks. After printing, seal was die-cut into a circular shape. **(Courtesy of Chief Display Print Corporation, Chicago, Illinois)**

unit or press. As is true with decals, each printed pressure-sensitive label should have printed directions for its application to surfaces.

While it is not an adhesive product, the printer should be familiar with electrostatic transparent sign material which is pressure-applied. The printed material adheres to glass by static electricity and is simply installed by peeling off the backing sheet, placing on desired spot of window, and smoothing sign out against glass. This material has no adhesive and will adhere to glass in sunlight. It is weather-resistant and has exposure of 3 to 6 months in a window.

Figure 138 shows an emblem screen printed on pressure-sensitive

Figure 141. Three decals or transfers screen printed on permanent pressure-sensitive polyester sheet material. Six colors were printed on the "Ducks Unlimited" emblem on .002″ (.00508cm) thick stock. The other two emblems each .005″ (.01270cm) thick, were screen printed with transparent gold ink first, the varied required opaque colors were printed over the gold, the two emblems were embossed, and finally die-cut. **(Courtesy of Chicago Decal Company, Chicago, Illinois)**

reflective sheeting. Reflective sheeting is a flexible material made of millions of tiny glass lens-like beads which are covered with a smooth plastic. When light strikes these glass elements, the light is bounced or reflected back to its source with a brilliance that is much brighter than a perfectly white painted surface. Because of its day and night usefulness, reflective sheeting may be employed wherever it is intended to communicate a message day and night—around the clock. When reflective sheeting is screen printed with transparent colors, the print and sheet are brightly visible in light beams, especially of passing vehicles, at night in the same shape and color as during daytime. On the other hand, areas on reflective signs which are to be "blacked out" or not seen may be printed on with opaque screen printing inks.

Figure 139 shows a cross section of pressure-sensitive material; Figures 140 and 141 present sample prints done on pressure-sensitive materials intended for permanent application to varied surfaces.

Chapter 23

FLOCKING AND SCREEN PRINTING

Flocking is not a novelty anymore but an accepted method used to decorate, coat surfaces, and in general to supplement finishing. Fashion designers constantly "rediscover" flocking, since flocked products are now washable and dry-cleanable. Flocking is a process in which finely cut rayon, wool, and cotton fibers commonly known as flock are applied to a surface upon which the correct adhesive has been coated. Rayon, nylon, polyester, acrylic, fluorocarbon, wool, and cotton flock is applied on banners, greeting cards, wallpaper; for enhancing designs in the textile field (especially on sportswear; on walls, cabinets, caskets, and jewelry cases; for acoustic purposes; for exhibits; for insulating; for imitating suede, velvet, embroidery, etc. Flock covers completely, since the nap covers cracks and slight imperfections. While flocking in the past was used on occasion to cover up imperfections, today's flocking is used for its creativity in design, its utility as a finish, and for its many end uses.

While flocking has been used for many years, it originated commercially in the United States in about 1930 by the Behr-Manning Company. After 1945, with the development of flock cutting and electrostatic flocking, the flocking industry began to grow so that today it is another process used by screen printers. The screen printer and the textile industry have used flocking to produce suede and velvet-like fabrics for apparel, carpeting for institutions and homes, high pile furlike fabrics, sound absorbing fabrics, curtains, draperies, upholstery materials, and for applying designs with impact on plastisol inks printed on sportswear, etc.

Flock is available in fiber length sizes from about 1/64"(.0397cm) to about 1½" (3.81cm). Most common lengths of flock in use are about 1/32" (.079cm) and 1/16" (.159cm). Flock is available in all colors of the spectrum and may be used on any surface to which the correct adhesive can be applied. Almost any screen printing supply house stocks flock in the following colors: white, black, silver, gold, red, yellow, orange, green, brown, and purple. Other colors may be obtained by applying flock of one color over an adhesive that is of another color. Also, flock of one color may be mixed with flock of another to produce a third color. However, it is advisable to use an adhesive which is the same color or nearly the same as the flock. Generally, rayon flock is the most used because it produces a better nap, since it is cut to more uniform lengths, and is transparent. Also, rayon is best to use when it is necessary to show a color under it. A good grade of flock is one that is of uniform length, of uniform color, one that will wear well, will adhere permanently, and will produce a good nap. Flock must not be stored in damp places nor allowed to become wet, as it will form into lumps and be difficult to spray or apply. Damp flock fibers may be dried by exposing them to about five or six infra-red lamps, moving lamps over flock slowly. When it is necessary to store flock fibers in damp places or climates, then calcium chloride should be stored in the vicinity of the flock fibers. Calcium chloride is a white solid substance that is deliquescent, that is, it absorbs moisture. The flock fibers may be spread out thin on racks and the calcium chloride, placed near it, will aid in keeping the fibers dry.

While the adhesive for flocking may be applied by means of screen printing, passing stock through a coating machine or rollers, hand brushing, or dipping the object in the adhesive, the screen printer may use printing, spraying the flock on, vibration or beater bars, and electrostatic application. The surface must be perfectly clean before applying adhesive. Where more than one color of flock is applied, each color must be run separately and allowed to dry completely before coating the next adhering coat and running the next color of flock. Regardless of the method of applying the adhesive, the thickness of the adhesive coat must be controlled and uniform. The longer the fiber of flock to be applied, generally, the thicker the film of adhesive should be. Usually, a thicker flock coat will be obtained if this adhesive coat is thicker.

To obtain a thicker coat of adhesive, the screen fabric used should be anywhere from about a Number 6 to a Number 10 mesh or its equivalent. The screen plate used must not be dissolved by the adhesive printed. Printing the adhesive slightly off-contact will assure better adhering of flock and a more dense coating. In off-contact printing, the screen fabric normally does not touch the material being printed when the screen is down in printing position. Contact between screen and material only occurs where the squeegee forces fabric down on stock. A double impression with less pressure in pulling the squeegee over the screen a second time will also print a thicker coat of adhesive.

The adhesive used may be any one that will serve the given purpose best. Adhesives used for flocking are water soluble ones (such as glue), enamels, lacquers, and synthetic adhesives. Adhesives may be obtained in any desired color or in clear. Transparent adhesives used are glue, lacquer, and alkyd resin. Shellac was employed originally but it sets too quickly and is not as good as the present adhesives. Adhesives may be applied over flock of one color so that a second coat of another color may be adhered. Where flock is to be coated on textiles that are to be washed, then the adhesive must be one that is waterproof. Textiles should be stretched well and flat to insure that the adhesive is better applied. The adhesive employed should be slow drying, have a minimum of penetration, thus producing a coat to which the flock will adhere. Where material is very absorbent, a sizing coat must be applied first, allowed to dry, and then the adhesive applied.

Plastisols, rubber type, or stretch inks (originally developed for printing on mesh fabrics, denim, and the like), besides being printed directly on fabrics, are also used as flocking adhesives. They produce an embossed effect after being printed directly on the material. After the plastisol is printed and flocked, the printed design must be baked and flocked at about 240 to 325 degrees Fahrenheit (116 to 163C) for about 3 to 8 minutes. After being cured, the flocked design will resist washing.

The flock fibers should be applied after the application of the adhesive and while the adhesive is still wet enough to allow the fibers to penetrate the adhesive. The method of application varies depending on the quantity of the objects to be flocked, shape, size of object, and material being flocked. Flock may be applied manually by sifting through hand sifters, by spraying both with hand and compressed air spraying guns, and by means of vibrating machines or vibrating tables. There are regular flock air guns used for spraying which emit narrow or wide streams which can be adjusted as desired and which operate on pressure of twenty pounds or more. Ordinarily, the pressure used for flocking varies from about 40 to 60 pounds. In any application of flock, the flocking should be done in a booth or in an enclosed area for the protection of the operator and to aid in reclaiming the flock. Where flock is sprayed, it is suggested that the individual doing the spraying wear a respirator mask to prevent breathing in of the minute fiber particles.

The larger screen printing shops and those specializing in such work as printing and flocking of curtains, draperies, bedspreads, flame resistant drapery material, printing bolt materials, and the like, use automatically operated flocking machines or tables in which the flock is fed in at one end of the machine at the top and into a flock tank or hopper built directly over a conveyor upon which adhesive coated objects are placed or moved. The conveyor may serve two purposes: to move the adhesive coated and flocked objects along and as a vibrator or agitator. See Figure 142. As the conveyor passes over the vibrator or agitator bars, the bars produce a vibrating action on the flocked object or material, causing bouncing which in turn anchors the flock deeply and uniformly into the adhesive coating and makes the flock fibers stand on end. The vibrating bars are square, hexagonal, or octagonal in cross section and are generally built under the conveyor at right angles to the motion. These bars are usually attached to an electric

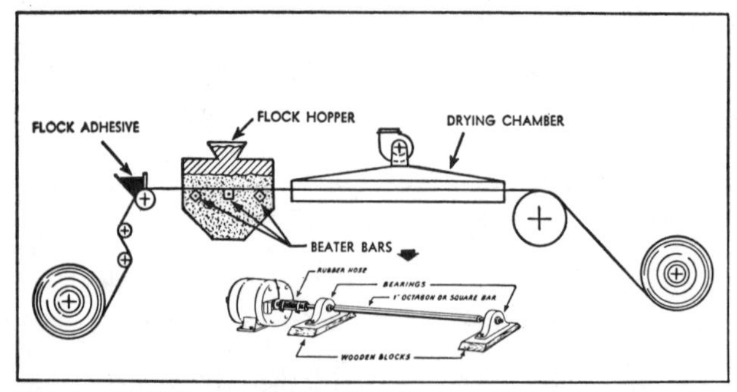

Figure 142. Vibration method of flock application is shown in this basic schematic diagram. Detailed drawing at bottom illustrates assembly of components of simple beater bar. **(Courtesy of Cellusuede Products, Inc., Rockford, Illinois)**

motor which turns them at the required speed. One or more bars may be built in under the conveyor. The conveyor, vibrating bar, and flock are enclosed so that flock will not be blown about into the air.

Besides the hand methods and flocking machine or vibration methods of flock application, there is also the electrostatic method. In this method, electrostatic flocking machines are employed to create an electrically charged area as the adhesive coated surface passes between two electrodes as illustrated in Figure 143. Each of the electrodes has a different or opposite charge. When the flock is introduced between the electrodes or in the electrostatic field, the fibers become electrically charged and are attracted to the adhesive being embedded end-wise

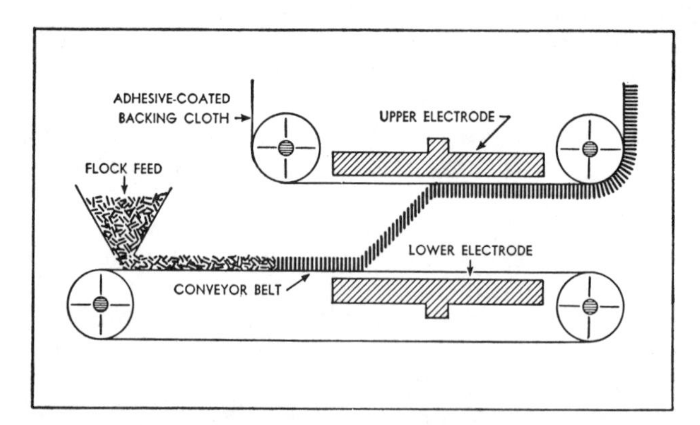

Figure 143. Electrostatic method of flock application is outlined in this simple diagram. Parallel lines denoting flock show how fibers erect themselves along lines of force and are projected endwise onto surface of adhesive coated material above. **(Courtesy of Cellusuede Products, Inc., Rockford, Illinois)**

or end first into the adhesive surface. It is possible to deposit up to about 300,000 fibers per square inch (about 118,000 per square cm). Information on flocking machines is available from screen printing suppliers and from manufacturers and suppliers of flock. Flocked objects may be allowed to dry naturally in about 4 to 24 hours, depending on the type of adhesive printed. However, flocked material and objects may be force-dried in about 3 to 30 minutes depending on the type of heat and on the adhesive printed. Forced drying may be employed by using ovens for drying and curing through which the flocked material may pass. Convection ovens with forced hot air have proven practical for this purpose, the heat being supplied by gas, electricity, or oil. Forced drying may also be accomplished by using an infra-red unit attached over the vibrating and conveying unit. However, manufacturers of drying and curing ovens for flocking recommend that for practical reasons two oven zones be used—one zone for adhesive drying and one zone for adhesive curing. The correct temperature and time for forced drying may be obtained from the flock supplier. Some flocked surfaces may be force-dried up to about 120 degrees Fahrenheit (49C) while others may be force-dried up to about 350 degrees Fahrenheit (177C). In forced drying, the correct heat temperature and time should not be exceeded, since the flocked surface may be scorched. Flocked surfaces should not be handled until the drying process is definitely complete.

Flock fibers left as excess may be reused. In the vibrator machine, excess flock is removed with suction hoses or by means of gravity, that is, just allowing the fibers to fall into a drawer or tank under the machine. In racking flocked objects or surfaces for drying, it is advisable to rack or stack the objects vertically and not too closely, since flock retards drying. It must be understood that a flocked coat takes longer to dry than an ordinary printed coat.

Where large flocked exhibits or objects are to be exhibited for long periods of time it is suggested that colored flock rather than white flock be used, since colored flock does not show dust and dirt as quickly as white flock.

Reflective glass beads, tinsel, cellophane spangles which come in varied colors and which are used for decorating displays, posters, greeting cards, etc., are all applied over an adhesive similarly to flocking. They are affixed or sprinkled on after the adhesive has been applied. Since beads, tinsel, etc., are more solid material than flock, the adhesive used for affixing them must be flexible enough so that the film will not crack off after application of decorative coating. These may be mixed with one another or with flock to obtain desired effects. Beads and the like should not be imbedded in the adhesive, since this may cut down on their reflective qualities. Some screen printers sift the beads onto the adhesive covered material so that adhesive is covered (but not excessively) with the beads. A coarse silk screen may be used for sifting beads. Simple experimentation will produce acceptable results.

Figure 144 presents an example of flocking and decal printing. The designs were printed in one stroke with one screen with a clear enamel ink on top of simplex decal paper and the flock was then applied to the tacky clear enamel. In this type of printing, any color flock may be applied to the varied designs, flocking a whole sheet at one time.

Figure 144. Varied designs of screen printed and flocked decals. **(Courtesy of Chicago Screen Print, Inc., Morton Grove, Illinois)**

Figure 145 shows a different treatment where flock is used on a greeting card.

Figures 146, 147 and 148, illustrate some practical flocking machines used in screen printing and flocking.

Figure 145. A 29″ x 36″ (73.7cm x 91.4cm) greeting card printed in eight attractive colors, then an adhesive is applied for receiving a red fluorescent flock coating to supplement the impact of the greeting effect. **(Courtesy of Superior Silk Screen Industries, Inc., Chicago, Illinois)**

Figure 146. An R-K Automatic Printing and Flocking Machine on which garment is automatically printed, flocked, de-flocked, transferred to dryer belt and dried, cleaned, and manually removed for packing. **(Courtesy of R-K Electric Company, Inc., Cincinnati, Ohio)**

Figure 147. A complete mechanical unit for application of flock to objects and materials such as textiles, paper, plastics, wood, metal, foam material, and the like. Machine design permits components to be added and rearranged to suit customer's needs. Machine may be designed to handle material up to 12 feet (3.658m) in width or more. **(Courtesy of Indev, Inc., Pawtucket, Rhode Island)**

Figure 148. Combined equipment for 4-color screen printing and flocking allowing for contact pressure and angle of squeegee adjustment while loading and unloading is done manually. Equipment may be used for such garments as T-shirts. **(Courtesy of Kopal Industries, Inc., Seabrook, Texas)**

Chapter 24

SCREEN PRINTING ON PLASTICS

The endeavor for perfection and for creation of plastics materials by plastics manufacturers, engineers, chemists, and research laboratories has brought about developmental growth in the plastics industry which has a positive effect on the screen printing industry. Plastics are synthetic materials consisting of large molecular weight organic substances which are solid or semi-rigid in the finished state but at some stage in their manufacture may be formed into various shapes through the application of heat or heat and pressure. While originally plastics were considered substitute materials, today plastics are accepted as important industrial and structural materials and their use permeates many industries and processes. The screen printer who is reluctant to accept printing on plastics substrates must realize that it is no longer a question of printing on this material but how much effort should be put into this type of printing. It must be stressed that captive or in-house shops do very much printing and decorating on plastics materials.

The constant important developments in plastics make it imperative that the screen printer make objective choices in their use for printing and thermoforming. It is suggested that the printer, especially the beginner, maintain close contact with his suppliers and approach each subject on an individual basis so that practical preferences will emerge based on objective printing evaluation. Also, because of the constant emergence of new inks and substrates, the screen printer should pretest the ink and substrate for adhesion and other properties before doing a production run. Testing should be done where any doubt may exist, since a plastic material may vary even from batch to batch. Sometimes an ink manufacturer may even recommend that testing be done after print has been allowed to react with the substrate for about 24 hours.

Although today we generally consider plastics to be synthetic substances used industrially, plastics may be synthetic or natural materials. Casein, cold molden, lignin, and shellac are natural plastics. However, the word "plastics" in the modern sense is a commercial term describing a class of industrial materials whose use overlaps into many industries. Modern plastics are man-made materials produced from high molecular weight synthetic or natural substances which are capable of being shaped or flowing under heat and pressure into desired shape at some stage of their manufacture. In modern plastics we are concerned chiefly with materials that may not be found directly in nature but are manufactured from organic matter. Organic matter consists of materials that have hydrocarbons as part of their formulations and plastics are based on organic chemistry. Because there are many formulations and the average screen printer cannot ask for some "oxybenzylmethylene-glycolanhydride" from a supplier, plastics manufacturers have been forced to develop practical scientific nomenclature and trade names for plastics. It is necessary to deal with plastics generically to obtain the specific chemical formulation. For example, the term "Tyvek" represents the DuPont spun-bonded polyolefin derivative, "Lexan" is the General Electric polycarbonate derivative, "Plexiglas" is the Rohm and Haas methyl methacrylate, etc.

Despite the many trade-named plastics, they are normally classified into two general types: *thermoplastics* and *thermosetting.* Thermoplastics are substances which are capable of being repeatedly softened with application of heat or heat and pressure and are hardened by cooling. Generally, they undergo a physical change and not a chemical change. The thermoplastic material "Celluloid" (cellulose nitrate), the first American plastic, was developed by a young printer John Wesley Hyatt in 1869, who was looking for a substitute material for manufacturing billiard balls because of the shortage of ivory. A thermoplastic has an "elastic or plastic memory" which implies that it may be reheated repeatedly to a forming temperature as in thermoforming or vacuum forming, and will revert to its original flat condition when reheated to its forming temperature. Thermoforming is a process in which a thermoplastic sheet is heated and pulled down onto a mold surface forming a three-dimensional object. See Chapter 28. Thousands of items of thermoplastics such as polystyrene, polyethylene, polypropylene, and polyvinyl chloride (PVC) are formed into items such as containers and decorated by screen printing which must remain on the container throughout the expected life of the product.

Thermosetting plastics (see Figure 149) are materials that undergo a chemical reaction by the action of heat, catalysts, etc., producing a relatively infusible material, generally making the material impervious for further application of heat. Because thermosetting substances undergo more of a chemical change when made into a product, once they are hardened they cannot be softened again. Although the temperature at which the two classes of materials may be worked may be the same, yet heating a thermoplastic material will soften and melt it, while heating the thermosetting material above the working temperature may charr it. The thermosetting material was developed by Dr.

I. THERMOPLASTICS
1. Acrylonitrile Butadiene-Styrene (ABS)
2. Acetal
3. Acrylic
4. Fluoroplastics
5. Ionomer Resins
6. Phenylene Oxide
7. Polybutylene
8. Polycarbonate
9. Polyimide (Thermoplastic)
10. Polypropylene Oxide
11. Polystyrene
12. Polyurethane
13. Polyvinyl Chloride (PVC)
14. Sulfone polymer

II. THERMOSETTING RESINS
1. Alkyd
2. Allyl
3. Amino
4. Epoxy
5. Furan
6. Melamine
7. Phenolic
8. Polyester
9. Silicone
10. Urea
11. Urethane

III. CELLULOSICS
1. Acetate (Cellulose Acetate)
2. Butyrate (Cellulose Acetate Butyrate)
3. Propionate (Cellulose Propionate)
4. Ethyl (Ethyl Cellulose)
5. Nitrate (Cellulose Nitrate)

Figure 149. A list of some thermoplastic and some thermosetting plastics.

Leo Baekland of Yonkers, New York in 1909. Figure 149 lists some thermoplastic and thermosetting materials.

Plastics are manufactured by being molded, cast, calendered, extruded, or laminated to almost any specification and it is possible to print on any of these. These materials may be obtained in any size, shape, thickness, color (even simulated brilliant metallics) and property. Both thermosetting and thermoplastic substances can be screen printed. Most screening on flat surfaces is not patented and may be printed in similar fashion to general screen printing, employing general screen printing equipment. However, some screen printing on complex and cylindrical surfaces is proprietory (produced on equipment developed in captive or in in-plant shops).

There is no one universal plastic that possesses the best properties for all specific screen printing applications. Any plastic product which is to be decorated by screen printing should be designed with attention paid in advance to the processes involved in decorating. The printer should make decorating or printing on a plastic surface or product a part of the total standardized process. While screening today represents an obvious answer to decorating plastics, the difference in chemical and physical properties of the substrates and inks may lead to some confusion in the printing, if complete pre-testing and pre-planning are not done. Inks serve a labeling and decorative purpose and are designed to enhance a plastic product by providing contrasting colors, impact at point of sale and by providing a finish not possible with the substrate material by itself. Ink may also serve a more functional and protective purpose in which it may be used to cover defects or to protect a surface, as in circuit printing. Plastics and screen printing inks are chemical products and consideration must be given to the use of each. The manufacture of plastic screen printing inks, while technically advanced, has become a highly specialized and integral part of screen printing. The screen printer may print with an ink that is recommended for more than one type of plastic, or he may print with an ink that is formulated for a specific plastic. For example, a supplier may have an ink formulated for printing on Mylar (Du Pont polyester) which he may also recommend generally for printing on vinyl or on pyroxylin; or a styrene lacquer formulated for printing specifically on styrene which he may also recommend for printing on rigid vinyl, cellulose acetate butyrate, acrylics, and ABS (acrylonitrile butadiene-styrene) plastics. Here again, it is suggested that the printer pretest ink when using an ink not recommended specifically for the plastic. When in doubt, the screen printer should make sure that the ink meets such pretest requirements as adhesion, water and humidity resistance, acid resistance, stretch, salt and weather resistance. Also, reliable ink manufacturers generally suggest that a sample of the plastic material to be printed be forwarded to the manufacturer for testing before doing a production run. Ink and plastic manufacturers are interested in the correct use of their products. It is interesting to note that it took about 15 years for producers and suppliers of acrylic plastics to educate sign painters in the proper screen printing of this thermoplastic material. As is true in general screen printing, the end use of the product may govern the printing procedure and type of ink which may best be used for printing.

Where a new plastic is being printed, it is suggested that printing conditions be recorded, including type of plastic (trade name or chemical name and manufacturer), type of screen fabric and mesh, type of printing screen, whether off-contact or contact printing is used, viscosity of ink, toxicity, odor, drying rate and method of drying, color retention of ink, squeegee stroke and pressure, atmospheric conditions, etc. Such a record is especially useful for the novice for accumulation of objective information and for any possible reprint of job.

Since most plastics are non-absorbent, non-porous, smooth, and highly polished so that ink adhesion may be difficult, choosing the correct type of ink is important. The printer should have enough knowledge of the material being printed so that it will be easier to choose the correct ink. Ink must dry correctly, not cause curling of sheet, nor stick to one another when piled. Ink adhesion must be compatible with the specific plastic being printed. In many cases, adhesion is obtained by creating a chemical bond with the substrate and ink must remain on the product throughout the life of the product. Sometimes adhesion of a plastic surface may be impaired if there are mold release agents or silicone lubricants on the surface which have not been removed with correct cleaners or solvents. Although much information on screen printing may be obtained from the ink or plastic supplier, a simple compatibility test of product and ink can be made by immersing the printed product in the questionable solvent. However, the advantage of using a plastic material such as polyethylene may be that it is chemically inert and insoluble in most solvents at room temperature. It is the chemical inertness that makes ink formulation a difficult task. In the untreated state, polyethylene and polypropylene have a waxy surface to which printing ink may not adhere satisfactorily. Since about 1955, pretreatment of polyethylene has helped solve the problem of more permanent adhesion in screen printing. This may be done by oxidizing the surface by means of direct flame treating, by corona discharge (electronic bombardment), or by chemical treatment to produce molecular attraction between plastic and ink. While in general inks are formulated for printing on treated polyethylene, there are some inks which are recommended for printing on untreated polyethylene and polypropylene plastic substrates. However, a sample of untreated polyethylene or any questionable plastic material should be tested completely with the recommended ink before eliminating pretreatment or other recommendation.

Screen printing plastics ink is based on preparing a pigmented or dye colored solution of similar plastic or resin used in the manufacture of the plastic to be printed. For example, a practical ink for polyvinyl chloride (PVC) film should be based on a resin that is compatible and a PVC powder may be dispersed in a suitable vehicle. Pigments often are especially tailored for the specific type of plastic to be printed. The pigment is part of the film former or the portion that remains and colors the plastic. The ink on plastics may create a chemical bond and the final print should exhibit similar properties to wear conditions common to the plastic being printed. Often inks are specifically formulated for the particular type of plastic so that the ink penetrates into the plastic and becomes an integral part of the final material. For example, a rigid non-plasticized PVC may require a different type of ink than a soft or highly plasticized PVC.

Inks or coatings may be printed on the "first" or "second" surface of a plastic sheet. The first surface is the front surface on which a printed design is intended to be seen. The second surface is usually the back of a transparent or translucent sheet on which the design may be applied. The first or second surface may require different ink treatment to obtain necessary effects. For example, a non-glossy ink may be used on the second surface with gloss being produced by the front surface of the plastic itself. See Figure 150.

Most inks used for printing on thermosetting substrates are of the baking type, since the heat distortion point of thermosets is not very critical. Alkyd enamels, epoxy inks, and epoxy esters are printed on thermosets, and may adhere to the plastic by mechanical bond and may be dried by oxidation and/or polymerization. Lacquer type inks generally may be used on such thermoplastics as acrylics, PVC, polyvinyl butyrate, and on cellulose acetate, cellulose acetate butyrate, ethyl cellulose, and nitrocellulose plastics. The effect on thermoplastics may be more critical. For example, ink may craze styrene while it may not affect a phenolic part. Crazing consists of very fine cracks which may extend as a network under a surface or through a layer. Crazing may also be caused by incorrectly thermoforming or vacuum forming a thermoplastic material. Screen printing on plastics demands proper choice of plastic, ink, correct mesh in printing, perfect preparation of printing screen, and care in drying printed matter.

Generally, photographic printing screens or water-soluble hand cut film screens may be employed for printing on plastics. Direct, direct-indirect, and indirect printing screens may be used; these screens may be prepared on nylon polyester or stainless steel fabric. The mesh employed would be governed by the detail to be printed. For example, about 200 to 250 mesh per inch (78 to 98 mesh per cm) may be used for preparing screens for printing opaque colors, while about 300 to 350 mesh per inch (118 to 138 mesh per cm) may be used for preparing screens for printing transparent colors. A sharp squeegee may be employed using off-contact printing.

In summary, decoration by screen printing today is a common method which contributes to the total packaging of products. The quality obtained generally is excellent. The process is economical, has color versatility, may be used for long and short runs, and is practical for both small and large copy. Products may be printed by automatic

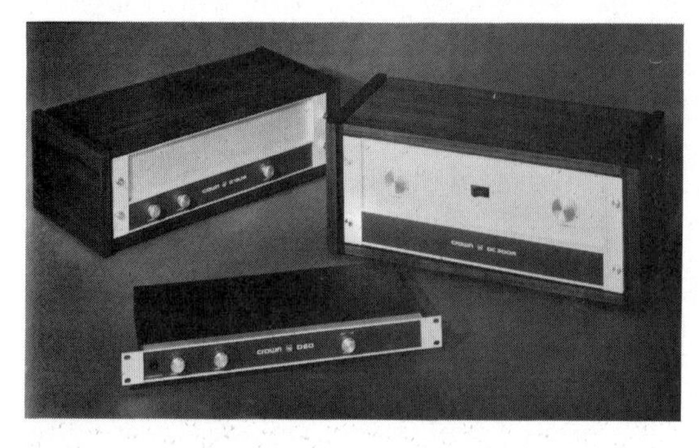

Figure 150. The faceplates on the audio electronic equipment were made from second surface or back surface decorated polycarbonate plastic. Printing on the back surface produces a more durable and attractive product. **(Courtesy of Crown International, Inc., and General Electric Company)**

means, semi-automatic, or produced manually. Since manufacturers normally do evaluate their own materials, they should be consulted concerning the use of a questionable ink on a substrate. Because essentially the process employs chemicals and different substrates, complete evaluation of a job must be a prerequisite of printing. Today's screen printer must realize that the future will bring positive change and that he must keep abreast of emerging conditions, materials, equipment, and technology which affect his process.

Chapter 25

SCREEN PRINTING ON TEXTILES WITH DYES

Although it is maintained that screen printing was done on textiles as far back as 1920 and that the felt pennant was historically the first object screen printed in this country, general screen printing on textiles developed more slowly. This type of printing really emerged as the chemistry of screen printing inks and dyes developed. Also, generally, printing on surfaces such as paper and cardboard was more lucrative and caused fewer printing problems. However, ultimately screen printing on textiles proved practical both in the general screen printing shop and in the specialized shop. Although T-shirts and the like were screen printed before the 1940's, the impact of screen printing on these items and other similar garments in the 1970's produced unusual growth in this phase of printing. While textile screen printing is more of a specialized field, the constant and emerging changes of color styles in printing, and the varied inks and formulae of color application have made possible this type of printing also in the general shop.

Dyeing and printing are two main methods of applying color to textiles. One differs from the other only in the method by which the ink, color, paste, or dye is applied. Generally, when being dyed, the fiber, yarn, or fabric is immersed and saturated with a solution of dyestuff or material used as dye. When a piece of cloth is dyed, it is given a new and permanent color by being impregnated with a dyestuff or coloring agent. In printing, the desired design is applied onto the cloth by the use of a colored ink or dye in paste form. "Textile printing" is the general term given to the process of applying designs and color patterns onto natural, synthetic fabrics, onto various mixtures of fabrics, or onto materials which are woven, knitted, felted, braided, knotted, crocheted, or bonded. Textile printing is employed to enhance the value of the material either practically or aesthetically and to eliminate the monotony of the original fabric.

Ordinarily, the method of printing depends upon the fiber or material being printed, upon the color, type of ink or dye being applied, and upon the purpose for which the fabric is to be employed. Printing on textiles is being done by various means: (1) by direct method from engraved rollers; (2) by hand blocking; (3) by means of ordinary stencil printing; (4) by discharge printing; (5) by means of direct screen printing on fabrics; and (6) by indirect or transfer type textile screen printing.*

Printing from rollers is the most common and the most employed method of textile printing. It is a machine method of printing color designs on fabrics at the rate of thousands of yards per hour. The roller is as long as the width of the cloth to be printed. The design to be printed is engraved on the rollers, generally in intaglio fashion so that the design is incised or cut below the surface of the roller, a separate roller being needed for each color of the design. The printing is done mechanically as the cloth passes over a series of these rollers, each roller revolving in a pan or vat of the dyestuff. After printing and drying, the printed cloth is passed over hot rollers, or steamed, or both, to set the color, and then washed and mangled to make the fabric ready for sale.

Hand blocking, the oldest method of printing on cloth, is a method in which the dyestuff is applied in paste form to a design carved on a wood, linoleum, rubber, or metal block. The block is then pressed down on the fabric by various means, imprinting the design in the required area and in the desired color. A different block must be employed for printing each color.

Stencil printing is another old method in which the stencil representing the required design is cut out in stencil paper, cardboard, wood, plastic sheet, or thin metal sheet and the dye is brushed or sprayed through the stencil onto cloth.

The principle of batik printing is similar to machine resist printing. The batik process involves painting out with a resist, or substance which will resist the dye, all those areas which are not to receive the dye; all those areas which are to be dyed are not covered with the resist. Resists are applied in design form either by hand or machine onto the cloth and the fabric is immersed in the prepared dye or passed through the dye. The dye covers only the parts that are not covered by the resist paste. After dyeing, the resist is removed with a prescribed solvent. Batik screen printing has been done by printing the resist onto cloth, using a transparent base that has been thinned out with a reducer. After printing or dipping the cloth in the dye, the cloth is dried and the resist may be removed with a solvent supplied by the manufacturer of the resist.

Discharge printing is a method in which the fabric is first dyed generally a darker solid color and then desired areas or parts of the color or dye are taken out or discharged from the cloth. Discharge printing may be done by machine or by hand. The design is the part

* The following book covers the general subject of screen printing on textiles more completely: Kosloff, Albert, *Textile/Garment Screen Printing*. ST Publications, Book Division, Cincinnati, Ohio.

that is usually discharged. Discharge printing is also being done successfully by employing screen printing as illustrated in Figure 151.

Although more printing of textiles is being done by the machine roller method than by any other method, there are times when it is essential that textiles be screen printed. Since the development of screen printing and especially since the introduction of direct fadeproof screen printing dyes in ink form at the end of World War II, hand blocking and plain stencil printing has given way almost completely to screen printing. The latter printing method stresses the general textile printing trend which is toward increased fastness and brightness of color and simplification of processing. Screen printing on textiles is done basically to apply particular and individualized designs on white and colored surfaces and not to dye the complete cloth in one color. This method, then, is both a printing and dyeing process; hence, the

Figure 151. Dress and novelty silk neckties decorated with varied colors by means of screen printing employing direct transparent and opaque dye inks. Numbers 1, 2 and 3 present ties in which discharge printing was used to print lighter colored designs onto darker backgrounds. Number 4 presents a tie which was printed with an opaque yellow dye ink onto a dark green fabric. **(Courtesy of Sherman Textiles, Inc., Chicago, Illinois)**

beginning printer must know not only about screen printing techniques, printing screens, inks, screen fabrics, etc., but also about the various properties of dyes he plans to use. Although the initial set-up cost for this process is much less than for other comparable commercial processes, the technical know-how is just as great, since it takes much experimentation with printing on different fabrics with dyes, inks, varied printing plates, solvents, and finishing techniques before one can guarantee the same results each time under the same conditions. Successful textile printing establishments spend a large portion of their income and time for research and experimentation.

Screen printing, however, offers certain distinctiveness, exclusiveness, and unusual color impact. There is no limit to the new design ideas and to the items that may be printed with this method. The following have been screen printed successfully for commercial and other purposes: varied towels, robes, tablecloths, table runners, scarves, luncheon sets, chair backs, place mats, bridge sets, decorative and novelty aprons, dress and novelty ties, teenage socks, nylon hosiery, overalls, coveralls, signs, felt souvenir banners, pictures on regular textiles and on washable window shades, T-shirts, bathing suits, shower curtains, drapes, sweaters, pillow slips, handkerchiefs, drawstring bags, murals, valances, smocks, shorts, slipcovers, phone book covers, beach bags, beach umbrellas, shopping bags, skirts, blouses, rugs, yard goods, napkins, printed-to-match fabrics with screen printed wallpaper, etc. Besides commercial printing, screen printing on textiles has definite educational, recreational, and physical therapy applications. Screen printing on textiles may be accomplished by either hand or machine methods or, according to design and scope of the project, a combination of both.

Besides the above advantages there are other advantages for employing this process for printing on textiles. Screen printing is generally better suited to print orders that call for variety, especially in smaller orders. There is no limit, however, to the number of colors which can be printed and the runs may vary from one item to thousands, from one yard to thousands. There is a heavier deposit of ink and more complete penetration of the ink into the cloth, thus eliminating *duplex* printing or printing and registering the dye on both sides of the fabric, as is often used in drapery fabric machine printing. The thickness of the ink coating may also be governed by using more than one stroke of the squeegee. It is less fatiguing and less expensive than other hand methods and gives sharper printed lines and detail where they are desired. It produces large area printing and detail printing with equal facility. With the perfection of the varied photographic printing plates or printing screens, fine detail can now be produced. It is an advantage, too, that screens may be saved and reused.

Material of any width and very large designs may be screen printed as compared to roller printing where material width is limited to the length of roller which the machine will accept. Length of repeating designs is governed by circumference of the roller which can be placed in the machine, but there is no such limitation in screen printing. The printed notation of "hand screen printed," "silk screened," or "hand printed" on the selvage or extreme outer edge of the cloth carries a definite sales appeal. Also, the printing on some textile objects may supplement the printing on other materials in the general screen printing shop. The screen printer may do quality work manually, semi-automatically, and may also produce quantity work with the available specialized textile screen printing machines and textile printing presses.

Generally, textile screen printing may be done by screen printing directly on the material, or it may be accomplished by an indirect method or transfer method by first printing the patterns on transfer paper and then transfer the printed patterns from the paper to the desired cloth material. This is done by employing varied heat transfer machines using heat and temperature in the transferring process.

Thus, we see that the versatility of screen printing produces a versatility of advantages. The progressive printer whether he prints on textiles or not, should be well informed about its potentialities. Textile printing is a definite phase of screen printing.

Textile Inks or Dyes

Dyestuffs for screen printing are essentially the same as other dyes used in textile printing. A dye is a chemical which is made to adhere to a textile fiber and which gives the fiber a definite color that is reasonably fast. By the fastness of a dye is meant its resistance to action under different conditions such as laundering, light, wear, weather, perspiration, ironing, etc. In textile printing, the dye combines with the cells or molecules of a fiber in such a way that the color cannot be removed without damaging the fiber.

There are varied types and classifications of dye inks, paste dyes, and paste assistants and compounds used by printers to print on textiles. The inks may be classified as to (1) method of application; (2) the properties exhibited such as crocking, fastness to light, etc.; (3) method of finishing the dye, that is, whether the ink is to be steamed or aged; (4) composition of ingredients; (5) opacity or transparency; (6) the effect that the ink produces: flat, flocked, or luminescent; (7) and whether the ink is meant for direct printing or for transfer printing on transfer paper. Although the exact classification is the chemical classification, from the dyer's viewpoint it is customary to divide the dyes into as few groups as possible based on methods which yield the maximum color value. However, practically and generally, textile inks used by screen printers come under three classifications: (1) the direct type of ink which does not require application of heat treatment and is used directly from the container; (2) the direct type which is used directly from the manufacturer's container but has to be given simple heat treatment after printing; and (3) the hundreds of various dyes or inks in paste form such as vat colors, stabilized azoic dyes, etc., which have to be processed more specifically and finished according to formula, to type of dye, and to specific directions of the manufacturer of the dye. All these inks and dyes are obtainable from screen printing suppliers and from dyestuff manufacturers and suppliers.

Regardless of the type of ink, the printing ink or printing paste employed or recommended for screen printing should be free flowing. It should not dry in the printing screen, should not clog the design area of the screen, should not freeze, and should not settle out on standing. The ink should dye the fabric in the desired restricted area, forming the required colored pattern. The dye inks used should produce the same results after final processing as dyes do in actual dyeing. Also, the ink should be easily cleaned off the screen with standard solvents. Print pastes prepared from dyes should have stability also in long storage. The inks should be printed with standard available printing screens. Generally, the dye inks used in printing have kept pace with dyes used in dyeing.

The first class, that which is used directly from the container and does not need heat treatment, includes lacquers, resinous inks, and luminescent inks. The first two have been employed for printing on textiles for quite some time. They are satisfactory for many jobs but they will not withstand indefinite laundering and dry-cleaning and do have certain "hand" or stiffening of the fabric. These types of inks have been used in printing on felt, sign cloth, daylight luminescent cloth, denim novelty printing such as children's overalls and coveralls, T-shirts, window shade material, and other such materials. The resinous inks may be used also as a base on cloth for flocking. These inks have good adhesion, dry quickly, and generally do not require heat, except perhaps in the hastening of the drying process immediately after printing. They are quite non-crocking, that is, the ink or dye will not rub off a fabric when the fabric is exposed to friction or wear. An ink that penetrates to the center of the fiber in textile printing generally will better resist this rubbing or crocking.

There are textile lacquers which are suitable for white and light colored fabric and are soft and flexible; there are opaque lacquers which are formulated for darker materials and are stiff and heavily pigmented. Both may be used directly from the container and may be cleaned off the screen with a standard solvent obtainable from screen printing suppliers. In this first group may be included too, the daylight luminescent colors which are suitable for novelty printing on ordinary textiles and also for printing contrasting colors on luminescent dyed cloth.

Almost any type of printing screen may be employed for printing the inks in the first class. Where the printer is in doubt about an ink's effect on a screen, a pre-test run should be made to test all printing, drying, fastness of ink, and other related properties. Also, of course, the screen should be tested for its ink resistance.

In all cases where the printing must be varied from the normal, regardless of the type of ink, directions of the manufacturer must be followed accurately, since printing with textile inks and dyes is a chemical process once the dye or ink is applied on the fiber.

The second class of textile inks, that which requires simple heat-setting or heat-curing came into use after World War II, about 1947. It has opened up new fields for the screen printer and has added to the versatility of screen printing. This type of ink enables the average printer to print on textile materials satisfactorily, using normal screen printing equipment. It is resistant to fading, washing, and is generally fast and alkali proof. There is very little "hand" or stiffening of the fabric after printing, which usually disappears after the first washing. However, if the printer does not wash the material after printing, it is suggested that he notify the consumer by means of a label or in some other fashion that this "hand" effect will be eliminated after the first washing. Most of the inks in this class consist of a pigment dye which is dispersed to a very high degree in a suitable vehicle which has high drying characteristics.

This class of inks may be employed for printing on most textiles and also on surfaces other than textiles especially those which have a tendency to absorb large amounts of ink. The writer has found this type of ink practical for such surfaces as calcimine and for coloring and staining wood. The colors are transparent and may be made more transparent. Different colors of the same manufacturer's inks may be mixed together to form varying shades and pastels. This should be done, however, according to manufacturer's directions or according to results obtained from complete experimentation.

The inks may be employed for single or multi-color printing. It is also possible to print one color ink over another to produce a third color. The inks are procured in proper consistency for printing. Some are simply mixed by the printer by mixing a concentrated color with a clear base or clear extender base which serves as the vehicle and prepares the color for squeegee consistency.

The inks must air-dry after printing for about one-half hour or more, or for the time recommended by the manufacturer, to evaporate the volatile parts before heat-setting the ink and fabric. The setting of the color is a simple process but should be done throughly and throughout, since the color must impregnate the fiber completely.

The curing, heat cycle, or heat setting of the color makes the printed ink more brilliant and resistant to washing, fading crocking, etc. The heat cycle may vary from about 30 seconds to about 5 minutes, depending upon the type of ink being printed, upon the thickness of the fabric being printed, upon the type of fabric, and the type of heat used. The heat source may be that obtained from a convection type oven, infra-red heat, a hot flat pressing iron, or a steam clothes pressing machine. Although there is some variation with regard to the different inks, the temperature for curing or heat-setting the printed material ranges from about 250 to 375 degrees Fahrenheit (121 to 190 degrees Celsius). For example, when one prints on synthetic fabrics such as rayon, the temperature must be in the lower range and held for a slightly longer heat-setting period. Here again, the recommendation of the ink manufacturer or the results of experimentation will determine which type of heat is most practical and which range of temperature is best. Where many small-piece textiles such as T-shirts, towels, or napkins are being printed, infra-red lamps placed over a conveyor have proved practical; however, the material must be in constant motion under the lamps so that the lamps do not scorch the material. Conveyors are generally designed so that the heat source is shut off automatically when conveyor belt stops moving. This prevents printed material from being overheated, scorched, or charred, especially if infra-red lamps are used to heat-cure. A steam clothes pressing machine is also practical for heat-curing. Regardless of heat source, if much printing is done, adequate ventilation must be provided for quick removal of fumes.

Some time ago, as an experiment, the author printed a monogram on kitchen towels which were set by dampening the towel and applying heat from a medium hot pressing iron for 4 minutes. This particular towel, which was an experimental job trying out a new textile ink, has been washed at least 150 times, in all types of laundry soaps and detergents. Figure 153 presents a T-shirt printed with textile inks. The T-shirt was printed with three different colors and the colors were made fast by infra-red heat application.

Where there is a sizing or filler in a fabric, it is suggested that the fabric be washed first, since sizing may absorb the color and most of the color may disappear after the first washing. Final printing should be done only after a complete test has been finished, including printing,

Figure 152. A cotton T-shirt printed with yellow, red, and black textile screen printing inks which require simple heat treatment. **(Courtesy of David A. Frindell Signs, Milwaukee, Wisconsin)**

printing plates, application of heat and washing material first where necessary.

Since the 1970's *water-soluble* or water-base textile inks have had great impact; these may also be used on surfaces other than textiles. These inks are water-soluble, lead free, have no unpleasant odor, are formulated to have the appearance and handling properties of solvent-based ink and are not flammable; they are safe enough to use for teaching purposes in schools. Unlike the older oil-and-water system inks, the newer water inks contain no petroleum-based solvent.

The inks are available for printing on such garments and materials as T-shirts, dresses, drapery material, cotton, rayon, fiberglass, polyester, synthetics, etc. The inks are obtainable in varied transparent colors, opaque, and fluorescent colors. They are thermosetting types and generally consist of a binder, resin and pigment dyestuff, and are designed for printing on fabrics which ordinarily have not been sized or finished to prevent the color from adhering to the fiber.

The transparent water-soluble inks may be printed wet-on-wet to produce multi-color prints. The inks are available in ready-to-use form and also in a form that may be mixed with an extender. Using the extender correctly produces shades of colors, obtains lighter shades, and if necessary, water may be employed to thin the ink. The opaque type ink is formulated for printing on dark colored fabrics such as cotton, polyester, and blends of cotton and polyester. Curing the inks is similar to curing petroleum-based ink. If not cured, the ink may also be air-dried to produce a fast print. However, the printed fabric should be heat-cured for about 2 minutes at 300 to 325 degrees Fahrenheit (148 to 163 degrees Celsius) to produce fastness of color and resistance to washing and dry cleaning.

Inks of the second class which require heat curing may also be printed through regular printing screens such as knife-cut film, photographic, washout or tusche and glue, tusche and enamel printing screens, and blockout screens. The inks may be washed off with regular mineral spirit type of solvent or a solvent recommended by the supplier. The use of these inks does not require a knowledge of chemistry.

Plastisols, rubber type, or stretch inks are interesting applications of inks that are heat-cured. These inks are designed for direct printing on dark and light knitted and woven fabric for producing an embossed, highly elastic type of coating. They may also be printed on transfer paper and transferred with the aid of heat and pressure to fabric.

After the inks are printed and heat-cured, they become inseparable from the fabric and remain flexible. They may be printed on cotton, linen, denim, wool, felt, and most open mesh fabrics that are subject to stretch. They are widely used for athletic wear such as sweat shirts and jerseys were opacity, flexibility, and washability are required. However, because they are thermoplastic and are softened by heat, the printed material should not be washed in hot water nor should it be dry-cleaned. Lukewarm water is recommended for washing. The inks are practical textile adhesives for flocking and for printing flocked designs on the above type of textiles.

Plastisols do not air-dry but have to be heat-cured. Most manufacturers recommend curing time of three minutes at about 300 degrees Fahrenheit (149 degrees Celsius); shorter periods may be used if temperature is higher. A coarse printing screen is generally used (about 2XX to 8XX) and any screen that is resistant to lacquers may be employed. It is suggested that the screen printer pre-test this textile ink under his shop conditions before printing large volume commercial jobs.

Plastisol inks may be used for printing directly on material or for printing single and multi-color designs on transfer release papers for transfer as iron-on decals onto fabrics. When printing on release paper, the prints should be cured for about 1½ to 2 minutes at 225°F to 250°F (107°C to 120°C). Lower temperature and less curing time is used for heat-curing transfer paper, since printing on the release paper is temporary. The transfer is transferred to fabric by placing paper, ink side down, and then heating transfer in a heat-transfer machine for about 10 to 15 seconds at about 375 degrees Fahrenheit (191C). While there are varied heat transfer machines, Figures 153 and 154 present two types that the beginner and advanced printer may use. The release paper should cool before releasing paper from fabric. If a heat-transfer machine is not available, the transfer may be made with a warm pressing iron. However, the heat and timing may be more difficult to control.

While plastisols may be printed directly on textile materials and also on transfer paper, *sublimation* dye printing may be done only on transfer paper. This printing may be done manually, semiautomatically and automatically. Although the principle of sublimation dyes

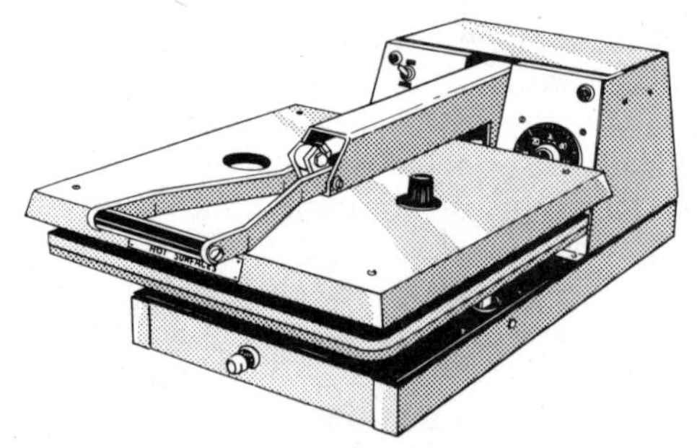

Figure 153. A simple illustration of the Roach Semi-Automatic heat transfer press for application of heat transfers to garments. The press has an automatic timer that opens the platen upon which garment is placed for application of transfer; the press has a 15″ x 15″ (37 x 37cm) platen with a coating pad that is impervious to heat, pressure, or soiling; unit has a manually adjusted pressure control through knob on the front of the machine. Simple directions for its use are available for the beginner. **(Courtesy of Roach, Division of Perma-Trans Products, Columbus, Ohio)**

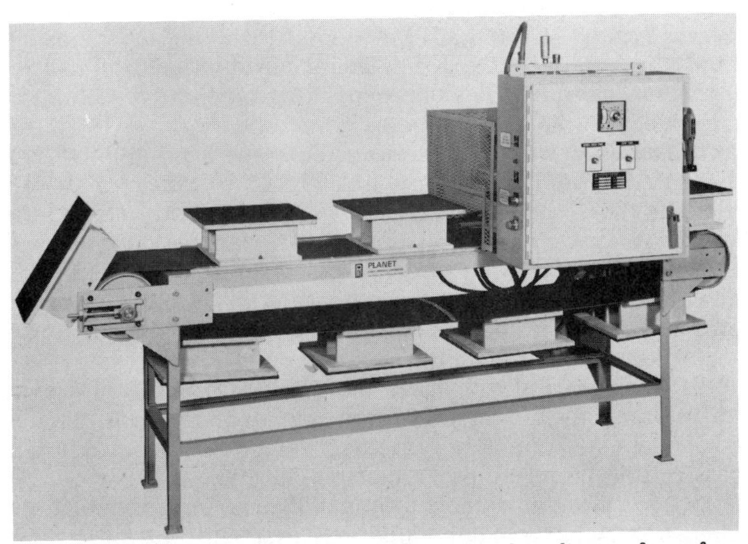

Figure 154. An Auto-Transfer Automatic High-Speed Applicator of transfers to T-shirts, garments, novelties, canvas bags, and the like. Item and transfer are placed and located on elevated pallet, as item moves on conveyor, heat, and pressure are applied and item is allowed drop on to inclined cooling conveyor (not shown). Unit produces up to 12 items per minute. **(Courtesy of Planet Products Corporation, Cincinnati, Ohio)**

or vapor phase process was known in the 1920's, this type of heat transfer printing did not become a reality until 1968, when it was introduced by Sublistatic, SA, a Swiss firm. The desired designs are first printed by gravure, screen printing, flexography, or screen printing and lithography on a special transfer paper. The dry designs are then transferred to the textile material with the aid of correct heat and pressure and the dye prints remain permanently on the fabric.

The word "sublime" refers to a disperse type dye which transforms directly from a solid phase to a gas without passing through the liquid state. The dye or inks sublime or vaporize and transfer directly to the textile. The dye ink is printed in reverse on the transfer paper so that when it is transferred the design will appear right side up.

The sublimation printing process generally requires (1) a special dye or ink, (2) a transfer release paper on which the original design may be screen printed, (3) a heat transfer machine for transferring pattern from paper to the fabric, and (4) the correct type of fabric onto which the design is to be transferred. While polyester and blends of polyester and cotton accept transfer images best, nylon and acrylic material may be used. However, the screen printer should always test the material onto which the transferring is to be done. The transferring may be accomplished manually or automatically on a simple flat bed heat transfer machine, automatic heat machine, or rotary transfer machine. See Figures 153 and 154. Most heat curing on machines is done in about 15 to 30 seconds dwell time from about 370 to 480 degrees Fahrenheit (188 to 249 Celsius), depending on the dye color and the cloth to which transferring is being done.

Sublimation or vapor phase transfers have been applied on many items varying from T-shirts to upholstery and drapery material. The process has grown because it prints solid areas and detailed designs including four-color halftones. Printing on transfer paper has better dimensional stability than printing on knitted material. Also, it is more practical to store than printed costly material. Sublistatic printing is also known as dry printing, since there are no after-finishing processes. In most textile or conventional dye printing it is necessary to print, dye, steam, wash, and dry again the printed material. However, the screen printer may obtain help from manufacturers and should test material completely including the transfer of the printed design and fastness of print before doing a commercial job.

The third type of screen printing inks in the form of powders, dye pastes, and paste compounds and assistants to aid in printing, include fast dyes such as vat dyes, acid, basic, aniline dyes, dispersed dyes, pigments, etc. These inks which are partially or completely prepared or mixed by the screen printer or dyeing plant, require experimentation, a knowledge of chemistry or a desire to learn, a cognizance of printing techniques, and a knowledge of heat-curing or ageing methods. The specialist shop and larger printing establishments have a chemist do the mixing of colors and ingredients. The preparation of dyes for screen printing is more of a science than an art. With the scientific development and mixing of coal tar dyes, the mysterious formula secrets of the color mixer, like the past secret techniques of screen printing itself, are gradually disappearing. Although ordinarily the printer will mix ingredients, it is suggested that the making of dyes be left to the dye industry.

A dye ink not only has color but must fix that color under proper conditions onto or in the desired fiber. Textile colors or dyes are chiefly organic compounds and today most of them are man-made or synthetic. From ancient times up to about 1856, all dyestuffs were of natural origin, such as indigo, cochineal, and woad. However, when William Henry Perkins, an English chemist, accidently succeeded in making the first coal tar dye (mauve) in 1856 when he was trying to make quinine from a coal tar derivative known as aniline, the practical start of the first modern synthetic dye occurred. Since then, various classes and hundreds of dyes have been developed in this country and abroad.

A common way of classifying dyes is according to the way the dye is applied to the cloth. Dyes are also classified as *direct* dyes, *mordant* dyes, *acid, basic,* and *vat* dyes.

Direct dyes or inks are those that dye the fiber without the aid of a fixing agent or mordant. The word "mordant" comes from the

Latin "mordere" meaning to bite. Mordant dyes require an agent known as a mordant to bite into the fiber; they are not direct dyes. The final insoluble color is the chemical result of the combination of the mordant, dyestuff, fiber, and treatment. Logwood, tartaric, and tannic acid, or salts of tin, iron, or other metals, and basic iron sulphate are mordants. Acid dyes are direct dyes and are applied in an acid bath or in certain acid dye-liquid solutions. Basic dyes are so called because chemically they are generally an acid salt of a color base. These are but simple definitions of products which would require voluminous treatment.

Vat dyes get their names from the fact that originally, in the making of the old indigo dyes (one of the first natural vat dyes), the dyestuff had to steep or ferment for some days in a large vessel, cistern, tub, or vat before it could be used. Vat dyes are superior fast dyes which are generally resistant to light, washing, acids, alkalis, and bleaching. While the dye is in the process of application or printing, it is reduced to a soluble form. After printing, the printed material is given a treatment or an oxidizing bath to bring out the color so that it is insoluble or in resistant form.

There is encouragement for the beginning textile printer. Although some printers guard the specific formulae which they individually developed and guard specific techniques of application of design, dye formulas are becoming more standardized and manufacturers of dye inks invite requests for technical assistance from printers genuinely interested in textile printing. Most manufacturers of dyes have studied their colors carefully and have attempted to devise the simplest and safest method for their application.

There are various dyes available today in the United States for printing on any material including plastics textiles and mixtures of weaves of various fibers. Since the composition of the print paste is an important factor, reliable dyestuff manufacturers sell their products with suggested directions for mixing various formulae (generally 100 or 1000 parts equaling 100 per cent of the formula). For example, a 15 per cent standard vat printing paste would contain 15 parts of a vat color paste and 85 parts of vat thickener or thickening agent. The thickening agent may consist of correct proportions of wheat starch, British gum, potassium carbonate, glycerine, and an additive. For best results the printer must follow the manufacturer's directions and suggested conditions under which the color is to be prepared, proportions of ingredients to be mixed, order in which the ingredients are to be added, treatment of goods before printing, treatment of goods after printing, fixation time and temperature for color, and other data.

Dye inks generally consist of a color or color paste and thickening agent. The thickening agent is employed in screen printing as a vehicle in which the color is carried to aid in squeegeeing the dye onto the textile and to prevent the color from spreading so that sharp detailed penetrating printing is obtained. Thickening agents may consist of such

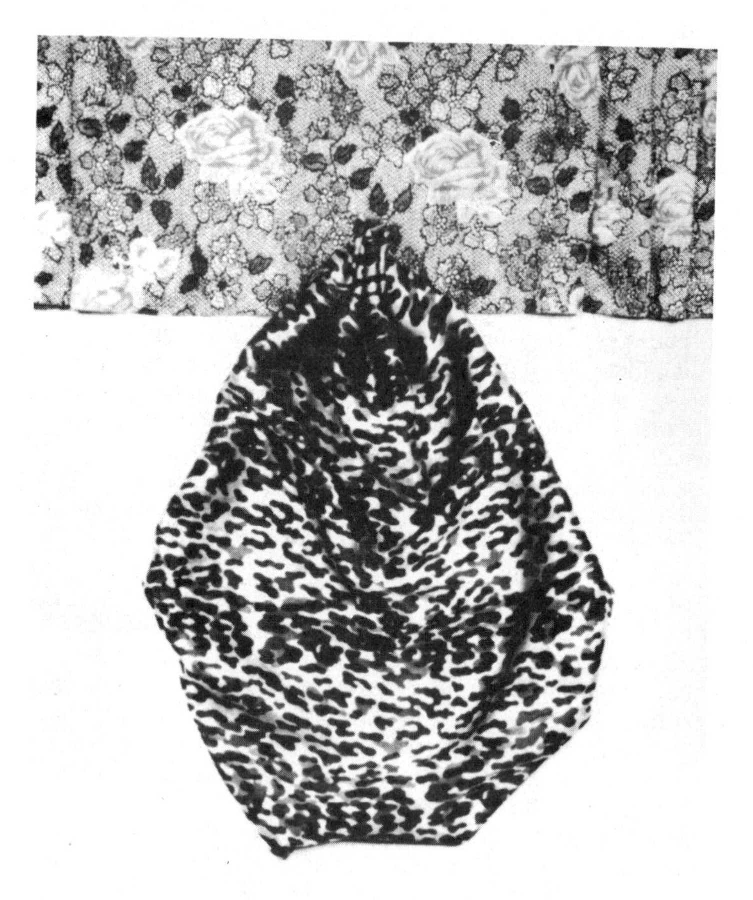

Figure 155. Two samples of silk satin yard goods, each screen printed with four different colors of vat dyes and heat-set with steam in a steam chamber. During the printing operation, the bolt of material was stretched and attached to printing table longer and wider in size than the bolt. **(Courtesy of Sherman Textiles, Inc., Chicago, Illinois)**

substances as gum tragacanth, locust bean, wheat starch, arabic gum, British gum or a combination of these. Some printing dyes consist of a thickening agent, mordant, and color. Where special additives are employed, their use must be based on directions of the manufacturer, on the type of cloth being printed, on type of heat-curing, or on results of definite experimentation. Additives may interfere with the use of printing pastes for dyeing and, therefore, complete investigation in their use is essential. The screen printer who intends to specialize in this phase of printing must keep an accurate record of the standard and also peculiar results obtained during experimental printing. The printer to a certain extent, must control each step of the printing. Textile printing is a challenging type of printing.

Figure 155 presents screen printed yard goods printed with screen printing dyes.

Equipment for Screen Printing on Textiles

Dyeing of textiles is generally accomplished in two ways—by moving or passing the material through the dyestuff or dyeliquor or by circulating the dyeliquor through the stationary textile material. In screen printing on textiles, the printing screen which contains the dye, ink, or printing paste may be carried manually or moved mechanically to the desired spot when dyeing or printing the ink as illustrated in Figures 156 and 157. Also, the fabric being printed may be either stationary or in motion regardless of the movement of the printing plate or printing screen.

There are three general units employed for screen printing on textiles: (1) the ordinary printing screen attached to a base or table which can print on such small items as felt and other textiles, pennants, T-shirts, scarves, and the like; (2) the printing units shown in Figures 157 and 158 which afford a means of producing varied types of colorful and large repeat patterns in single color and multi-color on different bolt material or yard goods; and (3) the printing machine which is developed by the textile specialist, often at a great expense, to answer a specialized need.

The ordinary printing screen is familiar to the average printer. The main precaution in its use is to employ a printing plate or printing screen that will resist the dye ink and not be dissolved during the printing process. This type of printing unit is generally employed for experimental printing, especially in trying out new screen printing inks or paste dyes and in experimenting with new resists or block-out materials for printing screens.

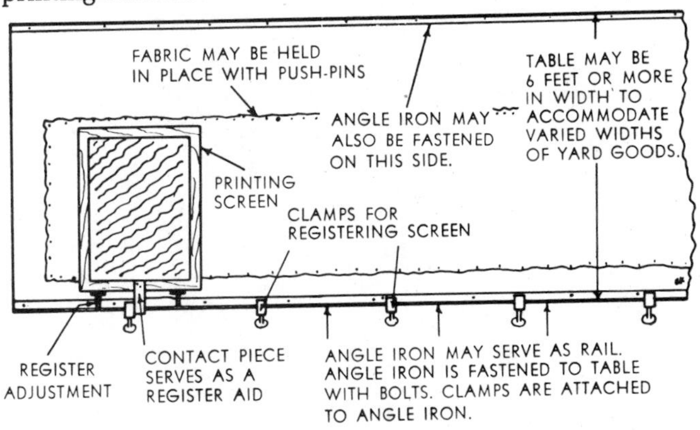

Figure 156. Top view of a table for hand printing and registering varied colors on textiles.

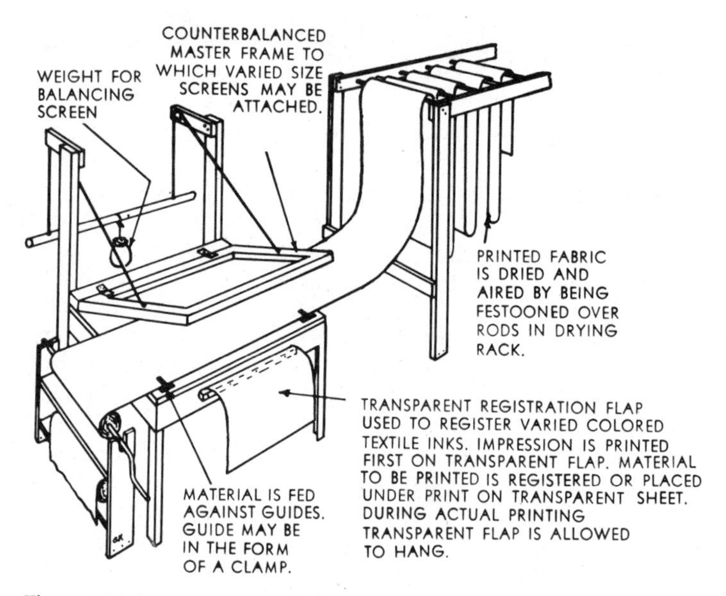

Figure 157. A master screen hand printing unit for registering and printing varied colors on textiles.

The unit consisting of the long smooth textile printing table shown in Figure 156 is used by textile printers in the United States and abroad. The length of this table may vary from about 75 to 300 feet (22.88 to 91.5m), depending on the length of the average bolt of material printed in the shop. Its height is about 30 to 33 inches (76.2 to 83.8cm) and the width depends upon thé width of the material being printed or upon the size of the average printing screen used. For example, if a

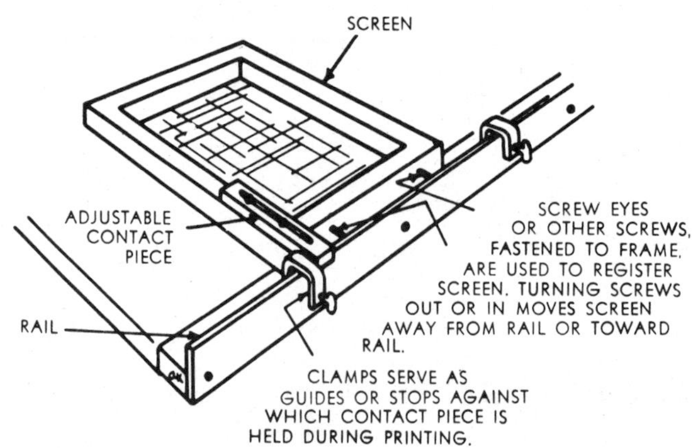

Figure 158. Method of registering screen for printing each color of a repeat pattern in hand textile printing on a table unit.

36-inch wide (91.4cm) fabric is to be printed, then the screen should be about 44 to 46 inches (111.76 to 116.8cm) long and the table should be about 6 inches (15.2cm) wider than the length of the screen. If the average material is wider, then the table should be wider in proportion. The top of the table should be level and may be made of boards, plywood, or any smooth, good quality pressed board.

The textile to be printed is fastened to the printing table in various ways. The older method, which is still used, is to employ a table covered with a padding consisting of a soft wool felt that is about 3/16" (.48cm) thick. The felt is covered with a top layer of oil cloth or a plastic sheet material such as koroseal or polyethylene. Prior to printing, the top layer is covered with an inexpensive cotton material or "back grey" which is used to absorb the excess dye that may go through the fabric being printed. The term "back grey" comes from the machine roller textile printing and refers to a cloth that is placed next to the textile being printed for absorbing excess color that penetrates the textile. The whole padding should be stretched in such a way that a smooth, taut surface is produced.

To insure that the yard goods does not move under the action of the squeegee, the material is fastened to the table in semi-permanent fashion either with pins or with an adhesive that does not affect the dyeing process. Although pinning is still being used, the adhesives or pasting method is being employed more and more. The latter method makes registration of colors easier in printing, since the cloth is held more fixed and prevents shrinkage of cloth during printing. However, either method will work if used carefully. The pinning of the fabric to the top of the layer on the table must be done carefully and the printer must be cautious not to place the screen on top of the pins during printing, as this may damage the printing screen.

In the adhesive, wax, gum, or paste method, the adhesive or wax applied to the smooth table top serves as the adhering agent for holding the cloth down during printing. The most practical wax or gum to use is one that will hold the cloth to the table and yet not be picked up by the fabric, since this may present difficulties in washing the material after it is finally processed. Gum arabic and dextrine paste have been used for this purpose, although the dyestuff manufacturer may recommend the adhesive to be used. The adhesive is applied to the table with a special jig or device which melts the gum or wax during application. The wax coating may be cleaned off the table by rubbing with a cloth that is saturated with water and a detergent or with a solvent. There are mechanical devices which both remove the old adhesive and apply the new adhesive for the next job to be produced. However, loosely woven material is not practical for adhesive application since the paste or ink would be excessively deposited onto the wax and thus may spoil the cloth.

The printing of repeat patterns or designs on the long table is done generally by one or more operators. Where the fabrics are not wide, one operator may work on one side of the table. Where wider fabrics and patterns are being printed, two operators may be required, one on each side of the table. In order to insure that the design is printed in the exact desired spot on the material, the screen is registered as illustrated in Figures 156 and 158. When the operator is printing on the long table, the screen is lifted and carried to the next stop or guide, or the screen may be moved semi-automatically on two rails over the cloth. The printer may print one design in one color, printing the odd numbered stops first. Another, or the same operator printing with a second color, may print the even numbered stops. By the time the operators reach the end of the table, the ink will have set enough so that there will be no chance of the ink's being offset or smeared by the screen in the next color printing. The first operator may then print the even numbered stops and the second printer may print the odd-numbered stops with his color.

The textile printing unit illustrated in Figure 157 has the advantages that it requires less area, does away with long tables, requires less material for its construction, and offers the printer a method of printing and registering more than one color on irregularly shaped or flexible material. The writer has adapted the transparent registration flap to this unit in order to do multi-color printing. It is a practical unit for printing detail that is not too fine. It has the advantage of allowing the printed material to pass over the rods of the drying unit or "festooner" so that the side of the material that is not printed is pulled over the rods of the unit, thus eliminating "mark-off" or offsetting when the fabric is being aired and dried. This printing unit may also be used for printing wallpaper, vinylite, oilcloth, window shade material, and on any other material in roll or bolt form. After the printed material has been aired and dried enough to allow the volatile substances to evaporate, the fabric may be made ready for the aging or steaming process, if this is necessary. The material may also be dried by heating the room, using banks of infra-red lamps which are placed over a conveyor on which the cloth moves, or heating the printing table (for example, with electric blankets).

Figure 159 presents a manually operated screen printing unit used by printers in the United States and Canada to print more than one color, printing one color immediately after the other. The writer has added a transparent registration flap to the unit to allow for more perfect registration, should this be necessary. Although the unit shows room for three screens or colors, if transparent ink is used and overlapped in printing, more than three colors may be obtained on the final printed item. This printing table may be used to print textile dyes and other inks, on textiles, wood, porous material, etc. The unit prints colors, one after another, without stopping for each color to dry completely and without stopping to rack the object after each impression.

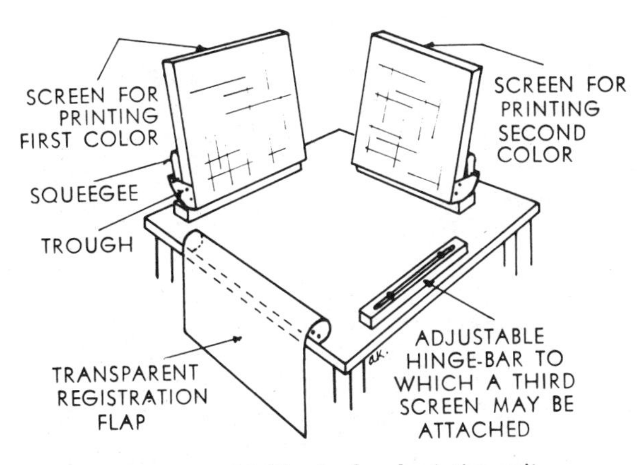

Figure 159. Multi-color hand printing unit.

After the desired colors have been printed, the printed object may then be racked to allow complete drying or air drying, as in the case of textile printing.

This space saving unit may be constructed on one table and built to suit the particular shop or situation. After printing the extra required colors, the extra screens may be removed from the base and the table used for one screen printing. The screens may be attached to a hinge-bar, as illustrated, or they may be fastened directly to the base. It is suggested that the printer attach a wooden prop bar or leg to the frame to keep the screen in a raised position when necessary. The trough for each of the screens may be made of tin, aluminum, plastics, or cardboard. It may be attached to the frame with screws or tape. Each squeegee should have nails driven in the ends of its handle so that each nail on each end of the squeegee extends past the wall of the trough and prevents the squeegee from falling into the ink when the squeegee is in the trough.

Although this printing set-up is planned more for printing large area designs lacking detail, the transparent registration flap will aid to register detail and more complex designs. The flap is used in similar fashion to the one illustrated in the master screen hand printed unit illustrated in Figure 157. The flap may serve as a guide in registering such flexible items as ties, scarves, towels, terrycloth apparel, and to print a color that may be difficult to register in a desired area on material.

There are also commercial semi-automatic textile printers similar to that shown in Figure 159. These will print accurately up to seven colors, print on all types of fabric and weights, and after initial setup, garment will automatically register in proper printing position.

As far as printing machines are concerned, printers have used and developed machines to answer individual needs. Where the textile material is an object such as a stocking or sport shirt, it is possible to stretch the object over a rigid form in order to make register of colors possible in multicolor printing. These may be printed by using regular screen printing presses or by employing semi-automatic methods. However, in some progressive shops, both in the United States and abroad, machines or printing jigs have been developed which operate on the principle of having the material that is being printed move on a conveyor toward the printing screen. The textile material is attached to, or combined with, a rubber or another type of sheet which moves toward the printing screen or printing screens on the conveyor unit. The combination of the textile and rubber sheet does away with the flexibility of the cloth, makes registration of colors simpler, and allows for variations in printing the material. (See Figures 160 and 161).

One mechanical unit offers the printer an arrangement having one or more screens placed next to the other. This unit may also be used with semi-automatic squeegees now available. The printing may be done by one or two operators, each operator handling one or two screens, or one operator printing on one screen. Another mechanical arrangement that has been employed, consists of having the printing screens placed vertically, one above the other, each screen being moved out of the way after the impression is made. Other textile printing machines may use the principle of the round or cylindrical printing screen over which the textile material moves speedily in similar fashion to printing done on a web press.

Figure 160. Precision "Midas" textile printer, an automated screen printing machine, will print 36" (91.4cm) repeat patterns at 800 to 900 yards (720 to 819m) per hour up to 120" (304.8cm) panel prints at 1800 yards (1638m) per hour. **(Courtesy of Precision Screen Machines, Inc., Hawthorne, N.J.)**

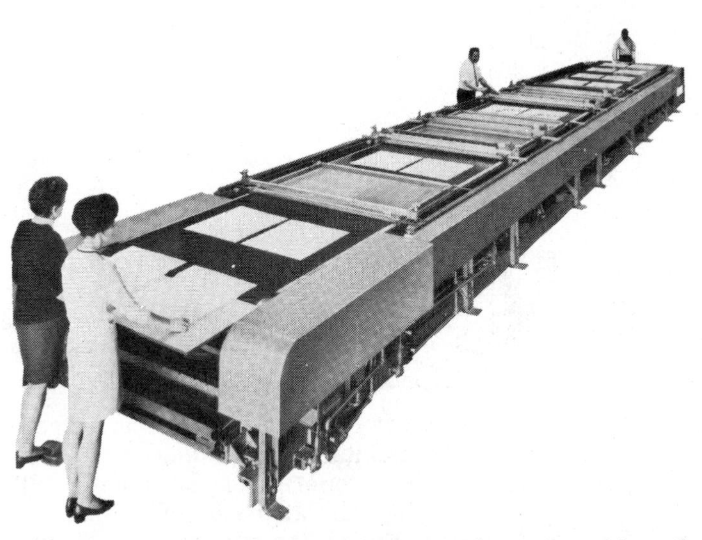

Figure 161. The Caravelle Fabric Printer, a custom designed textile screen printing machine for speedy and efficient printing of dyestuffs and pigments on cut pieces of every type, size, and shape. Four to eight screens may be set up and registered quickly and machine has a spot gumming system for positioning adhesive under garment and holding garment in register during the printing. **(Courtesy of Precision Screen Machines, Inc., Hawthorne, N.J.)**

Regardless of the printing unit employed, the processes following the printing vary, depending upon the material being printed and the type of dye ink being used. Where lacquers are printed on textile materials, then just airing and drying are sufficient. Some printed textiles are dried and then steamed or dried and exposed to infra-red heat, some are aged or steamed without pressure, while other materials are steamed under pressure. The recommendations of the manufacturer of the printing dye or paste must be followed in the post-printing processes. Where post-printing or after-printing processes are recommended, they are necessary to make the color fast, more brilliant, non-crocking, and resistant. Generally, the print must be dried, steamed, and washed.

Aging (ageing) or steaming is a process which enables dyeing to take place by placing the printed goods in a warm atmosphere or in an atmosphere of steam which provides the heat and moisture needed for the dyestuff to be absorbed by the fibers. Aging is a very important operation in screen printing on textiles. Although there are other types of steamers, the tower or vertical ager of the type shown in Figure 162 is being used. The vertical ager consists of a vertical shaft, the height of which is about 40 feet (12.2m), but may vary depending upon the yardage of cloth that is to be aged. As illustrated in Figure 162, the ager has single rollers at the top and entrance and exit slots through

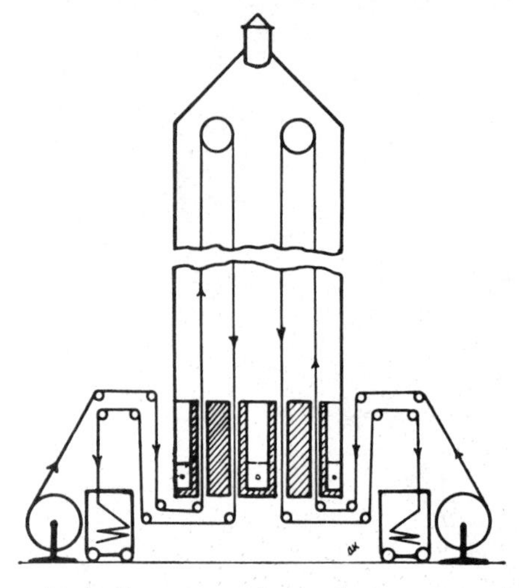

Figure 162. A tower or vertical ager. **(Courtesy of Ciba Company, Inc., New York, N.Y.)**

which the printed goods pass at the bottom. There are also heating coils and a steam supply for maintaining an atmosphere of steam in the vertical ager. The printed material which is wound on the one roller enters through one of the slots at the bottom, goes to the top over the roller and goes out through the exit slot. At all times, the back of the printed cloth is in contact with the roller and the front or printed side does not touch anything so that there is no danger of mark-off or offsetting. This is especially safe and desirable for screen prints where a heavy deposit of ink is used. The speed of travel of the goods is dependent on the length of time that the cloth is to be in the ager. If the top roller is 35 feet (10.67m) from the bottom of the ager, the ager will contain 140 feet (42.7m) of fabric at one time. This ager is suitable for the heat-curing or steaming of most types of colors.

The time of exposing the cloth in the steam atmosphere may vary from about 5 minutes to 1 hour or up; the pressure may range from no pressure at all to about 5 pounds.

After steaming, the prints are rinsed in water or in a solution specified by the dye manufacturer and dried. Each of the last steps such as rinsing, extracting, and drying is part of the complete process and must be done according to tested procedures or based on manufacturer's specifications.

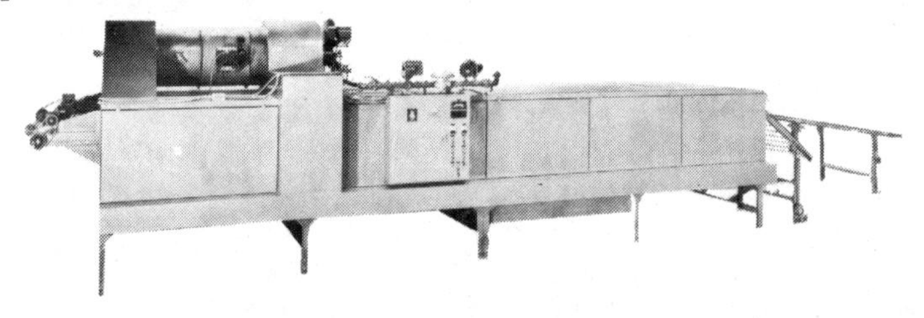

Figure 163. Precision gas fired textile dryer, designed to dry and cure cut pieces, terrycloth, or linen towels, T-shirts, and similar materials. Two printing machines may be used to feed the two conveyors of the dryer, simultaneously or independently, allowing the two machine conveyors to permit separate drying cycles. Dryer can dry 120 to 150 dozen pieces per hour. **(Courtesy of Precision Screen Machines, Inc., Hawthorne, New Jersey)**

The completely specialized textile screen printing shop may employ screen printing automatic machines of the types illustrated in Figures 160 and 161. These machines employ adhesive coated moving belts on which the material is moved or laid, registered, printed, and dried. They do multi-color dye printing, depositing wet colors on top of wet colors. The machines dry and finish the printed material automatically or the printed material is removed and placed on a conveyor-drier.

Printing Screens for Textile Printing

One of the factors which has given the textile designer and printer a new freedom in printing is the variety of the printing screens that he may use. He may prepare these himself or have the screens made by specialists. Originally, 6XX to 10XX silk fabric (76 to 110 mesh; 30 to 43 mesh per centimeter) was used as the fabric for the preparation of the screen. Today's screen printer may use equivalent and other numbers of multifilament and monofilament polyester, nylon, and metal cloth, since these are more resistant to dye inks especially when coated with direct and direct-indirect emulsions. Also, nylon and polyester gauzes are available in the followng thicknesses (letters) which distinguish different thread thickness—"S" light quality thin threads; "M" medium quality; "T" heavier quality; and "HD" heavy duty or extra heavy quality.

Every type of printing screen has been used and is being employed for printing on varied textile materials. Every type of screen, however, cannot be used for printing with every type of textile ink. The same factors govern the choice of the correct printing screen as in other screen printing methods. The screen to be used is determined by the textile ink or dye to be printed. For example, water-soluble inks should be printed through a screen that is resistant to water. The filler or blockout used to fill in the screen must not be dissolved in any fashion by the ink or dye during the printing process. When in doubt as to what screen filler will best resist an ink or dye, specifications of the ink manufacturer should be followed.

Although the early printer who printed on textiles seemed to favor the wash-out method (resist or tusche-glue type of screen) of screen preparation, the modern textile printer uses the simplest screen that will answer his purpose. Where detail is not too fine, where direct lacquers, resinous inks, or direct pigmented emulsion type dyes are being printed, the printer may still use washout screens, knife-cut film screen, knife-cut paper screens, and varied types of photographic screens. As far as photographic screens are concerned, generally direct screens and direct-indirect screens are employed; although photographic screen printing films that have been treated with a hardening agent, polyvinyl alcohol-polyvinyl acetate, and trade named products.

The Washout Screen

The washout screen which is explained in detail in Chapter 13, also known as tusche-glue, tusche-enamel, or tusche-lacquer is employed for printing textile inks and dyes by the printer who enjoys preparing his own printing screens. It has been used and is used by artists, designers, and screen printers to prepare screens for printing water-soluble inks and other types of dyes. It is a practical screen for the designer or artist who plans to print wallcoverings and matching textile materials such as drapes and the like.

Tusche and synthetic enamel, tusche, and lacquer, and tusche and vinyl lacquer or vinyl ink may be used for printing with water-soluble dyes. Tusche and the filler glue or a water-soluble filler may be used for printing inks consisting of flexible lacquers, vinyls, oil colors, and direct pigmented emulsion type dyes.

Making Screens more Resistant to Inks

Since some dye pastes or ceramic pastes have a tendency to dissolve gelatinous, indirect, and even some direct screens, it is essential that the screen be treated in some fashion to counteract this. While there are available commercial compounds or solutions for this purpose, the screen printer may make screens resistant by coating the emulsion with acid resistant, alkali resistant coatings, or with lacquers or synthetic enamels, which will resist printing paste, solvent soluble dyes, and inks.

Waterproofing screens is similar to making screens more resistant to ceramic inks. This is accomplished by spraying or brushing one side of the screen (top side or inside) with a coat of lacquer that will not be dissolved by the ink used in printing. Then the open parts of the design in the screen are wiped carefully on the other side (underside) of the screen with a cloth dampened with a lacquer thinner. When the lacquer on the top side of the screen is dry, the bottom or underside of the screen is coated and then wiped on the top side. The lacquer or filler used on one side of the screen should be a different type than that used to coat the other side of the screen. The solvents employed for the wipings should differ from one another so that the second solvent used will not dissolve the first coating. Both coatings or lacquers, however, must resist the dye or ink being printed.

Manufacturers of inks and lacquers may give advice as to type of best pair of fillers or lacquers for application of protective coatings. There are also special hardening agents and coatings sold by screen printing suppliers for this purpose.

Another method that the beginning printer may use to make a screen more resistant to certain types of inks and dyes is to place the screen on a soft paper blotter material or any absorbent material.

He then squeegees the resisting coat, epoxy ink, or lacquer on the inside of the screen over the design areas. The squeegeeing should be done just once so that the coat will be absorbed through the open parts of the screen by the blotting material. An air spray or a vacuum cleaner may then be used to blow out the open parts of the design. When the resist coat dries on the inside of the screen, the same procedure may be repeated on the underside of the screen.

Direct Photographic Printing Screens

Screens produced by application of protective coatings over gelatinous emulsions give practical service except that occasionally the coatings have a tendency to separate from the gelatin layer. This disadvantage has brought about the development of synthetic sensitized coatings such as polyvinyl alcohol and polyvinyl acetate.

The polyvinyl alcohol printing plate is used by the textile printer because it is insoluble in organic solvents after correct preparation; it is simple to prepare and has general resistance to inks and dyes. Although polyvinyl alcohol is soluble in water, after being processed and exposed to actinic light, it becomes resistant to water-soluble inks. It is a direct screen and consequently a tough screen as is evidenced by the fact that it is employed for printing ceramic inks and on abrasive surfaces. It will last for thousands of impressions, especially if prepared on metal fabric.

Polyvinyl alcohol is sold as a fine white powder; medium viscosity type powder is recommended for the preparation of printing screens. Although the printing plate specialist prepares polyvinyl alcohol as a film screen also, the textile printer uses the direct screen method, that is, he coats the prepared emulsion directly onto the screen fabric.

Generally, the procedure* is to dissolve the fine polyvinyl alcohol powder in cool water and then add potassium bichromate powder or ammonium bichromate powder to the completely dissolved polyvinyl alcohol solution. The polyvinyl alcohol solution without the bichromate will keep indefinitely. It is suggested that the printer dissolve the powder in small jars in the correct amount of water and use the dissolved solution as needed. A little blue or green inert dye or inert powder may be added to this mixture to aid in processing and developing the photographic screen after exposure.

There are varied formulae for mixing polyvinyl alcohol; the writer has found the following one practical for most purposes: 1 ounce of polyvinyl alcohol powder dissolved completely in 10 liquid ounces of water to which is added ¼ ounce by weight of potassium bichromate or ammonium bichromate powder. The dissolved polyvinyl alcohol is

* A complete treatment of the preparation of polyvinyl alcohol and other screens is found in the book: Kosloff, Albert. *Photographic Screen Printing,* St Publications, Book Division, Cincinnati, Ohio, 45202.

heated in a double boiler to assure that the powder is completely dissolved and the bichromate is added to the dissolved solution in the boiler. The mixture is heated but not boiled. The mixture should be strained through several layers of silk to eliminate air bubbles before applying to screen fabric. The solution is applied while it is still warm.

Although it is not necessary, it is advisable to apply the first coat on the inside of the screen. This coat serves as a basic base for the next coat. The second coat and third coat, if necessary, may then be applied on the underside of the screen. The coating may be done under subdued light; however, the screen should dry in complete darkness or in a darkroom. A fan may be used to hasten drying. If a whirler is available, the coated screen may be whirled in similar fashion to a screen prepared for printing ceramic inks.

The coated and dried screen is exposed to a carbon arc, "black light" unit, or to photofloods. The time of exposure and the distance from exposing light is similar to the exposing of other screens. After the correct exposure, the screen is washed out in water that is about 110 degrees Fahrenheit (43C).

The above information is presented to the screen printer who may wish to prepare his own printing screens. However, varied commercial direct photographic emulsions, polyvinyl alcohol-polyvinyl acetate screens, modified polyvinyl plastic screens and other products are offered to the printer who does not wish to prepare his own emulsions.

Chapter 26

SCREEN PRINTING ELECTRONIC CIRCUITS

The screen printing industry is not in its infancy; nor is it completely mature. The versatility of its applications makes maturity difficult because of the varied new principles that are constantly developed. With civilization grown more complex, the transfer of ideas and principles from one industry to another has been quickened. Screen printing has become more of a technology than a craft. Screen printing in its relationship with industry has shown many facets and has made possible the application of various principles. One of these, the principle of printed electronic circuits, was known as early as 1921. This type of printing was motivated when the Army Ordnance Department* in February, 1946, released developments of screen printing of printed circuits in a proximity fuse. This type of fuse was used in trench or artillery shells. This release tended to place stress on printed circuits as a practical process rather than as a laboratory curiosity.

Circuit printing is a process in which a simple or complex system of "wires" in the form of electrical conductive film coatings are applied on a surface or base of plastic, ceramic, glass or other substrate material that does not conduct electricity. More specifically, a *printed circuit* is a predetermined printed electrical circuit produced by direct or indirect printing an electrically conducting pattern on a base or substrate. The base may be rigid or flexible. The purpose of the printed electrical circuit is to produce an electrically conducting pattern on an insulating material, the material serving as a medium for holding the printed circuit and the miniature electrical parts that may be connected to it. Printed circuits make possible the printing of wiring, resistors, capacitors, and inductance.

This process, wherever possible, replaced the maze of wires and conventional point-to-point wiring with the simpler technique of screen printing special conducting ink or using a metal laminated plastic material. Although printed circuits are no cure-all and will not replace wires

* Brunetti, Cledo and Curtis, Roger W. *Printed Circuit Techniques.* National Bureau of Standards Circular 468, United States Department of Commerce, U.S. Government Printing Office, Washington, D.C. 20025.

in all wired circuits completely, the future of circuit printing is as great as the potential of the electronic industries.

This type of printing has become a reality because it stresses ruggedness, uniformity of production, efficiency of design, reduction of cost, improvement of reliability, motivation of research, and miniaturization. The latter process—miniaturization—has reference to the manufacturing of very small equipment and parts and generally to the reduction of the size of parts. Miniaturization produces compactness, saves weight and space, and does away with excess soldering tools, brackets for storing parts, and amount of floor space needed. This type of printing tends to eliminate wiring errors since once the circuit is designed, it can be reproduced by semi-skilled and unskilled workers almost indefinitely without error. The advantages of miniaturization for military and civilian use are obvious.

In the circuit printing industry screen printing of circuits is also known as "thick film" circuits to distinguish them from thin film circuits. A thick film circuit generally is a screen printed circuit produced by applying inks, pastes, or coatings on substrates or bases and firing the printed patterns to change their properties. While thick film circuits are about 50 times thicker than thin films (thin films are about .00002" to .00004" thick; .00051mm to .00102 mm), the difference is in the method in which the two types are made. Thin film elements are not screen printed but are vaporized or sputtered in a vacuum chamber and the vaporized material deposited on a substrate or base. Sometimes, the screen printer may just do the thick film printing after the thin film has been applied.*

Although the coating making up the conductive circuit may be applied or affixed to a surface in various ways such as paint, metal spraying, die-stamp process, etching, and electroplating, screen printing, because of its versatility, is advantageous to use. This process makes possible, easier, and more exact applications of circuits on flat, round, and irregular surfaces. Because of the heavy coat it applies, the circuit may be printed on decalcomania paper, the decal applied to the desired surface, and the decal fixed by firing, leaving the circuit on the required surface. There are varied practical types of printing screens, resists and photoresists for printing large area and detail designs. This type of circuit printing makes possible printing or placing of parts very close together and allows for variation of designs and almost any circuit configuration. There are ready-mixed inks available for printing conductors and for printing resists on metal laminated plastics or on ceramic bases to counteract etching solutions. Since the screen printed circuit is really bonded, molded, or fused to the supporting surface, there is elimination of moving parts. Mass production becomes a matter of screen printing and assembling.

* The following book deals with circuit printing more completely: Kosloff, Albert, *Screen Printing Electronic Circuits,* St Publications, Book Division, Cincinnati, Ohio.

Besides requiring a knowledge of expert general and photographic screen printing, circuit printing also involves knowledge and experience in electrically conducting materials, in ceramic arts and engineering, resistance materials, metallized ceramics, fabrication of plastics, experimentation, and finally an exact standardization of the complete processing to obtain the desired product. The electrical properties of the finished printed circuit is dependent on the choice of the base insulation or surfaces printed on, the selection of a metal conductor or ink employed for printing, the selection of the resist for printing (if printing is done on metal laminated plastic), and the way in which the circuit and the base are bonded together. Although much of the experimentation and practical work is being done by private establishments under controlled and trade secret conditions, the printer who has a general background, who can mix screen printing inks, who is industrious, and who can control his processes, should be able to do circuit printing.

Generally, the printed unit consists of a supporting base with the printed circuit applied to the base. The base may be in the shape of a disc, flat plate, or tube. The following materials have been and are being employed as bases or substrates: titanates, steatite, glass, thermosetting plastics, plastic impregnated cloth, specially prepared paper, and ceramoplastics which may be ceramic or mica combined with plastics, and glass-mica products. Where the base is not of ceramic material, it should allow for the required electrical properties, good machineability and be sturdy. The base should have high insulation resistance, low moisture absorption, and low electrical loss. The size and thickness of the base is determined by the design of the part and the circuit design. Generally, where plastics are employed as the base, they are about $\frac{1}{64}$ to $\frac{1}{8}$ inch (.054cm to .218cm) in thickness and are of the thermosetting variety. The design, the engineering of the product, and the supplier of the product or base material help solve many problems involved in the printing.

The coatings for direct screen printed circuits, thick film or hybrid circuits are generally of four types: conductors, resistors, insulators, and dielectrics. Each of the latter materials contains a glass, organic binder and an organic solvent. For example, conductors in ready-to-use paste form may consist of a finely divided precious metal powder, glass powder, a temporary organic material, and a solvent portion. Generally, conductor inks may contain the following metals: gold, platinum-gold, palladium-gold, palladium-silver, or silver. Thus, the screen printer may be printing a conductor coating which may consist of a finely ground silver powder, a low melting point glass in a liquid solvent and an organic vehicle to serve as a binder, and to hold the silver to a substrate surface. The silver becomes the conducting material once it is printed on the base and processed correctly.

Resistor inks differ from conductor inks generally because the glass-to-metal ratio is considerably higher in resistors; whereas in con-

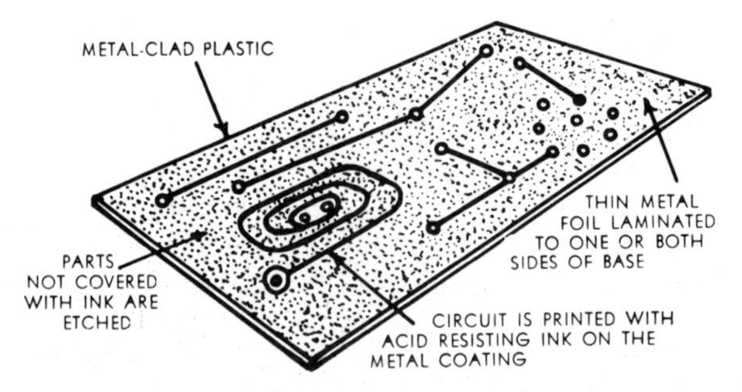

Figure 165. The circuit design printed with an acid-resisting ink on top of the metal-clad base material. The exposed portions (shaded in the diagram) are later etched away by acid or another chemical leaving the circuit design.

ductors the metal part is high in order to obtain low resistance. There are also resistor inks or coatings which may consist of carbon or graphite dissolved in a binder or in a varnish and may be applied to ceramic, phenolic, or to special paper sheets.

The conducting ink may be printed directly or deposited indirectly onto the base. The direct method consists of printing the ink in the design representing the circuit directly on the prepared base through a printing screen. Two general methods are employed for printing a circuit by the indirect method. In one method, an acid-resisting ink is printed onto the base surface and the circuit design is left open. The open and exposed parts making up the circuit are then electrochemically coated with the desired metal thickness coating. This process is controlled, and requires screen printing equipment and electroplating equipment, since the coating is really electroplated onto the base. The second method, which is used more, is a printing and etching method. See Figures 165 and 166. In this method, an acid-resisting ink is also

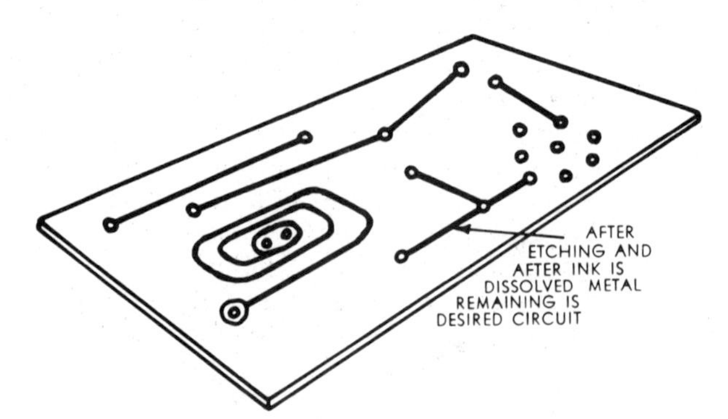

Figure 166. Printed circuit panel after etching shows the printed "wires" on the insulating base material.

printed on a thermosetting plastic base which is metal-clad, laminated, or molded with an exact thickness of copper or aluminum coating. Examples of plastics employed for bases are phenolics, melamine-fiberglass, teflon-fiberglass, and epoxy-fiberglass. The pattern printed onto the base with the acid-resisting ink represents the desired circuit design. The open areas or those parts of the base which are not covered with the ink are eaten away with an acid or chemical; those parts covered with the ink are protected from the acid. After the metal lamination has been etched away, the ink is dissolved away from the base and the desired circuit is left on the base. The printing may be done on both sides of the base, since the metal-clad bases are available in varied thicknesses of metal coatings, coated on one side or both sides of the base. After the circuit is printed, the desired leads or parts are connected by soldering, with rivets, eyelets, or special fastening devices developed for circuit printing, and the entire assembly may be embedded or cast in a suitable resin to protect the parts from dust corrosion, electrolytic corrosion, humidity, etc.

Besides printing on rigid base material, screen printing is also used for flexible printed wiring and for multi-layer wiring. The flexible printed circuit consists of a film or glass reinforced insulating (dielec-

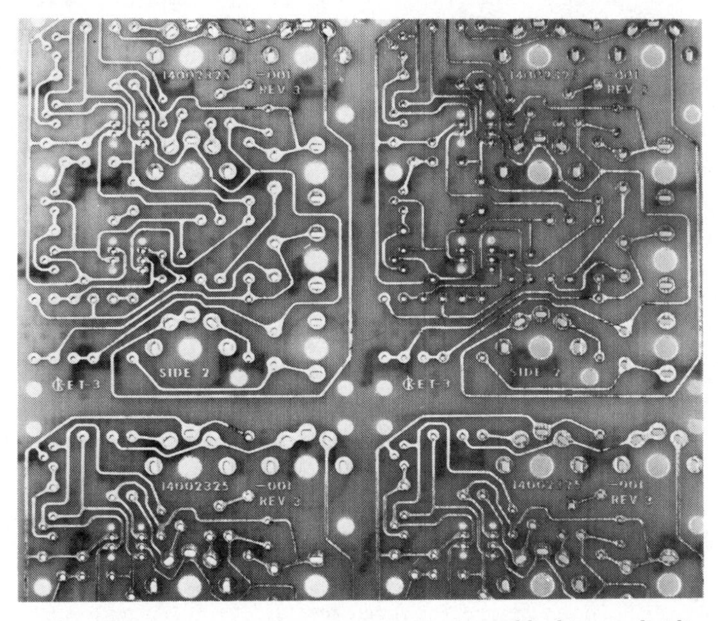

Figure 167. Four circuits for a computer, prior to blanking or dividing into four individual units, printed with one screen. Circuits were first produced by etching out copper laminate on epoxy base, then circuits were plated with tin over the copper. **(Courtesy of Kalmus and Associates, Inc., Broadview, Illinois)**

tric) material, which is easily bendable, conforms to curves, and allows for bending without breaking. Multi-layer circuits consist of two or more layers of separate and different circuit patterns which are laminated together under heat and pressure to produce a strong and resistant unit.

Figure 167 shows four units of a printed circuit to which ultimately components or parts will be connected by soldering or by other methods. Figure 168 stresses the accuracy of screen printing in relation to circuit printing.

General Procedure

Analysis of factors involved in circuit printing leads to the conclusion that each individual manufacturer doing this type of screen printing improves and develops methods of printing peculiar to and necessitated by his finished product. Studies of manufacturers' techniques indicate, however, a certain standardization. It is this standardization that is the common factor found in varied plants and these standards are forwarded as information. Because there are variables that are not possible to depict, the printer or novice going into this type of work must realize that screen printing of circuits is an inter-dependent printing process. Initial experimentation which is necessary for one attempting it must be complete and thorough from start to finish, including the final use of the printed circuit which should test the ability to

Figure 168. A full-size electronic circuit produced by screen printing. The circuit lines are .0085" (.216mm) wide and the spaces between the lines are .0115" (.292mm) wide. Some of the circuit lines have been screen printed with a resist for protection from solder during the soldering step. **(Courtesy of Kalmus and Associates, Broadview, IL)**

withstand rigors of service. This initial experimental printing will make the printer familiar with the specific materials and equipment used and where they may be obtained.

The general procedure of this type of printing consists of the following steps: (1) designing the circuit; (2) producing of photographic positives; (3) producing of printing plate; (4) printing; and (5) assembling parts.

Designing the Circuit

The production of the printed circuit starts with a schematic drawing or with an engineering wiring drawing, from which an outline drawing or a pencil layout may be made. The latter rough layout should have all the specifications on it such as overall dimensions of circuit board and circuit, conductor thickness, conductor width, space between conductor lines, plus and minus tolerances, dielectric material to be used, hole size and tolerance, thickness of plating in holes, number of holes, type of resist to be printed, type of plating and thickness of plating, type of testing, etc. From the outline drawing the artwork is produced. The artwork is a configuration of the circuit and may be made in black-on-white or with tape-up characters and symbols, generally drawn very large to exact scale. The black-on-white pattern is used for the production of the positive.

The layout of the design, of course, would vary depending on whether the circuit would be used for radio, television, guided missile, hearing aid, radar computer, automatic business machine, etc. It must be stressed that the printed circuit is only as good as the original design. Lines should be clean and sharp and layout may have register marks on it outside the circuit area as an aid in printing. Although it is advisable that the original design be kept as large as possible, since reduction in size eliminates or reduces faults, the proportions employed for circuit printing artwork may be two to ten times the size of the printed circuit. Often where parts of the circuit are to be thousandths of an inch or minute parts of a millimeter, the original artwork may be 50 times the size of the final printed circuit. The lettering or numbering which is part of the printed circuit should be to scale and legible. The process in every step of progress, must carry out specifications exactly in this type of work and in this type of screen printing.

Photographic Positives

Although knife-cut film is also employed for this type of printing, photographic screens, as a rule, are used for printing circuits. This implies that photographic positives are needed for the production of the printing plate or printing screen. The making of the positives is similar to making positives for other printing screens. However, when the positive is reduced, it should be verified by checking with specifications. The positive design used for making the printing screen is the same size as the circuit to be printed. Although one positive may be used for making one printing screen, more than one positive is generally "ganged up" or included on one printing screen.

The Printing Screen

The direct printing screen is a common printing screen employed for circuit printing because it is a tough and resistant screen which meets the demands of relatively large production and is not difficult to prepare. Any practical screen, however, including direct-indirect or direct-film screen, or indirect or transfer type screen printing film, may be employed, depending on the type of ink to be printed.

Regardless of the printing screen used, the printer must standardize the processing of the screen based on trials. The direct and direct-indirect screen (which consists of two parts: a dry emulsion film and a sensitized liquid emulsion) may be used on stainless steel fabric. Commercially developed solid metal etched screens, which are very resistant and last for thousands of impressions, are also used. If the ink used to print the circuit is an abrasive type, it is suggested that a direct screen be employed and metal screen fabric be used for the screen. If, however, the resist method is used in circuit printing or an acid resisting ink is printed onto the metal part of a metal-clad base, then any photographic screen or hand-prepared screen that will not be dissolved by the ink or resist may be used.

Monofilament nylon and monofilament polyester screen fabrics equivalent to Number 6 to Number 18 silk are used as fabric for the printing screen. Stainless steel cloth up to 450 mesh is used depending on the design to be reproduced and the ink that is to be used in printing. A common metal screen fabric used is about 165 mesh or 165 woven wires to the lineal inch (about 65 threads to the centimeter). Because circuit printing is precision printing, screen fabric used for circuit printing such as metal cloth, nylon or polyester must be stretched tight. It is suggested that either the two-floating bar frame or the four-floating bar frame be used or a commercial frame designed for this purpose be employed. The screen fabric area should be approximately twice the image or printing area. Where a silver conducting ink or paint is employed for printing a not too detailed design directly onto a base, a coarser screen may be used. Where a resist ink is printed onto a metal-clad plastic base and then the metal coating is etched, the screen fabric used for printing the resist may be of a finer mesh. The same care and skill must be exercised for making these types of screens as for printing other specialized products in the screen printing industry.

Shops specializing in circuit printing either make their own screens or have them made by specialists who cater to the trade. Where resistant screens have to be used and it is necessary to employ less resistant screens, the screen may be reinforced with a hardening agent or solution available from screen printing suppliers. The reinforcing may be done by placing the screen, underside down and in contact with newsprint or blotting paper. The solution is poured along one edge on top of the screen fabric and the solution is squeegeed across the screen with two strokes of the squeegee. The screen is then turned over and the mesh in the screen is wiped out with a lintless soft cloth that has been dampened with a recommended solvent, wiping away just the design parts on the bottom of the screen. However, with the resistant types of screens available commercially, it is suggested that the beginner use a commercial emulsion in the preparation of the screen.

Printing

The actual printing of circuits is not different from other screen printing. The inks used do require careful mixing and care must be taken in using them. Some of the inks are air-dried at room temperature; some are baked at higher temperatures to permit proper bonding of the ink to the metal surface; and some inks have to be fused to the base in kilns or lehrs at temperatures up to about 1400 degrees Fahrenheit (760 Celsius). Ceramic substrates or supports upon which the conductor or resistor inks or compositions are printed are an important part of thick film circuits and belong to the latter class. They have to be dried or baked and fired in such ovens as illustrated in Figures 169 and 170.

If the printing is being done on a copper-clad plastic base, then

Figure 169. A BTU high volume production furnace for accurate firing of thick film substrates or screen printed conductors, resistors, and dielectrics; furnace has an 8″ (20.3cm) wide belt, 5 individually controlled zones with 90″ (228.6cm) of heated length, an operating firing range from 752 to 2012 degrees Fahrenheit (400 to 1100 degrees Celsius), and a control accuracy of plus or minus ½ degree Celsius. **(Courtesy of BTU Engineering, Waltham, MA)**

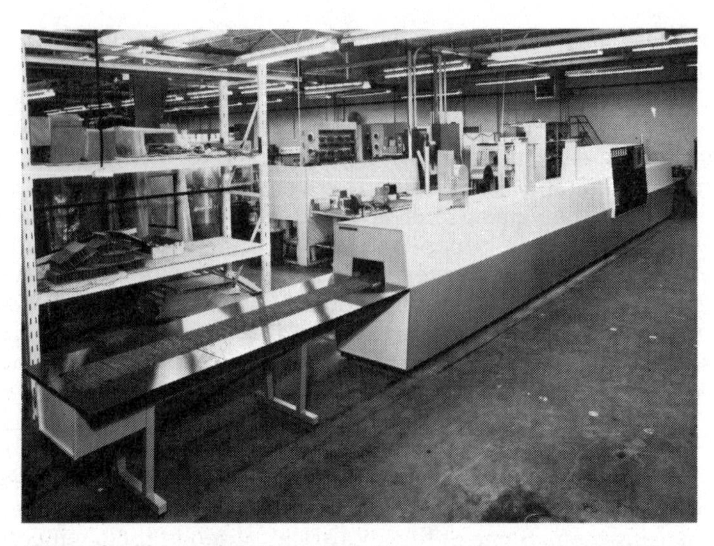

Figure 170. The Lindberg Hevi-Duty Conveyor Furnace designed for firing thick film electronic circuits and related firing. Furnace can be heated up to 1100 degrees Celsius (2012 degrees Fahrenheit), has a heated length of 156″ (396cm) which is made up of 7 zones of control. The furnace has a cooling chamber, a furnace interior that is isolated from the room air, and precision control of firing. **(Courtesy of Lindberg Hevi-Duty, Watertown, Wisconsin)**

the copper surface must first be cleaned thoroughly to insure proper bonding and proper drying of the acid resisting ink. It is important that the ink adhere perfectly to the copper surface. After the design is printed with the resist ink and dried, the coating is inspected before the etching process is begun. After the etching is completed, the whole panel is washed with warm water and is placed in a solvent which removes the resist, leaving the metal surface in the shape of the desired circuit. The solvent used, of course, is of the type that will not affect the copper coating, the circuit design, or soldering of the parts to the metal, if soldering is to be used in the assembly work. Sometimes the solvent used will just soften the ink and the ink may be wiped off easily with cloths.

Circuit printing requires accurate registration, especially where one circuit design is printed on one side of the base or panel and another circuit design is printed on the other side of the panel. An aid in this type of registration is to employ a transparent sheet of plastic or paper for proofing the circuit print.

Where more than one circuit is printed or ganged up on a panel or base, the panel is cut into the individual designs after the printing is completed. See Figure 167.

Some screen printing shops just specialize in printing the acid resisting ink onto the metal-clad plastics bases and allow the manufacturer to do his own etching. This is an advantage for the manufacturer and the printer, since each is doing his own specialty.

Assembly and Finishing

The assembly of parts of the printed circuit is as varied as the complete process. It is assumed that testing and inspection of parts is part of processing in each step of the total process. A common method of assembly may be to drill or punch holes in the base to facilitate the attachment of sockets, condenser, resistors, and related printed circuits hardware. After the leads and other parts are fastened with special fasteners or soldered to the metal parts on the base, often with one dipping operation in the solder, a phenolic plastic coating may be added to the assembly by a dipping or spraying process. The coating provides resistance to moisture, elements, dust, and other forces.

Chapter 27

CHEMICAL MACHINING AND SCREEN PRINTING

One of the main characteristics of the technological advances which have dominated the years since World War II is that, for every development made in industry, more advances come to meet the needs of the first development. It is an interesting cycle; and today's industry and society thrive on it.

One of the major technical breakthroughs in screen printing is chemical machining. It is a relatively new "industry" which employs design, graphic arts, and metal technology. It is a process by which material is formed, shaped, or changed—with the aid of screen printing or photochemistry—by the removal or addition of material.

More specifically, this is accomplished by applying screen printing resists or photosensitive resists either by photographic means or by screen printing the resist on the substrate. The resists are applied to desired areas on a material surface. Some areas are left uncovered so that they may be removed later by etching or built up by plating. Chemical machining involves first the application or transfer of a precise photographic or printed image to an object.

While this technique is relatively new (developed in the early 1940's), its principle is the same as that used in photoengraving. This type of machining produces parts to an exacting tolerance by chemical means rather than by conventional machining operations or milling. The process may be used to produce intricate, small, thin parts where precision is an important factor. See Figure 172. It may be employed to make one or thousands of parts and almost any flat part can be produced. It produces such parts as nameplates, printed circuits from TV-set size to subminiature size, dials, aircraft parts, and instrument panels. Any metal, alloy, plastic, glass and ceramic material which can be attacked chemically may be worked with the process. It is used for decorative etching or chemically machining fine art work, as illustrated in Figure 171, and, of course, in printed circuit work. Parts which require etching entirely through the metal can vary in thickness from .0001 to about .062 inches (.0025mm to 1.57mm). While

Figure 171. Decorative etching similar to nameplate etching makes use of chemical machining. **(Courtesy of Chemcut Corp., State College, Pennsylvania)**

those parts which do not require complete etching through the metal (for example, fine art work or nameplates) can be any thickness as long as depth of etch does not exceed the maximum limit.

This process is growing and becoming an important part of industry because it is reducing tooling expense and time compared to conventional metal working processes. It eliminates stresses, strains, and distortion on very thin metals as may result with general die and punch methods. Chemical machining does not affect the hardness of the metal, does not introduce edge stresses, produces burr-free edges on small parts, and therefore, eliminates the need of subsequent operations. It allows for hardened metal to be chemically machined, thus requiring no heat treatment after fabrication. Extremely fine detail not possible with traditional methods may be produced and because fine dies are not needed in the process, there is also a reduction of maintenance costs. It produces consistent dimensional tolerances where the production of new thin metal and complex parts may prohibit conventional machine processing. Any configuration on adequate frame or tab supports can be made. See Figure 172. Design changes may be made easily by altering the original copy or design.

The versatility of this process has brought about varied terminology to describe it; it is also known by such names as chemical milling, photoetching, chemical cutting, photochemical duplicating, photofabrication, photomechanical reproduction, etc. It must be noted that chemical machining is a subtractive process, that is, it removes material as compared to electroforming, electrodeposition, electroplating, printing which prints resist coats or inks on surfaces. Photosensitive resists are liquid formulations of resins which become light-sensitive when dry; they have chemical resistance and hold exact detail. The screen printer who plans to do photofabrication should also have knowledge of these resists and their correct use to supplement screen printing.

Chemical machining has great potential in screen printing for the production of parts that may not be practical to make with other processes. It must be stressed that general screen printing has advanced to the point where it can develop specialized knowledge research, and standardization of precise printing. As with other processes, there are limitations. Before the screen printer attempts to do this type of work commercially, he must experiment and standardize procedures so that precision work may be done without guess-work, as often the work involves screen printing or photographic reproduction having a tolerance of plus or minus .002″ (.051mm) and even less if possible.

While more than one metal or alloy may meet requirements for the manufacturing of parts, the screen printer should choose a material that can be processed with the least difficulty. This type of precision printing requires close control in design of copy, in camera work, preparation of printing screens, in machine screen printing the same film thickness consistently, and in etching of resist-printed pieces. The printer must develop care and safety in all his processing and develop methods in eliminating or decreasing pollution.

Before the screen printer starts on this type of venture, he will have to purchase etching equipment or make an etching unit to suit his specifications. If he does not have a process camera, he will need these services for preparing negatives and positives and for enlarging or reducing copy. He should have a screen printing press for doing precision work. The screen printer will have to develop generally the following steps in working with chemical machining: (1) preparation of master drawing or artwork, (2) producing photographically a negative

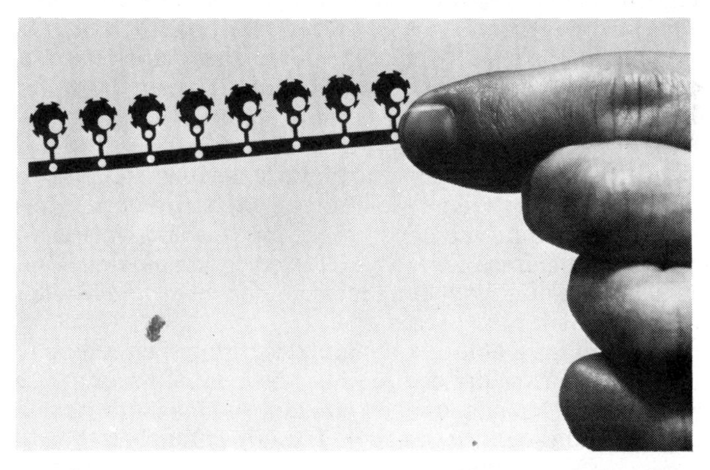

Figure 172. Seven small chemically machined thin stainless steel parts for hearing aids. Very many of these parts were screen printed in one impression. **(Courtesy of of Kalmus and Associates, Inc., Broadview, Illinois)**

or positive from the artwork, (3) applying resist by screen printing image on prepared metal or material, (4) etching or plating, and (5) removal of resist or photosensitive resist.

Artwork

The artwork, original master, or engineering drawing may be drawn on paper or cardboard, on polyester film, scribing film, or knife-cut film. Also artwork may be bought, paste-up copy may be employed, or it may be prepared by a draftsman by cutting a facsimile of the part on a coordinategraph (coordinate layout machine). Some of the methods employed for this type of artwork are similar to that used in the preparation of copy for printed circuits.

Artwork or design configuration may be made, greatly enlarged, on knife-cut film, in similar fashion to preparing knife-cut film printing screens. The knife-cut film which is of the correct transparent color is then reduced photographically, eliminating any errors in the photographic reductions. The original size of the copy will depend on the camera, accuracy of reproduction, and desired reduction. To assure accuracy of photographic reproduction the size of the artwork master may vary from two to 200 times actual size. However, most artwork is prepared about 10 to 20 times actual printing size, since precise accuracy is required and reducing copy does produce more accurate images.

The completed artwork is reduced photographically and the designed parts are reproduced as a negative on photographic film in a process camera. The negative may be put in a step-and-repeat machine or may be repeated in another fashion in order to duplicate the design on one large piece of film for "gang-up" screen printing or printing of more than one object or image in one impression.

While they may be a limit to how wide thin metal sheets may be and still hold dimensional tolerances, the more parts that can be ganged-up and fitted on the negative the more economical the process. A microscope or stereomicroscope is used in shops which specialize in this type of work for inspecting finished negatives and also for examining screen print.

In designing for etching of nameplates, printed circuit boards, fine art work and the like, the etching may be done on one side and not through the metal. However, where etching is done on thin metal material completely through the material (under .010 inches thick; .254mm thick), one side of the material is screen printed with the desired design. Where thicker metals are produced, both side of the material must be printed and images must line up perfectly on both sides so that the etching through the metal is done accurately, reproducing parts with sharp burr-free lines.

Printing Screen

A photographic positive is made from the negative and the positive is employed to make the printing screen. Direct emulsions, screen printing films and direct films (indirect-direct screens) may be used to make the printing screen. While metal mesh (about No. 150 to 325 per inch; about 60 to 128 per cm) is usually employed for the screen fabric, monofilament or polyester fabric also may be used.

Because the printing must be very accurate, the fabric must be stretched tightly onto the frame. Usually commercially built metal frames are used for this type of work. Where this screen printing is standard procedure, regular stretching machines or devices are used to stretch the fabric. Unlike general screen printing, where the printer may use more latitude, the coating of the emulsion or film application, drying, exposure, and washing out of the printing screen for chemical machining must be done under controlled conditions to assure perfect image reproductions in the screen and perfect screen printing.

Preparation of Surface for Machining

The metal surfaces are cleaned perfectly to remove scales, oxides, lubricants, grease, finger marks, and the like so that perfect adhesion of screen printing resists may be obtained. Cleaning tanks or solutions may be used for this purpose and surfaces rinsed off with water and allowed to dry. Where automation is essential, scrubbing machines are available through which panels pass and may be cleaned, polished, rinsed, and dried on both sides of the panel.

The metal surface should not be touched until the screen printing step. The printer must inspect the sheets to assure that there are no buckles, kinks, or other imperfections that would prevent adhering of ink resist to surface. Slight curvature of the flat material can be overcome in screen printing by printing on a vacuum table, whether done by hand or by machine. One of the methods of testing for flatness of surface is to place material between two pieces of glass and inspect to see that glass touches all over.

Printing

There is no one resist or ink that can be used for all types of work. The function of the screen printed resist or of a photoresist is to protect the desired areas on a surface from planned etching or plating. The screen printed resist must have excellent definition—it must print very sharp detail the same thickness each impression. The resists are generally mechanically printed in similar fashion to other inks, except that the screen printing must be controlled, since precision detail must be obtained. Some available resists may be used both as a resist for etching in chemical machining and also as a resist for plating in electroforming. The printing is generally done "off-contact"—that is, only that part of the screen which is pressed down by the squeegee touches the surface being printed; the rest of the screen does not touch the work. The limitation to the fineness of the print is dependent on whether sufficient thickness of resist is printed to withstand the etching solution. The limitation to fineness is dependent also on the type of mesh used in preparing the screen and the control in the preparation of the printing screen.

The printed image may dry either naturally or with the aid of heat or heat and air in a dust-free atmosphere. Generally, most resists dry in about three to 120 minutes at temperatures varying from about 150 to 300 degrees Fahrenheit (66 to 149 Celsius), depending on the job, print thickness, and type of resist. Where ultraviolet curing is recommended for a job, the recommendation of the resist or ink manufacturer must be followed.

After the material has been screen printed and the piece has been etched, the resist may be removed from the surface with the correct solvent. Some resists may require forced spray of solvents; others may be removed by simple immersion in a tank containing the solvent. Available and more economical stripping formulations not recommended by the manufacturer of a resist, should be tested completely for compatibility with the particular surface. Lacquer thinner or aromatic hydrocarbons such as xylene or toluene may be used to wash the resist or ink off the printing screen. There are also resists which may wash off with water and a caustic solution. This solution is then completely removed with sprays of water.

Etching

After the resists are dried or dried and baked onto the surfaces, the printed panels are generally put through conveyorized etching machines or etching tanks where both or one side of the panel may be sprayed with the necessary etchant. Generally, the thinner the metal the easier it is to etch. All areas not protected by resists are dissolved and the finished parts are left held together by frame supports or metal tabs which are incorporated in the original design. The printed ink or resist must resist such etchants as ferric chloride, ammonium persulfide, cupric chloride, and chromic sulphuric acid. Caution must be employed in mixing and handling the etchants.

There are generally three types of etching methods used: immersion, splash method, and spray etching. In the first method, the parts to be etched are placed in a ceramic or plastic tank which contains the correct etchant and the parts are left in the tank until the etching is completed. This method is generally the beginning method used by the screen printer but is not as accurate as the other two methods.

Figure 173. Chemcut Chemical Machining System, an etching system, using oscillating spray to apply more etchant on material transported on a variable speed conveyor. Such parts as instrument panels, nameplates and the like made from virtually any available commercial metal or alloy are etched with controlled temperature and designed specifically for chemical machining. **(Courtesy of Chemcut Corporation, State College, Pennsylvania)**

Figure 174. The DEA etcher, a high volume, automatic, conveyorized etching machine for the production of rigid and flexible printed circuits, nameplates, and chemically milled parts, for etching single and double sided work up to 40 inches (102cm) in width, with control enclosure shown at the left. Conveyor in unit transports materials at variable speeds, passing through top and bottom spray banks. The modular design allows for multiple chamber construction for very high production. **(Courtesy of Philip A. Hunt Chemical Corporation, Palisades Park, N.J.)**

In the splash method the parts are in an enclosed area or machine and are splashed with the etchant. For the large majority of chemical machining spray etching is used. Spray etchers are faster acting and the screen printer may obtain any type etcher from etching equipment manufacturers. There are horizontal, vertical spray, horizontal rotary etchers, vertical rotary etchers, and conveyorized etchers. See Figures 173 and 174. Regardless of method of etching and type of etching, the metal should be etched in a well-agitated solution.

After etching, the parts are washed off with water sprays, and then passed through a solvent for removal of screen printed resists. Where fine art work and nameplates are processed on one side of metal, the etched areas may be filled in with a contrasting attractive color of screen printing ink and excess ink wiped or rubbed off from rest of surface. Etched areas may also be plated with a different metal for decorative purposes.

Figure 175 shows very small to medium size parts, chemically machined or photofabricated into complex designs from different metals of various thicknesses. Each one of the parts was intended for a different product.

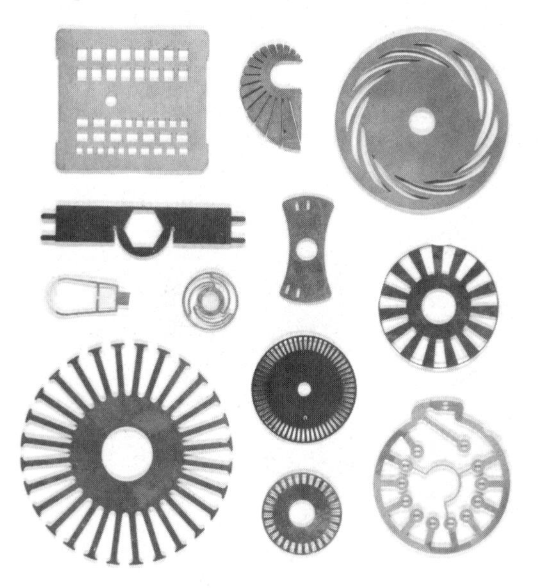

Figure 175. Small varied intricately designed parts, chemically machined from different thin metals for varied purpose. A dry film photoresist of uniform thickness, employed with special equipment designed for photofabrication, was used in completing the processing. **(Courtesy of Fotofabrication Corp., Chicago, Illinois)**

Chapter 28

VACUUM FORMING AND SCREEN PRINTING

Thermoforming or vacuum forming, as it is called in screen printing, is a process of shaping or forming heated sheet plastic material into desired shapes by applying a vacuum or air pressure to the heat softened material and bringing the material into contact with a mold or pattern surface. Vacuum forming is a process which changes flat sheets into useful shaped products.

Forming or shaping of thermoplastic sheet plastic material by means of vacuum was done in about 1917 with pyroxylin sheets. Thermoplastics materials, of course, are those that are resoftened by reheating, that can be reshaped again and again, and are hardened when cooling. Rigid, weather and impact resistant light-weight thermoplastics are employed in vacuum forming and screen printing. Polystyrene (styrene), cellulose acetate butyrate, acrylics, acrylonitrile-butadiene-styrene (ABS), or polyvinyl chloride (PVC) may be used for screen printing and forming. These materials are available in sheet or flat shapes to enable forming to take place. While many thermoplastics are available, some are not suitable for vacuum forming. The proper flat sheet in relation to size of sheet involved should be used. About 10 to 60 mils (.010 to .060 inches; .254 to 1.52mm) in thickness may be employed.

Although one of the earliest records of drawing thermoplastic sheet material is U.S. Patent 669,331, issued in 1901, it was not until about 1950 that the growth of vacuum forming accelerated because heating, forming, mechanical time controls, general equipment, and economic forming production became a possibility.

The selection of the forming method depends on the type of job to be produced, choice of plastic, the shape of the final product, thickness of sheet, required tolerance, optical qualities required (as in signs), equipment available, end use of product, and if screen printed, the choice of ink. Surface smoothness, shrinkage, resistance to elements and to vandalism are also important in producing vacuum formed parts. It should also be possible for the final formed and printed sheet to be drilled, sawed, welded, cemented, ground, or polished. While stock

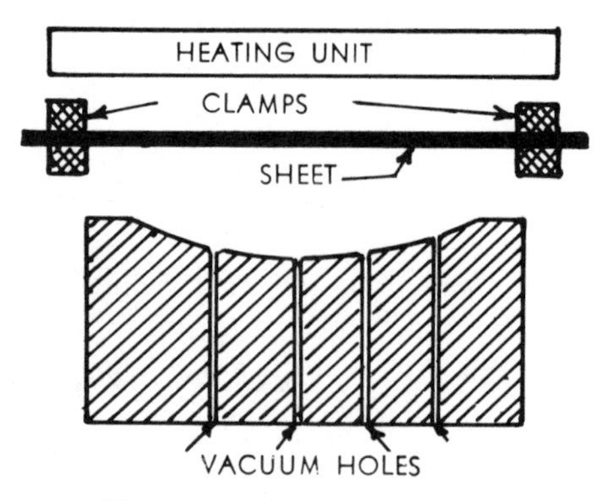

Figure 177. Sheet being heated.

is generally available with a 10 per cent plus or minus in thickness, the thickness used may depend on the depth of draw into the mold.

Generally the process involves clamping the plastic sheet of the correct thickness in a frame, heating the sheet between about 260 to 360 degrees Fahrenheit (127 to 182 degrees Celsius) for a predetermined time, and drawing it down by means of air pressure of a vacuum into or over the intricate contours of a mold. After the sheet is heated, a vacuum is made by means of small holes in the die, and atmospheric pressure forces the heated and formed plastic against the desired shaped mold, producing a three-dimensional effect. See Figures 177 and 178. As the air in the cavity between sheet and mold is evacuated, the external pressure on the softened sheet forces it into the mold—thus the term "vacuum forming." After a short cooling period, the plastic sheet reproduction is removed.

In ordinary vacuum forming it is atmospheric pressure alone that shapes or forces the heated and softened sheet against the mold surface. However, often it is necessary to pre-stretch and form the plastic sheet as fully as possible and at the same time avoid thin spots in the formed sheet. In this type of shaping, drape forming is used. In drape forming, the plastic sheet is heated and pulled down or draped over the mold to its lowest surface before applying the vacuum. Generally, drape

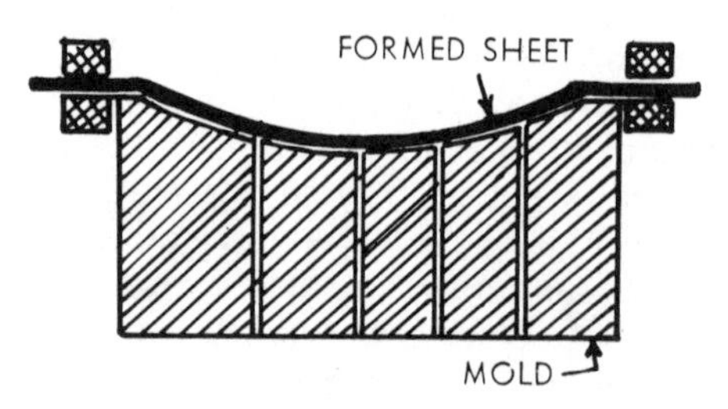

Figure 178. Sheet being formed.

forming is employed for plastics with thick wall sections. This is only one of the examples of the various types of vacuum forming.

Formed plastic parts today are used for such products as refrigerators, clock faces, maps, washing machine parts, airplane and automobile parts, for lighting and illumination, for architectural design, for counter and window displays, blister-forming or visual packaging displays, signs, Christmas displays, toy, automobile association emblems, and the like. The screen printer may be involved in printing on any of the above parts. Vacuum forming of plastic shapes for display use is a significant point-of-purchase device which attracts attention and has impact because of color and three-dimensional effect. Varied colored plastics, transparent plastics, translucent, opaque, metallic plastics, and variations of these are formed. By varying the color of plastic and ink, the screen printed design is made to stand out clearly against the formed lustrous plastic. Flocking can be done to supplement forming and printing. Normally, the sheet flocked is of an opaque color and is slightly darker than the color of the flock. Flock may be applied prior to forming or after forming.

A very interesting type of forming is "blister, bubble, or skin" forming. In blister forming, visual packaging, or skin packaging transparent plastic thin sheet or film is formed so that it fits over a product. The product is placed on a sheet and may be heat-sealed, stapled, or glued to the backing sheet, with the product between the bubble and sheet. While the formed sheet covers the item completely, it makes the product visually available. This type of forming is employed for packaging razor blades, ball-point pens, sparkplugs, thread, novelties, and almost any small or medium-size item that may be seen at a point-of-purchase area in a modern self-service market. The transparent blisters often are produced as multiple forms with as many as 100 to 1000 pieces to the die. While transparency and clarity are important in displaying as well as protecting the product inside the formed blister, screen printing may be done on blisters for adding messages and varied important effects. This type of forming is not old, and the printer who may do printing on the blister parts should select equipment for use with extreme caution. Plus screen printing, the printer must know transparent plastics, packaging, and related equipment, machinery, and processing. As in purchasing other equipment, the printer will find that manufacturers of vacuum forming machines have overcome many problems in this field and their knowledge is of great value in aiding the selection of proper equipment.

Generally, there are two classes of machines employed for thermoforming: (1) vacuum forming machines or those employing atmospheric pressure to form or shape a sheet as illustrated in Figures 179 and 180; and (2) pressure forming machines or equipment that employ hydraulic pressure, compressed air, mechanical pressure, or a combination of these. Ordinarily, vacuum forming machines are easier to

Figure 179. The Comet Star vacuum forming machine illustrating the forming of printed maps; machine is designed for production and laboratory work, provides for 17 combinations of forming techniques, has an independent control panel, a temperature sensing device, and is available in mold areas up to 30″ x 36″ (76.2cm x 91.4cm) with larger sizes available on request. **(Courtesy of Comet Industries, Bensenville, IL)**

operate and employ less expensive and simpler dies as normally used with screen printing. Vacuum forming equipment is available in a range from the simple laboratory type hand pump machine to specialized automatic machines (see Figures 179 and 180) made specifically for doing forming in controlled situations. There are commercial vacuuming machines that will handle sheets up to 16 by 10 feet (4.877 × 3.048 meters) and will form plastic into contours about 2½ feet (.752m) deep. Machines are available with multi-zoning for accurate heat control and push-button control. While the printer may purchase machines which are either sheet fed or roller fed, screen printing shops normally employ sheet fed machines.

Pressure forming machines are more complex and, as a rule, are custom made. However, some printers, after much experimentation, have made jigs and machines for forming the sheet mechanically after heating the sheet, for example, in forming acrylic sheets, either before or after printing. Ordinarily, the sheet may be heated by infra-red lamps or high frequency current.

As far as the plastic itself is concerned for vacuum forming—it should be one that will heat up and form easily, quickly and uniformly. It should produce detail accurately and should heat and cool quickly.

Figure 180. A vacuum forming machine designed to form varied types of thermoplastics sheets up to 10 x 16 feet (3.048 x 4.877m) in size up to a depth mold of 30 inches (76.2cm); unit may be used for forming very large outdoor signs for motels, restaurants, hotels, and the like. **(Courtesy of Plasti-Vac Inc., Charlotte, North Carolina).**

After forming, it should remain tough and resilient; it should have weather resistance, dimensional stability; and it should be available in unlimited colors and color effects including transparent, translucent, and opaque. The plastic sheet should be available in thicknesses up to about .125″ (.32cm), and, very important, the plastic should have compatibility with the screen printing ink or finishes to be applied to it. In choosing the correct plastic sheet for forming, the printer is also concerned with cost and preprinting on sheet. Fortunately, the screen printer today may have his choice of plastics to suit any of the above requirements.

Vacuum forming molds and dies for screen printing are inexpensive compared to molds for injection machines and may be made quicker. The tooling is less expensive because the forming often requires one set of dies, either male tools or plugs, or female dies or dies with cavities. In the preparation of the mold, the general procedure is to make a full-size three-dimensional solid from the original artwork or design. If the pattern is detailed, a sculpture is made, a flexible rubber mold may be made from the sculpture, and plaster is poured into the rubber mold. The dry plaster cast may then be employed for making the final die. Another technique used to make the die is to make the solid full-size design and then heat up a plastic sheet and form it over the full-size design. This female formed sheet is used to make the mold from a material such as epoxy resin. The epoxy resin is then placed on a base and the unit used as the die to form all the needed vacuum formed pieces.

Molds may be made from plastic epoxy material, phenolic plastic, from plaster, special mold compounds, from hardwood, rubber compositions, or plastic compositions. A commonly used mold material consists of epoxy resin, a catalyst, and aluminum powder. The material can be polished and machines easily. From some of the above molds may be made sprayed metal molds for long production runs. Vacuum holes are placed in molds so that the air will be drawn out and thus allow the air to flow rapidly out of the areas around the mold.

The printer employs vacuum forming to shape plastic parts either before screen printing or after printing. Much forming has to be done after parts are printed, and when a part has complex curves, the printing may become quite challenging.

Generally, vacuum forming done by the printer not only requires a knowledge of forming and plastics but also of screen printing and its intimate relation to the complex process. Forming requires the same type of planning from an engineering production and printing standpoint as any other very specialized screen printing process. In spite of the apparent simplicity of the vacuum forming process there is much standardization and a great deal of technology necessary to develop successful forming and printing. Each new application requires knowledge of product design, mold materials, mold design, plastics, temperature control of sheets, development of a forming cycle, and very important—preprinting and postprinting with compatible screen printing inks. Also, good equipment, trained personnel, and constant guidance in the actual work are necessary. The beginner must realize, however, that the plastic supplier, the vacuum forming machine manufacturer, and the ink manufacturer are in a position to give him much help before he starts actual vacuum forming.

Printing on Vacuum Formed Parts

While a vacuum forming demonstration may appear simple to the novice, the method may be misleading. The average printer who attempts printing and vacuum forming operations may take about six months before he is able to develop ideas into actual products. Therefore, the printer interested in doing forming and screen printing should first attempt a simple design, involving minimum and shallow draw depths. To obtain some experience it is suggested that the printer first form uncoated or unprinted plastic; then one color printed jobs; then two or more color jobs. Some practical experience may also be obtained by doing simple blister molding, as already explained.

Generally, the steps in screen printing and vacuum forming consist of: (1) creation of design to be reproduced into a three-dimensional product; (2) choosing the sheet plastic that will be best for the reproduction of the design; (3) transforming the original design into a mold or sculpture, depending upon the design; (4) developing a distorted print pattern on a plastic sheet as a guide for printing and making printing screens; (5) actual screen printing; (6) vacuum forming; (7) die-cutting and finishing the plastic formed pieces to shape; and (8) post-decorating processing, if design calls for this. It must be stated that every job has different requirements in printing, heating of plastic, forming, evacuating the air, and cooling the plastic. Also, the correct molding cycle for each job must be predetermined by tests. While the above tests appear simple, each sheet forming job is different, depending on the design, the plastic to be formed, the ink printed on the plastic, and the end result of the job. The printer may do only the printing for this type of work, or, if he is a specialist in vacuum forming, he may do both printing and forming.

The ink chosen for the job is very important and it is no accident that screen printing inks are employed for vacuum forming. They do have good adhesive qualities. Also, screen printing generally does not require clear protective over-coating for protection of printed design as is often necessary where the ink deposit is very thin. Inks specifically designed for vacuum forming are available from screen ink suppliers. Normally, the ink employed to print on a plastic should contain a liquid or solvent which is at least a partial solvent for the sheet plastic to be printed. Inks used should have perfect adhesion, should have some flexibility, and should be practical for over-printing over another color, should this be necessary. They should dry quickly and should have the desired common working properties found in the inks used for general screen printing.

There are screen printing inks which are formulated specifically for printing on plastics. There are inks and finishes for printing on acrylics, on cellulose type materials, styrene, epoxies, vinyls, polyethylene, ureas, phenolics, etc. The ink employed for printing on plastics is made of a pigmented or dye-colored solution or resinous liquid which is chemically similar to the plastic that is to be printed and formed. However, there are single inks that may be used on different types of plastics. For example, the printer may use a modified acrylic ink for printing-forming operations on acrylic sheets, cellulose acetate, cellulose butyrate, styrene, and rigid vinyl. However, it is suggested that in order to select the proper ink, the printer send a sample of the plastic material to the ink supplier to assure that the ink will have all the required qualities, since often the same type of plastic from one manufacturer may vary from batch to batch.

Although heat forming may improve the adhesion of some colors to a vacuum formed plastic, it is necessary to check the suitability of a color or ink for the depth of draw desired in vacuum forming. Also, at least 24 hours should elapse after test printing before evaluating the practicality of an ink for a plastic being printed. It is always necessary to determine the suitability of these inks for the draw of depth desired in order to standardize processing. A heavy coat of ink is normally necessary, as vacuum forming stretches ink as well as plastics.

In printing for vacuum forming as in other plastic printing, the ink must bind or weld to the plastic for the permanent life of the article; it should have chemical resistance equal to that of the plastic; it should pass through the common meshes of screen fabric; it should not fade; and generally it should be as color-fast as inks normally employed for screen printing. The ink should be practical for large area printing as well as for detail printing. It should not craze the plastic after printing. Using the wrong solvent or wrong additive may tend to produce crazing. Crazing is the development of fine cracks which may appear on or under the surface or through the layer of the plastic. The printer must realize that he cannot doctor up inks unless this is recommended by a reliable ink manufacturer after the manufacturer has printed on a sample of the material which was submitted by the screen printer. The printer must also realize that solvent resistance of plastics varies and that vacuum formed parts are to a certain extent internally strained. Therefore, excess use of solvent, for some reason or other, during printing operation may cause distortion, buckling, and damage to the surface of the plastic.

If possible, it is suggested that the printer print some multi-color detail jobs on the same day (under the same atmospheric conditions). For example, large plastic sheets which absorb moisture or are more hygroscopic may contract or expand with very extreme changes in atmospheric conditions. This may cause difficulty in registering detail on a large plastic sheet.

Generally, screen printing inks printed on vacuum formed items dry quicker than oil-vehicle inks. The inks may be allowed to dry naturally or drying may be accelerated. However, too rapid drying on some plastics may form a crust on the surface with solvent remaining under the crust. Also, since high heat tends to soften thermoplastics, the printer should use care in applying heat that is higher than about 100 degrees Fahrenheit (38 degrees Celsius) to accelerate drying. As correct drying is a very important part of any screen printing, the drying procedure should be pretested.

Screen printing is intimately related to vacuum forming operations. Printing may be done either before or after forming, depending on the complexity of the design, the number of colors printed and on the general processing, or a product may be printed first and then post-decorated as illustrated in Figure 182. The most challenging step, especially for the beginner, is the printing of a distorted pattern of the design on a flat plastic sheet and then forming the plastic sheet over the mold so that the parts and print appear exactly as desired and not distorted. Much screen printing involves printing the distorted pattern in the desired colors on a flat sheet and then forming the sheet into a product on which the design does not appear distorted and at the same time appears in perfect register. In doing this type of work, inks used should be those which have been tested for stretch, abrasion, and general durability.

One of the incentives which has increased the use of screen printing on vacuum formed plastic sheets is the accelerated growth of all types

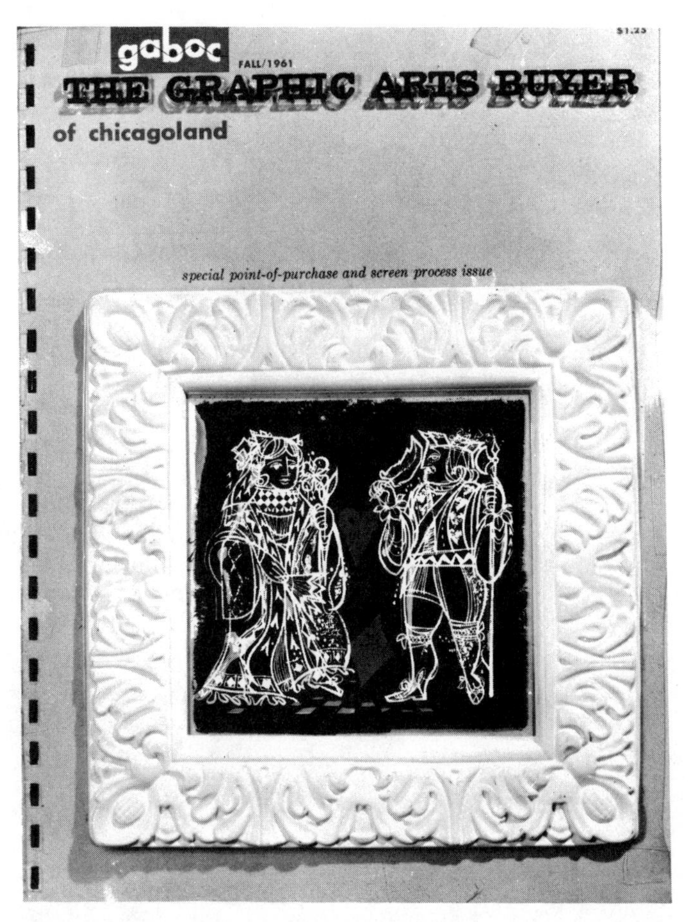

Figure 181. An attractive, unique, and detailed vacuum formed and screen printed magazine cover done on clear cellulose acetate butyrate plastic. Of the four colors printed on the cover, one color was printed on the back side and the other three colors on the front of the cover. The raised letters "The Graphic Arts Buyer" were roller-coated on. **(Courtesy of The Institute for Printing Sales, Chicago, Illinois)**

and sizes of plastic signs. In vacuum forming of plastic signs or other types of shapes the printer must determine how much to allow for stretching of the plastic. One of the ways of obtaining a print and a shape of a vacuum formed sign is by a trial and error method. In this method, especially if the object does not have too much draw, several formed signs are decorated either by hand brushing or spraying, using the exact inks and colors which are to be printed. Some printers pencil in the colors and determine register in printing from the penciled lines. Sometimes pencilling may be enough for preparing the printing

Figure 182. A large red styrene plastic sheet vacuum formed into a point-of-purchase display. The formed plastic then was screen printed in red ink in the required areas on the sheet. **(Courtesy of Burke Communications, Industries, Inc., Chicago, Illinois)**

plate. Then the formed decorated signs are placed in clamps and reheated until the formed sheet returns to a perfectly flat shape. The flat sheet will have the design on it in distorted fashion. A thermoplastic has what is known as "elastic memory"; that is, if the formed sheet is heated, it will become perfectly flat. The printing screen or

Figure 183. A large vacuum formed and screen printed window display made of high impact white styrene. The multicolor display was first printed and then vacuum formed of .020 inch (.051cm) styrene. The forming cycle consisted of 8 seconds for heating the plastic and 25 seconds for cooling. **(Courtesy of Burke Communication Industries, Inc., Chicago, Illinois)**

screens are then made from the varied colored design areas on the best flat sheet.

However, a more practical, exact, and more interesting way of obtaining a complex form and complex print for vacuum formed items is to employ what is known as the "grid method." In this method the printing is done before vacuum forming, as it may be too difficult to print on the object after forming. In the grid method a plastic sheet

Figure 184. The preprinted and preregistered plastic sheet is loaded into the vacuum forming machine. **(Courtesy of Liebig Industries, Beaver Dam, Wisconsin)**

Figure 185. Printed plastic sheet being pulled down mechanically over the positive mold forms prior to applying vacuum. **(Courtesy of Comet Industries, Inc., Bensenville, Illinois; and Liebig Industries, Beaver Dam, Wisconsin)**

Figure 186. Formed sheet is removed after forming and cooling.

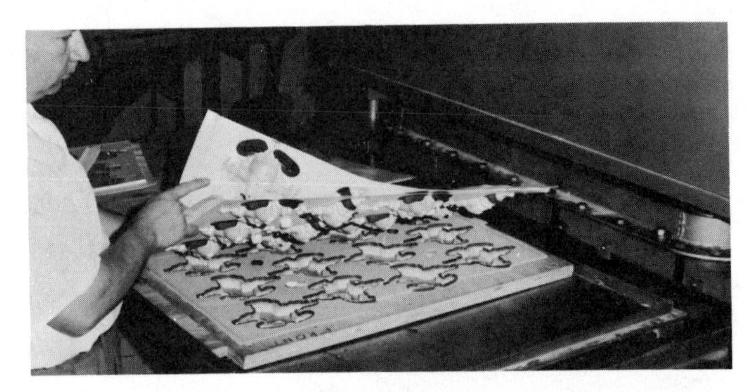

Figure 187. Die-cutting of the printed and vacuum formed clowns using steel dies on a Comet pneumatic trim press of 80 ton capacity. **(Courtesy of Comet Industries and Liebig Industries)**

of the material being formed is graphed or printed with parallel vertical and horizontal grid lines that are about ¼ inch (.635cm) apart. The graphed sheet is formed over a mold or pattern of the product to be reproduced. The full-size artwork of the job to be printed is also lined with squares corresponding in size of squares and numbering of lines to the squares on the plastic formed grid sheet. The artwork is then copied on the grid vacuum formed sheet so that the design in the squares of the artwork corresponds to the identical squares on the formed plastic sheet. After the artwork has been outlined on the formed grid sheet, the sheet is heated so that it returns to its original flat shape. The flat plastic grid sheet with its distorted design is used to make the printing screens and to aid in registering the varied colors on flat sheets before the sheets are vacuum formed. In forming the grid sheets a heat cycle of slightly less time than the production cycle is used. In heating the grid sheet great care should be taken not to overheat. The

Figure 188. The front and back of the finished clown. **(Courtesy of Comet Industries, Inc., Bensenville, Illinois)**

critical factor in vacuum forming and screen printing is time control for heating the plastic sheet. However, automatic time controls on vacuum forming machines have made this type of printing-forming a practical means of production.

Once the printing is started with vacuum forming operation, salvaging the pieces becomes almost impossible and mistakes in printing and forming must be avoided, since labor is costly and sheets are generally large. (See Figure 182).

As far as printing screens for vacuum forming-printing are concerned, any tough screen that will resist the inks being printed may be used. Direct photographic and direct-indirect printing screens prepared on synthetic fabrics and metal cloth, and water-soluble hand-prepared knife-cut films are employed.

Figures 183 and 188 present two interesting but very different vacuum formed and printed products which were printed before forming. Figures 184 through 187 show forming operations; Figure 188 presents the finished printed and vacuum formed job.

In summary, vacuum forming is an art based on experience and is also a science governed by the properties of the plastic, ink, preparation of printing screens, preparation of printing of trial sheets, and the total processes involved in the interdependence of each step.

Chapter 29

CERAMIC SCREEN PRINTING

Some of the principles of ceramic processes and arts are secrets which are lost in antiquity. While the ceramic principles may differ from those of screen printing, the service offered by the latter process to ceramics forms a useful link between the two.

Because of the efficient mechanized, semi-automatic, and hand production, screen printing has become a very important and practical method for decorations and finishing permanently and semi-permanently varied surfaces and shapes of earthenware, porcelainware, glassware, and building material. The versatility and flexibility of this printing process, the variability of designs made possible by photographic printing screens, the expertly hand-prepared knifecut screens, and the colorful ready-made ceramic inks and colors have increased the quality and quantity of ceramic screen printing in varied parts of the world.

Ceramic screen printing* is an inexpensive technique considering the results obtained. The printing produces uniformity of work without requiring specially trained workers. It presents many creative opportunities and makes possible the printing of artistically and industrially acceptable large solid and detailed areas with ceramic colors, porcelain or vitreous enamels, rare metals, and glass ceramic enamels. Besides printing varied thicknesses and coatings, it is superior to the older methods of hand painting and stenciling of glaze and ceramic materials. The ceramic coatings have chemical resistance to acids, alkalis, and resist the caustic attacks of strong washing solutions at temperatures that normally wear away ordinary organic inks or paints. Screen printing applies and adheres designs to surfaces so that the coating does not run off the surface or ware before or after firing. However, the applied colors can be removed before firing by washing the color off with simple solvents or by buffing.

This expanding branch of screen printing produces a variety of

* A complete treatment of ceramic screen printing is found in the book: Kosloff, Albert, *Ceramic Screen Printing*. St Publications, Book Division, Cincinnati, Ohio 45202.

shapes and designs on ceramic products such as tiles for decorating and building purposes, cosmetic containers, fired-on permanent labels for all types of bottles, glass, ash trays, cigarette boxes, permanently labeled tiny medicine ampoules, gas ranges, refrigerators, vases, lamp bases, signs, coffee tables, novelties, ceramic decalcomanias, and numerous other items.

Ceramic screen printing is done in two general ways: (1) by printing directly with printing screens onto ware and objects and (2) by printing ceramic decalcomanias or transfers on decalcomania papers. While direct printing is essential and may be preferred in many cases, the convenience of being able to handle detailed designs in the form of a decal, being able to print the decal in many colors, and being able to print many decals with one printing screen in one operation does away with some problems common in printing directly on ceramic products. The decals, which are designed for later application onto ceramic products, are generally transferred to more complex surfaces which are not practical for direct printing. Decals are also printed by the printer upon order and specifications of the ceramist who applies the decals to his ware for firing. Decals are widely used in the decoration of dishes, tableware, and tiles for building and for novelty purposes.

In order to understand, to be able to relate, and to compare this type of printing with other methods, the printer should become acquainted with the terminology that is peculiar to ceramics and the related screen printing. It is also essential that one understand the type of inks or colors that are printed on ceramic surfaces; the properties of these inks; the firing or fusing of the printed designs onto the ceramic, glass, or metal surfaces; and the equipment that the printer will need for doing this type of printing.

The screen printer prints on glazed and unglazed surfaces, on porcelain-enameled surfaces with porcelain or vitreous enamels, on glassware with glass inks or colors that are fused to the glass, and he prints with ceramic inks on decalcomania papers.

The coating, decoration, or chemical composition of color applied by the printing screen is dependent on the surface and material being printed and upon the proposed use of the product. Although surfaces such as ceramic, glass, or glazed materials, and metal, each being different, require different formulations of inks and different processing, ceramic screen printing is similar to other screen printing. The difference in the ceramic color porcelain enamel, or frit ink is in the chemical composition and in the fact that each of these colors must be fired or fused to the printed surface after the printing is completed. Temperatures range, method of firing, chemical composition of ink or colors, thickness of printed color, type of printing screen used, color or colors desired, and general processing are directly or indirectly controlled by firing. Also, since the inks must be fused or welded into the surface, it is necessary to use an ink or color for permanent printing that has similar composition to the surface being printed. Since practical results can only be seen after the firing has taken place, any color formula worked out by the printer must always stand the final test—that of being fired in an oven such as a kiln or lehr.

The inks or colors employed for ceramic screen printing bear similarity to the following: glazes, overglazes, frits, glass enamels, porcelain or vitreous enamels, and royal metals such as gold, silver, and platinum which have been compounded in such a way that they can be printed by means of screen printing. Although the lower temperature baking organic type glass enamels are greatly used for temporary and semi-permanent use, these are not included in this discussion, since they are not of ceramic composition.

Ceramic Inks or Colors

Most ceramic inks or ceramic colors are really glazes. Volumes have been written on the subject of glazes and the term is not easy to define. However, for practical purposes, a glaze, basically, is a glass coating composition, prepared so that it will adhere and fuse permanently to a ceramic surface after the glaze-coated article has been fired to the required temperature for a specific time length. Glaze colors have and are being used because they make an article more durable, more waterproof, and more attractive. The printer prints glaze compositions mostly for decorative purposes. Generally, glazes contain powdered glass, a flux for lowering the firing temperature or for increasing the fluidity of the molten glaze, and a substance to give the glaze viscosity so that it will not drain off during firing. For screen printing another ingredient is necessary—a vehicle or viscous liquid for holding the finely ground ingredients so that these may be printed through the printing screen.

There are generally two types of glass used: raw glass and frit glass. Frit is composed of materials similar to glass such as silica, feldspar, sand, and borax which acts as a flux. The latter mixture of ingredients of correct proportions is placed in a crucible and heated from about 2300 to 2500 degrees Fahrenheit (1260 to 1731 degrees Celsius). The high temperatures form a molten glass which is quenched or poured into cold water. This quenching operation or *fritting* causes the glass to shatter into tiny particles known as "frit." The frit is then ground in special mills with clay water, ceramic pigments for color, and a suspending medium for holding the particles in a thick liquid which is used for dipping, spraying, or for screen printing. In some cases, metallic oxides such as oxides of antimony, manganese, tin, etc. are added for color during the grinding operation. A frit does not have objectionable raw materials found in ordinary raw glass, since these have been burned out in the preparation of the frit. A frit has less tendency to crack in firing. Also, fritting changes many soluble materials into insoluble forms. Consequently, many of the ceramic colors used in screen printing are prepared with frits, since they give more uniform results in color and in firing.

The early screen printing experimenters used clear screen printing lacquer as a vehicle into which was mixed a powdered colored frit, a plain frit, or a shattered glass powder. Then to a pint of this paste, the printer added approximately one-half liquid ounce (14.787cc), or about 10 drops of oil of cloves. Butyl lactate was added to the well mixed ingredients to obtain proper screening consistency. The oil of cloves aided in preventing blistering, pinholing, carbonizing, and other defects. Today's screen printer may buy his colors ready for screen printing or may obtain standard ingredients from suppliers with specific directions for mixing.

Ceramic inks or colors, after being standardized by the printer, whether formulated by the printer or bought from a supplier, must withstand certain tests and should give standardized results under similar processing. The fired ink should have the desired color appearance, should be insoluble, and resistant to use and weathering. The ink should have such viscosity during firing that it will cover defects and will not run off the object being fired. At the same time, the fired ink should keep the printed detail. In firing, it is desirable that the ink have a wide enough firing or maturing range to take care of slight variation in temperature. It should not be necessary to maintain firing temperatures too near the critical point of the ware that has been printed or coated. The printed color should expand approximately at the same rate as the glaze or ware on which it was printed; otherwise the print may craze or crack. Also, under the same firing conditions the same color should be produced each time after being fired.

The ink should have approximately the same printing qualities as other screen printing inks. It should print sharp detail, depending on the design, printing screen, and ink employed. Ceramic colors should not clog the screen and should be cleaned easily off the screen. The vehicle or the liquid in which the color and ingredients are mixed before applying to the surface must fire or burn away completely and not be left as a residue on the ware and not cause blistering, crawling, or other defects. It should be possible to shade and also produce pastel colors; however, this mixing should be done according to recommendations of the manufacturer or based upon the results of the printer's experimentation. Ceramic inks must be ground fine enough to pass easily through the finest screen fabric that the printer will use. For example, if the printer will employ a 300 mesh screen, (about 118 mesh per centimeter) then the solids in the ink should be ground finer than 300 mesh. Of course, there should be no objectionable or toxic odor given off by the ink in the complete printing and finishing operation.

Glaze coats fire from about 1250 to 2400 degrees Fahrenheit (677 to 1316 degrees Celsius) depending on the type of ware to which the coating is applied, whether the coat is underglaze or overglaze, how thick the coating is, and other variable factors. The time of firing screen printed work varies from about 3 minutes to about 6 hours and is governed by the ceramic ink printed, the thickness of the coat, the type of ware, and the type of oven used.

Glaze colors are applied by dipping the object in glaze solution, by pouring the glaze color over the article, by brushing, spraying, and screen printing. Glaze mediums are available in varied colors, in transparent, opaque, and in gloss and matte finish. Although transparent gloss colors may be made opaque by the addition of certain ingredients and glazes may be changed somewhat, this addition should be done only as specified in the manufacturer's directions. Also, a softening or hardening flux added to a mixture either to lower or raise the firing temperature should be done according to manufacturer's specifications or printer's results of experimentation. As a rule, articles are coated with underglaze before the printer prints the overglaze colors or ink on them. However, the printer may also print glazes directly on unglazed ware or clay that has been fired.

An overglaze is a color (or a glaze and a color) used for decoration on top of a glaze. As the name signifies, overglazes are applied after the body glaze or underglaze, usually of a transparent type, has been fired, while an underglaze or body glaze color can be used either over or in a glaze. The printer planning to print with underglaze and overglaze colors should purchase these from the same manufacturer or supplier to insure that the overglaze fits the underglaze in every respect.

Overglaze colors for screen printing are obtainable in paste-form ready and mixed for screen printing. The use of paste-form ceramic inks is an advantage since it eliminates the need for milling and grinding of colors and milling equipment necessary for the accurate mixing of colors. They are also available in powder form and must be mixed by the user according to specifications with the correct vehicle to the required paste consistency so that the color may be squeegeed normally through a printing screen. Many colors of overglaze type may be applied but each color must dry thoroughly before the next one is printed or applied.

After using some glaze colors, such as those containing lead, the hands should be washed well, since lead composition colors may be detrimental to the health of some individuals. Also, the printer who makes a practice of using continually and daily finely ground powders such as silica or other ceramic products should keep the dust content of the air at a minimum.

Porcelain or Vitreous Enamel

Porcelain or vitreous enamel is not an organic paint but is a ceramic material which is a combination of glass and a metal. The glass part of this combination in the porcelain enameling industry or in screen printing is frit.

Porcelain enameling is the process of applying and fusing the glassy material onto a metal surface. Although white enamel is common, almost any color frit and transparent frit may be obtained for screen printing of enamels. The fusing enamel may be applied to enameling iron, aluminum, or to copper, onto stainless steels, and gold. Vitreous enamels screen printed on aluminum produce very vivid effects. They are applied either directly onto the prepared aluminum surface or over a semi-transparent ground coat which has been previously fired. A very important and related part is the correct cleaning and preparation of the metal surface by means of "pickling" or etching to do away with dirt and grease. Generally, enamels for steel and iron are opaque and cover the underlying surface completely. Opaque enamels are also used to produce designs on enamel coats.

As is true with glaze colors, porcelain enamel colors are compatible and may be blended with others to obtain intermediate shades. Color enamels are made by adding metallic oxides to the frit. Different oxides of metals produce different colors when fired.

Screen printing colors for porcelain enamel are fluxed dry powders which are ground by the printer with "squeegee" oil or a screen printing oil to a paste. The paste may be screen printed onto enamel that has been fired. Several colors may be fired at one time. However, each color must be hardened or baked lightly before the next color is screen printed. Usually the screen printing oil or vehicle requires a slow heating at first to allow the vehicle or organic material to burn out before the enamels fuse.

These enamels are fired from about 1000 to about 1600 degrees Fahrenheit (538 to 871 degrees Celsius), depending on the enamel, surface printed, the oven, and the length of the firing cycle.

Permanent enamels for printing on varied shaped glass surfaces are available as inks for screen printing application and as powders to be mixed by the printer into inks. These enamels are the inorganic or ceramic type not the organic enamels that are baked on glass at temperatures varying from about 400 to 600 degrees Fahrenheit (204 to 316 degrees Celsius); organic enamels are not designed for permanent use.

Besides organic or paint type colors used for nonpermanent screen printing on glass, two general types of ceramic colors are employed for more permanent printing on glass: (1) conventional ceramic glass colors and (2) "hot color," thermofluid, or thermoplastic ceramic colors.

The ceramic type glass enamels come in varied brilliant colors, have a high gloss, good working properties, and may be fired from about 1000 to 1250 degrees Fahrenheit, (538 to 677 degrees Celsius), the range of firing being dependent on whether the glass enamel is to be applied to surfaces that are to have resistance to acids or alkalis or whether resistance is not important. Glass articles that are to be used again and again such as milk bottles, soft drink bottles, or glasses are printed with resistant colors. See Figure 189.

The glass enamels are formulated so that the coefficient of expansion is close to that of glass and therefore no strain is present during firing. The colors are used for printing and decorating lighting fixtures, flat glass, tumblers, bottles from about ¼ inch (.635cm) in diameter to 5 gallon (22.024 liters) sizes, lamp bulbs, and convexing glass printing. Convexing glass enamels are generally screened on flat glass and are fired at the same time the product is convexed or formed in a mold.

Glass ceramic enamels are available in opaque, transparent, gloss and matte colors of all types. Where the powder is mixed with the screening vehicle or oil, it is done simply but carefully as specified by the manufacturer or supplier of the glass enamel.

As with other ceramic colors, glass enamels should be mixed thoroughly before printing onto surfaces. Gloss enamels may be screened over each other without firing separately each applied color. However, each applied color should be dried perfectly before the next color is printed.

In working in a specialized printing field such as ceramic printing, the printer must form the habit of using rigid controls, standardizing his processes, keeping records of all performances, especially at first, watching firing temperatures and time cycles, recording formulations or mixtures of inks, keeping printing surfaces clean, and, in general, striving for standardized quality work.

In the hot color type of ceramic screen printing, a formulated ceramic color is dispersed in a low melting wax type vehicle. The ceramic

Figure 189. A four-color halftone ceramic screen print of "By The Seashore" by Renoir, screen printed with glass enamel on flat glass, including a gold border on the four edges. **(Courtesy of Wire Cloth Enterprises, Pittsburgh, Pennsylvania)**

color is solid at room temperature, but becomes liquid when the ink is heated during the printing step at temperatures ranging from about 130 to 200 degrees Fahrenheit (54 to 93 degrees Celsius). Generally, the hot printing is done with an electrically heated stainless steel screen; although heat has been applied above the screen with infrared energy. The hardening takes place immediately as the ink is printed on the glass object. There is no time consumed in drying and the object may be fired immediately after printing.

Most printers who start in ceramic screen printing start on a small scale and as they progress standardize each step in the process completely. The printer must be sure of his processes, techniques, and equipment under controlled conditions before he can assure a constant service to his clientele. This involves standardization of the printing so that he can assure reproduction of colorful designs.

Ceramic printing like most screen printing starts with the design to be reproduced. Almost any design from simple one-color line copy to multi-colored designs reproduced by means of halftone screen printing exemplified in ceramic decalcomania printing may be used. For the beginner it is suggested that the design be a simple but attractive two color job, one that is not too difficult to register, one that may be printed with ready-to-use commercial screen printing ceramic pastes manufactured for printing directly on the product, and one that may be printed with a screen fabric that is equivalent to about 123 mesh per inch (about 50 per cm).

Although hand-prepared screens may be used in ceramic printing, the photographic method is employed wherever possible. This implies that the artwork must be finished, since imperfections will show up in the final photographic positive used for making the printing screen. Artwork for ceramic printing usually is two or three times the size of the finished print. Decreasing the size of copy photographically to printing size eliminates slight imperfections and allows for better preparation of designs, especially small designs. The usual photographic positive is required for each color to be printed. The positive is the actual size of the final printing job. The positive is not only used for making the printing screen but also may be employed as an aid in registering the colors, especially on tiles, ash trays, and the like.

Before doing an actual production run, some shops first hand paint an imitation of the original design onto the actual ceramic surface to be printed with the ceramic ink or color to be used. The hand-painted job which the final screen printed job approximates in detail and other phases, is fired under the normal firing conditions planned for the job.

The unknown quality in screen printing is how the colors in the printed design will look after the design has been fired. Therefore, in using a line of colors it is practical for the printer to try out his colors first before even attempting a trial firing on a job. This may be done by printing coarse and detailed designs in colors on test ceramic surfaces under the standard shop conditions through the various screen fabric mesh which it is felt will produce the best results. The firing of these test printed samples is done under the conditions recommended by the color manufacturer. Specifically, where the test sample of colors has to be exact, the printer may print the sample through three printing screens, one screen employing the actual screen fabric mesh intended for the job, a second screen having a fine screen mesh, and the third screen having a fabric that is coarser than the desired screen. For example, if it is desired to use Number 14 screen fabric or an equivalent metal or synthetic fabric for the final printing screen, then the sample printing should be done through a Number 12, 14, and Number 16 screen fabric. This is advisable and is obvious in very fine detail printing, since each fabric number will deposit a different thickness coat which may fire out slightly different.

Kilns and Lehrs

Firing, which is really a heat treating and important process necessitates planning, since poor firing procedure will destroy the best printing. These are various types and styles of kilns used in the ceramic industry and in screen printing for firing and fusing materials and coatings onto ceramic surfaces.

The choice of equipment for firing depends upon the type and amount of ware the printer plans to decorate, the shop space available, the type of fuel that is economical and practical in the locality, the largest size piece to be printed in the average run, industrial zoning regulations, and other factors.

The printer employs two general types of kilns, a periodic or portable type illustrated in Figure 190 and the tunnel or lehr type shown in Figure 191. The periodic kiln is one in which the firing cycle is accomplished in steps or periods; that is, the kiln is loaded with the printed ware, the ware is fired, allowed to cool, unloaded, the kiln loaded again with ware, and then fired again. The beginner ordinarily uses kilns of the periodic type. These are available in any needed size or style. They may be portable, have electric heating elements which may be replaced when they burn out, and may be installed wherever standard electric power is available. These beginner kilns or experimental kilns can be obtained with three-way switches for low, medium, and high temperatures. Kilns may be fired or heated with gas, coal, electricity, or oil. The fuel used depends on local availability and cost.

The lehr or tunnel kiln is used for continuous operation and is found in larger industrial shops which do much ceramic work and printing on glass and other such items. The lehr consists of a metal woven wire or metal belt conveyor on which the printed objects are placed for continuous firing. The ware travels slowly on this moving belt through the heat area where it comes in contact with zones of

Figure 190. Dyna-Trol front loading kiln or electric furnace provides firing temperatures up to 3000 degrees Fahrenheit (1649 degrees Celsius), with firing chamber up to 24″ x 24″ x 24″ (61cm x 61cm x 61cm), and may be used for experimental and production work. Kiln is equipped with pyrometer for determining temperature at all times, and furnace may also be used for enameling, glass annealing, and the like. **(Courtesy of L and L Manufacturing Co., Twin Oaks, Delaware County, Pennsylvania)**

Figure 191. A Surface Combustion decorating lehr for firing varied shaped glass containers, decorated tumblers, precious metals, lighting fixtures, and the like. Units up to 300 feet or more may be built to the screen printer's specifications, using modular construction with individual controlled heat zones, employing direct or indirect fired heat. **(Courtesy of Surface Combustion Division, Midland-Ross Corp., Toledo, Ohio)**

increasing temperatures. The firing zone is generally near the middle of the tunnel. The conveyor speed corresponds to the length of time it takes for the printing to be fired. The printed ware approaches the first zone or preheating zone, moves to and is fired in the firing zone, and then cools gradually before reaching the other end where it may be removed and packed. The firing cycle is dependent on the speed of firing which in turn is governed by the speed of the conveyor or tunnel car if a car is used to hold the ware instead of a conveyor. The speed may be controlled.

Lehrs vary in size from about 25 feet (7.62 meters) to about 200 feet (60.96m) in length with a firing chamber of 4 feet (1.219m) in width and 7 feet (2.134m) in height. Lehrs are ventilated so that any type of fuel may be used and so that gases formed in firing will not tend to distort or destroy the printing. The open-fire method, which is widely used in industry for the firing, employs natural gas, fuel oil, or propane as the fuel. Lehrs are equipped with automatic controls or with recording and indicating temperature controls.

The temperature for firing commercial kilns varies. For example, the manufacturer of tiles who may make tiles by means of a two-fire process, first may fire the bisque clay (unglazed clay) at a temperature that may exceed 2100 degrees Fahrenheit (1149 Celsius). The second firing which is done at a lower temperature matures the glaze coating and makes it hard and dense by fusing the glaze to the bisque tile. The printed design which would be printed on the glaze coating would be fired at a slightly lower temperature. Thus it becomes evident that the kiln is dependent on the type of work that will be done in the particular shop.

The printer who plans to build a kiln or have one built should first of all experience firing the various types of jobs that he will print. He should obtain advice of ceramic engineers, brick manufacturers, or others in the field, since once the kiln or lehr is built it will represent quite an investment and will have to be serviceable and practical. If he is planning to purchase one, he should experience firing so that the best type may be obtained for his use and demands. A poor kiln or incorrect firing procedure will damage the whole printing job, produce undesired color results, consume time and labor, and in general will not be economical.

Although a kiln may be found outside the shop premises, firing away from one's shop is costly and often difficult, since it involves packaging and transporting the pieces. More important, the printer is dependent on outside service for his completion of the printing process. This is not always an efficient method of printing.

The rule for firing is that the printed matter on the ware be fired at such a temperature that the design will not be distorted by the heat and the product itself will not be destroyed or its shape changed. The firing temperatures are recommended by the manufacturer of the color printed. However, firing temperatures are also determined by the composition of the piece screened. Best control for firing, either in a kiln or lehr, is obtained by gradual firing, that is, increasing the temperature gradually up to the maturing temperature.

Measuring Temperature

Pyrometers and pyrometric cones are used to measure temperature in kilns when firing. Pyrometers are heat registering instruments which record lehr and kiln temperatures. Pyrometric cones are common measuring temperature devices and are used with or without pyrometers. These are slender triangular pyramid shaped cones about 3 inches (7.62cm) in height placed in a conspicuous location in a firing area and are used for observing and for guiding the proper firing progress of all types of kiln-fired ceramic products. Their composition is similar to the ceramic product being fired. They are manufactured so that they bend, deform, or melt at known temperatures. Each cone is usually marked indicating its temperature equivalent. Some ceramists and printers employ a series of three cones in aiding in the firing process. The cones generally are placed one after the other, near each other. The middle or second cone is selected because it bends or melts at

TEMPERATURE EQUIVALENTS OF CONES

Cone Number	Cent.	Fahr.	Cone Number	Cent.	Fahr.
022	585	1085	01	1110	2030
021	595	1103	1	1125	2057
020	625	1157	2	1135	2075
019	630	1166	3	1145	2093
018	670	1238	4	1165	2129
017	720	1328	5	1180	2156
016	735	1355	6	1190	2174
015	770	1418	7	1210	2210
014	795	1463	8	1225	2237
013	825	1517	9	1250	2282
012	840	1544	10	1260	2300
011	875	1607	11	1285	2345
010	890	1634	12	1310	2390
09	930	1706	13	1350	2462
08	945	1733	14	1390	2534
07	975	1787	15	1410	2570
06	1005	1841	16	1450	2642
05	1030	1886	17	1465	2669
04	1050	1922	18	1485	2705
03	1080	1976	19	1515	2759
02	1095	2003	20	1520	2768

Figure 192. Table of standard pyrometric cones and temperature of each numbered cone. **(Courtesy of The O. Hommel Company, Pittsburgh, Pennsylvania)**

or near the temperature at which the kiln is to be heated and the ware is actually to be fired. The first cone melts just below the desired temperature and the third cone just above the desired temperature. The kiln is shut off when the middle cone bends over. The table in Figure 192 illustrates standard pyrometric cones ranging from Number 022 to Number 20 and their equivalent temperatures in Fahrenheit and Centigrade degrees. No printer is likely to use all these cones. For example, the printer who prints with overglaze colors only will probably use cones Number 020 (1157 degrees Fahrenheit; 625 degrees Celsius) to Cone Number 010 (1634 degrees Fahrenheit; 890 degrees Celsius).

Other Equipment

As the printer continues to grow in this type of printing he will find that he will need more equipment than a kiln in order to offer a service. In the past screen printing schops designed and built equipment based on individual shop requirements and results of experience and experimental work. Today equipment may be obtained from screen printing suppliers and from ceramic products suppliers.

Although the large very specialized shop does its own grinding of colors, every ceramic printer at times will have occasion to do some mixing, milling, or grinding of ceramic colors and powders for trial or special jobs. Whether it's mixing color or actual printing, orderly and clean procedure is essential for ceramic printing. See Figures 193 and 194.

The printer will need a burr mill or color grinding mill for general mixing and grinding of colors and a scale for weighing accurately the ingredients. Burr mills are simple to operate and are available with hopper capacity of ¼ gallon (1.1012 liters) and up to any practical size. As an aid in doing grinding and weighting it is suggested that the novice become acquainted with metric system weights and measurements, since this system generally makes the calculating easier and more practical. The printer will also need well-designed storage equipment and space for colors and for storing the ware before it is printed and after it is fired. Where a lehr is employed for firing the printer may package the printed and finished ceramic article in a carton upon removal of ware from the conveyor.

Ceramic powder colors must be kept dry and should be stored in a warm dry place. Moisture in colors may produce difficulty in obtaining clean prints.

Printing of Precious Metals

Bright genuine gold is being printed in some shops both directly on ware and on decal papers. While some of the gold is being printed on cylindrical glass shapes with machines, it is also being printed by

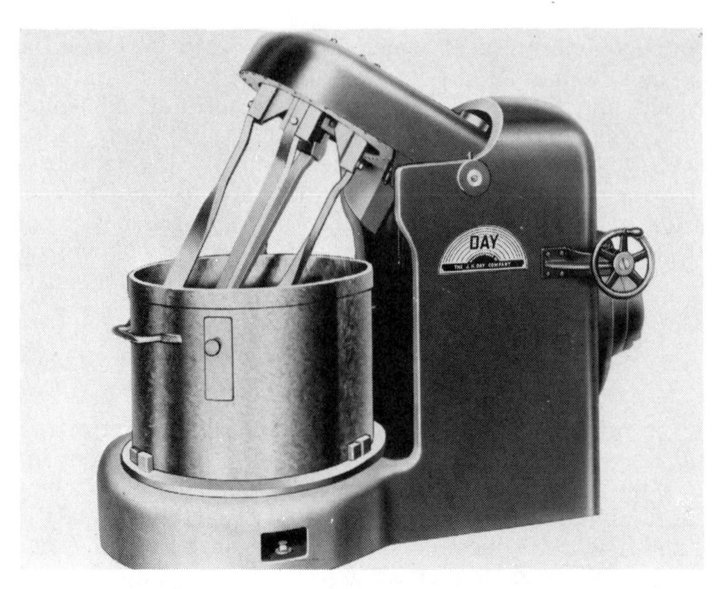

Figure 193. A gearless type pony mixer with tilted head for premixing colors, pigments, fillers, and vehicles. **(Courtesy of The J. H. Day Company, Cincinnati, Ohio)**

hand on glazed tiles, lamp bases, serving trays, novelties, and other glazed ware.

The screen printing of gold is similar to other ceramic screen printing, except that in screening gold, it is suggested that the printing screen be made of a tough thin good quality screen fabric. The combined thickness of the fabric and the sensitized screen printing film or coating should be thinner than normal. While some manufacturers of bright gold ink recommend that a special silk made specifically for gold printing be used, the finer woven metal cloth and monofilament nylon or polyester may also be employed. As far as the gold ink is concerned, it is recommended that the gold ink be purchased, since it is made especially for screen printing and requires chemical knowledge and technical skill for its manufacture and compounding. The gold is formulated in an organic vehicle which burns off in the firing process.

The printing should be done on ware that is made of glass or is glazed. The ware must be perfectly clean and dry. Like most ceramic printing, gold is printed by means of the off-contact or line-contact method. Since in this method the screen rests about ⅛ to ¼ inch (.32 to .64cm) above the article being printed, the screen fabric only touches the article when the squeegee is pressed down and only in the spot where the squeegee comes in contact with the article. As soon as the squeegee pressure is removed, the screen fabric springs away, thus eliminating a smeared line and producing a sharp print. A hard sharp

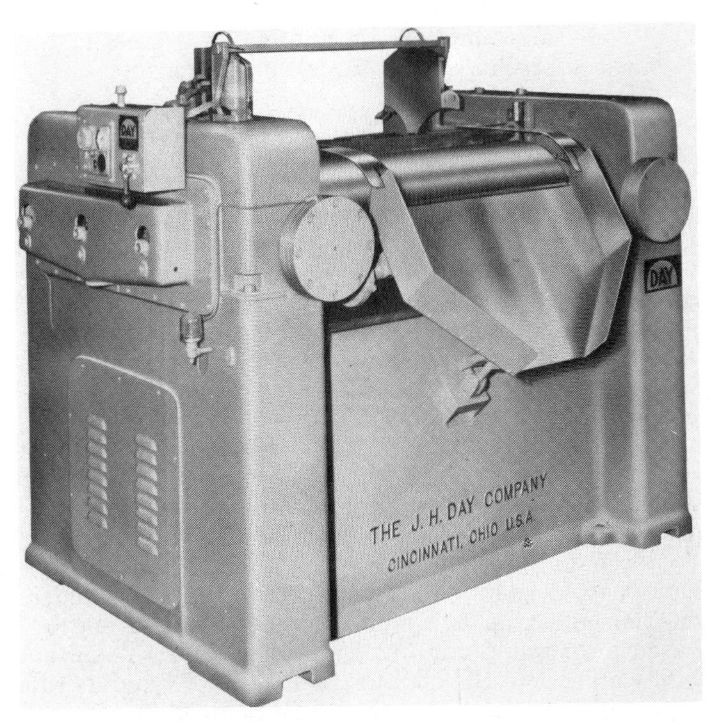

Figure 194. A Three Roll Mill with hydraulic roll set and transfer blade for dispersing all types of inks and removing air from paste materials. **(Courtesy of The J. H. Day Company, Cincinnati, Ohio)**

rubber squeegee blade should be used with uniform pressure for each stroke. Should the gold ink become too stiff for squeegeeing, a few drops of oil of lavender may be added to the mixture.

A thin coat of gold generally fires out brighter than one that is deposited thicker. Thick coats may fire out so that the print looks dull. In firing gold it is suggested that the temperature by 150 to 200 degrees Fahrenheit (66 to 93 degrees Celsius) lower than that used for firing the color or surface upon which the gold was printed. Good ventilation is essential for firing gold. The firing cycle is not as long as for firing ceramic color or pottery. However, the firing should be gradual. A lehr or a kiln may be employed for firing. The higher the temperature, the lower should be the time of firing. Depending on the ware or article, the time of firing in some cases may be from 5 to 10 minutes. Temperatures for firing range from about 1050 to 1500 degrees Fahrenheit (566 to 816 degrees Celsius). In some cases a 5 to 10 minutes preheating of the ware is necessary at about 400 to 500 degrees Fahrenheit (204 to 260 degrees Celsius). After the preheating, the printed gold may be flash-fired or fired.

Truly, the techniques of screen printing have brought the beauty and enjoyment of precious metal to the common man.

Printing Screens for Ceramic Screen Printing

Industrial methods and processes must be mutually adapted to each other. Although ceramic colors are ground to a very fine state, they still have some abrasive action in printing because of their glass-like composition. Therefore, the best quality screen printing films or coatings should be used and the best and most practical screen fabric should be employed in the preparation of the printing plate. Although at first direct screens were used for ceramic screen printing because they were tougher and longer lasting, direct, transfer films, and direct-indirect screens may be used. Knife-cut film is employed where the design is not too detailed and where the thickness of ink deposit is not of much concern. However, where detailed design is to be reproduced and where deposit of the ink has to be thin, photographic printing screens are generally used.

Double-X (XX) quality silk, metal fabric such as stainless steel, and monofilament nylon and monofilament polyester are the screen fabrics used for ceramic printing. Depending on the detail and upon the type of work, about No. 6XX to about No. 25XX and its equivalent screen fabric may be used. The screen fabric used in each case must be one that will allow the ink to pass easily through the mesh. It stands to reason that if the ceramic color is made of a powder that has been sifted originally through a Number 250 screen wire mesh, that the number of the screen fabric used for the printing would have to be less than Number 250 metal wire and the openings in the screen fabric would have to be larger than Number 250. Although metal screen fabrics are used, metal cloth does leave a heavier deposit on the ceramic ware. This may not be practical for printing detail, since too heavy a color deposit may have a tendency for the impression to peel away from the printed surface during firing. However, in printing on glass bottles with ceramic glass enamels, metal fabrics may be used. For printing genuine gold inks, silk and nylon may be employed, although the silk must be tough and thin.

As far as the screen fabric is concerned, the screen printer must make sure that the ceramic color or ink used is finely ground. Also, in choosing a screen fabric, the printer should choose one that he has tried and found practical for specific types of jobs. With the direct coatings used for preparing screens or where a screen printing film has been given a protective coating to make it more resistant to printing, it is possible to obtain as high as 7500 impressions, especially where metal fabrics are used.

Direct Printing Screens

Direct printing screens* used for ceramic printing may be coated with commercial coating emulsions, with polyvinyl alcohol solutions, modified polyvinyl plastics, polyvinyl alcohol-polyvinyl acetate, and gelatinous compositions. The emulsions may be obtained from reliable screen printing suppliers with directions for their preparation. Generally, the coatings consist of two stock solutions which may be prepared—an emulsion and a simple sensitizer such as potassium bichromate or ammonium bichromate or diazo type sensitizer. The stock solutions will keep. However once they are mixed together, then they should be used as specified in the manufacturer's directions.

In the preparation of the direct screen, the printer must make sure that the screen fabric is clean, that is, free of inks, grease, oil, or any other foreign matter, and that the screen is taut and of the correct mesh. For the average ceramic printing, numbers 120 to 140 mesh per inch (47 to 55 per cm) may be used for preparation of direct screens. If a halftone is to be reproduced, depending on the halftone dots, 140 to about 170 mesh (55 to 67 per cm) may be employed. However, the printer should have tested the printing and firing quality of any ink before using a specific type of screen fabric. Where metal fabric is used, either for direct or indirect screens, Number 140 to 250 mesh (55 to 98 mesh per cm) wire may be used with Number 165 mesh (65 mesh per cm) being used for most work. Also nylon, monofilament polyester, and special silk may be employed for the screen.

With most solutions, the coating onto the screen fabric should be done under subdued light (15 amperes incandescent bulbs or less may be used). However, it is best that the screen be dried in complete darkness. The coatings generally are not light-sensitive when in solution but are light sensitive when dried in the form of a coating. Therefore, after the first coating dries and when it becomes necessary to apply another coat over the dried coat, it is best to do the coating in a darkroom or in a dark area.

The sensitized solution may be applied with a piece of cardboard, with a squeegee, by being poured onto the screen fabric, by means of a coating trough (see Figures 195 and 196) or with the aid of a device such as that illustrated in Figure 197.

A common way of coating is to pour a little of the solution at one end of the screen and to squeegee the solution across with a clean squeegee or with a sharp edged cardboard. The first coating is applied on the inside of the screen since it will serve as a base for coats which are to follow. It is very important that each applied coat dries

* The following book covers photographic printing plates: Kosloff, Albert, *Photographic Screen Printing.* ST Publications, Book Division, Cincinnati, Ohio, 45202.

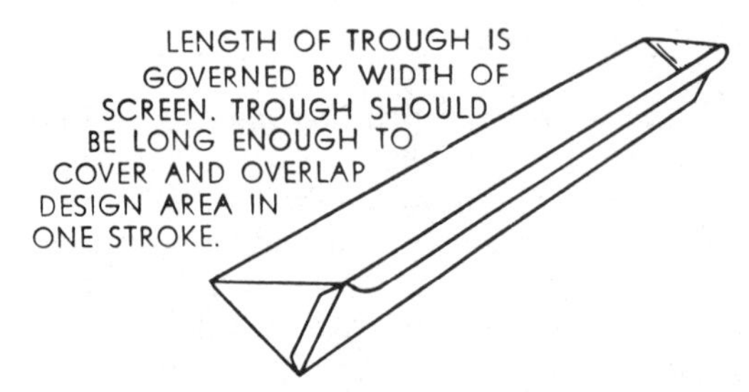

Figure 195. Coating trough for applying sensitized solution to screen fabric.

thoroughly before applying the next coat. Where the printer may be in doubt about the preparation of a screen, it is suggested that he refer to the sections on their preparation in this book.

In the trough method, a coating trough is filled with enough solution to complete each coating. The screen is held rigid in a vertical position with the inside surface toward the printer. The working edge or coating edge of the coating trough is placed at the bottom of the screen on the inside and the trough is tilted so that the solution comes in contact with the screen fabric. The trough is brought forward upward in a tilted position (see Figure 197) using some pressure, so that an even coating is deposited. After the first coat dries, a second coat or even a third coat may be applied, if necessary. Most printers apply the second and third coats on the underside or outside of screen fabric in order to produce a more even and smooth coating. The coats may be dried naturally or with the aid of a fan. The coating should not be touched until it is dry and then only in a spot which will not come in contact with the positive during exposure.

Although with today's available emulsions it may not be necessary, some shops have made a practice of using a whirling device suggested in Figure 198 in preparing printing screens. These whirling devices may be purchased or built according to one's need. For screen printing purposes the whirler rotates from about 250 to 350 revolutions per minute, depending on the size of the screen. Usually small and medium size screens are whirled. The screen placed coated side up on turntable

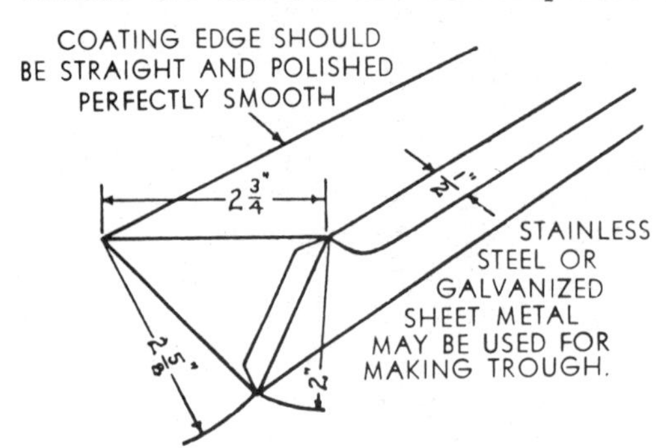

Figure 196. Suggested dimensions for coating trough.

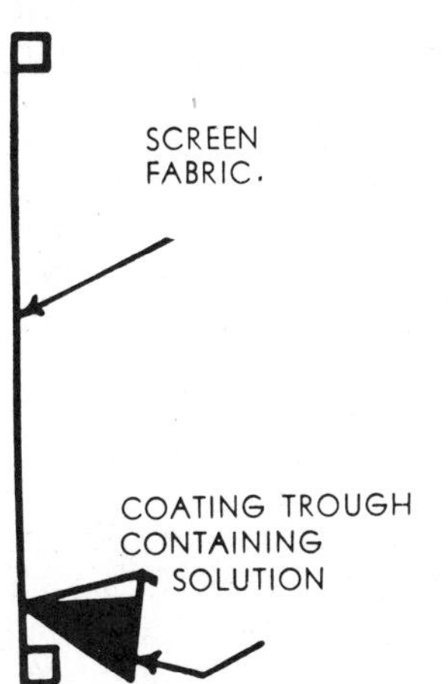

Figure 197. Position of coating trough in coating screen fabric with direct method of sensitized solution.

of the whirler produces uniform distribution and even coating over the screen fabric. The whirling may last from 10 to 20 seconds. The screen is then allowed to dry completely in the dark.

After the screen is dried, it is exposed, washed-out, and prepared for printing in similar fashion to other type direct screens.

Transfer Type Screen Printing Films

The use of direct screens for ceramic printing has developed because they are tough and resistant and also because of custom. The recent developments in the varied screen printing films are making

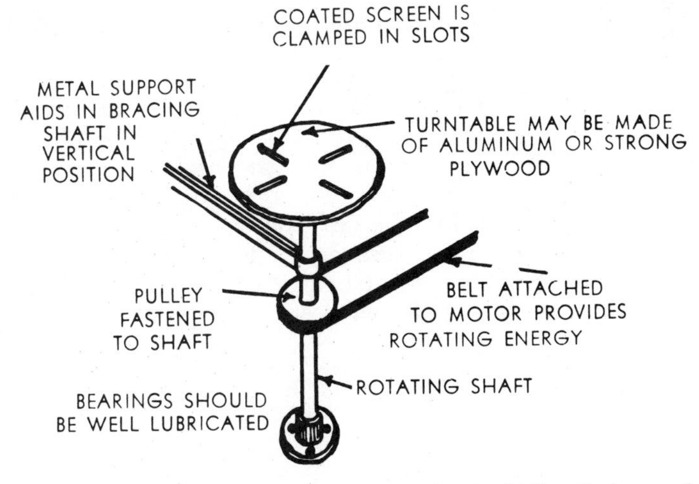

Figure 198. Mechanical details of a suggested whirling device used for evenly coating screens indicate construction simplicity.

more common the use of transfer films for ceramic printing. These are available commercially with simple directions for their processing.

Making Screens More Resistant to Ceramic Inks

Where a printer may be in doubt as to the durability or toughness of a film or the effect of an ink on the film or coating, he may apply a protective coating or solution over the screen printing film or even over a direct screen where it may be necessary to protect the film from being dissolved by the solutions in the ink. The coating may be applied on the inside of the screen after the film has been processed and adhered permanently to the underside of the screen fabric.

To do this, the screen is placed film side down and in contact with blotting paper or newsprint paper. The protective solution, which may be any coat that will not be dissolved by the ink or one that will resist the ink, is poured along one end of the screen and is squeegeed across the screen and back again to the starting point. The screen is turned over and the open parts of the design are wiped carefully on the film side with a soft cloth that has been dampened with the required solvent.

Transparent or colored lacquers, screen printing synthetic enamels, vinyl inks, or special hardening solutions may be used for the coatings. A colored coating is more practical to use, since it is more visible and therefore easier to wipe away from the open parts of the design.

On occasion it may be necessary to protect a screen on both sides, that is, directly on the film and on the side opposite the film. This may be accomplished by spraying or brushing one side of the screen with a coat (say of lacquer) that will not be dissolved by the ceramic ink used in printing. The open parts of the design are wiped then on the underside of screen with a cloth dampened with a solvent such as a lacquer thinner. When the lacquer on the top side is dry, the underside of the screen is coated and then wiped on the top side. The lacquer or filler used on one side of the screen should be different from that used to coat the other side of the screen. The solvents used for wiping should differ from one another so that the second solvent employed would not dissolve the first coating.

As in the preparation of screens for textile printing, the printer may use an air spray or a vacuum cleaner to blow the protective coating out of the openings in the design areas, before allowing protective coating to dry.

Chapter 30

SCREEN PRINTING OF WALLPAPER AND WALL COVERINGS

The versatility of screen printing is producing an ever increasing amount of general screen printing and also specialized printing. Printing of all types of wallpaper and wall coverings on such materials as burlap, grass cloth, linen, foil, vinyl, paper-backed vinyl, shade cloth and the like for varied purposes is a specialized phase of the industry. This implies that the entire processing from the drawing of the original design to the final rolling-up of the product into rolls may be done in a single shop using hand printing, one-arm squeegees, and screen printing machines. Screen printers paint wall coverings from simple singe-colored paper to many-colored and intricately designed papers and coverings for almost any purpose. There are establishments which print just vinyl and paper wall covering; while some also create and print bolts of drapery material and scenic panels to harmonize with the wall coverings, the complete architecture of the room, and its furnishings.

It may take up to six months before a screen printer begins to screen wall coverings. Whether he uses automated equipment or hand printing tables in his shop, the printer must standardize his procedures before doing production work. This type of printing requires a knowledge of design and interior decoration; a knowledge of techniques involved in the actual printing; information about the affixing or wallpapering process; and a financial investment involved in maintaining sufficient stock on hand, in filing and in storing of large screens, in shop working space, inks, labor, in selling, service, etc. Although this type of printing has many of the problems that are common to other screen printing, it also has problems peculiar to it. Therefore, lack of complete experimentation in this specialized phase of printing may destroy the confidence of even the most undaunted and produce very unsatisfactory technical and financial results. The results of an incomplete trial printing forced one concern to burn a large quantity of wallpaper simply because it had no desire to sell inferior paper to its trade. This paper was printed with the wrong type of ink on a heavy coated paper, in quite a few colors, one color overlapping another. Upon being applied to the wall and even upon being unrolled, the paper had a tendency to crack in spots.

Another negative example involved a five-color design where the very effective small design was concentrated in one small area of the paper in repeat pattern fashion with an excess of blank space between the pattern. When the paper was affixed to the wall, the parts of the wallpaper upon which the design was printed pulled away from the wall causing obvious bumps in the paper. This involved the removal of the wallpaper, changing the design somewhat, printing the paper over, and finally wallpapering again. The purpose of the above two examples is to stress the completion of the trial printing, especially when techniques or materials are changed. This also includes a trial application of the wallpaper to the wall or surface before merchandising the paper to the trade.

The history of wallpaper and wallpapering indicates that paper hangings or wallpaper were invented to supply inexpensive substitutes for the ancient costly tapestry, leathers, brocatelles, etc. employed in palaces and homes of the rich. History credits the Chinese with being the first to have employed paper for wall coverings long before the English claim of introducing wallpaper in Europe and before the French claim of producing beautiful wallpaper in sheet form. Regardless of its historical background, wallpaper today is used universally not only for paper and scenics affixed to walls, but is finding increased supplementary uses, such as for advertising brochures, fireplace screens, for items such as lampshades, wastebaskets, for the binding of books, greeting cards, etc.

Of the hand-printed wallpaper and wall coverings, very little paper today is being printed by hand from wood blocks; most of the paper and wall coverings are hand screen printed, since screen printed wallpaper offers the usual advantages of the process. The process produces opaque colors and the rich three-dimensional effects of screen printing inks; it offers long lasting, fadeproof, brilliant, multi-colored, and washable paper; it can be made grease-proof, sound-proof, and occasionally treated so that it is vermin-proof. Any size papers and scenics may be printed with the process. Also, paper may be printed to order in small quantities to suit or match almost any furnishings. Very fine detail, even including the repeat pattern of the photograph of one's favorite grandchild, may be reproduced. Some very excellent flocked papers in varied colored flock application and beaded coverings may be printed and processed.

Most of the printing in shops is being done on coated wallpaper stock; very few screen printing shops coat their own stock. Thus, the printer, even if he prints a one-color mural, panel, or wallpaper, actually ends up with a two-color job, since the background coating makes up the second color. The wallpaper employed for screen printing work is hard sized to resist moisture in coating and pasting and has "tooth"

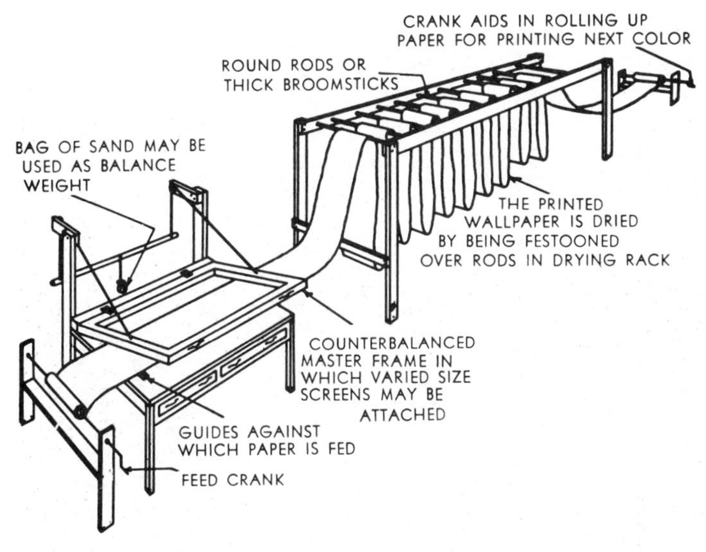

Figure 199. A set-up for screen printing on wallpaper.

which enables it to be printed either by hand, on special jigs, or machines. The paper is obtainable in almost any desired colored coat, varnished, or in other effects. Although there are 18-, 22-, 24-, and 30-inch (45.7, 55.9, 61, and 76.2cm) width rolls being printed, generally printers print on the 30-inch (76.2cm) roll. Occasionally the term "hanging-paper" is employed for wallpaper; technically, this term refers to the raw stock used in the manufacture of wallpaper.

Although vinyl inks, metallic inks, and other inks may be employed, the inks ordinarily used are of the synthetic oil-vehicle types. Generally, they are of the quick air-drying variety. Because this type of printer uses many colors to reproduce his work, he may, on occasion, just buy flat white ink to which he may add desired pigments.

Any type of printing screen may be employed for reproducing the wallpaper, depending on the detail of the design to be printed. For fine detail printing any type of photographic screen which will resist

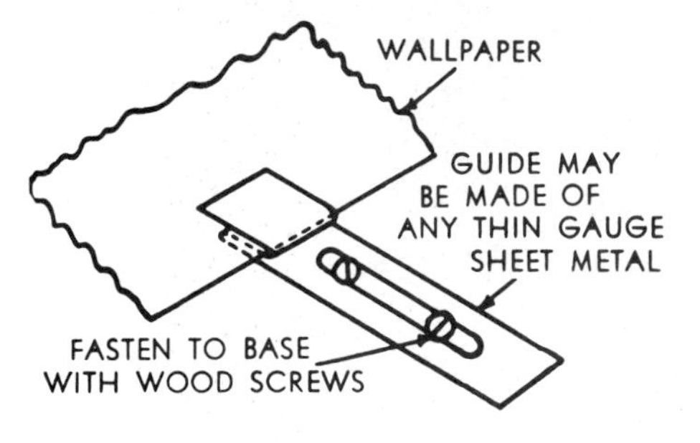

Figure 200. A suggested guide for registering wallpaper.

the ink being printed may be used. Of the hand-prepared screens, usually the knife-cut film and the tusche-glue screen are the most used. If a printing screen is also to be printed on textiles or such materials as grass cloth or window shade materials, the most practical and resistant printing screen should be used. Often the printer may include hand prepared screens in order to obtain a deliberate hand look.

Figure 201. Two distinctly different designs; upper left, a cartoon style rendition of "Nellie the Train"; lower right, a series of separate illustrations in repeating design frames taken from very old woodcut style motifs. **(Both designs are products of Carson Handprints, Cowell, California)**

Most screen printers start out by doing manual printing and may use such equipment as a one-man squeegee with a vacuum table, or long tables similar to those used in hand textile printing, or a basic set-up for printing wall coverings and wallpaper illustrated in Figure 199. This set-up consists of (1) a feed crank upon which the roll of paper to be printed is placed; (2) a printing unit large enough to print the wallpaper, scenic, or section of a scenic; (3) a festooner or drying arrangement; and (4) a roll-up crank. The whole set-up or printing equipment may be built by the printer in permanent or portable fashion, or it may be constructed by a carpenter to individual specifications. It is suggested that the festooner or drying arrangement be built just high enough so that the average worker will be able to rack and arrange the paper at the top of the festooner. Usually, one individual does the printing and another one racks and arranges the roll of paper over the festooner as illustrated. As quick drying inks are employed for printing, by the time the wallpaper reaches the roll-up crank the paper is dry enough to be rolled up, or to be cut into smaller rolls or to be printed with the next color.

Figure 200 shows a guide that may be used for printing wallpaper and wall coverings.

Figure 202. The Stork Rotary Screen Printing Machine designed for continuous screen printing of all types of wall coverings and wallpaper, may have manual or automatic operating device and can be operated by two or three operators. Machine may consist of one section for single color effects and may be enlarged by more units as desired. **(Courtesy of Stork Inter-America Corp., Charlotte, N.C.)**

Some shops which print on textiles and wallpaper do the printing on tables which are described in the chapter on printing on textiles. The paper to be printed is taped semi-permanently over a layer of newspaper and one or two printers do the printing, either both printing on one side of the long table or one operator printing on one side and the other printer printing the same or another color on the opposite side. As with textile printing, in the long table printing unit the printing screen is not hinged to the table but is carried to the next register spot for each impression. The wallpaper is left on the table until it is completely printed and dried.

Figure 202 presents a rotary screen printing machine designed for screen printing automatically all types of wall coverings with the varied inks used for this type of decorating. Machine has rotary cylindrical stainless steel seamless screens which has a maximum printing width of 31 inches (78.7cm). The machine dries material automatically, applies a base coat, embossing effect, design, and a full finish in one operation.

Chapter 31

HAND-MADE INTAGLIO PHOTOGRAPHIC POSITIVE

Any positive used for photographic work, whether made by hand or photochemically, should be opaque enough to block out undesired light in the copy or design, must appear *positive* or exactly as it will look in the finished job, must be on transparent or translucent material, and must reproduce the exact detail of the original. The hand-made intaglio positive presented here is one that may be made by anyone who is able to trace accurately; will reproduce fine detail; is ideal for copying designs and parts of large designs; may be used to reproduce fine art work represented by thin lines as illustrated in Figure 203 through Figure 206; and offers an excellent hand method for producing screen printing plates in an emergency. No photographic equipment or supplies are necessary to make the positive. It is a method that the writer has used and is original with him for making hand executed photographic positives for screen printing.

The procedure for making the positive is the same as that explained in the writer's book (Kosloff, *Celluloid Etching*) on making a celluloid drypoint etching plate. Actually, the positive described in this chapter is a drypoint or intaglio etching plate in which the design in the form of grooves are inked and the surface is wiped carefully in such a way that the ink is left in the grooves which form the design or the opaque areas on the positive.

Specifically, the materials needed to make the positive are a piece of transparent rigid plastic sheet that is about .015″ to .025″ (.381mm to .635mm) thick (acrylic plastic, celluloid nitrate, or celluloid acetate may be used); an etching needle that may be bought in any art or hobby shop or made as illustrated in Figure 207; some masking tape or tacks, ink that is opaque when it is dry; and a piece of soft cloth.

Making the Positive

Lay and tape design, face up, on a drawing board, thick cardboard, or any flat surface. Center over the design a clean piece of transparent

Figure 203. Design for hand-made positive. **(Courtesy of Samuel Bingham Company, Chicago, Illinois)**

plastic larger in size than the design to be reproduced, and tape plastic at corners to the flat surface. In tracing fashion, begin drawing or scratching with the etching needle, the design onto the plastic, reproducing the details in scribing fashion on top of the plastic surface. The needle is held in the same manner as a pencil and the lines are scratched evenly, slowly, and carefully. To obtain shadow effects with the needle, crisscross or cross-hatch lines. Where heavier lines are necessary the needle is pressed at an angle and more pressure is put on it. For thin and delicate lines the needle is held more vertically to the plastic. After a few minutes of practice the printer will find the method easy.

As the work progresses hold the board with the plastic positive on it at an angle to see scratched or intaglio lines. Although it is not

Figure 204. Hand-made intaglio positive made by the writer from the design illustrated in Figure 203.

Figure 205. Print made from photographic printing screen which was produced from hand-made intaglio positive.

Figure 206. Print made on a handkerchief with a fast red textile ink using printing screen prepared from hand-made intaglio positive.

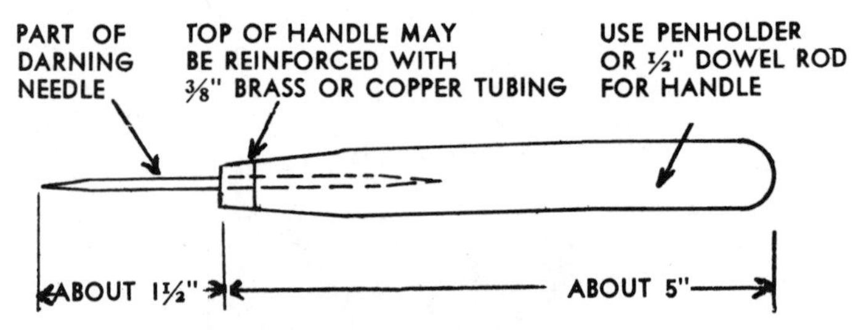

Figure 207. A hand-made etching needle.

necessary, should there be difficulty in seeing the lines, ordinary writing ink may be rubbed over the scratched lines. A mixture of a little lamp-black and vaseline rubbed into the lines is ideal for this purpose.

After the whole design has been copied onto the plastic, the scratched side of the positive is cleaned with a little benzine or naphtha and some ink is rubbed into the scratched or intaglio lines in order to make the lines opaque to light. The preferred ink to use is dark red or ruby red screen printing opaque ink that is opaque when it dries. However, any opaque dark colored screen printing oil-vehicle or enamel ink, heavy bodied ordinary printing ink, or etching ink that has not been mixed with too much plate oil may be used. The ink may be applied with the finger or with a soft cloth onto the plastic over the entire area where the lines were traced with the needle, filling in all the small grooves. The cloth, in rubbing the plastic, will also remove unwanted protruding burrs along the scratched lines. When the wiping is completed, the plastic must be perfectly clean on the surface outside the grooves. The ink must *not* be wiped out of the grooves. The positive may be inked and wiped a second time to insure that there will be enough ink in the lines to make them absolutely opaque. The ink, when dry, will produce a very fine opaque line. The opaqueness may be easily inspected with a pocket microscope, a magnifying glass, or a hand magnifier of the type used by photoengravers. For anyone planning to do much photographic inspection work the latter magnifier will be best as it will magnify lines ten to twenty times their original size.

Exposing Positive

The intaglio positive may be exposed as any other positive. However, the exposing time for this type of positive is approximately the same length as that of a halftone positive, since detail in this handmade positive is very fine and the length of exposure would be less than for ordinary line copy positives. Exposing may be done with a carbon arc lamp, a pulsed xenon lamp, a black light fluorescent unit, or a plain Number 2 photoflood lamp.

This positive may be exposed in contact with a direct screen, a direct-indirect screen, or in contact with a carbon tissue or gelatinous type screen. The positive may be exposed in contact with the transparent support of film or in contact with emulsion side of film. As illustrated in Figure 208, in exposing, the hand-made positive is placed on the glass of the photographic contact frame, scribed or scratched lines of positive up, and the film support or transparent temporary support is placed over and in contact with positive. If carbon tissue or a similar photographic emulsion is used, the temporary support may be a transparent plastic sheet such as polyester or vinylite, about .003" (.076mm) thick, since these do not require waxing before transferring carbon tissue or image to it. Celluloid of the cellulose nitrate type is better than cellulose acetate as cellulose nitrate generally does not curl up in the warm or hot water when developing exposed tissue. The celluloid type temporary support must be waxed well on the surface that is to receive the carbon tissue or emulsion film. If a vacuum contact frame is available, the positive and tissue or film may be exposed in it, since this type of frame will give better contact. However, an ordinary photographic contact frame will give good results also. The positive shown in Figure 204 was exposed to a carbon arc lamp at a distance of three feet for two minutes to produce the prints illustrated in Figures 205 and 206.

In exposing a direct screen, the positive is placed in direct contact with underside of coated screen, scribed side of positive in perfect contact with screen, and exposure is made so that light strikes positive first.

Making a Thicker Positive

Exposing a hand-made positive as shown in Figure 208 will produce fine results for most screen printing work. However, where it is absolutely essential that no light seepage occur in exposing, a positive may be exposed in direct contact with the tissue or emulsion film as illus-

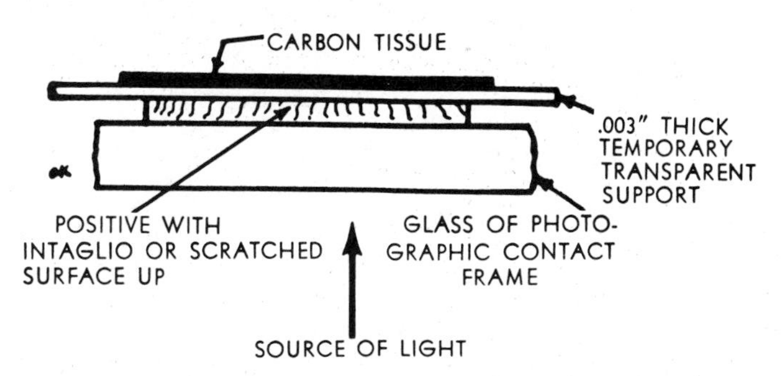

Figure 208. Exposing positive through the temporary support.

trated in Figure 209. A positive exposed in this manner should be coated with a transparent coating applied over the intaglio side of the positive (over the emulsion side of a regular photographic positive) to insure that the tissue or emulsion coating will not stick to the positive when the emulsion image is being adhered to the screen fabric. For the intaglio positive Number 14 to 18 silk (about 140 to 170 mesh per inch; 55 to 67 mesh per cm) or equivalent, screen fabrics may be used for the printing screen; although for this type of screen a finer mesh may be preferred.

The procedure for making this positive is similar to the first method. This positive may be made on thicker stock, if desired, since heavier lines may be scratched in and the positive will be easier to handle. After the positive is completely finished, it must be coated with a spraying lacquer, acrylic spray, a transparent varnish, or with collodion on the scribed side.

Applying a Transparent Coating on Positive

The protective coating of spraying lacquer or acrylic spray may be applied with a hand spray, with a spray gun, with a spray can, or with a brush on the scribed side of the positive. When the coating is dry, the surface is waxed perfectly by applying wax on the coated surface. When waxing and polishing is completed, the waxed side is placed in perfect contact with the carbon tissue, film, or screen, and exposed.

If a spar varnish is used as the transparent protective coating, it should first be applied on a sample positive, as the ingredients in the spar varnish take longer to dry, the varnish may not be too transparent, and to assure that the varnish does not dissolve or blur the ink in the positive.

Another transparent protective that has been used on occasion is collodion; it may be coated on other positives and negatives when it is desired to expose them in direct contact with film as illustrated in Figure 209. Collodion is a solution that is made by dissolving pyroxy-

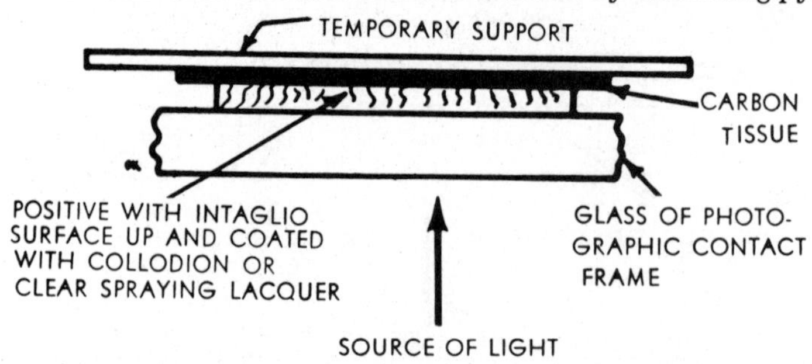

Figure 209. Exposing coated positive in direct contact with tissue.

lin, which is a form of nitrocellulose or soluble cotton, in a mixture of equal parts of grain (ethyl) alcohol and ether (concentrated). It should be used with care. The collodion used by screen printers is the plain collodion, colorless, transparent when it dries and forms a protective film, and may be obtained from screen printing suppliers, photographic shops, photoengraving suppliers, etc.

Collodion in the solution state is poured onto the face side of the positive and allowed to dry or harden. In coating, it is suggested that it be poured onto one corner of the positive and flowed over the entire surface of the positive by tilting positive. The coating must be uniform and the excess can be flowed back into the container. Do not allow collodion to flow back over a spot. When the collodion is hardening the positive should not be bent or handled, as small cracks or crazing will develop in the collodion coating. When using a thin flexible positive it is best to tape it down around the edges to a hard support such as a piece of glass to keep positive from buckling when collodion hardens. Ordinary room temperature (about 65 to 70 degrees Fahrenheit (18 to 21 degrees Celsius) is best working temperature for collodion. As collodion gives off inflammable vapors, it should not be used near an open flame. To test collodion for dryness touch a spot at the edge of the coated positive with the finger.

After the collodion is dry, the plate may be waxed perfectly by applying wax on collodion coating. When waxing is completed the waxed side of the positive is placed in perfect contact with the sensitized film or screen and exposed.

As explained in Chapter 16, the cement method of exposure may also be used in exposing the hand-made intaglio positive.

Hardening Solution

In spite of the fact that the printing screen produced from a hand-made intaglio positive may be quite resistant, sometimes it is desirable to produce a harder and more durable film or direct screen. This may be done by using a hardening agent or solution which is applied on top of the screen fabric, on the inside of the screen, directly over the emulsion coating or film, after the film has been applied and has dried. These solutions are available from screen printing suppliers. The hardening solution may be applied with a brush and left on for about five minutes. The excess solution on top of the silk should be blotted away.

The following formulations make practical hardening solutions. For screens that are made in the summertime, the solution may be composed of 112 ounces (3.312 liters) of distilled water to which has been added 12 ounces (354.89cc) of a 40 percent formaldehyde solution, and 4 ounces (119.9cc) of glycerine; in the wintertime, the following mixture may be used: 96 ounces of distilled water (2.839 liters), 16 ounces (473.2cc) of a 40 per cent formaldehyde solution, and 16 ounces

(473.2cc) of glycerine. Each of the above mixtures will make up a gallon (3.785liters) solution which may be used as needed and will keep indefinitely if stored in a well corked bottle. The proportions of the ingredients may be reduced to make a smaller mixture. The solutions may be used as hardening agents for most carbon tissue and gelatinous type screens.

The prints illustrated in Figures 205 and 206 were made from a photographic screen to which the first of the above hardening solutions was applied.

Chapter 32

MAKING DIRECT PHOTOGRAPHIC POSITIVES FOR SCREEN PRINTING

Autopositive Film

Ordinarily, photographic printing screens are made from photographic positives. A film positive is the opposite of a film negative in which light and shades are opposite to the original copy. See Figure 210. A photographic positive is a design or copy that is similar to an original being reproduced, with the exception that the positive is on a transparent plastic film or glass support. All areas that are dark on the original are dark or black on the photographic positive. Normally to produce a photographic printing screen the original design is photographed, a negative is made, a positive is produced from the negative, and the printing screen is prepared by photochemical means from the positive.

The autopositive film* or direct contact positive film is a product used to produce a direct film positive which eliminates the intermediate step of making a negative and does away with cameras used in the making of negatives. It is accurate and differentiates between the fine black and whites in a copy, if ordinary care is used in its processing. It may be developed and processed with ordinary photographic solutions that are easily available in photographic and graphic arts supply establishments. The film can be handled and processed in daylight and is exposed in a simple contact photographic printing frame in direct contact with the original that is to be reproduced. The film can also be used for making duplicate negatives and positives. The screen printer who has processed film will have no difficulty in working with autopositive products.

However, because the film has to be exposed in direct contact with the copy it will produce positives that are the same size as the original copy. Where it is necessary to reduce or enlarge originals,

* Eastman Kodak Company, Rochester, New York.

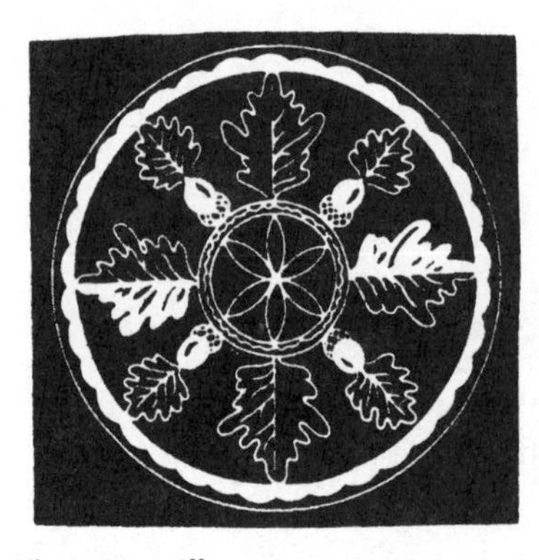

Figure 210. Illustrates a negative print on the left and a positive print of the same design on the right. The design for these prints was made with a screen that was prepared with a direct emulsion on Number 230 nylon and screen was exposed 16 weeks later to a black light fluorescent unit for 4 minutes.

then enlarging or reduction must be done before making the direct positive.

The film comes with a matte or dull finished surface on both sides. It is colored brown on one side and gray on the other. The gray colored side is the emulsion side. The film is obtainable in any size and in rolls ranging from 24 inches (61cm) wide by 30 feet long (9.144m) to 44 inches (111.76cm) in width by 100 feet (30.48m) in length. Wider films rolls are available on special order. It is possible to write or draw with India ink or pencil on either side of the film after the film has been developed and processed. Also, photographic eradicator solution may be used to remove portions of a design on the developed and processed film, should this be desirable.

The principle of the autopositive film is that the film has been already "exposed" in its manufacture. In producing a desired positive from the autopositive film the original exposure is taken out by placing a transparent yellow sheet or yellow gelatin sheet over the film when the autopositive film is exposed in direct contact with the original copy to an arc light or to a photo-flood lamp. The theory is to burn out the original exposure in areas where white copy reflects light back to the film. The black portions will reflect too little light to burn out the original exposure. If the film were developed out of its original container it would develop out absolutely black. To test for maximum opacity or blackness or to test a developer it is suggested that a sample of the unexposed autopositive film be developed in the dark. To test for different degrees of opacity, it is necessary to vary the time of exposure or the distance of the film from the exposing light.

A good copy or original design is essential for this process. The copy employed should be black and white, printed or drawn on perfectly white paper, preferably enameled or calendered paper. Perfectly white paper is desirable, since the light in exposing goes through the yellow sheet, the autopositive film, strikes the copy, and is reflected back by the white in the copy. The black in the copy has a tendency to absorb the light, therefore, it does not reflect light back and the parts of the film that are over the black areas on the copy remain black. Where typewritten material is used as copy the typewriter ribbon used must be perfectly black and each character should be struck twice.

Although directions given here for the film are detailed intentionally, the actual processing of the film is simple. Most of the photographic chemicals are powders and are easily mixed with ordinary water. Most water that is fit to drink may be used to make the mixture. If ordinary clean water is not available, then clean rain water or distilled water may be used. All that is necessary are three trays for holding the solutions, each tray being big enough to hold the film. Any of the following trays must be used: glass trays, pyrex dishes, stainless steel trays, procelain enameled tray, bakelite, or glazed trays. When processing the film, arrange the three trays containing the processing solutions in the following order: first, the tray with the developer; then the tray containing the rinse or stop-bath; and last the tray with the fixing solution. The last tray should be nearest to the sink, since the film can then be washed in the sink. Basically, the process of making direct positives consists of the following steps: preparation for exposing; exposing; developing; rinsing; fixing; and washing.

Preparation for Exposing

To prepare the film for exposing place the original design or copy face side up. Over the copy place the autopositive film, emulsion side or gray colored side down, and in contact with copy. Place yellow sheet over film. The whole sandwich consisting of the original, film, and yellow sheet, with the film in the center, is placed under the contact frame glass (see Figure 211), the yellow sheet being in contact with the glass. The writer has found that a more practical way of exposing the unit is to place the copy under the film and the film directly under the contact frame glass and then lay the yellow sheet on top on the outside of the frame glass, covering the film area. The important thing is that the yellow sheet be placed between the light source and the film. Make sure that there is perfect contact between film and copy. Hold film by edges when handling it, since finger marks and oil marks may produce unwanted spots on film. The yellow sheet must also be handled by edges to keep it clean.

If a vacuum contact frame is available, it should be used instead of an ordinary photographic contact frame, since the former does produce better contact between original and film.

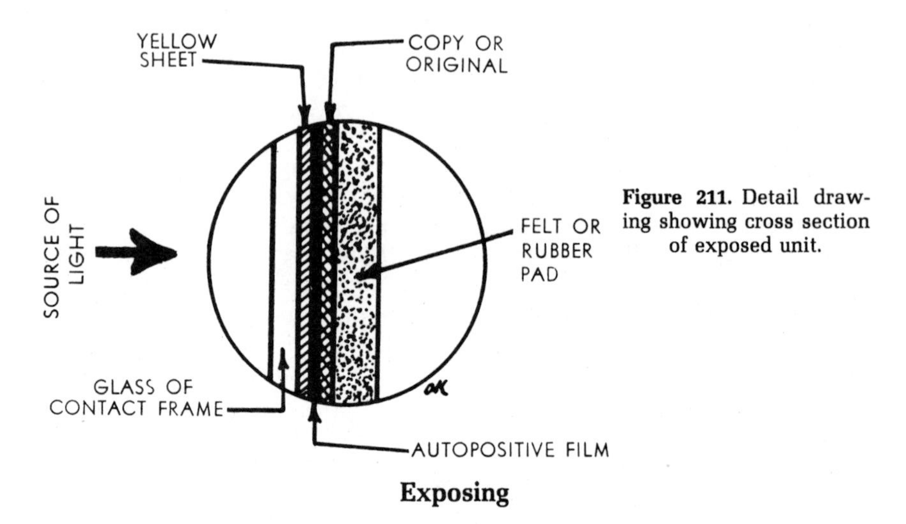

Figure 211. Detail drawing showing cross section of exposed unit.

Exposing

The film may be exposed to a carbon arc lamp or to a plain Number 2 photoflood lamp, being careful that the lamp or carbon arc does not have hot spots in it and that the light strikes with the same intensity on all areas of the contact frame. When exposing film to a carbon arc expose film for about one to one and one-half minutes at a distance of about 4 feet (1.219m) from the light. When exposing to a Number 2 photoflood lamp, keep film about 4 feet (1.219m) from light source and expose for about two minutes. A little experimentation will determine easily for the beginner the time of exposure and the distance of exposure. A tint of gray or fog over the background of the copy or design indicates insufficient exposure and more exposure is necessary.

Developing

Developing of a film refers to producing a visible image or design on film. The autopositive film may be developed with normal photographic solutions. Different developers will develop out the film at slightly varying lengths of time. It is suggested that the screen printer use developers recommended by the manufacturer of the film.

Developers are mixed according to the directions on the containers. If developers are made into stock solutions, the solutions may be stored and used as needed. Generally developers consist of two powdered chemicals which are first dissolved in smaller portions of lukewarm water about 90 degrees Fahrenheit. The chemicals must be stirred until they are completely dissolved. When the chemicals are completely dissolved the rest of the required water is added to the dissolved portion to make up a stock solution. The stock solutions will keep, if each solution is stored in a well-stoppered bottle. However, once the two stock solutions are mixed, they are good for a given time up to about a half day, depending on the use. In using any of the developers, the solution should be discarded when it turns yellow or brown. The temperature of the developing solution for developing film should be about 68 degrees Fahrenheit (20 degrees Celsius), which is approximate room temperature.

To prevent uneven development and production of streaks when using a developing solution, agitate solution slightly. Pour enough developing solution into tray to cover film completely when it is placed in tray. Keep film under solution at all times and keep in developer until image or design shows up very clear. The time of development may vary from about 15 seconds to about one minute, depending on the developer used. When image on the film is black immerse film in rinsing solution or stop-bath.

If the printer decides to use developers other than those mentioned then he should try them out under his regular working conditions. It must be kept in mind that a positive for screen printing work must be more opaque than for most other reproductive work.

Rinsing

The purpose of a rinse or stopbath is to stop development immediately and prevent streaks and stains on film. Fresh water may be used or an acid bath may be made for the stop-bath. The stop-bath that the writer has used is a simple acid bath consisting of one part of 28 per cent acetic acid and seven parts of water making a total of eight parts. The 28 per cent acetic acid solution may be bought in any photographic shop or drug store. The film should be left in the stop bath for about 10 to 20 seconds at room temperature (about 65 to 75 degrees Fahrenheit; 18 to 24 degrees Celsius) before placing it in fixing solution. The 28 per cent acetic acid solution will keep indefinitely, if the bottle is well stoppered. The Kodak Stop Bath SB-1a may also be used for rinsing the film. The printer may try other stop baths if he so desires.

Fixing

After rinsing the film is immersed in a fixing solution for two or three minutes. The purpose of the fixing solution is to remove any sensitive substance that has not been acted upon by the light or developer and to make the film inactive as far as light and handling is concerned. The fixing solution is mixed easily with water according to directions on the container. The writer has obtained good results with Kodak Fixer. The fixing solution may be used over and over, provided it is kept in a well stoppered bottle. Fixing solutions such as Kodak Rapid Fixer or Kodak Fixing Bath and of course, other fixing solutions may also be tried by the printer.

Washing

After the film is fixed it should be well washed to remove all traces of chemicals. The film may be washed by placing it in a tray of cold water or it can be left in the sink in which there is a spray of running cold water. Leave film in water for at least ten minutes.

Normal film drying and storing procedures should be followed.

High Speed Duplicating Film*

The screen printer may also use a High Speed Duplicating film which is designed for making negatives from negatives and positives from positives. It will duplicate line copy and halftone copy on transparent or translucent material such as scribed images, or ink, pencil or crayon lines. Film may be exposed by contact method for same size reproduction or in a process camera for same size reproduction, and enlargement or reduction from varied copy.

Exposed film may be processed manually or in a processing machine. Film is used with normal exposure and processing procedures in similar fashion to autopositive film. When duplicating film is exposed, it is placed so that base side of positive or negative is in contact with emulsion side of duplicating film. For reversed duplicates, the emulsion side of the positive or negative should be in contact with the emulsion side of the duplicating film. The film is available in sizes from 8 × 10 inches (20.32 × 25.4cm) to roll sizes 48″ × 100 feet (121.92cm × 30.48meters).

* Eastman Kodak Company, Rochester, New York.

Chapter 33

COLOR SEPARATION AND SCREEN PRINTING

Photography is used by the screen printer because with it he can produce detail or an actual likeness of an original subject or copy. With its aid he makes use of line copy and half-tone copy. Line copy consist of originals that are made of solid larger areas, of dots, and lines. Halftones are used by the printer to reproduce middletones and variations of tones or color. As the name implies, halftones (half tones) reproduce not only the black and white of copy but also the varying and intermediate shades of copy, photographs, or an actual object. Photography makes it possible for the printer to enlarge or reduce the size of original copy; to make positives and negatives; and most important, he can reproduce the original colors of copy or an object with the aid of the color separation process.

Color is a part and property of light which causes objects to have different appearance to the human eye. Since color separation involves a general knowledge of light and color, the printer should become acquainted with it. There are theories about light and although it is definitely not known what light actually is, scientists are agreed that it is a form of energy and they do know its behavior. Because it is something that can do work, the screen printer like all those in the graphic arts is making light work for him by employing it to produce changes on specially prepared light sensitive plates or emulsions.

Sir Isaac Newton (1642–1727), the English mathematician and physicist, proved that white light is a mixture of all colors by passing a narrow beam of light through a triangular glass prism. He showed that white light separates into a spectrum or band of the following colors: violet, indigo, blue, green, yellow, orange, and red as illustrated in Figure 212. Newton's discovery of the light or solar spectrum started the vast field of research by such men as Clerk Maxwell, Ducas du Hauron, Charles Cros, William H. Wollaston, Joseph Von Fraunhofer, whose contributions of the study of light and color has aided the production of today's graphic arts. The physicist accepts light as a form of waves and as a part of a group of waves known as the Electromagnetic Spectrum. Each group of waves of the Electromagnetic Spectrum has

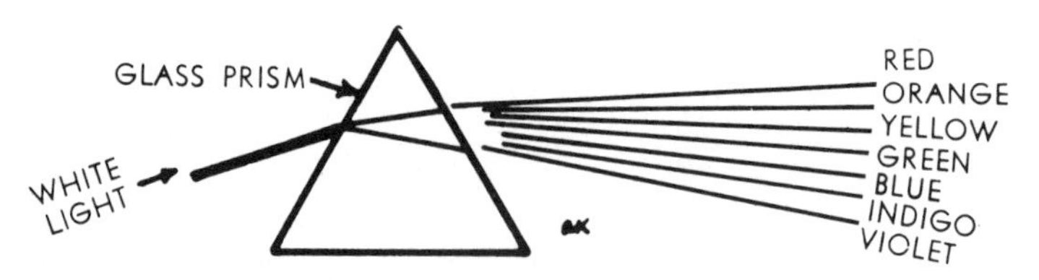

Figure 212. Sunlight separated into the spectral colors to which the eyes are sensitive.

been standardized and has been measured to have its own wavelength. Those waves that affect the eye and cause a sensation of vision are between .00004 and .00008 of a centimeter of length (400 millimicrons to 800 millimicrons) and travel approximately at the speed of 186,000 miles per second. Although the camera can record other wavelengths of rays, the eye is sensitive only to visible light. Figure 213 illustrates the electromagnetic spectrum and shows an enlarged detail of the spectral or light colors.

By observing Figure 213 the reader will notice that where red and green overlap yellow is produced and the overlap of green and blue produces blue-green. Although there is no sharp break or distinction between one color and the one immediately next to it in the color spectrum, colors are grouped into three classes because of the results that can be obtained with these three classes. The three color classes or colors are spoken of as blue (blue-violet), green, and red. These

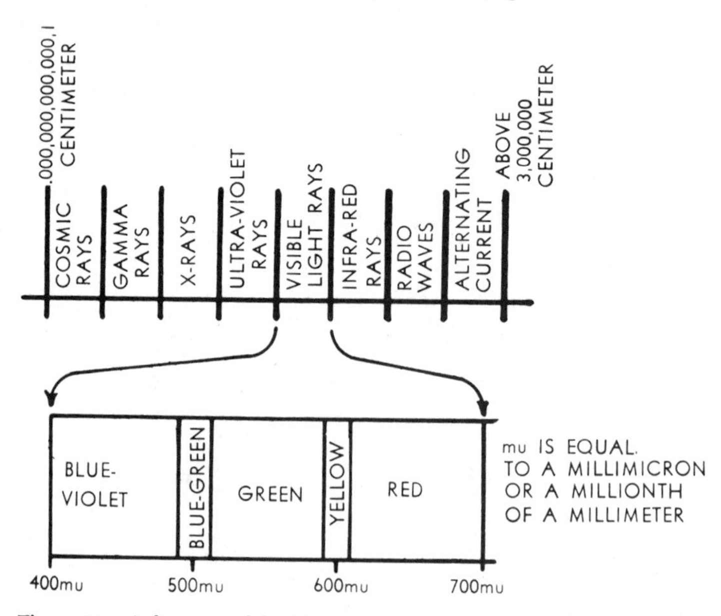

Figure 213. A diagram of the Electromagnetic Spectrum and visible light.

three colors are known as the primary colors of which white light is composed. They are the first or primary colors because with them it is possible to produce other colors.

Combining different colored light produces different results than combining colored pigments. However, just like the primary colors of pigments are mixed to produce different pigments so the three spectral or light colors may be mixed to produce other light colors.

In doing its work light reacts differently when it strikes varied colored materials. When light rays strike a blue colored opaque object, the object absorbs most of the other colors except blue; in a green object most of the other colors are absorbed and green is reflected to the eyes; anything red absorbs all colors except red, etc. Thus, we see that, generally the color of an object is what is left over and reflected after some white light is absorbed by the object. A green object, then, is not one that reflects green light, but one which has absorbed red and blue light; a red object is one that has absorbed blue (blue-violet) and green; and a yellow object is one that has absorbed blue light and reflects red and green which stimulate the eyes to produce the sensation of the color yellow.

Transparent colored objects or objects through which light passes have a different effect on light. A transparent colored material has two effects on light; the material absorbs some of the light which is reflected from an original and it allows some of the light to pass through. Generally, the color of an opaque colored material is governed by the light it reflects; the color of a transparent material depends on the light it transmits or lets through. See Figures 214 and 215. The transparent material is named for the light it lets through. For example, glass appears red to the eye when red light rays pass through it. A transparent colored material that allows some light to pass through and absorbs the rest is known as a filter.

Filters allow all colors to pass through except the color of which a photographic negative is wanted. They react similarly to filter paper; the filter allows the required parts to pass through. Generally, the different types of filters, or separation filters as they are called and which have been carefully developed after much experimentation with color

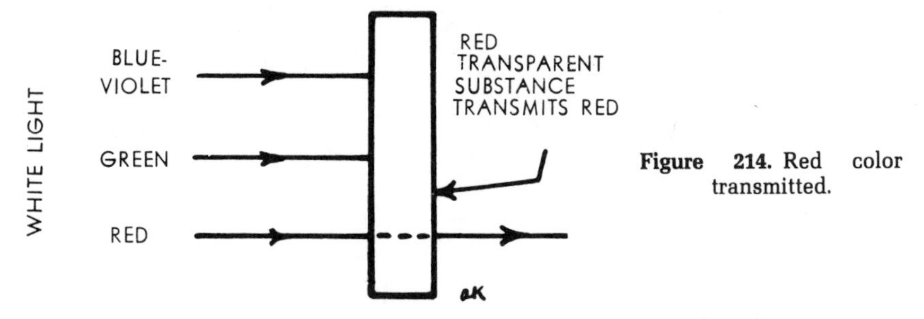

Figure 214. Red color transmitted.

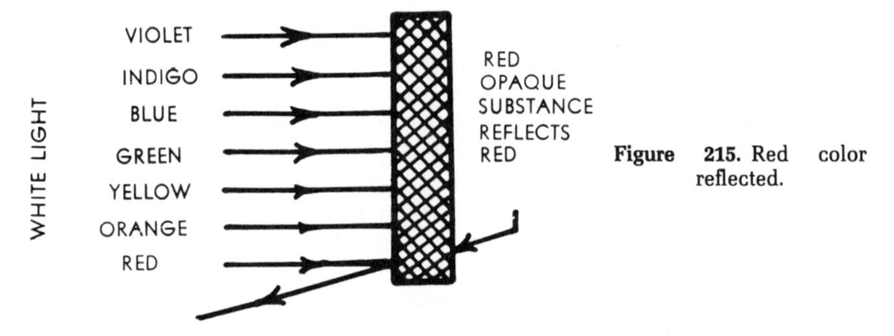

Figure 215. Red color reflected.

and light, are of two types: simple dyed gelatin films and dyed gelatin films accurately cemented between sheets of optical glass. The simple dyed gelatin films are more used at present.

By passing light through different colored filters we can absorb some colors and allow others to pass and be deposited on specially prepared light sensitive negatives or panchromatic plates. Panchromatic plates or films are those that are sensitive to the visible colors of the spectrum and can be used with photographic filters. The absorbed colors are not visible, seem to disappear, and have no effect on the sensitized film.

In the three-color process three different negatives are made with the aid of filters; in the four-color process the pigment black is added and printed after the other three pigment primary colors to aid in improving register; to add strength to the finished job, to darken the detail more in the completed job, and to print type matter in a completed job. Also, three-color printing inks are transparent and are usually thin so that by combining the three colors a perfect black will not be obtained. In the two-color process either two colors or a color plus black are reproduced. Some of the big screen printing shops are doing "full-color" work also. This involves the use of the three-color or four-color process to which are added other colors or effects with the aid of hand-made printing plates, photographic printing plates, or shading effects. The purpose of a filter, then, is to record on a sensitized negative the color which is complementary to the inks in which the screen printing plate is to be printed. The filter transmits its own color and absorbs the complementary color.

When dealing with light or spectral colors a complementary color is one that is added to another color to produce white light. In other words, the spectral colors represented in a pigment produced by a screen printing plate and the light color in the complementary filter represents the complete spectral colors. Each filter, therefore, is a combination of two printing colors, since it absorbs one color and transmits the rest. Colors that are absorbed by the filter appear lighter on the photographic negative; colors which pass through filter appear darker on the sensitized negative or film.

In pigment colors a complementary color is one that shows the greatest contrast or one that is opposite another color on a color wheel. See Figure 216. If a color is a mixture of two primary pigment colors, the complementary color is the remaining primary color. Two complementary colors include all the primary colors. In a color wheel complementary colors are always a primary color and a secondary color, or two opposite terliary colors.

The scale of gray or darkness obtained through three filters on the negatives must be exactly the same on each negative. If the negatives show different degrees or values of gray or density, the final color values in the pigment print will not be correct and an imperfect color reproduction will be obtained. The precise photographic screen printer or photoengraver will use the correct filter factor; a gray-scale, wedge, or step-wedge; and a densitometer to overcome the above difficulty. The filter factor is the ratio or the amount that the exposure must be increased when using a given filter. Since the filter absorbs some light, it is necessary to increase the exposure. A gray-scale is a range of grays from white to black and serves as a measuring device

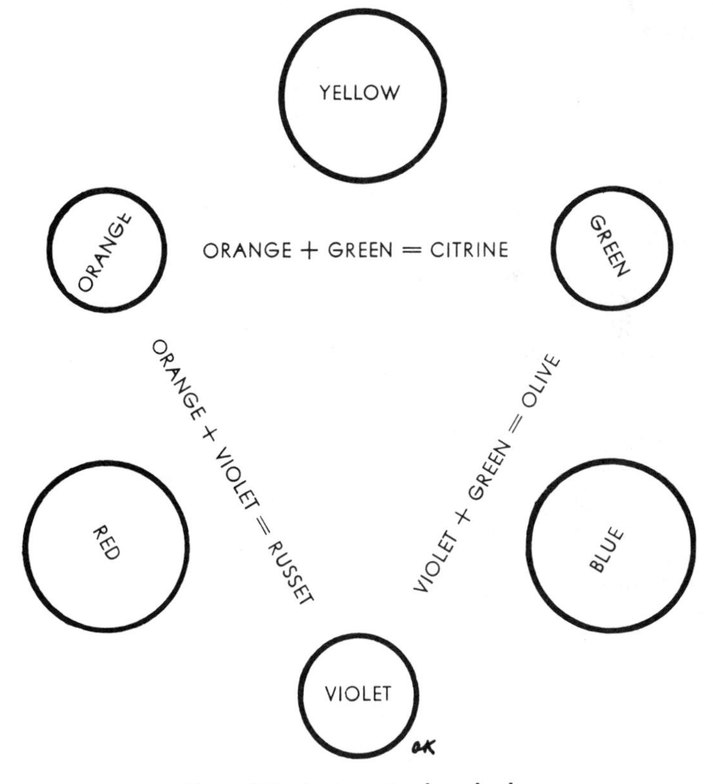

Figure 216. A pigment color wheel.

for each negative to make sure that the grays on each negative will match. The gray-scale is attached to the original on the copyboard of the camera, on a side near the original, but not too near the edge of the original, and serves to determine the accuracy of grayness or blackness of exposure. A densitometer is a very accurate instrument used to measure the density of negatives and positives. All these may be obtained from photographic supply houses and from photoengraving supply houses.

To make sure that the three negatives are each registered in relation to one another and that the final printing plate be proved and registered, register marks in the form of cross bars or commercial register marks are attached to the original, one at each end or on diagonal ends of the original on the copyboard. These register marks will not show in the final screen printing. The register marks save time in proving and in superimposing of pigment colors.

In other words, by employing filters and placing them in the camera in such a way so that light has to pass through them before it strikes the sensitized film we produce what is commonly known as color separation for use in the graphic arts and in screen printing. Printing from printing screens that are the result of color separation is based on the principle that all colors can be reproduced with the three primary pigment colors: yellow, red, and blue, and that these primary pigments really complete or are complementary to the colors which were recorded on the negatives. When a halftone is made from each color separation and each halftone is printed or superimposed on a white surface in its own primary pigment color, a colored reproduction of the original is obtained.

Thus, in summary, the colored object, original, or picture to be screen printed by the three-color process is photographed through three colored filters or separated into the three desired primary colors. These colors are filtered in such a way that three black and white negatives are produced. Positives are then made from the negatives and the final printing screens are prepared from the black and white positives. The three photographic screens are each printed separately with transparent screen printing inks. Usually, the yellow pigment is printed first, then the red, and finally the blue to produce the colors of the original. The printing in the bigger shops is being done on screen printing machines; in smaller shops the printing is done by hand. It is more difficult to reproduce this process by hand printing.

Chapter 34

REPRODUCING HALFTONES BY MEANS OF SCREEN PRINTING

Photographic screen printing work employs both line copy which consists of lines or full tones, and single-color halftones and multi-color halftones which consist of printed varied size dots. The screen printer, like the photoengraving industry (which has been employing the halftone principle since about 1890), uses the halftone principle to reproduce originals that have varied tones in them. Halftone copy may be reproduced in one color, two, three, or four colors, employing color separation photography for multi-color printing. Photographs, wash-drawings, pencil, pen and ink, oil paintings, sprayed work, colored copy, and prints from other graphic arts processes may be reproduced by means of halftones. The copy for screen printing with halftones must be distinct, sharp, and clear. Background on photographs for screen printing work should be light. Reproducing the background involves the breaking up of the image into dots, dark shadows on the copy forming large dots and the light shadows forming smaller dots.

Generally, the procedure for making a halftone negative is similar to that of making a line or solid tone negative, with the exception that in producing a halftone negative a "halftone screen" is placed in the camera in front of the photographic sensitized plate. In thinking and talking about screens, the printer must not confuse the halftone screen with the actual printing screen.

The whole basis of photographic reproduction is the camera. Basically, the *process camera,* as it is called, consists of a camera which has three basic parts: (1) a copyboard to hold the original or copy in front of (2) a lensboard containing the lens, and (3) a film holder in back of the lensboard. There are two types of process cameras used to produce negatives and positives in the screen printing shop—horizontal and vertical. Horizontal process cameras have the basic parts mounted horizontally (see Figure 217); the vertical camera has the three parts mounted vertically with the copyboard at the base of the camera, the lensboard above the copyboard and the film holder above the lensboard. Either type camera may be a gallery or a darkroom camera.

Figure 217. A Robertson 41″ (104cm) Tri-Color Overhead Darkroom Camera designed to reproduce any type of copy. Camera has a 50″ x 50″ (127cm x 127cm) glass covered copyboard, a transparency opening of (25½″ x 33½″; 44.8cm x 85cm) for transparent or translucent copy reproduction, and a screen mechanism for holding circular or rectangular glass halftone screens with precision instruments for controlling precise reproduction. **(Courtesy of Robertson Photo-Mechanix, Inc., Desplaines, IL, and William Feather Company, Cleveland, OH)**

The gallery type gets its name from the fact that it is stationed in the gallery or photographic department—located outside the darkroom. (See Figure 218). A darkroom camera illustrated in Figure 217 is one which is located entirely in the darkroom; often the wall of a darkroom is built to serve permanently as the rear section of the camera.

Cameras vary in the sizes of photographic negatives and positives that they reproduce. An 8″ × 10″ (20.32cm × 25.4cm) gallery type camera complete with accessories or an 8″ × 10″ (20.32cm × 25.4cm) view

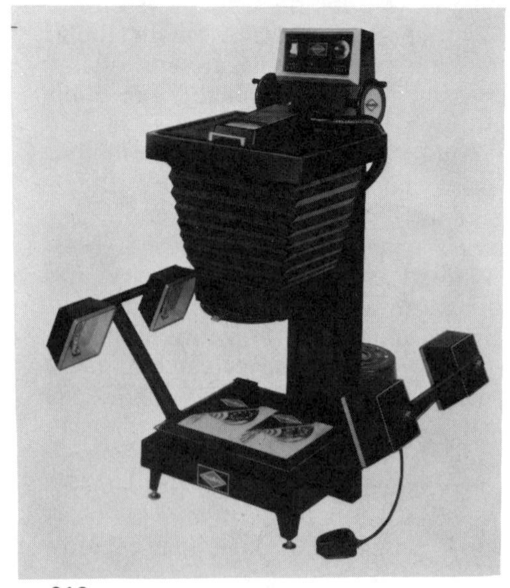

Figure 218. nuArc Vertical Camera which produces 14″ x 18″ (35.6cm x 45.7cm) images, has automatic focusing and sizing, can be operated as a gallery or darkroom camera, will reproduce negatives, positives, halftone, and enlarges and reduces copy. **(Courtesy of nuArc Co., Inc., Chicago, IL)**

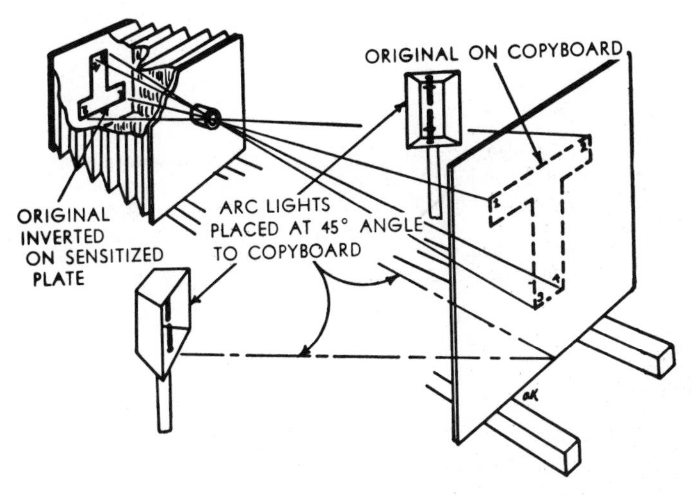

Figure 219. Showing simple camera, copyboard, and illumination.

camera may work in the small shop under expert workmanship. However, the large screen printing shop is forced to use larger cameras, many of them up to a size that reproduces images up to about 46″ × 64″ (117cm × 162.5cm).

The matter of light illumination is very important and arc lamps, pulsed xenon lamps, or mercury vapor lights are used to spread an even light on the copy being reproduced. The lamps are designed so that they can be attached to the camera bed or the lamp may be attached to its own individual portable counterbalanced stand. One, two, and four lamps may be used to illuminate the copyboard. For most work, two lamps are employed, each placed in front of the copyboard, at an angle of about 45 degrees to the copyboard and about two to four feet from the copy as illustrated in Figure 219.

Figure 220 presents a projector which some screen printers employ, especially beginners, to supplement their service, and to enlarge and reduce copy or artwork, onto horizontal or vertical surfaces.

Halftone Screens

A halftone screen consists of a transparent material upon which very uniform opaque lines are etched in glass at right angles to one another, leaving square transparent openings between the crossed lines. See Figure 208. When an exposure is made through the halftone screen a formation of small evenly spaced dots is produced on the halftone negative or positive. By means of halftone screens the dark tones of originals are reproduced into a series of dots that are very close together; while light tones of the original produce small and smaller dots

Figure 220. The Artograph Projector, a mobile unit which can be used as an artist's projector over a drawing board with a range of 50% reduction to 5X enlargement of copy to be reproduced; it can enlarge onto a vertical surface (to 30X at 25 feet). It projects opaque, small objects, or color transparencies from 35mm to 5″ x 7″ (12.7cm x 17.8cm). **(Courtesy of Artograph, Minneapolis, MN)**

spaced wider apart. The eye sees the formation of dots in the final inked print as a solid tone and the printer upon examination of the print with a magnifying glass can easily see the formation of dots.

Although there are many sizes and types of halftone screens, basically, there are two types of halftone screens in use: those that have to be separated from the sensitized plate during exposure (glass screens) and those that can touch the plate or film during exposure (contact screens). The Levy screens and the Buckbee Mears screens represent the first classification; the Eastman Kodak Contact Screens represent the second type.

Some screens in use by photoengravers and screen printing shops are the type used universally and developed by Max Levy of Philadelphia in about 1888. These screens consist of two sheets of optically clear glass, each sheet having been etched with very regularly spaced parallel lines, depending upon the number of lines required per inch. After the etched lines are filled in with a dark opaque pigment, the plates are cemented together, face to face, in such a way that the lines cross each other at perfect right angles. The Buckbee Mears screens are made on a single sheet of specially selected plate glass with the etched lines made opaque by filling in with a deposit of ferric oxide. The latter screens were developed as a result of the experimentation in making precision optics for ordnance use in World War II and were first used successfully in 1947.

The Eastman Kodak Contact Screens which were introduced in 1941 are just what their name implies. They consist of films and are used in direct and closest possible contact with the sensitized material or plate and do away with figuring the distance of halftone screen from the sensitized plate. They may be employed for producing negatives and positives and may be used either in a camera or in a vacuum printing frame. Contact screens consist of patterns of dots (round dot, square dot, and elliptical dot) printed on a film base. They are also

	DOUBLE-SHEET GLASS SCREEN		SINGLE-SHEET GLASS SCREEN	CONTACT SCREEN
LINES PER INCH	50 LINES TO 400 LINES		55 LINES TO 150 LINES	32 LINES TO 350 LINES
SIZE OF SCREEN IN INCHES	RECTANGULAR	CIRCULAR		
	4″ × 5″ TO 32″ × 40″	13½″ TO 55″ IN DIAMETER	8″ × 10″ TO 20″ × 24″	8″ × 10″ TO 39″ × 39″

* Usually there is a ½″ margin on most sizes.

Table III. Showing range of lines per inch and sizes of halftone screens.

available as special effects screens, as illustrated in Figures 222 and 224. Contact screens have proved to be very practical for the screen printer; generally this is the first type of screen he will use.* Table III shows the range of standard lines per inch and the size range in inches of the three types of screens. To obtain the lines per centimeter for the screens, it is suggested that the given dimensions be divided by 2.54.

Screens are classified by the number of etched lines or lines per inch, ranging from about 45 lines per inch to 400 lines per inch. This means that a 45 line screen would produce 45 times 45 dots to the square inch or approximately 2025 dots to the square inch and 400 line screen would produce 400 times 400 dots per square inch. The finer the screen or the higher the number of lines per inch, the less obvious is the breaking up of the design into dots in the final print. There are many other sizes available from manufacturers, photoengravers, and photographic equipment suppliers.

Glass halftone screens come in two general shapes—square and round. The round or circular screen which is attached to a rectangular frame so that it can be inserted in process cameras, can be rotated in its frame to different angles which are necessary for making halftones in order to eliminate the objectionable pattern effects in actual printing. Regardless of shape of screen, either screen is placed in the camera in such a way that the plane of the screen is perfectly parallel to the sensitized plate. Generally, the area of the opening in the screen is equal to the thickness of the opaque lines as shown in Figure 221.

In actual production of the halftone negative, the original or copy is attached to the copyboard and focused the same as in line or solid reproduction. The copy and the ground glass in the camera are carefully adjusted to produce the best dot formation, after which the sensitized plate is placed in the plate holder of the camera. In large screen printing

* The subject of contact screens is treated more completely in the book: Kosloff, Albert, *Photographic Screen Printing*, St Publications, Book Division, Cincinnati, Ohio 45202.

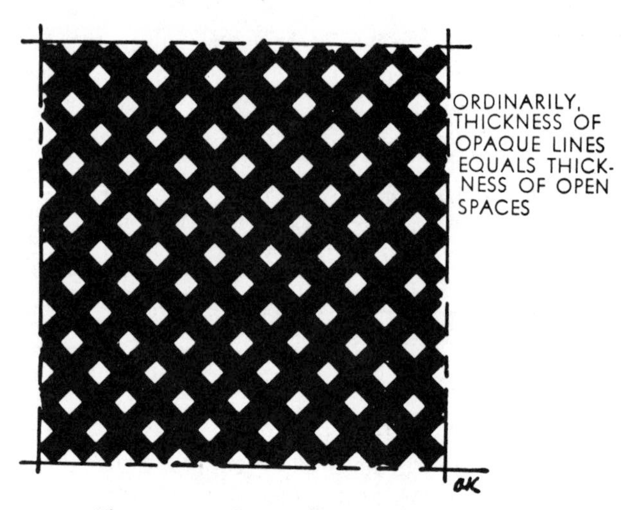

Figure 221. Enlarged detail of halftone screen.

shops the cameras used for making halftone negatives and positives are of the type that have exact mechanical adjustments for obtaining the distance of the copyboard from camera, the lens from the sensitized plate, and the halftone screen from the sensitized plate where such a distance is required. All these distances must be exact, especially that of the halftone screen from the sensitized plate, in order to produce the correct dot formation on the final halftone. The printer who has a home-made set-up for his camera has to consider four main items which are related to each other in figuring the screen separation or screen distance from the sensitized plate. They are the exact distance of the actual halftone screen rulings to the sensitized plate or film; the diameter of the lens opening; the camera extension or the distance of the stop in the lens to the sensitized plate; and the size of the halftone screen ruling. Each camera manufacturer supplies tables and ratios for obtaining systems of exposure. The plate, the halftone screen, the copy on the copyboard, and the plane of the lens must all be perfectly parallel to one another to obtain a good halftone.

However, where the screen printer uses a contact screen to obtain his halftone negative, he does not have to bother with screen separation or screen distance and may expose his negative either in a vacuum frame or in a process camera.

Halftone Printing

Of all screen printing, halftones are the most difficult to reproduce, since their production requires precise camera equipment, a darkroom, a knowledge of techniques that are common to this type of printing, and experimentation. Although halftone printing is not practical for the one-man shop, the large screen printing shop can supplement the other graphic arts and continue developing another field of printing by handling short run jobs of about 3,500 impressions and less in any of the larger sizes ranging from about 8 x 12 inches (20.3 x 30.5cm) to about 40 x 60 inches (101.6 x 152.40cm).

For reproducing halftones in screen printing, generally about 123 to 171 mesh to the inch (48 to 68 mesh to the cm) or a good quality of Number 12 to Number 18 silk may be used for the printing screen. Finer screen fabrics may be used with a finer halftone screen or dot. Generally, if the screen printer plans to print 85 lines to the inch, then he should use a fabric that is approximately a 340 (about 4 times 85) mesh fabric so that the halftone dots will better cling to the fabric. Direct emulsions, direct-indirect products, commercial screen printing films, and carbon tissue may be employed to make the printing screen.

The range of halftones used in screen printing varies from about 10 to about 133 lines per inch, the very coarse screens being obtained by means of enlargement. For inside posters about 65 to 85 line screens may be used. For the first job it is advisable to try a 55 to 65 line halftone screen of about 9 x 12 inches (22.9 x 30.5cm) or an 11 x 14 inch subject (27.9 x 35.6cm), using an indirect or direct photographic emulsion, applying film or emulsion to a Number 140 to 170 mesh per inch (55 to 68 mesh per cm), printing the first job in one color. After the one color halftone printing has been standardized, the screen printer may work with two-color halftones or duotones.

Halftone transparent inks for screen printing must be used to do the actual printing. The ink must dry fast, not spread, as this may eliminate the dot structure and distort the picture, and the printing should be done off contact. The different colored dots in the job produce color illusion by being printed one next to another, or by overprinting one colored dot on top of another colored dot. The ink color must print on top of another color without building up or producing an embossed effect. Usually, the prints are heat dried in about one or two minutes. This is essential, especially where machines do the printing. The size of the dot is determined by the material upon which the printing is to be done. Some of the shops do this printing on stock that is easy to print and then mount the stock on any light weight board for display purposes.

Four color process work may also be done by starting with four actual letterpress printing plates or cuts. This method is ideal where a job has to be enlarged and where the actual printing plates are available, as the letterpress plate already has the halftone dots on it. First, very good black and white proofs are made of each of the printing plates. The proofs are then enlarged to the required size producing the negative from which a positive is made for the screen printing plate.

In running duotones, duographs, or any pleasing two color jobs; three color; or four color jobs always have a trial run of the complete job to check results and to avoid difficulties. The duotone process, which may also be employed in the printing of line and Ben Day effects, is an economical method of printing, using two color combinations. The printer has hundreds of two-color combinations to choose from in using this method. In planning the job it is necessary to eliminate an undesirable pattern or *moire* effect, which is caused when one set of very close parallel lines cross another group of parallel lines at a wrong angle. Some printers overcome this undesirable difficulty by stretching the silk on the silk screen frame at an angle with the frame. In elimination of this pattern the screen printer must be aware of two things. First, is to place the halftone screen at the correct angle for each color so that each halftone screen will be turned to the required angle in the camera. Where a camera has a circular screen, the screen can easily be turned to the required angle. Where it is not possible to turn the halftone screen it is a simple matter to rotate the original copy on the copyboard to the required angle. The angles shown in Table IV are those generally used in screen printing shops for halftone screen angles.

Then to complete elimination of a pattern effect on the final print, lay the halftone positive on the clean screen fabric of the screen over a light table or a light source, fabric side up, and rotate the positive against the fabric until the moire pattern disappears. Then mark the angle at which the clearest image is obtained in relation to the screen fabric threads. When the screen printing film or printing screen is made from the positive, place and attach screen printing film image in the same position as the positive was marked.

<table>
<tr><th rowspan="2">COLOR OF LIGHT FILTER</th><th rowspan="2">PIGMENT COLOR USED IN SCREEN PROCESS PTG.</th><th colspan="3">ANGLE OR HALFTONE SCREEN OR COPY</th></tr>
<tr><th>4 COLORS</th><th>3 COLORS</th><th>2 COLORS OR DUOTONE</th></tr>
<tr><td>BLUE</td><td>YELLOW</td><td>90°</td><td>15° OR 105°</td><td rowspan="4">FOR STRONGEST COLOR HALF-TONE SCREEN OR COPY IS PLACED ON 45°; SECOND COLOR IS ROTATED 30° AWAY FROM FIRST ANGLE</td></tr>
<tr><td>GREEN</td><td>RED</td><td>15° OR 75°</td><td>75°</td></tr>
<tr><td>RED</td><td>BLUE</td><td>75° OR 105°</td><td>45°</td></tr>
<tr><td>LIGHT YELLOW</td><td>BLACK</td><td>45°</td><td></td></tr>
</table>

Table IV. Showing filter color, color of printed pigment, and angle of halftone screen or copy on copyboard.

The positive halftone that is made from the halftone negative must be perfectly opaque and very dense, and black to produce a good printing screen. The positive should be inspected with a pocket microscope to make sure that it is opaque, otherwise the screen printing film or image that is made from the positive may not develop and etch out as desired. A halftone positive that is not opaque should be discarded.

Although there are many types of halftone screens, it does not follow that shops will invest in many screens, as they are expensive. Neither is it suggested that the printer try to make his own by means of photography or by scratching lines on transparent plastics and filling in the lines with an opaque pigment. Much time will be lost with home-

Figure 222. A print made from a printing screen which was prepared by coating a direct emulsion on No. 16 silk. The printing screen was exposed to a positive; positive was made by exposing film in contact with a pebble-grain effect screen. **(Negative courtesy of Caprock Developments, New York, New York)**

made screens and they will turn out to be costly in the long run. However, with the aid of one or two halftone screens, the screen printer may enlarge the negative where necessary, since this phase of screen printing is well adapted for large poster work. For example, the printer who owns one small 120 line halftone glass or contact screen may print a poster job that is 24 x 30 inches (61 x 76.2cm) in size. The printer could make the color separation negatives or have them made on the outside, each 8 x 10 inches (20.3 x 25.4cm), as a finer screen will reproduce better tone values and will show contrast and detail better than a coarse screen. If each of the color separations is enlarged 3 times its original size, it can readily be seen that more detail will be recorded on the enlarged halftone, a 40-line screen will result, and the dots in the final print will be larger and therefore will anchor and attach better to the mesh of the screen fabric.

Halftones may be combined with other types of copy in screen printing such as line copy, Ben Day shading effects, or hand-made printing plates. The line positive and the halftone positive may be made separately and then combined together or the halftone negative and line negative may each be made separately and the final positive made from both negatives.

Where very large outdoor posters or displays are to be made in which very coarse dots are to be reproduced then the halftone may be broken up into as many parts as are practical to print. In cutting or dividing a halftone, it is suggested that it be divided in the spot or area where the details in the halftone will be easy to match together in the final print. Where a job is too large to print full size with one screen, as in some 24-sheet posters used for outdoor advertising, then a separate screen may be made for each halftone part and each part printed separately. Each part is printed with a border on it so that parts will be easier to join or paste together on a hard smooth surface to produce the final printing job.

Special Effect Screens

Halftone screens with special patterns on them are designed for use by the graphic arts industries to produce halftone effects from continuous tone copy. These screens are known by the effect they produce in actual printing, such as straight-line, wavy-line, pebble-grain, spiral or circle-effect, and mezzotint or mezzograph screen. For example, the latter effect is produced by a screen which has a grain formation instead of the usual halftone parallel lines.

These screens are used in screen printing for producing varied effects on different surfaces and at the same time for eliminating the undesirable moire patterns in printing. The screens are available as regular glass screens and as gray and magenta contact screens. The employment of these contact screens has grown in use. They are availa-

Figure 223. A four-color screen printing halftone reproduction of a scene of the old West entitled "Top of the Divide" **(By Dan Muller and screen printed by Frank Mayer and Associates, Inc., Grafton, Wisconsin).**

ble in sizes comparable to various halftone dot sizes and in different pattern films. See Figure 224. The screen printer may enlarge or reduce the pattern, depending on the job being printed.

The contact screens may be used in a process camera equipped with a vacuum back, in a photographic enlarger, or in a projector of the type illustrated in Figure 220. When used in a process camera,

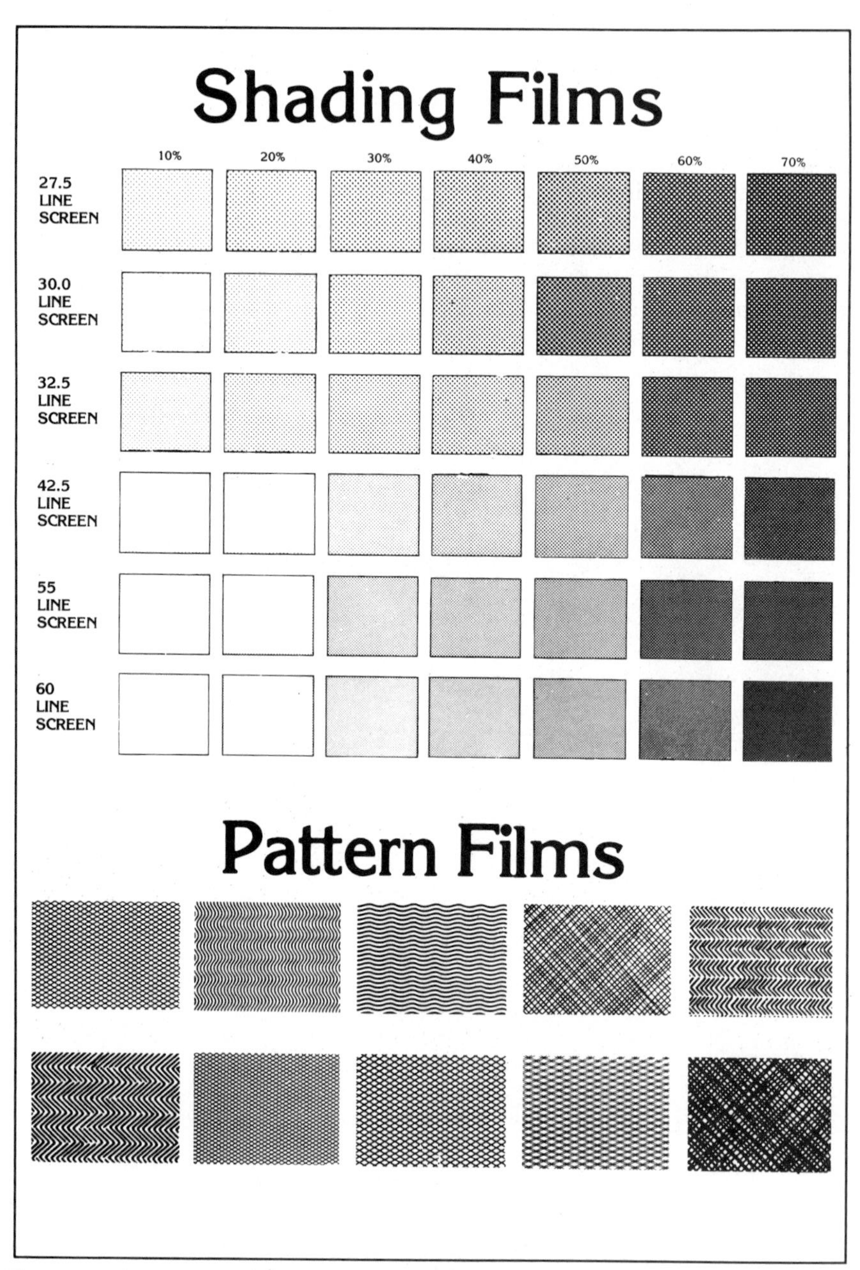

Figure 224. Some contact halftone shading films of different halftone lines per inch with varied percentage of shading in the different halftone lines, and also some pattern films that the screen printer may use to obtain halftone and special effects.

the sensitive film is placed on the back, with contact screen over film, emulsion side of film in contact with emulsion of screen. The film is then exposed to copy on the camera copyboard. When using an enlarger, the copy is projected through the enlarger onto the vacuum table which holds the screen in contact with the sensitive film, emulsion to emulsion, and film under the screen.

While obtaining special effect negatives and positives is not difficult, it does require care in processing negatives and positives and standardization of each step in the photographic processes, in the production of the screen printing table, and in the actual screen printing. Direct emulsions, direct-indirect screens, and screen printing films may be used in the preparation of the printing screen.

Figure 210 presents a reproduction of a four color halftone screen printing job of fine art work.

Chapter 35

ORGANIZATION OF SCREEN PRINTING

From the start of screen printing up to about 1922 when the first screen printing supply firm* was formed the pioneers in the industry produced the varied work which they were capable of doing with the materials and equipment that in most instances were developed by the individual doing the work. Not many workers were found in each shop and each shop guarded its techniques of production behind locked doors. However, today there are different types of organizations, each working for the constant development of screen printing. These organizations consist of the (1) manufacturer and supplier; (2) exclusive screen printing shop; (3) specialized screen printing shop; (4) screen printing department or captive plant; (5) the one-man shop; (6) educational and hobby group; and (7) the Screen Printing Association. All of the above organizations contribute to the development of an international, interdependent, and integrated industry. It is a difficult task to decide which of these groups or organizations is most important. All of them are contributing to the industry by making this phase of graphic communication one that can print anything which cannot be handled normally to practical advantage by other methods.

The Screen Printing Manufacturer and Supplier

The screen printing manufacturer and supplier cater to the industry in this country and in the world by taking raw materials and converting them into the necessary supplies and equipment needed by the rest of the screen printing organizations and related industries. This group is made up of the general screen printing supply companies, specialized firms, and divisions or subsidiaries of larger companies. The general establishment is one that can supply the screen printer almost everything that he will need in his shop for his work, including information on the correct use of products. The specialized firm has done its job expertly by developing one item, such as the manufacturing of screen

* Naz-Dar Company, Chicago, Illinois 60622.

printing inks, or knife-cut film for printing screens, or photographic printing screen materials, tusche, screen printing machines and the like. The larger general manufacturers and suppliers have organizations in varied parts of the country and in different parts of the world in order to give service, information on products, and better supply larger areas.

As is typical of most American concerns, many of these establishments started with an idea and very little financial backing and developed its product into something needed by industry and society. The large concerns generally carry on research, give technical advice on the use of its products, work with the screen printing industry by attempting to improve and vary the printing, and are in a position to help the individual shop in many ways. Most of the manufacturers and suppliers do all types of screen printing in their testing programs.

The Exclusive Screen Printing Shop

The exclusive screen printing shop is a general shop organization that is capable of doing most types of screen printing and dares to handle every type of job. It is the largest of the shops doing screen printing and may take on jobs that have never been attempted before. It prints on every type of material and is capable of doing such work as glass printing and mirror etching, printing on metal and plastics, decals and pressure-sensitive materials, flocking work, die-cut work, process color work, etc.

Physically, this organization consists of a large size area shop, sometimes occupying one floor and many times more than one floor; having a photographic department; a very well equipped darkroom for making halftones, negatives, positives, reductions, and enlargements, screen printing machines, drying equipment, air conditioning, anti-pollution devices, office spaces, etc. Some of these shops have art and design departments; others may have their art work done on the outside. Generally, this type of organization is set up to produce hand prepared and photographic printing screens for its own use.

Its workers may be knife-cut film cutters, photographers, artists and designers, office workers, woodworkers, carbon tissue workers, makeready men, printing machine operators, squeegee pushers (operators), rackers, packers, machinists, chemists, delivery crews, etc. The work done by workers in this type of shop may be specialized, each worker doing one or two types of jobs. This type os organization reflects a financial investment.

Specialized Screen Printing Organization

This specialized screen printing shop is an organization that caters to a certain phase of screen printing. It may be a shop that does one or two specialties such a decal printing; textile printing and sportswear printing; glass etching; electronic printing and plating; two, three and four color process work; flocking; signs, etc. Ordinarily, this type of shop will produce its own hand prepared plates and sometimes will make it own photographic screens. If the specialty work of this type of organization is photographic type of printing then it will have a photographic department and a darkroom; if it is flocking, then it will have equipment and supplies, etc. Many of the specialized shops have printing machines and drying equipment for speeding up work. The size in area of this type of shop may vary, depending on the type of specialization. Some of the specialized phases are point of purchase organization; textile printing; close tolerance, electronics, and container phase; decal shops; and heat applied graphics phase. The specialized shop generally is growing, since there is tendency for the general shop to specialize.

Screen Printing Department or Captive Shop

The screen printing department is found in large display companies, department stores, chain stores, theatre chains, toy companies, radio and television companies, and the like. Often it is a "captive plant" or part of a larger parent company. Usually, it is an organization within a big organization and its work consists of doing the required and necessary screen printing for the larger organization. For example, the screen printing department for a chain of theatres will do the printing of signs, posters, and displays found upon entering any movie house of that chain; the screen printing department of a chain food store will do the printing that is visible in the windows of such stores; in manufacturing of electronic circuits the screen printing section will do the varied resist printing and other printing necessary for production. The screen printing department is usually large and well equipped to do its work. Generally, it buys its supplies and equipment and does the simpler preparation of printing plates.

The captive shop may be a specialized or a general shop. It is an organization designed to meet production requirements of an establishment which often is forced to do screen printing on its own premises in order to be able to complete its product manufacturing more economically and efficiently. An example is the radio or television firm which must do its own electronic circuit printing. This type of shop has grown because of general technical advances in the screen printing industry, of more technical information being available, and because suppliers of equipment and materials have been able to standardize their products for this type of organization. Often this type of shop will develop techniques and processes which are peculiar to the processing of its general product.

The One-Man Shop

This type of organization is often the starting point in commercial screen printing work. An individual who has learned enough about screen printing work, either by working for someone else or in another fashion, will start by doing screen printing. Because of the versatility of the nature of screen printing and the need of help of other workers, it ultimately becomes obvious that the one-man shop is limited in the scope of work that it is able to turn out. This type of shop, generally, is not large enough in area and does not have enough equipment to handle more than one or two have enough equipment to handle more than one to three phases of general work. Signs, greeting cards, banners, printing on T-shirts, and the like are common products in the one-man shop.

Because of the owner's ingenuity and skill, many of the one-man shops are producing excellent work. Usually, the owner is a jack-of-all trades. He does the art work, sells the printing, prepares the printing plates, prints, racks, packs, does the delivering, billing, etc. It is quite common for the owner of the shop to have a helper during busy times. The individual who is successful in this type of shop will work up into one of the larger organizations. However, many of the one-man shop attempts have failed because the owner lacked knowledge of cost of material and equipment, did not charge for his own labor, had no business personality, no knowledge of promotion of business, and in some cases did not even make a practice of using a cost estimate sheet when quoting a price for printing.

Educational and Hobby Group

The educational and hobby groups are always important prospective groups in any industry, as they both aid the industry in a very positive way. It consists of the individual or groups who do screen printing in industrial arts, vocational, and art classes in public and private schools where the teaching of the principles of screen printing as a part of the graphic arts is attempted; and the individual who does this type of printing as a hobby.

The schools of our country are inseparable from the society they serve. In industrial and vocational education the schools desire to develop in each individual an interest in industrial life, a respect for the products of labor and management, a development of consumer knowledge, a desire to assist others in constructive group undertakings, an appreciation of good workmanship, and the development of leisure-time interests. The objectives of the schools of the country definitely aid the objectives of any industry.

The equipment in the school or in the expression of the hobby usually is just enough to do the limited work and may consist of a table to which may be attached a varied number of screens either with loose pin hinges or with C-clamps. In most of the industrial arts classes and vocational classes the simple equipment will be made; in fine arts classes and those who print as a hobby will ordinarily buy kits from the screen printing supplier. The educational or hobby group prepare the printing plates. Usually, handmade printing plates are used. More and more schools in the country are beginning to teach screen printing as a vocation, as a phase of graphic communication, and also as a phase of fine arts. Junior colleges, liberal arts and technical colleges, and even graduate departments of universities are attempting to teach screen printing. As a matter of fact, many instructors not only belong to their individual education organization but do join local and international screen printing organizations.

Screen Printing Association

The Screen Printing Association International (SPA) is a phenomenon in American industry. Its organization in October 22, 1948 in Chicago, Illinois, as the Screen Process Printing Association was an excellent expression of a democratic society in which screen operators, firms engaged in screen printing work, and manufacturers and dealers of materials and equipment used by screen printers met and set up a constitution with the following as its objectives: (1) Conduct an educational and promotional program to expand and benefit the industry: (2) acquire from and disseminate among the members any industry information which might be desired by the members from time to time; (3) promote the standardization and simplification of materials by the industry; (4) establish and maintain research facilities for the general advancement of the industry; (5) establish and maintain a central office to coordinate the industry program, and to cooperate with other industries for the benefit of the screen printing industry; (6) to promote the development of unexplored markets beneficial to the industry; and (7) to act as a neutral agency to assist the industry in the solution of mutual problems.

When the term "screen printing" became more common than "screen process printing" the association dropped the word "Process" from its name and became known as the Screen Printing Association, International, in 1967.

The Screen Printing Association in the United States and in other countries, together with the journals published specifically for the industry (such as *Screen Printing Magazine* in the United States and *Point of Sale and Screen Printing* in England) have been communicating and motivating forces for the constant solving of problems. These forces have encouraged and aided in research; motivated industrial surveys; provided data on cost accounting, management, and other problems; developed courses in screen printing instruction; organized a technical information center; introduced yearly screen printing conventions which were attended by thousands of association members and nonmembers; developed an academy of screen printing technology (consisting of knowledgeable individuals of varied countries) which publishes current technical subjects and other information of interest to screen printers; and the Screen Printing Association International generally guides activities which tend to assure the constant growth of the most versatile method of graphic communication—*screen printing.*

EQUIVALENT VALUES OF SOME UNITS IN THE ENGLISH (U.S.) AND IN THE METRIC SYSTEMS OF MEASUREMENT

Data for the following units are included should the reader have occasion to convert units from the English (U.S.) system to the metric system.

	English or U.S. System		Metric System*
(1)	.3937 inch	(1)	1 centimeter
(2)	1 inch	(2)	2.54 centimeters
(3)	1 inch	(3)	25.400 millimeters
(4)	39.37 inches	(4)	1 meter
(5)	.0328 foot	(5)	1 centimeter
(6)	1 foot	(6)	30.48 centimeters
(7)	.10936 yard	(7)	1 centimeter
(8)	1 yard	(8)	91.4402 centimeters
(9)	1 yard	(9)	.9144 meter
(10)	1 point printer's measurement, .0133889 inch)	(10)	.03528 centimeter
(11)	1 nonpareil (printer's measurement, 1/12 inch)	(11)	.21166 centimeter
(12)	28.3441 points	(12)	1 centimeter
(13)	1 pica (printer's measurement, 1/6 inch)	(13)	.42333 centimeter
(14)	1 ounce (avoirdupois)	(14)	28.3495 grams
(15)	1 pound (avoirdupois)	(15)	453.5924 grams
(16)	2.2 pounds	(16)	1 kilogram or 1000 grams
(17)	1 ounce (U.S. liquid)	(17)	29.5735 cubic centimeters
(18)	1 pint (16 ounces, U.S. fluid)	(18)	.473168 liter or 473.168 cubic centimeters
(19)	1 quart (57.75 cubic inches, U.S. liquid)	(19)	.946358 liter or 946.358 cubic centimeters

(20) To change Fahrenheit temperature readings *to Centigrade* readings use the following formula: (Degrees F—32) × 5/9 = degrees Centigrade.

(21) To change Centigrade temperature readings *to Fahrenheit* readings use the following formula: (Degrees C × 9/5) + 32 = degrees Fahrenheit.

(22) To change degrees Centigrade *to Kelvin degrees* use the following formula: Degrees C + 273.1 = Kelvin temperature. *Note*—Another name for the Centigrade scale is "Celsius" scale.

* The metric system is based on the *meter* as the unit of length, *gram* as unit of weight, and *second* as unit of time. The prefixes in the metric system are: DECI (one-tenth, .1); CENTI (one-hundredth, .01); MILLI (one-thousandth, .001); and KILO (one thousand, 1000).

INDEX

M

N

O

P